The Early Poetry
of Charles Wright

ALSO BY ROBERT D. DENHAM

*Charles Wright: A Companion to the Late Poetry,
1988–2007* (McFarland, 2008)

*Charles Wright in Conversation: Interviews,
1979–2006* (McFarland, 2008)

The Early Poetry of Charles Wright

A Companion, 1960–1990

ROBERT D. DENHAM

McFarland & Company, Inc., Publishers
Jefferson, North Carolina, and London

Excerpts *The World of the Ten Thousand Things* by Charles Wright. Copyright © 1991 by Charles Wright; reprinted by permission of Farrar, Straus, and Giroux, LLC and of Charles Wright. Excerpts from Charles Wright, *Country Music: Selected Early Poems* © 1982 by Charles Wright; reprinted by permission of Wesleyan University Press and of Charles Wright. Quotations from *Halflife: Improvisations and Interviews, 1977–1987,* copyright © 1988 by University of Michigan Press; reprinted by permission of Charles Wright; passages from the interview with Carol Ellis in *Halflife* are reprinted by permission of the *Iowa Journal of Literary Studies.* Quotations from *Quarter Notes: Improvisations and Interviews,* copyright © 1995 by University of Michigan Press; reprinted by permission of Charles Wright; passages from the interview with David Young in *Quarter Notes* are reprinted by permission of *The Iron Mountain Review.* Translation of lines from Cesare Pavese's *Verrà la morte e avrà i tuoi occhi* (*Death Will Come and Will Wear Your Eyes*) appeared in *Modern Poetry in Translation,* new series, no. 18, 2001; reprinted by permission of the translators, Marco Sonzoghni and David Wheatley, and by the editors of *Modern Poetry in Translation.* Translations of Dino Campana's *Oscar Wilde a San Miniato* (*Oscar Wilde at San Miniato*) and *Nocturno teppista* (*Hoodlum Nocturne*) appeared in *Canti orfici e Altre poesie / Orphic Songs and Other Poems,* trans. Luigi Bonaffini (New York: Peter Lang, 1991); reprinted by permission of Luigi Bonaffini. The passages from Giacomo Leopardi's *Poems* are from the translations by Jean-Pierre Barricelli © 1963 by Las Americas Publishing Co.

LIBRARY OF CONGRESS CATALOGUING-IN-PUBLICATION DATA

Denham, Robert D.
The early poetry of Charles Wright : a companion, 1960–1990 / Robert D. Denham.
    p.   cm.
Includes bibliographical references and index.

ISBN 978-0-7864-4198-3
softcover : 50# alkaline paper ∞

1. Wright, Charles, 1935– —Criticism and interpretation—Handbooks, manuals, etc.   I. Title.
PS3573.R52Z64   2009   811'.54—dc22   2008050004

British Library cataloguing data are available

©2009 Robert D. Denham. All rights reserved

No part of this book may be reproduced or transmitted in any form or by any means, electronic or mechanical, including photocopying or recording, or by any information storage and retrieval system, without permission in writing from the publisher.

On the cover: Detail from Vittore Carpaccio, *Vision of St. Augustine,* Scuola di S. Giorgio Degli Schiavoni, Venice, Italy
(*Cameraphoto Arte, Venice/Art Resource, NY*)

Manufactured in the United States of America

McFarland & Company, Inc., Publishers
Box 611, Jefferson, North Carolina 28640
www.mcfarlandpub.com

For Jeff Daniel Marion, who knows the Holston

Table of Contents

Preface   1

List of Abbreviations and Shortened Forms   3

A Charles Wright Chronology   5

Introduction   9

Part I. The First Trilogy:
Country Music: Selected Early Poems

Chapter 1. *The Grave of the Right Hand* and *Hard Freight*   17

Chapter 2. *Bloodlines*   39

Chapter 3. *China Trace*   58

Part II. The Second Trilogy:
The World of the Ten Thousand Things:
Poems 1980–1990

Chapter 4. *The Southern Cross*   88

Chapter 5. *The Other Side of the River*   115

Chapter 6. *Zone Journals* and *Xionia*   138

Appendix 1: Reviews of Wright's Books, 1968–1990   177

Appendix 2. Secondary Sources on Wright's Poetry   181

Index   187

Preface

This *Companion*, which is a sequel to *Charles Wright: A Companion to the Late Poetry, 1988–2007* (McFarland, 2008), is a reader's guide or handbook, intended to be consulted alongside Wright's poems. It begins with *Country Music*, a selection of Wright's early poems (1963–1982), and continues through the volumes collected in *The World of the Ten Thousand Things* (1990). Wright conceives of these two collections as trilogies, even though each contains work from four separately published volumes: *Country Music* contains four prose poems from Wright's apprentice volume, *The Grave of the Right Hand* (1970), and *The World of the Ten Thousand Things* reprints work that appeared in *The Southern Cross* (1981), *The Other Side of the River* (1984), *Zone Journals* (1988), and *Xionia* (1990). The present study contains commentaries on the 166 poems in these two collections.

The commentaries follow the order of the poems as they appear in Wright's books. After the title of each poem I give its original place of publication, the page number in the book in which it was collected, and its formal pattern, meaning the pattern formed by the number of lines in each stanza and the number of stanzas. For example, "5 × 3" means that there are three stanzas of five lines each. When the place or setting and the time (usually a month or season) can be determined, I also note these.

Wright sometimes separates parts of his poems by an asterisk or a centered short rule. I have referred to the parts so separated as "sections." Otherwise, those parts separated by a single blank space are referred to, conventionally, as "stanzas." I have used italics for poem titles, including those that originally appeared within double quotation marks in interviews and other prose texts.

In quotations the double virgule is used to indicate the place where Wright drops down a line without returning it to the left margin, as in "Released in his suit of lights, // lifted and laid clear." These dropped-down lines appear occasionally in *Country Music*; they are omnipresent in *The World of the Ten Thousand Things*. References to Wright's comments in interviews that are not included in *Halflife* and *Quarter Notes* are cited by the interviewer's last name, the full bibliographic record for which is in the list of abbreviations and shortened forms below. When seeing an image, especially of paintings, is crucial for a full appreciation of a poem, I have provided an internet link, the URLs being current at the time of publication.

I record my deep thanks to Charles Wright for his graciousness, for the immense pleasure and instruction his poems have given me, and for generously responding to all my queries.

List of Abbreviations and Shortened Forms

"Book"	"The Book That Changed My Life," *The National Book Foundation.* http://www.nationalbook.org/bookchanged_cwright.html
BY	Charles Wright. *Buffalo Yoga.* New York: Farrar, Straus and Giroux, 2004.
C	Charles Wright. *Chickamauga.* New York: Farrar, Straus and Giroux, 1995.
Cantos	*The Cantos of Ezra Pound.* New York: New Directions, 1970.
Caseley	Martin Caseley. "Through Purgatory to Appalachia: An Interview with Charles Wright." *PN Review* 27 (September–October 2000): 22–5.
Clark	"A Conversation with Miriam Marty Clark and Michael McFee." *Arts Journal* (February 1989): 8–13.
CM	Charles Wright. *Country Music.* 2nd ed. Hanover, NH: Wesleyan/New England Press, 1991.
CT	Charles Wright. *China Trace.* Middletown, CT: Wesleyan University Press, 1977.
DA	Charles Wright. *Dream Animal.* Toronto: House of Anansi, 1968.
Davis	Peter Davis, ed. *The Poets' Bookshelf: Contemporary Poets on Books That Shaped Their Art.* Selma, IN: Barnwood Press, 2005.
Farnsworth	Interview with Elizabeth Farnsworth, National Public Radio, 15 April 1998.
Genoways	Ted Genoways. "An Interview with Charles Wright." *Southern Review* 36 (Spring 2000): 442–52.
GRH	Charles Wright. *The Grave of the Right Hand.* Middletown, CT: Wesleyan University Press, 1970.
Halflife	Charles Wright. *Halflife: Improvisations and Interviews, 1977-87.* Ann Arbor: University of Michigan Press, 1988.
HF	Charles Wright. *Hard Freight.* Middletown, CT: Wesleyan University Press, 1973.
Hix	H. L. Hix. "Charles Wright and a Case of Foreshortened Influence." *Notes on Contemporary Literature* 18, no. 1 (January 1988): 4–6.
NB	Charles Wright. *Negative Blue: Selected Later Poems.* New York: Farrar, Straus and Giroux, 2000.
Profile	*Wright: A Profile.* New Poems by Charles Wright with an Interview and a Critical Essay by David St. John. Iowa City: Grilled Flowers Press, 1979.

QN	Charles Wright. *Quarter Notes: Improvisations and Interviews*. Ann Arbor: University of Michigan Press, 1995.
Remnick	David Remnick. "An Interview with Charles Wright." *Partisan Review* 50, no. 4 (1983): 567–75.
Rubin	"'Metaphysics of the Quotidian': A Conversation with Charles Wright," an interview with Stan Sanvel Rubin and William Heyen, in *The Post-Confessionals: Conversations with American Poets of the Eighties*, ed. Earl Ingersoll, Judith Kitchen, and Stan Sanvel Rubin. Rutherford, NJ: Fairleigh Dickinson University Press, 1989. 25–38
Schuldt	Morgan Schuldt. "An Interview with Charles Wright." *Sonora Review* 43 (2002): 74–80.
SHS	Charles Wright. *A Short History of the Shadow*. New York: Farrar, Straus Giroux, 2002.
Spiegelman	Willard Spiegelman. "Interview." *Literary Imagination: The Review of the Association of Literary Scholars and Critics* 2 (2000 Winter): 108–21.
ST	Charles Wright. *Scar Tissue*. New York: Farrar, Straus and Giroux, 2006.
Storm	*The Storm and Other Poems*, trans. Charles Wright. Oberlin College: Field Translation Series 1, 1978.
Suarez	Ernest Suarez and Amy Verner. "Interview with Charles Wright," in *Southbound: Interviews with Southern Poets*, by Ernest Suarez with T.W. Stanford III and Amy Verner. Columbia: University of Missouri Press, 1999. 39–61.
Turner	David Cross Turner. "Oblivion's Glow: The (Post)Southern Sides of Charles Wright" [an interview]. *storySouth* (Summer 2005). http://www.storysouth.com/summer2005/wright_interview.html
UP	Charles Wright. *Uncollected Prose: Six Guys and a Supplement*. Salem, VA: Roanoke College, 2000.
Vadnie	Rebecca Swain Vadnie. "Interview with Poet Charles Wright: In Writing, I Just Follow the Pencil." *Orlando Sentinel* 11 October 2002: E3.
VN	Charles Wright. *The Venice Notebook*. Boston: Barn Dream Press, 1971.
WTTT	Charles Wright. *The World of the Ten Thousand Things*. New York: Farrar Straus Giroux, 1990
Zawacki	Zawacki, Andrew. "Charles Wright." *The Verse Book of Interviews*, ed. Brian Henry and Andrew Zawacki. Amherst, MA: Verse Press, 2005. 18–29.

A Charles Wright Chronology

1935	Born on his father's birthday, 25 August, in Pickwick Dam, Hardin County, Tennessee
1936	Moves to Knoxville, Tennessee
1937	Moves to Corinth, Mississippi
1941	Moves to Hiwassee Village, North Carolina
1943	Moves to Oak Ridge, Tennessee
1945	Moves to Kingsport, Tennessee
1948–50	Attends summer camp at Sky Valley School, Hendersonville, North Carolina
1950–51	Attends Sky Valley School
1951–53	Attends Christ School, Arden, North Carolina
1953	Takes a summer job as police reporter for the *Kingsport* [Tennessee] *Times-News*
1953–57	Attends Davidson College; graduates with a degree in history
1957	In October, spends three weeks in New York; purchases the *Selected Poems of Ezra Pound*
1957	Commissioned as a 2nd Lt. in the U.S. Army Intelligence Corps; reports for active duty to Ft. Holabird, Maryland, November 2
1958	Studies Italian at the Presidio's Army Language School, Monterey, California
1959–61	Works for the 430th CIC Detachment, U.S. Army, in Verona, Italy. Discharged with rank of captain
1959	In March visits Catullus' villa on the peninsula of Sirmione, Lake Garda. Reads Pound's *Selected Poems*
1961	Turns down acceptance for study at the Columbia School of Journalism in order to study creative writing
1961–63	Begins study in the creative writing program at the University of Iowa
1961	Begins translating Montale's *Motets*
1963	Receives M.F.A. from the University of Iowa
1963	Publishes *The Voyage* (Iowa City: Patrician Press)
1963–65	Studies at the University of Rome as a Fulbright student; reads Dante with Maria Sampoli; completes translation of Montale
1964	Publishes *Six Poems* (London: Royal College of Art)
1964	Death of mother, Mary Winter Wright, at age 54, on 5 June
1965–66	Returns to the University of Iowa for further study
1966	Begins teaching in the Creative Writing Center at the University of California, Irvine
1968	Publishes *The Dream Animal* (Toronto: House of Anansi)

1968–69	Serves as Fulbright lecturer at the University of Padua, Italy
1969	Publishes *Private Madrigals* (Madison, WI: Abraxas Press)
1969	Marries Holly McIntire, April 6
1969	Receives the Eunice Tietjens Award from *Poetry* magazine
1970	Publishes *The Grave of the Right Hand* (Middletown, CT: Wesleyan University Press)
1970	Birth of son, Luke Savin Herrick Wright
1971	Publishes *The Venice Notebook* (Boston: Barn Dream Press)
1972	Death of father, Charles Penzel Wright, at age 67
1973	Publishes *Backwater* (Santa Ana, CA: Golem Press)
1973	Publishes *Hard Freight* (Middletown, CT: Wesleyan University Press)
1974	Receives National Endowment for the Arts Award
1975	Publishes *Bloodlines* (Middletown, CT: Wesleyan University Press)
1975	Receives a Guggenheim Fellowship
1976	Receives the Melville Cane Award from the Poetry Society of America and the Edgar Allan Poe Award from the Academy of American Poets—both for *Bloodlines*
1977	Publishes *Colophons* (Iowa City: Windhover Press)
1977	Publishes *China Trace* (Middletown, CT: Wesleyan University Press)
1977	Writer in residence at Oberlin College
1977	Receives the Academy-Institute Award, American Academy and Institute of the Arts
1978	Oberlin College publishes Wright's translation of Eugenio Montale, *The Storm and Other Poems* (Field Translation Series 1)
1978	Begins systematic reading of Dante's *Commedia*
1979	Publication of *Wright: A Profile*. New Poems by Charles Wright with an Interview and a Critical Essay by David St. John (Iowa City: Grilled Flowers Press)
1979	Receives the PEN translation award for *The Storm and Other Poems*
1980	Publishes *Dead Color* (San Francisco: Meadow Press)
1980	Receives the Ingram Merrill Fellowship in Poetry
1981	Publishes *The Southern Cross* (New York: Random House)
1982	Publishes *Country Music: Selected Early Poems* (Middletown, CT: Wesleyan University Press)
1983	Publishes *Four Poems of Departure* (Portland, OR: Trace Editions)
1983	Receives the National Book Award for *Country Music*
1983	Visits London, September–December
1983	Begins teaching at the University of Virginia and settles permanently in Charlottesville
1983	Receives National Endowment for the Arts Award
1984	Publishes *The Other Side of the River* (New York: Vintage/Random House)
1984	Oberlin College publishes Wright's translation of Dino Campana, *Orphic Songs* (Field Translation Series 9)
1984	Nominated for the National Book Critics Circle Award for *The Other Side of the River*
1985	Publishes *Five Journals* (New York: Red Ozier Press)
1985	Spends part of the summer with Mark Strand at an Italian villa, Cà Paruta
1987	Receives the Brandeis Creative Arts Citation for poetry

A Charles Wright Chronology

1988	Publishes *A Journal of the Year of the Ox* (1988)
1988	Publishes *Zone Journals* (New York: Farrar Straus Giroux)
1988	Publishes *Halflife: Improvisations and Interviews, 1977-87* (Ann Arbor: University of Michigan Press)
1988	Appointed Souter Family Professor of English at the University of Virginia
1988	Travels to China to attend meeting of American and Chinese writers at the 4th Sino-American Writer's Conference, 12 April
1990	Publishes *The World of the Ten Thousand Things: Poems 1980-1990* (New York: Farrar Straus Giroux)
1990	Publishes *Xionia* (Iowa City: Windhover Press)
1991	Becomes a member of the Fellowship of Southern Writers
1991	Is the subject of the annual Literary Festival at Emory & Henry College, Emory, VA
1992	Receives an Award of Merit Medal from the American Academy of Arts and Letters
1992	Serves as distinguished visiting professor, Universita Degli Studi, Florence, Italy
1993	Receives the Ruth Lilly Poetry Prize
1993	Receives Distinguished Contribution to Letters Award from the Ingram Merrill Foundation
1993	Reads at the Library of Congress, December 16
1995	Publishes *Chickamauga* (New York: Farrar, Straus and Giroux)
1995	Publishes *Quarter Notes: Improvisations and Interviews* (Ann Arbor: University of Michigan Press)
1995	Oberlin College publishes *The Point Where All Things Meet: Essays on Charles Wright*, ed. Tom Andrews
1995	Elected to membership in the American Academy of Arts and Letters
1996	Receives the Lenore Marshall Poetry Prize from the Academy of American Poets
1997	Publishes *Black Zodiac* (New York: Farrar, Straus and Giroux)
1997	Receives the Book Prize, *Los Angeles Times*, and National Book Critics Circle Award for Poetry—both for *Black Zodiac*
1997	Receives an honorary Doctor of Letters degree from Davidson College
1998	Receives the Pulitzer Prize for Poetry, the Ambassador Book Award, and the Premio Antico Fattore Alla Poesia—all for *Black Zodiac*
1998	Receives the Ambassador Book Award from the English-Speaking Union for *Black Zodiac*
1998	Publishes *Appalachia* (New York: Farrar, Straus and Giroux)
1999	Publishes *North American Bear* (La Crosse, WI: Sutton Hoo Press)
1999	Begins two-year stint as poetry editor of the *New Republic*
2000	Publishes *Negative Blue: Selected Later Poems* (New York: Farrar, Straus and Giroux)
2001	Publishes *Night Music* (Exeter, Devon, England: Stride Publications)
2001	Italian translation of poems (*L'altra riva del fiume* [ExCogita Editore] and *Crepuscolo americano e altre poesie 1980-2000* [Jaca Book]) presented by Gaetano Pramapolini and Barbara Lanati at Salone del Libro, Turin (19 May)
2001	Attends a discussion of his work on May 25 at Fondazione Il Fiore, Florence
2002	Publishes *A Short History of the Shadow* (New York: Farrar, Straus and Giroux)
2002	Elected as a fellow of the American Academy of Arts and Sciences

2003	Receives the Rome Prize Fellowship, awarded by the American Academy of Arts and Letters
2004	Publishes *Buffalo Yoga* (New York: Farrar Straus Giroux)
2005	Publishes *The Wrong End of the Rainbow* (Louisville, KY: Sarabande Books)
2005	"Charles Wright at 70: A Celebration and Retrospective," Vancouver, BC, 31 March. Annual Meeting of the Associated Writing Programs
2006	Publishes *Scar Tissue* (New York: Farrar, Straus and Giroux)
2006	Oberlin College Press publishes *High Lonesome: On the Poetry of Charles Wright*, a revised and expanded edition of *The Point Where All Things Meet* (1995)
2007	Publishes *Littlefoot* (New York: Farrar, Straus and Giroux)
2007	Receives the Griffin Prize for *Scar Tissue* (2006)
2007	Receives the Leoncino d'Oro award at the Palazzo Comunale of Pistoia
2008	McFarland & Company, Inc., publishes *Charles Wright: A Companion to the Late Poetry, 1998–2007*
2008	McFarland & Company, Inc., publishes *Charles Wright in Conversation: Fifteen Interviews*
2008	Receives the Rebekah Johnson Bobbitt National Prize for Poetry
2008	Receives the Premio Internazionale Mario Luzi Award for lifetime achievement

Introduction

As the title of this book implies, it is a reader's guide, intended to be used alongside the poems. While it may offer some assistance to the professional critic, its primary audience is the common reader. Its aim is to enhance the reading experience of Wright's early poems. For each of the poems in Wright's first two collections, it provides a commentary. The commentaries combine varying degrees of paraphrase, analysis, explanation, and interpretation. Their focus is on what Aristotle calls the formal and the efficient causes—what the poems say and how they say it. Because Wright's early poetry is often private and elusive, my observations on the individual poems often contain conjecture. As with any major poet, the poems naturally invite unlimited commentary.

Each of Wright's poems can be read as a discrete work, but each is also part of an expansive quest begun in the early 1970s. Accordingly, the commentaries often provide the occasion to reflect on the contours of the whole—Wright's poetic pilgrimage. Because the scope of the present enterprise is to remark on each of the 166 poems, the length of the commentaries has had to be restricted.

The commentaries frequently point to links among the poems, and they occasionally include brief thematic essays. When Wright himself has remarked on an issue in his prose writings or interviews that seems to me apposite to the poem under consideration, I have reproduced the passage, ordinarily under the heading "Wright on Wright."

Wright's first published poem appeared in 1962. Since that time thirty-four books, including the chapbooks and limited editions but excluding the translations, have made their way into print, and still another (*Sestets*) is forthcoming. The attention this substantial body of work has received continues to expand. A selection of the secondary material—essays and reviews—has been collected in *The Point Where All Things Meet: Essays on Charles Wright*, ed. Tom Andrews (Oberlin, OH: Oberlin College Press, 1995), and in the expanded version of this anthology, *High Lonesome: On the Poetry of Charles Wright*, ed. Adam Giannelli (Oberlin, OH: Oberlin College Press, 2006). Ten interviews with Wright can be found in the two collections of his prose, *Halflife: Improvisations and Interviews, 1977–87* (Ann Arbor: University of Michigan Press, 1988) and *Quarter Notes: Improvisations and Interviews* (Ann Arbor: University of Michigan Press, 1995). An additional fifteen interviews are in *Charles Wright in Conversation*, ed. Robert D. Denham (Jefferson, NC, and London: McFarland, 2008). For further discussion of Wright's work, readers are encouraged to consult the reviews, essays, and articles recorded in the appendixes, as well as Joe Moffett's *Understanding Charles Wright*, forthcoming from the University of South Carolina Press in 2009.

In the present book the notes that accompany most of the poems follow the usual conventions of annotation. They identify Wright's sources (he is a comparatively allusive poet), along with people, places, things, and events that might not be immediately obvious. They also point to perceived influences, parallels to other poets, biographical details, historical explanation, and other kinds of supplementary and expository information, and they translate the occasional foreign word and phrase, ordinarily Italian. Notes beginning with "Cf." are intended to point to parallels, not borrowings, direct influences, or allusions.

The *Companion* to Wright's late poetry (McFarland, 2008) was a reader's guide to his third trilogy, *Negative Blue*, and the four volumes that followed in its wake. The last four volumes I referred to, without any warrant from the poet, as the "fourth trilogy and its coda." The present *Companion* is devoted to the first two trilogies—the poems collected in *Country Music* (1982) and *The World of the Ten Thousand Things* (1990).

The poems in *Country Music* (Middletown, CT: Wesleyan University Press, 1982) come from *The Grave of the Right Hand* (1970), *Hard Freight* (1973), *Bloodlines* (1975), and *China Trace* (1977). *The Grave of the Right Hand* was Wright's apprentice volume, a series of technical experiments that reveal an interest, as he puts it, "in the tight weave of the surface only" (QN, 103). From this collection Wright chose to retain only the five prose poems at the beginning, which form a proem to the trilogy that was seven years in the making. Some of the poems in *The Grave of the Right Hand* had appeared earlier in two limited-edition books: *The Voyage* (Iowa City: Patrician Press, 1963) and *The Dream Animal* (Toronto: House of Anansi, 1968). *Hard Freight* contains eleven poems from *The Venice Notebook* (Boston: Barn Dream Press, 1971).

Wright describes the trilogy as a "sort of a past, present, and future, an autobiography by fragmented accretions, as it were. Books—and poems—about family, childhood, landscape, and place. And one, *China Trace*, about the future, a spiritual future. The trilogy also had a structural progression, from a book of disparate, individual lyrics [*Hard Freight*], through one of sequences [*Bloodlines*, especially the longer sequences of *Tattoos* and *Skins*], and ending with a book-length poem [*China Trace*]—granted, an odd one, but one who has a character that goes from the first poem, where he shrugs off childhood, to the last, where he ends up a constellation in the heaven of fixed stars—not enough belief to be able to get beyond what he can see, into the empyrean. Each poem is a chapter in the book, the book a little 'pilgrim's progress'—with a small 'p.'" (QN, 103). Wright provides similar versions of this tripartite structure in *Halflife* (75, 97, 107), and in the Preface to the second edition of *Country Music*.

"Country music" refers, of course, to the style of popular music, derived from the folk music traditions of the Appalachian mountains and other areas of the southern rural United States. This music, originally played and sung almost exclusively in the home, at church, or at local community functions, did not become commercial until after the 1920s. In *Dog Creek Mainline* Wright refers to the "old songs" (CM, 37) and in *Sky Valley Rider* to the "tinkly hymns" he heard at the Sky Valley School. But while *Country Music* has numerous lines about music, songs, and singing (see, for example, the elaborate musical metaphors in *Cancer Rising*), it makes no reference to particular country music songs. Wright's later poetry is replete with such references, and he often reproduces lyrics from country music, including gospel and bluegrass tunes. The title of the first trilogy has a broader reference, then, to Wright's lyrics as a whole, arising from the country landscape of his early years. It points to what he says in *Firstborn* streaks through and sings in the blood of his infant son: "The foothills of Tennessee, / The mountains of North Carolina, / Their rivers and villages /—Hiwassee and Cherokee, / The Cumberland, Pisgah and Nantahala, / Unaka and Unicoi—" (CM, 27). These places, along with the experiences of Wright's past in Tennessee and North Carolina, are the "country" of his lyrics. As he says in *Sky Valley Rider*, "The past, wrecked accordion, plays on / My song, its one breath my breath, / The square root, the indivisible cipher" (CM, 40). *Dog Creek Mainline* (1972) was an epiphany for Wright, revealing to him that the content of his poems could come from his own experience in the "country" of his early life. From then on, his poems began to reach beyond technical experiments toward the content of his own journey. This means that the phrase "country music" also extends to the lyrics that derive from his early sojourns in another country—the years spent in Italy: 1959–61, 1963–65, and 1968–69.

The World of the Ten Thousand Things: Poems 1980-1990 contains poems from *The Southern Cross* (1981), *The Other Side of the River* (1984), *Zone Journals* (1988), and *Xionia* (1990). *Xionia*, a slim though handsomely produced book, contained fifteen poems issued in a limited letterpress edition of 250 copies (Iowa City: Windhover Press, 1990). As these poems are of the same form as those of *Zone Journals*, Wright conceived of them as the third unit of his writing from the 1980s. Several other poems, or groups of poems, from the final part of the trilogy were published in limited editions: *A Journal of the Year of the Ox* (Iowa City: Windhover Press, 1988; 150 copies); *December Journal* (N.p.: Geary Press, 1990); and *Five Journals* (New York: Red Ozier Press, 1986; 100 copies). "Ten thousand things," a phrase commonly found in Buddhist and Taoist writings, refers to the plentitude of the material world. In the *Tao Te Ching*, for example, Lao Tzu says, "Tao produced the One. / The One produced the two. / The two produced the three. /And the three produced the ten thousand things" (chap. 42). Wright uses the phrase in *Night Journal*: "The Chinese say we live in the world of the ten thousand things, / Each of the ten thousand things // crying out to us / Precisely nothing, / A silence whose tune we've come to understand" (*WTTT*, 147), and he attaches "ten thousand" to other things in this volume—yards of glass (*WTTT*, 96), stars (*WTTT*, 103), and years (*WTTT*, 188)— and in later ones—matters (*NB*, 166) and miles (*SHS*, 77).

The lines from *Night Journal* just quoted are an improvisation on a passage from Annie Dillard: "The Chinese say that we live in a world of ten thousand things. Each of the ten thousand cries out to us precisely nothing.... You empty yourself and wait, listening. After a time you hear it: there is nothing there. There is nothing but those things only.... You feel the world's word as a tension, a hum, a single chorused note everywhere the same. This is it: this hum is the silence" (*Teaching a Stone to Talk* [New York: Harper & Row, 1983], 69, 72). One source of Dillard's comment is the *Tao Te Ching*, chap. 34): "The great Tao flows everywhere, both to the right and to the left. / The ten thousand things depend upon it; / it holds nothing back. / It fulfills its purpose silently and makes no claim. / It nourishes the ten thousand things, and yet is not their lord. / It has no aim; / it is very small. / The ten thousand things return to it, yet it is not their lord. / It is very great. / It does not show greatness, and is therefore really great." In Taoism "the ten thousand things" is a phrase referring to the outer world. In Zen Buddhism, similarly, "the thousand things" means all of phenomenal reality.

"The things of this world," says Wright, "are my only happiness.... As I once said in a verse, 'what gifts there are are all here, in this world' [*Italian Days*, in *WTTT*, 93]. I am a melancholy man by temperament, I fear, and my forays into it in my work are not so much 'literary' as personal, especially when I am concentrating on metaquotidian things. It's the things of this world that hold me in thrall, however, and set the mind to music and the heart to whatever happiness it is that the heart uncovers. And also one has to remember that a penchant for melancholy, a substantive and sustaining melancholy, becomes a thing in itself in the long run, tactile and rubbable, and becomes a living and generative part of the world of the ten thousand things" (Spiegelman, 119–20). The forebears of Wright's journey through the world of ten thousand things have been, especially, the poets of the T'ang dynasty, who patiently described the landscape they encountered. Wright says that the short lyrics of these poets, "which often centered upon the enduring problems of man's life[,] can be said to be large spiritual voyages as the Chinese looked around themselves and told how it was to be here at this time, in this place, letting the waters of the River of Heaven slide over their heads and the waters of the Yangtze slide under their feet. The enormousness of the material world and all the roads that wind through the ten thousand things!" (*QN*, 41).

The poems in *The World of the Ten Thousand Things* become much more expansive than those of *Country Music*: the lines begin to lengthen and the poems themselves are generally longer. A single poem in *Zone Journals*—*A Journal of the Year of the Ox*—has more than twice as many words as the entire volume of *China Trace*. The temporal pattern is like that of *Country Music*, as the three units focus, respectively, on the past, present and future. What Wright calls the *sottonarrativa* or submerged narrative becomes more foregrounded than before, and the pilgrimage, especially as it plays out in the "journal" poems, is more attentive to the seasonal cycle.

The dropped-down or low-rider line is used sparingly in Wright's earliest poems, but after *Portrait of the Artist with Hart Crane* (*WTTT*, 33) this stylistic feature becomes a visual signature of his lyrics. Only rarely does he not use it in the poems he has written from the late 1970s on: of the 265 poems in *Negative Blue, A Short History of the Shadow, Buffalo Yoga, Scar Tissue,* and *Littlefoot*, only eight bring all of the lines flush left. The white space before and after the dropped-down line reveals at a glance that these poems were written by Wright. It is a part of the significant style that Wright has said he yearns to achieve: "I want people to be able to look at a poem of mine on the page, read it, and to say, as though they had seen a painting on a wall, 'This is Charles Wright'" (*QN*, 104).

The dropped line is a spatial as well as a temporal feature, affecting both the eye and the ear. Its intent is to achieve "a kind of spatial negation, a visual power in absence that painters understand and employ, and which I'm interested in poetically. It's a sort of white hole that has a kinetic draw to it that the lines of the poem float on and resist. Part of my interest in the dropped line for me is that it sets up a bit of this power field within the line itself; a rhythmic jolt sometimes might appear, small as it is, that kicks the line and the poem along, keeping it alive over the top of a force that would founder and sink it at any time. But everybody knows this. You keep the composition apart just a little to let this energy in and out, and to let the poem in and out of the energy generated by this emptiness. It's all about the same thing, the power and domination of what's not there, the energy of absence" (*QN*, 173). Wright has developed no particular strategies for using the dropped line. It is rather a matter of his intuitions about the sight and sound of the line. If the line is "coming together and springing, then I'll drop it down. If it needs to have a little push, I'll drop it. If it seems to be breaking under its own weight, then I'll drop it to the next line. If it doesn't, I let it go. I don't have any program" (Genoways, 449). But the dropped line is a function of the entire page as well: just as a painter uses the entire canvas, so the dropped line enables Wright "to use both sides of the page at once, left and right hand margins, and you can carry the long line on as an imagistic one, rather than discursive or laboriously rhetorical" ("Color and Line," *Poetry East*, 13–14 [Spring–Summer 1984]: 76).

The stanzaic arrangements in *The World of the Ten Thousand Things* vary widely. In twenty of the poems the number of lines in the first stanza is repeated consistently throughout. For example, in six poems the five-line stanza is repeated three times. Such repeated patterns tend to disappear in the longer poems, though even in these poems the arrangement is anything but random. *A Journal of the Year of the Ox*, a poem of some 950 lines, has thirty-three parts. The stanzaic patterns in parts 16, 17, 18, 29, and 31 are irregular, but in the other twenty-eight parts some principle of repetition is at work. In part 1, for example, there are five sections, each of the twenty stanzas of which has four lines, forming this pattern: $(4 \times 6)\ (4)\ (4 \times 6)\ (4)\ (4 \times 6)$. Three of the parts—5, 22, and 23—have the same stanzaic scheme: five-line stanzas repeated four times. The remaining parts follow a regular pattern of some sort: eight-line stanzas repeated twice, ten-line stanzas repeated five times, five-line stanzas repeated five times, four-line stanzas repeated four times, and so on. And even in the irregular parts, some sections maintain patterns similar to these. Part 16 has one section with three six-line stanzas; part 17 has one section with five ten-line stanzas; and part 18 has one section with two twenty-line stanzas. Because the dropped-down line creates the same amount of space as that between stanzas, the stanzaic patterns do not appear obvious at first glance. But it is clear that Wright has been as attentive in constructing these stanzaic patterns as he has been in counting the number of syllables in each line. The repetition of stanzaic patterns is a regular feature of the poems in Wright's third trilogy, *Negative Blue*, and in the four books that followed.

These formal features are part of what the eye sees and the ear hears. They, along with other formal features of the lyric, are part of the microstructure of Wright's poems. The macrostructure of the two trilogies might be represented in the following schema, borrowed from a more expansive one in the *Companion* to Wright's late poetry:

COUNTRY MUSIC [1970s]

Condensed form; process of squeezing down; the pilgrimage moves upward; a book of separate poems

Hard Freight	Bloodlines	China Trace
• past • book of disparate individual lyrics • imagistic tone, narrative structure	• present • book of sequences • imagistic tone, narrative structure; imagistic structure, narrative tone	• future: movement toward a spiritual hope • a forty-six part poem beginning in childhood and ending in constellation of fixed stars • imagistic structure, narrative tone

THE WORLD OF THE TEN THOUSAND THINGS [1980s]

Long lines and longer poems; process of stretching out; the development of the autobiographical sottonarrativa or submerged narrative; the pilgrimage moves horizontally; the beginning of poems that follow the seasonal cycle

The Southern Cross	The Other Side of the River	Zone Journals and Xionia
• treatment of large concepts • focus on yesterday	• attention to narrative-based poems that are imagistically anecdotal • focus on today	• movement toward diaristic and quotidian reportage • focus on tomorrow

What we experience emotionally and intellectually in Wright's lyrics is a function, as just suggested, of what we see and hear. Seeing and hearing remind us that poetry is related to the arts of music and painting, which are respectively temporal and spatial arts. Music is a recurring thematic feature in Wright's poems, especially the later ones, and painters and paintings make regular appearances. But more generally the temporal feature of Wright's work is a narrative movement in the sense, not of story-telling, but of a poetic odyssey. This odyssey is a search for a transcendent vision by way of the landscape—the world of the ten thousand things—that presents itself to the poet's keenly observant consciousness. The narrative movement is often also cyclical, following the movements of the stars and moon, the seasons, the solar cycle of light and darkness, and the sacred places returned to time and again (the Appalachia of the poet's youth, the cities and gardens of Italy, the California coast, and the natural bounty of the poet's back yard). Such recurrent events lend a certain ritual quality to the pilgrimage. This temporal progression occurs along a horizontal axis. Wright calls his trilogy of trilogies "a kind of quasi-spiritual autobiography" (Suarez), so the narrative is structured as a succession of episodes in a confession, behind which hovers the book that most profoundly influenced Wright: "The iconic book of my life is the *Confessions* of Saint Augustine. The idea of that book, spiritual confessions, has had a pretty controlling hand over my imagination for many, many years. In my own way, I try to reproduce that sort of movement, or that sort of confession, and what such confession has led my life to be. It's not going to be the same thing as Saint Augustine, of course, because we don't believe in the same things. I did have quite a religious upbringing, however, and so some of that has, obviously, had to wear off on me. And that's okay, I don't mind. But to say that my poetry is a spiritual poetry is, I think, problematic. Of course, in the long run, I would like to think that others might think that" (Suarez, 44).

The spatial dimension or vertical axis of Wright's work is the entire body of his imagery. His images are taken largely from the natural world, and, as in all poetry, they typically organize themselves along an *axis mundi*, strung out between the upper cosmos and the underworld on a great chain of being that includes the human, animal, vegetable, and mineral worlds. This structure is explicitly apparent in *Skins* (CM, 82–102). Wright's images, of course, come under the transforming power of his fertile imagination, which recreates the landscape by way of metaphor and simile. The imagination for Wright, as for his great Romantic precursors, is both a perceptive and a creative faculty. Coleridge says that the imagination is "a repetition in the finite mind of the eternal act of creation in the infinite I AM" (*Biographia Literaria*, chap. 13). Such repetition amounts to a recreation of the thing seen, and Wright's recreative powers, which produce such startlingly original and often spectacular descriptions, are one of the principal reasons he is a major poet.

As a counterpoint to the ingenious descriptive passages are Wright's speculations on the self and other, grace and affection, the mystery of the transcendent (what he calls "the contemplation of the divine"), the search for enlightenment, the pull of the spirit that is lodged in the poet's interior landscape, the unseen world that emerges from the seen one, sacred space, the emptiness in the *via negativa*, the existential urgency to make some sense of life and death, and numerous other examples of what Horace called *res*, as opposed to *verba*. This is just as much a feature of Wright's pilgrimage as his attention to the quotidian, and it is a feature that becomes more insistent as Wright's poetry matures. His wit winks at us from almost every page, but poetry for him is serious business, and he remains unrelenting in his purgatorial quest through, in Keats's phrase, "the vale of soul-making." It is fashionable nowadays to snicker at Matthew Arnold's "high seriousness," but whatever one thinks of the canon of Arnold's great tradition, he was surely right in claiming that "manner" is insufficient in determining what we most value in poetry. Without "matter" we are left only with ingenuity, which produces delight but not instruction. Sir Philip Sidney's version of the twin pillars of poetry is the "example" and the "precept." The peerless poets, he says, have both. The intent of this *Companion* is to exemplify some of the ways in which the matter and manner, the *res* and *verba*, the precept and the example operate in the early poetry of Charles Wright, launching him in the direction of the peerless poets. The *Companion*, it is hoped, will, like Virgil, serve as a guide to the pilgrim poet.

PART I

The First Trilogy: *Country Music: Selected Early Poems*

The cover and frontispiece reproduce Giorgio Morandi's *1960, Landscape*, a pencil drawing done shortly after Wright had arrived in Italy for his army tour of duty. The dust jacket of the second printing of *Country Music* erroneously identifies it as the recipient of "The American Book Award for Poetry, 1982." It in fact received the National Book Award for Poetry in 1983. The correction was made on the cover of the second edition of the book, issued in 1991 by Wesleyan University Press, with a foreword by David St. John and a preface by Wright. The book is dedicated to Wright's wife Holly.

The epigraph from Hemingway is drawn from this passage in *The Green Hills of Africa*: "Now, being in Africa, I was hungry for more of it, the changes of the seasons, the rains with no need to travel, the discomforts that you paid to make it real, the names of the trees, of the small animals, and all the birds, to know the language and have time to be in it and to move slowly. I had loved the country all my life; *the country was always better than the people*. I could only care about people a few at a time" (New York: Scribner's 1935), [73]).

Chapter 1

The Grave of the Right Hand (1970) and Hard Freight (1973)

Five Prose-Poems from The Grave of the Right Hand

Wright on Wright: "My first book, *The Grave of the Right Hand*, was published ... some eight years after the earliest poem in it, *The Voyage*, was written in Iowa City in the spring of 1962. During these eight years I went through several 'changes of style,' several major convictions of 'how poems must be written,' and several major changes of inspiration and venue.... I didn't think there was a bad poem in the book. And, actually, I was right about that. What I hadn't yet figured out was the fact there weren't any particularly good ones in it either. Only the five prose poems now seem to me to have any quirkiness or interest in them. The rest—the syllabics and tight little blocks of what I thought of as free verse back then—seem poems that anyone could have written. It wasn't until 1971, ten years after I had begun writing seriously and with direction, that I came up with a poem no one else could have written, *Dog Creek Mainline*, as no one else had lived it" ("Symposium on First Books of Poetry," *Hayden's Ferry Review* 6 [Summer 1990]: 116).

The five prose poems from *The Grave of the Right Hand* all have to do with the beginning of Wright's poetic journeys—waiting for an epiphany, suffering anxiety because of late start, fantasizing about the imminent adventure, preparing for the voyage, and visiting a sacred place.

Aubade

Orig. pub. as *Corfu* in *Poetry Northwest* 4 (Autumn 1963–Winter 1964): 33.
DA, 21; GRH, 25; CM, 3
Time: ca. 1960
Place: Corfu

The setting for this *aubade* (from Old Provençal, *alba*, dawn) or early morning song is Corfu, the only large town on the island of the same name (a northerly Ionian island off the coast of Albania). The town, on the eastern shore of the island, overlooks Govino Bay to the north. As the poet watches the sunrise, he waits "calmly, unquestioning" and in silence for Saint Spiridion (d. ca. 348) miraculously to arise. Saint Spiridion, the shepherd Bishop of Trimithus (on the island of Cyprus, where he lived and died), was present at the Council of Nicaea in 325 with two other Cypriot bishops. His relics were removed in 1460 to the grove in Corfu where many miracles were said subsequently to have taken place. He became the patron saint of the island. On four occasions each year church leaders carry the coffin holding his mummified body with its richly embroidered slippers through the main city in a parade of joyful celebration.

The first poem Wright chose to preserve from his first collection begins with a description of landscape and ends in anticipation of the saint's resurrection, which coincides, and is perhaps in the poet's imagination even identified with, the rising sun. The poem is a single sentence, the subject of which is, significantly, "landscape." The poet's attitude is one of quiet repose: he surrenders to the silence and waits for the miracle to occur.

p. 3, l. 2. *Genova* (Genoa). A town in northwestern Italy.
p. 3, l. 4. *plane tree*. The North American sycamore.

The Poet Grows Older

Orig. pub. in *Midwest* 6 (1963): 25; rpt. in *Choice* 4 (1965): 33.
V, 18–19; DA, as *Departures II*, 26–7; GRH, 26; CM, 4

Reflecting on "the various disguises of a decent childhood," the poet, age twenty-eight, wonders wistfully why he cannot recall any imaginative adventures from his early life. Now, years later, as he sits alone in his room during a rainy April, he makes up for lost time. Spurred by his reading about ancient dynasties, rocket ships, and a recently sighted water dragon, his imagination effortlessly carries him away into fantasy adventures, including a gallop on camelback "along the miraculous caravan trails to Asia." Such fantasies were, of course, quickly disposed of, replaced by the internal adventures of the poet's own heart and spirit.

The Voyage

Orig. pub. in *Oberlin Quarterly* 2 (Winter–Spring 1964): 37–8.
V, 21–2; DA, as *Departures III*, 28–9; GRH, 27; CM, 5

The poet recalls how he had readied himself for the voyage, carefully assembling his maps, dictionaries, and guides. But uncertain of his destination and lacking clarity about the plans he had made, he was never able to shove off. During the subsequent period of waiting in his drafty attic, the careful plans he had made for his odyssey begin to dissolve and the perspectives that were once clear have become blunted. Later, he imagines that it might be possible to descend from his attic and set out on his trip, but this time it will be with fewer friends and with fewer charts and maps, dictionaries and guides.

"Most of my own work," says Wright, "has centered around pilgrimages of one sort or another" (*Halflife*, 123). *The Voyage*, written at about the time he was finishing his M.F.A. at Iowa, is an allegory of the poetic journey he is about to embark on. His destination is uncertain, but he realizes that it will require less baggage than his initial plans called for.

Nocturne

Orig. pub. in *Arena* 1 (October 1965): 17.
DA, 22; GRH, 28; CM, 6
Place: Sirmione, Lake Garda, near Verona

This evening song takes place at the ruins of the Grotte di Catullo, located at the tip of Sirmione on Lake Garda. The poet imagines that the strains of the lute and the rhythms of Catullus' verse can still be heard by "a strayed traveler, or some misguided pilgrim." The pilgrim is the poet himself. As Wright has said on numerous occasions, he dates the beginning of his poetic career from a moment in 1959 when he read Ezra Pound's poem *Blandula, Tenulla, Vagula* at Lake Garda. Pound had composed the poem there—on the tip of the Sirmione peninsula, which was said to be the site of Catullus' villa. Wright had bought a copy of Pound's

Selected Poems in New York in November 1957. More than a year later, after arriving in Italy, he loaned the book to his friend Harold Schimmel, who urged him to visit Catullus' villa and read Pound's poems. Wright obliged, and the experience was an epiphany for him. Sirmione was an earthly paradise for Pound (the poem begins, "What hast thou, O my soul, with paradise?"), and it became a sacred place in Wright's memory. Sirmione, reports Wright, is "still one of the most beautiful places I have ever been to, or expect to go to. Lake Garda in front of you, the Italian Alps on three sides of you, the ruined and beautiful villa around you, and I read a poem that Pound has written about the place, about Sirmione being more beautiful than Paradise, and my life was changed forever" (*Halflife*, 60).

Sirmione was known from ancient times for its health-giving spas, and Catullus' villa was an excellent example of a private structure of the Roman aristocracy, built in the early Imperial Era. Catullus was born near Verona, where he came under the influence of the teachings of Valerius Cato. Cato's circle included a number of fashionable intellectuals, of whom Catullus was the acknowledged guiding spirit. They engaged in such dissolute behavior that, as the poet indicates, even Bacchus wanted to dissociate himself from their debauchery.

On Wright's accounts of the experience at Sirmione, see QN, 36, 94–5; *Halflife*, 60, 149, 169; Remnick, 567; Genoways, 444; Farnsworth; and Vadnie.

Storm

Orig. pub. as *Sudden Storm* in *Arena* 1 (October 1965): 17.
DA, 23; GRH, 29; CM, 7
Time: ca. 1960
Place: Positano

In this brief prose-poem, written at the small town of Positano on the Amalfi coast of Campania, Italy, the poet retires to a basement room in the middle of a rain and hail storm to "study the various aspects of water" and to await the breakthrough of some adventurous vision "across the barren hills of his brain." The former—one of the essential elements of landscape—did become a part of the poet's project; the latter, an imaginative recreation of military heroism completely removed from his own experience, thankfully did not.

Hard Freight (1973)

The dedication: "For my Mother and Father." The epigraph, not included in *Country Music*: "What is the use of talking, and there is no end of talking, / There is no end of things in the heart." The lines are from Pound's translation of Rihaku (Li Po) in *Exile's Letter* (*Selected Poems of Ezra Pound* [New York: New Directions, 1957], 59 [ll. 70–1]). When the poem was published in *Poetry* (April 1915) it carried the note that Li Po was "usually considered the greatest poet of China" (Hugh Kenner, *The Pound Era* [Berkeley: University of California Press, 1971], 206). In the lines immediately preceding those quoted in the epigraph Li Po speaks of his regret at having had to part from a friend, saying "It is like the flowers falling at Spring's end / Confused, whirled in a tangle." Li Po's direct use of the landscape to express emotion will become a signature of Wright's poetry as well.

The photograph on the cover, by Holly Wright, is of a railroad track that has fallen into disuse. The upper half of the photo is of telephone lines receding toward the vanishing point, which directs the eye to an opening of light in a vaguely overcast sky. The track itself has been blocked off by six railroad ties stacked on either side of the track. The photo, which was actually taken in San Clemente, California, is emblematic of certain themes in *Dog Creek Mainline*.

Hard Freight, which was nominated for the National Book Award, contains forty poems, twenty-seven of which Wright included in *Country Music*. The title comes from a phrase in *Dog Creek Mainline*: "Hard freight. It's hard freight / From Ducktown to Copper Hill, from Six / To Piled High: Dog Creek is on this line" (CM, 37). The eighteen poems from *Hard Freight* that precede *Dog Creek Mainline* in *Country Music* are, except for the homages and *Firstborn*, more or less technical exercises. Wright has not yet discovered his poetic voice.

Homage to Ezra Pound

Orig. pub. in *Southern Review* n.s. 7 (Summer 1971): 881–2.
VN, [2–3]; HF, 11; CM, 11
Pattern: 7 × 6
Time: ca. 1960
Place: Venice

Following Pound's own footsteps through Venice, the poet makes his way east past the three churches mentioned in ll. 1–2, which are along the southern part of the city, just north of the Canal della Giudecca. The Zattere runs immediately to the south along the canal. The Dogana di Mare is the seventeenth-century custom house that sits on the left at the beginning of the Canal Grande—on the speaker's right. The poem was written in Venice during the time Wright was a Fulbright lecturer at the University of Padua.

Other poets "have led the way," says Wright, but they have died of natural causes or, like Cesare Pavese, committed suicide. But Pound has survived, though now he is a pathetic exile, shuffling along the Venetian canals, sitting in his "muffled rooms, / Wondering where it went bad," and remaining silent. The homage is to Pound as the "father of light," a phrase that Pound himself used to describe Jules LaForgue. Although "Awash in the wrong life," the poet, who addresses Pound in the second person, enjoins him to "Rise and be whole again," which recalls the resurrection theme of *Aubade*. Pound is the first of four writers who are the subjects of the four opening poems of *Hard Freight*. It is significant that at the beginning of his career, Wright pays homage to several of his literary forebears. His work will continue to reveal that literature is made out of other literature.

In May 1943 Pound was indicted for treason, arrested in 1945 in Rapallo, Italy (because of his radio broadcasts criticizing U.S. war policy, denouncing Roosevelt, supporting Mussolini, and the like), and placed in solitary confinement in Pisa. Later in the year he was flown to Washington, re-indicted for treason, found to be unfit to stand trial, and committed to St. Elizabeth's Hospital for the Criminally Insane. He continued to write during his twelve-year imprisonment. In 1958 he was released by the district court in Washington, largely through the intervention of Robert Frost, T.S. Eliot, Archibald MacLeish, and Ernest Hemingway. About the time that Wright began his three-year army tour near Verona, Pound returned to Italy, where he spent the rest of his life, dividing his time between Venice, Rapallo and the Brunnenberg Castle near Morano.

Wright on Wright, from an interview with J.D. McClatchy: "I came close [to meeting Pound] once, in 1969, when I was living in Venice.... We arranged to call on Pound on a particular Monday. This was on Wednesday, I think. Well, between Wednesday and Monday, Pound got a call about his honorary degree from Hamilton College and was already in the States by the time our appointment came around. Otherwise, I used to see him taking his walks along the Zattere off and on. I used to see him and [his longtime companion] Olga [Rudge] in Piazza San Marco.... He, as I recall, always wore (at least when I saw him) a beautiful camel's hair topcoat and a muffler. And a hat. He always wore a hat. I would see him occasionally, always with Miss Rudge, through the window at the odd restaurant. I remember wanting, early on, back when I was in the army [a decade earlier], to go up to Brunnenberg to see him.... All this, of course, was just so much fantasy. You must remember that I hadn't even published a book and that Pound didn't speak. The closest I ever came was when I stood anonymously next to him under the porticoes of San Marco, looking at the church and the piazza one evening. But what was there to say? 'I like your poems.' 'Is this the city of Dioce?' Besides, it was, in the end, the best thing, wasn't it? Standing side by side with him, looking at the most beautiful square in the world, in the city he taught me to look at in ways that would change my life. Water and silence. Some words, I guess, are better left unuttered" (QN, 96-7).

Wright has often acknowledged his debts to Pound, who taught him that there was a way to write (QN, 96) and that poetry required craft and careful attention to form (QN, 165). He had taken Pound's *Selected Poems* to Italy with him, and the first book of poems he bought there was *The Pisan Cantos*. "Pound contributed *Cathay* to listen to and *The Pisan Cantos* to look at. Conversational tone in a high mode in the former, emotional road maps in the latter. Italy prompted a realignment with the world and its attendant possibilities. Actually, I suppose it goes a bit further than that. Which is to say, if form imposes and structure allows, then Pound imposed and Italy allowed" (QN, 96). Pound also contributed *Blandula, Tenulla, Vagula*, which, as already noted, was the poem Wright was reading when he had his epiphany on the Sirmione peninsula in 1959, spurring him to become a poet. See *Nocturne*, above, and *Slides of Verona*, below.

On the Wright/Pound connection, see also QN, 93, 94-7, 165; *Halflife*, 63; Caseley, 23-4; Schuldt, 79; Spiegelman, 111-12; Suarez, 59.

p. 12, l. 6. *Dogana*. The Venetian Customs House of the Doge, the chief magistrate of the former Republic of Venice. At its top is a globe mounted with a statue of Fortune. See the reference to the Dogana in *Venetian Dog* in NB, 153.

p. 12, l. 2. *prophesy* should be *prophecy*.

Homage to Arthur Rimbaud

Orig. pub. as *Homage to Y* in *Iowa Review* 1 (Summer 1970): 18; rpt. as *Homage to Rimbaud* in VN.
VN, [4]; HF, 13; CM, 13
Pattern: 3-4-2-3-4-2
Place: Charleville

The setting is Charleville (in the Ardennes), Rimbaud's hometown, from which he fled to Paris at age seventeen, having stuffed a copy of *The Drunken Boat* into his pocket. Wright, age thirty-five, is drawn to the legend of the young Rimbaud—the legend of his turbulent life and his astonishing reputation in literary circles as a teenager. The poet is fearful of the end to which he and others might come by following the "brilliance" that Rimbaud affords. A large measure of the Rimbaud legend was shaped by Verlaine, who christened him a *poète maudit*. But for Wright, the legend has more to do with Rimbaud as a poet of light and flight than with the doomed poet of *A Season in Hell*. He has no illusions about being able to reach Rimbaud's "flame." But what he does have is knowledge of the liberation of Rimbaud's verse, of his sheer inventiveness and ecstatic visions, of the ineffable and dreamlike scenarios of *Illuminations*. What Rimbaud left behind, says the poet, is "what we deserve," which turns out to be in the final couplet a catalogue of five enigmatic codes—a part of the "alchemy of the word." But just as Rimbaud quit writing at about age nineteen, so Wright quits writing here, unable even to complete his parenthesis begun in stanza 4 and letting the catalogue of what Rimbaud has left us tail off into an ellipsis of silence.

Rimbaud makes cameo appearances in other poems. He is named, along with other of Wright's heroes and heroines (Dino Campana, Hart Crane, Emily Dickinson, and Paul Cézanne) as being resurrected from the winter night in *Self-Portrait* (2), *WTTT*, 19. In *Three Poems for the New Year* (*WTTT*, 94) Rimbaud is identified with the speaker. His "drunken boat" is used as a simile in *Venexia II* (*NB*, 66), and a Rimbaud metaphor appears in the title poem of *Buffalo Yoga* (15). See also *Ars Poetica III*: "Rimbaud, at the end, had got it right—/ Absurd, *ridiculous, disgusting., etc.—/* (Meaning his poems, meaning his life in literature) / But got the direction wrong. // That's not why you quit, but why you keep on, / Sky with its burners damped, husk and web" (*SHS*, 65).

Wright on Wright: "I look at things, look at paintings, look at reproductions. I'm much more interested in the visual. So I've tried, over the years, to retranslate that visual sense into a more written result. And so, naturally, childhood comes into play because we are so much more aware of things when we are children because it's all new. It's all just discovered. That's what made Rimbaud such a great poet. He was a child three or four years into the time of his mature writing period, so he had that incredible visionary newness from the age of fourteen through eighteen that most everybody else doesn't have because by the time they get mature enough to write well, it's gone, and they have to remember it. Nothing remembered is as good as the actual moment because you change it so much. Or it's better, but it's not the same thing; it's not the same electricity, and that's why Rimbaud is so fabulous, among other reasons" (Suarez, 42).

Some of the imagery in Wright's *Homage* corresponds to that in his translation of Eugenio Montale's *For an "Homage to Rimbaud"*: cocoon, black ice, risen flight. See Montale's poem in *Storm*, 87.

Homage to Baron Corvo

Orig. pub. in *Southern Review* n.s. 7 (Summer 1971): 879–80.
VN, [5–6]; HF, 14; CM, 14
Pattern: 10–(11–9)–11
Place: Venice

Baron Corvo was one of several *noms de plume* of Frederick Rolfe. Wright's note in *Hard Freight* (not included in CM) adds that "Baron Corvo was ... the author of *Hadrian VII* and *The Desire and Pursuit of the Whole*. Rolfe was born in England in 1860; he died in Venice in 1913" (67). Corvo was a rather self-deluded writer who scandalized society around the turn of the century. Although admired by D.H. Lawrence, W.H. Auden, Graham Greene, and others as a kind of eccentric genius, he was something of a crackpot, which is more than suggested in Wright's first stanza, hinted at in Corvo's writing for "vengeance only," and in the last stanza made explicit in his role as a "hustler" and "con" man. Corvo tried to become a priest but his bid was rejected. He was the author of historical romances, one of which was *Hadrian VII*, and a schoolmaster who took nude photographs of young Italian males. His *The Desire and Pursuit of the Whole* was a chronicle of Venetian life as Rolfe lived it in the person of Nicholas Crabbe (mentioned, along with Hadrian VII, in the last stanza). Corvo suffered from paranoia and had a very high regard for his own worth. He actually believed that all his troubles were the result of a Papist conspiracy against him: "There is, you said, / A collusion of things in this world." He ended his days sleeping on the streets of Venice and in gondolas, dying penniless and unknown in 1913, after biting every hand that dared feed him (section 2, stanza 1). A generous selection of his "indescribable letters," which include a mountain of quarrelsome correspondence with his publishers, is included in A.J.A. Symons's biography *The Quest for Corvo* (London: Quartet Books, 1993; orig. pub. 1934).

The poem opens and closes with the image of Corvo drifting out to sea as if headed for oblivion. The two middle stanzas, enclosed by parentheses, appear to arise from the poet's dream life. Corvo is clearly something of a curiosity for Wright ("a fascinating Englishman," he calls him in an interview [*Halflife*, 62]), motivating, in any case, a trip to his crypt on the island of San Michele, where Corvo's brother, Herbert Rolfe, had secured a permanent place for his remains. Finding no vase for the flowers he has brought, the poet scatters them on the lagoon. The shadowy Corvo is deserving of an homage because of the mysterious aura that surrounds him and because Wright is doubtless as captivated by his life as a writer as Symons was. The poet imagines him passing "On the canal, [his] pope's robes / Aflame in the secret light," an apparent allusion to *Hadrian VII*, a fantasy in which the hero, quite similar to Corvo himself, is elected Pope and sets off to right the world's wrongs. The final image—that of the toads with their fire-lit eyes—would have been an especially terrifying one for Corvo, who had an uncommon phobia of toads (Symons, 91–2).

Corvo makes a cameo appearance in *Rosso Venexiana* (BY, 43), and *Venetian Dog* opens with a Corvo metaphor (NB, 143).

p. 14, l. 8. *The quail-eyed fisher-boys / Sliding the craft.* For Corvo's own account of his sleeping in his *barchetta* and making voyages with his *gondoglieri* (the "fisher-boys"), see Symonds, *The Quest for Corvo*, 209–11.

Homage to X

Orig. pub. in *Iowa Review* 1 (Summer 1970): 18.
VN, [1]; HF, 16; CM, 16
Pattern: 5 × 4
Place: Prague

The first stanza of this homage to Kafka, set in Prague and in the Prague-Strashnitz Jewish cemetery where Kafka is buried, comes from three unrelated passages in Kafka's *Diaries*, noted below. Literature is always made out of other literature, and sometimes explicitly so. Wright will continue the practice throughout his career of incorporating the lines of other writers into his poems, appropriating them for his own ends.

Stanza two begins with an indeterminate "thing," which turns out to be whatever the metaphorical imagination chooses to identify the "thing" with. "In transit" suggests a transaction view of metaphor, where A is moved across to B: thus, "The vine is a blue light, / The cup is a star." The process is one of transformation.

In stanza 3 the poet addresses Kafka in the second person, just as he has so addressed Rimbaud and Baron Corvo, announcing that Kafka will see the archetypal city and garden. But these are of no concern to him. Kafka's attention rather is to be directed to the "dust," an image associated with both life, as in the creation story of Genesis 2, and death (the "belly-relinquishing dust" is what befalls Kafka's "Hunger Artist").

In the final stanza Kafka is displaced in space and time and is without identity. Whatever incarnation now bears his number (no. 137—section 21, row 14, tomb 33 in the Jewish cemetery) "Will not be new, will not be your own / And will not remember your name."

p. 16, ll. 1–2. *The red earth ... trees.* In his travel diary entry of 20 July 1912, Kafka wrote: "Morning in the words with Dr. Sch. The red earth and the light diffused from it. The upward soar of the trunks. The broad overhanging, flat-leaved limbs of the beeches" (*Diaries 1914-1923* [New York: Schocken Books, 1949], 312).

p. 16, ll. 3–4. *A cold, perpetual rain ... breast.* In his diary entry of 30 July 1917, Kafka wrote: "A cool, perpetual rain, a changing song, as if from a heaving breast" (*Diaries 1914-1923*, 171).

p. 16, l. 5. *O loved ones, O angels.* In his diary entry of 19 July 1916, Kafka wrote: "A singular judicial procedure. The condemned man is stabbed to death in his room by an executioner with no other person present. He is seated at his table finishing a letter in which he writes: O loved one, O angel, at what height do you hover, unknowing, beyond the reach of my earthly hand—" (*Diaries 1914–1923*, 160–1).

The New Poem

Orig. pub. in *VN*.
VN, [9]; *HF*, 19; *CM*, 17
Pattern: 3 × 3

Wright on Wright: This poem "was a reaction ... to the idea that everything in the sixties was going to be different and make our lives different and was going to change everything ... [and] a reaction to poems about the Vietnam War, that somehow they were going to make a difference. And they weren't going to make any difference at all, you know. At least in this country they didn't make much difference. And everybody was always talking about writing the 'new poem.' 'I'm going to write the new poem. This is the sixties, everything is thrown out, we need the new poem.' There was a lot of new stuff going on, there certainly was, and, as it turned out, a lot of productive stuff that was eventually assimilated. All the surrealists—the American surrealist movement that blossomed in the sixties—were eventually assimilated into the new body of American poetry and made it richer. Still, there was no new poem that was going to change everything. It would not be able to help us. So it was a youthful sort of gesture. It became the most anthologized poem I ever wrote. It was in a book called *The Grave of the Right Hand*, a book written during a ten-year period where I was trying to figure out what I was going to do, and what I was trying to get started on. I tried all different kinds of things, and that was one of the things I tried. It was the 'political' poem, but it was an antipoem" (Suarez, 58). The poem first appeared not in *the Grave of the Right Hand* but in *The Venice Notebook*. It was then reprinted in *Hard Freight*. See also Wright's commentary on the poem in Rubin, 27–8.

The poem consists entirely of negatives—of what the new poem will not *do* (the first two lines of each stanza) and not *be* (the third line of each stanza). The nine negatives, however, suggest something much broader than simply a reaction against a revolutionary poetry of political change. The last stanza, for example, is clearly meant to gainsay Matthew Arnold's view that poetry has replaced religion in providing in its criticism of life a "consolation and stay." The first stanza is a reaction against the conventions of both romance and realism. Line 2 hints at an anti–Marxist agenda: the new poetry will not celebrate the dignity of the working class after the manner of social realism. Line 4 implies that it will not be associated with a manifesto, like those of the Vorticists, Imagists, or Futurists. The new poetry will not dismiss completely the psychoanalytic dream—just those dreams "you can count on," apparently leaving the nightmares and wish-fulfillments you cannot count on as fair game for the muse. Finally, the new poetry "will not be photogenic," meaning that it abandons the ornamental rhetoric as we have it in, say, late nineteenth-century decadence. Thus, while Wright says that the poem "is only about political poetry" (Rubin, 27), its range of reference is wider than those of the read-ins against the Vietnam War.

The original poem returns, of course, to origins; the radical one, to its roots. Which means that the new poem, as Wright would discover, is always old.

Portrait of the Poet in Abraham von Werdt's Dream

Orig. pub. in *Poetry* 119 (January 1972): 216–17.
HF, 20; *CM*, 18

1. The Grave of the Right Hand (1970) *and* Hard Freight (1973)

Pattern: 10 × 3
Place: Venice

The first two stanzas of this clever poem describe a seventeenth-century south German printing office, taken directly from one of Abraham von Werdt's wood engravings—*Druckerwerkstatt* (ca. 1650). Wright has made von Werdt (the German form of his Dutch name, van Weerdt) the speaker of the poem, so the description comes to us almost as a dramatic monologue—almost, because there is no identifiable audience within the poem itself. A copy of the engraving can be found at http://www.poster.de/Von-Werdt-Abraham-p.html

In the engraving we see a type compositor; a warehouseman dampening sheets of paper; two pressmen, one (the beater) inking the type and the other (the puller) removing the printed sheet from the press while operating the rope that allows the frisket to drop onto the tympan; a proofreader; and, alongside him, a young girl. The hourglass on one of the shelves of the press's frame was used to indicate when it was time for the beater and the puller to change jobs. The furnishings are indeed "spare," as von Werdt has it, but the office contains various elaborate allegorical icons, some decorative and at least one, the griffin, functional. In his dream von Werdt misremembers several details of his engraving: the griffin rears not in the archway but atop the printing press; the cherubs are not on the far wall, but high up on an imposing structure that juts into the middle of the shop; the scene has been changed from a German to a Venetian one (von Werdt, who was from Holland, worked in Nuremberg from 1636 to 1680); and stars are said to appear through the open window, rather than the Baroque church and other buildings that we have in the engraving. But on the whole von Werdt gives an accurate description of his own wood engraving, including the details of his "disordered initials" in the oval supported by the cherubs and on one of the blocks in the lower left-hand corner: "W" placed above "AV." The force of the poem, however, lies not in the accuracy of the description, but in the Borgesian turn in the last stanza, where what has been completely spatial is suddenly invested with a narrative twist: von Werdt, the speaker, brings to life, Pygmalion-like, a person not in the engraving, a strangely clothed "sixth man" who is said to have been in the alcove. This character then thrusts what he has been writing into the wood engraver's hands, repeating "XYZ" aloud. What this unfamiliar person has been writing, we learn in the last line, is the poem before us. Moreover, as the poem is a "portrait of the poet," the scribe who comes to life and hands his manuscript to von Werdt, is Wright himself: he is the stranger whose clothes are "Centuries out of date." The poem, then, *koan*-like in the way it shifts our consciousness from ordinary description to narrative fantasy, is an example of both *ekphrasis* and *ars poetica*.

The poet's "XYZ" is the tail end of Wallace Stevens's "ABC of being," here representing the end of the alphabet—the poet has run out of letters. Perhaps it refers as well to the ordered grounding of the Renaissance world, where all people are performing their assigned functions. And just as the typesetter is obliged to get his letters and the printer his pages in the proper order, so the poet announces the completion of his own syntactic XYZ.

p. 18, l. 6. *griffin.* The griffin, which is holding ink-balls in its claws, is also found on the coat of arms of the German printers' guilds. In this print shop it serves as a counterweight, replacing the usual braces to the ceiling that hold the press stationary.

p. 18, l. 10. *Disordered initials.* What the "B" above von Werdt's reversed initials stands for is uncertain.

p. 18, ll. 16–18. *a third ... in front of a tub.* This person is actually stacking paper in the tub.

p. 18, ll. 18–19. *a fourth ... adjusts the unused type.* This person is a compositor. He is holding a composing stick in his left hand, and the text he is composing is attached to the case in front of him.

p. 18, l. 21. *sixth man.* von Werdt neglects to comment on the actual sixth person, a young girl standing beside the proofreader.

Chinoiserie

HF, 21; CM, 19
Pattern: 3 × 2

The extended form of the question that opens the poem is apparently, Why not write a poem in the Chinese style? The poet proceeds to do so, borrowing half of his lines from poets T'ang Yin (Ming Dynasty), Huang Kêng (Sung Dynasty), and Wang Chi-wu (Ch'ing Dynasty). The poem turns on the difference between the body of nature, with its mouths and knuckles and gasps, on the one hand, and all the artificial or material things that encumber us, on the other.

p. 19, l. 3. *Each year ... no one tends.* "Each year has its portion laid beneath the wild grass. / Beneath the grass how many are the tombs, high and low? / Each year has its half that no one tends" (T'ang Yin, *Song of a Life*, in *The Penguin Book of Chinese Verse*, trans. Robert Kotewell and Norman L. Smith [Harmondsworth: Penguin, 1962], 59).
p. 19, l. 5. *Stay half in love ... water reeds.* "The fullness of Autumn's colours that no man rules, / Is half in vassalage to the rushes, and half to the water reeds" (Huang Kêng, *The Village by the River*, in ibid., 55)
p. 19, l. 6. *Outside the body ... encumbrances.* "The whole world is not so great, the gourd is not so small; / All things beyond the body are an encumbrance" (Wang Chi-wu, *Hsü's Yu's Gourd*, in ibid., 66).
Wright's note (p. 67 of *HF*) indicates lines 3, 5, and 6 are variations on lines from different poems in *The Penguin Book of Chinese Verse*.

One Two Three

Orig. pub. in VN.
VN, [10–11]; HF, 24; CM, 20
Pattern: 10 × 3

The mood of this confessional poem is existential *Angst*. Nature (and everything else) conspires against the poet. What laps at his memory are "watery knots of light." He once thought of his poetic life as "an endless falling of seeds," the implication being that the seeds are no longer falling or have landed on barren ground. In stanza 2 the confession centers on the difficulty of self-recognition and the disjunction between word and self. Stanza 3 opens self-confidently with the poet's claim that he will be delivered by the wave, but, like Odysseus adrift at sea, his arms have nothing to grasp and his fingers nothing to attach themselves to. Deliverance, then, is replaced by the "idea of absence," and the completion of the poet's autobiography is projected ominously as "the stone / That no one will roll away"—which is death without resurrection.

The poem hurries along without any punctuation, and consistent with the theme is the syntactic fragmentation throughout. There are five clauses ("Everything works against," "places exist," "mirrors remain," "sofas ... rise," and "wave will deliver"). All of the other syntactic units are noun phrases without predicates—there are seventeen of them with varying degrees of complexity. This makes for a sense of incompletion and lack of coherence.

White

Orig. pub. as Whites *in* Lillabulero 13 (Spring 1974): 6.
HF, 22; CM, 21
Pattern: 3 × 5

This experimental lyric, which catalogues twenty images of things white (the word itself appears five times), both natural and artificial, reveals mostly the presence of the absence of color. The poem is dominated by the hard clarity of the objects, as in Imagism. The word "white" has conventional associations with innocence, purity, enlightenment, even inscrutability (Moby Dick). But the eight images, all white, that frame the poem—"Carafe, compotier, sea shell, vase.... Dogwood, the stripe, headlights, teeth"—have no subjective or symbolic import attached to them. What falls between the opening and closing lines is more complicated because those examples of whiteness do have emotional registers. The white clouds are "great piles of oblivion" that "darken whomever they please." The angel with "his left hand on your shoulder" appears to be, in the context of the white bones at the door, an image of death. And "for the last time in the mist" the poet writes the name of the anonymous "you." The connotations of these three little vignettes suggest, then, something other than the usual associations of "white." What helps musically to connect the discrete instances of "white" are the sibilants, as each object slides alliteratively over one caesura to the next. And lest all this become to sober, the meter of line 13—"White, and the leaf clicks; dry rock"—imitates the jingle "Shave and a haircut, two bits," or other versions of the seven-note couplet occasionally used to complete a musical performance.

Firstborn

Orig. pub. in *VN*.
VN, [13–18]; HF, 27; CM, 22
Pattern: (3 × 4) × 6

The epigraph, translated in the last line of part 6 of the poem, comes from John Scotus Erigena, the medieval Neoplatonist who declared that "all things that are are lights." The poem is addressed to Wright's newborn child, Luke, who moves in the first two parts from being jaundiced in the incubator to a robust "blossoming pink," the transformation paralleling and even seeming to be a part of the blossoming hibiscus and columbine outside the infant's window. Then in part 3, the poet struggles with what he might say to his son, lying beside him. He wants to find a "few felicitous vowels / Which expiate everything" (part 4), but his powers of verbal invention are postponed until parts 5 and 6, where a series of imperatives emerges. They have nothing to do with the man-of-the-world advice of a Lord Chesterfield or a Polonius. The poet enjoins his son rather to indenture himself to the land, to surrender himself to the law of nature, and to concentrate on the remembered earth. By so doing he will discover that "All things that are are lights." This advice turns out to be very much like the poetic credo Wright would adopt for himself.

p. 23, l. 1. *redress*. This word takes us in several directions. The bougainvillaea has decked itself out again, but in "Holding the earth together," it is also engaged in an act of restitution and atonement.
p. 23, l. 7. This is the first example in *Country Music* of Wright's "low-rider" or dropped-down line. The second example comes in *Congenital*, the penultimate poem in the selection from *Hard Freight* (CM, 47).
p. 27, ll. 4–6. *Hiwassee ... Unicoi*. The names here are places in east Tennessee and northwestern North Carolina.

Slides of Verona

Orig, pub. in *Seneca Review* 2 (December 1971): 3.
HF, 33; CM, 28
Pattern: 3-2-2-3-2-3-2-3-2
Place: Verona

This poem is a series of visual vignettes of Verona and various people associated with its history.

Slide 1. Catullus was born in Verona, a city to which he returned after a long sojourn in Rome. Wright dates the beginning of his poetic career from a moment in 1959 when he read Ezra Pound's poem *Blandula, Tenulla, Vagula* on Lake Garda outside Verona. Pound had composed the poem here on the tip of the Sirmione peninsula, which was said to be the site of Catullus' villa. Thus the association of Catullus with Verona in this first "slide." The Adige is the river that runs through Verona.

Slide 2. Lord Can Grande della Scala (1291–1329) was the Vicar General of the Principate of the Holy Roman Emperor in the town of Verona, the most famous member of the Ghibelline family that ruled Verona from 1277 to 1387. Dante's famous letter about the levels of meaning in *The Divine Comedy* was written to Can Grande, who was an eloquent rhetorician: thus, the "mellifluous ghost" that haunts Verona from his tomb (the "stone boat"), which is above the entrance to the small Romanesque church of Santa Maria Antica.

Slide 3. This "slide" is of the fresco *St. George Liberating the Princess of Trebizond* by Antonio Pisanello (1394–1455), located in the Pellegrini Chapel of San Anastasia in Verona. Even though water seepage badly damaged the fresco in the late nineteenth century, the people in the painting "still hold their poses." Pisanello (a.k.a. Pisano) lived in Verona at the beginning of the fifteenth century. For a reproduction of Pisanello's fresco, see http://www.artonline.it/img/large/i06g-113.jpg

Slide 4. The reference here is to Mastino della Scala, uncle of Can Grande and the founder of the Scaligeri dynasty. He became lord of Verona in 1260, failed to be reelected in 1262, but effected a coup d'état, having then to confront extended internal discord. He was killed by a faction of nobles in 1272. The slide refers to Mastino's sarcophagus in the Piazza die Signori.

Slides 5–9. In slide 5, "Whatever Will Come" is a personification of the future, which will have to get along without its baggage. Slide 6 recreates the image of the two hanged men in Pisanello's fresco (above). Slide 7, which like slide 5 has no direct reference to Verona, focuses on the star formed by the petals of the jasmine—a plant in Wright's yard at Laguna Beach; but whether the star is to be led or to be followed is uncertain. Stanza 8 is a slide of Adam's Expulsion from Paradise on one of the great bronze doors of the Basilica San Zeno Maggiore. The "white glove" in the last slide is the white glove of history, which, at some distance now from the poet's present circumstances, is cold and quiet.

The absence of all punctuation imitates the movement of the viewer's eye, the images of the slides running into each other without any break between their "syntactic" units.

Grace

Orig. pub. in *Crazy Horse* 10 (March 1972): 45.
HF, 34; CM, 29
Pattern: 3 × 3

This surreal personification of grace departs radically from the ordinary conventions of representing the virtue (as, say, in Raphael). Here the metaphors of the hair, arms, and face of the genderless grace are a parody of the traditional allegory: the hair as a matted weed displaces the flower and garden, and cold watery descent displaces warm plenitude—"Cold grace," as the poet would write a quarter century later (ST, 4). The ineradicable language of numerals that constitute the face of grace means that its "long soliloquy" is not something beyond the reach of art but, absent the language of images, simply unintelligible.

Negatives

Orig. pub. in *Poetry* 120 (July 1972): 214; Spanish trans. in *Plural* 50 (November 1975): 30.
HF, 35; *CM*, 30
Pattern: 7-6-6-7

From the simile of the photographic negative for the moon against the sky we move to other senses of "negative," represented here primarily by the nothingness associated with the spectral, dream-like night and with the sea. The poet wonders if this negative and almost indefinable vision is what awaits us. In the final stanza, the absence of sound replaces the visual negatives, and the poet suggests that this absence of all "positive" sights and sounds is what awaits us in death after we are ferried across the river.

The Fever Toy

Orig. pub. in *Poetry* 120 (July 1972): 215.
HF, 37; *CM*, 31
Pattern: 6 × 4

In this dream-like poem of metamorphosis the poet assembles himself into another form. The strange details of the transformation are catalogued in the first two stanzas, and in the third the poet discovers that he has become one with his "fever toy." But the self that emerges from the conjunction is so distant as to be unrecognizable: his sorrow and his body become a "foreign tongue," his "true name" notwithstanding. Wright has remarked that *The Fever Toy* is about suicide, which explains perhaps why we have witnessed something sorrowful, but the suicide is sufficiently displaced as to be almost undecipherable.

Notes for Oscar Wilde at San Miniato

Orig. pub. in *VN*.
VN, [19]; *HF*, 39; *CM*, 32
Pattern: 4-2-4-8

Oscar Wilde at San Miniato

Orig. pub. in *VN*.
VN, [20]; *HF*, 40; *CM*, 33
Pattern: 14

Nocturne

Orig. pub. in *Arena* 1 (October 1965): 17.
VN, [21]; *HF*, 41; *CM*, 34
Pattern: 1-2-3-5-6-1

These three poems were written "after Dino Campana," the Italian visionary poet (1885–1932) whose *Orphic Songs* Wright later translated. The first two poems are not literal translations but imitations. The third, *Nocturne*, is a translation of Campana's *Notturno teppista*. Many of the images and some of the lines in *Notes for Oscar Wilde at San Miniato* and *Oscar Wilde at San Miniato* come directly from Campana's own *Oscar Wilde a San Miniato*. In *Notes for Oscar Wilde* Wright takes several images from Campana—flames, Florence as a vortex, the cypress trees, the snake-like river—and reworks them into different contexts. Lying behind both Campana and Wright is Wilde's *San Miniato*, a poem written after his 1875 trip to Italy when he visited San Miniato, a Benedictine abbey on the Arno, about twenty-one miles from Florence. This was at the time when he began to be seriously attracted to Roman Catholicism. The upper order of the abbey church is surmounted by a thirteenth-century mosaic of the enthroned Christ between the Madonna and St. Miniato on a gilded background. The huge gilded copper eagle is above the mosaic, placed on top of the pediment. Here is the final form of Wilde's poem, which went through several versions.

See, I have climbed the mountain side
Up to this holy house of God,
Where once that Angel-Painter trod
Who saw the heavens opened wide,

And throned upon the crescent moon
The Virginal white Queen of Grace,—
Mary! could I but see thy face
Death could not come at all too soon.

O crowned by God with thorns and pain!
Mother of Christ! O mystic wife!
My heart is weary of this life
And over-sad to sing again.

O crowned by God with love and flame!
O crowned by Christ the Holy One!
O listen ere the searching sun
Show to the world my sin and shame.

Wilde reveals the desperate yearning for the intervention of the Virgin before his "sin and shame" are revealed. He aches for the Virgin to appear as she has done in one of the paintings of the Assumption by Fra Angelico (the Angel-Painter): heart-weary, he confesses that once he has seen the Virgin's face, then he would be willing to die.

Campana's surreal and altogether secular *Oscar Wilde at San Miniato* is intent in revealing what Wilde missed in climbing the mountain to San Miniato—the city of Florence itself, the River Arno snaking along below, the feverish, fiery upward climb of Campana and his companion. Campana turns the sing-song religiosity of Wilde's poem on its head. Rather than devotion to the Virgin Campana writes of "the melancholy and suicidal love of man," of a burning ship, of the fantastic city of Florence, of the drunken boys on the stairs below. Here is Campana's poem, as translated by Luigi Bonaffini:

Oscar Wilde at San Miniato

O fantastic city full of muted sounds ...
While on the stairs far away I climbed before
You aflame in lambent lines of fire
In the heavy evening, among the cypress trees.
I climbed with a solemn young friend
Who had been sacrificing since her early years
To the melancholy and suicidal love of man:
Down along the stairs
Willful boys drunk with mockery
Laughed over a circle around an invisible coin.
The monstrous river glistened listlessly like a scaly serpent;
We climbed, she oppressed and out of breath,
I with my eyes turned toward the funereal burning fever
Which set you ablaze, O black tower-masted ship
In the last fevers of remote times O city:
A bitter scent of laurel wafted muted from on high
Around the white sepulchral cloister:
But beautiful as you, boat burning in the high
Glorious breath of memory, I shouted O city,
O sublime dream to tender in flames

1. The Grave of the Right Hand (1970) and Hard Freight (1973)

> The bodies to the unsated chimera
> Most bitter funereal shudder before the muted lunar blaze.
> —*Canti orfici e Altre poesie / Orphic Songs and Other Poems* (New York: Peter Lang, 1991), 235.

Wright's *Oscar Wilde at San Miniato* omits a half-dozen lines from Campana's poem but is otherwise a faithful rendering of Campana's visionary poem. As indicated, Wright's *Nocturne* is a translation of Campana's *Notturno teppista* (*Hoodlum Nocturne*), to which Wright appends a flourish of ten ampersands, signifying apparently that Campana has still more to say about Florence. Here is Bonaffini's translation of *Notturno teppista*:

> Florence down below was a whirlpool of lights of muted tremors
> On wings of fire the long fleeting noises
> Of the streetcar soared: the monstrous sluggish
> River glistened like a scaly serpent.
> Over an uncertain circle the restless mocking faces
> Of the thieves, and I among the double long cypresses like extinguished torches.
> Harsher than to hedges cypresses
> Harsher than the quivering of box-trees,
> The love that from my heart,
> That from my heart, the love a pimp intoned and sang:
>
> I love the old whores
> Swollen leavened with sperm
> Who fall like toads on four paws over the red featherbed
> And wait and snort and pant
> Flabby as bellows.

Campana was one of the earliest Italian influences on Wright—along with Dante, Montale, and Pound. He was attracted to Campana as a visionary pilgrim and to the myth that had grown up around him as the Italian *poète maudit*. As Wright says in an interview, Campana represented the spirit of twentieth-century Italian poetry. "It was his desperate reaching and yearning for what he felt but couldn't ever write down or understand truly that has always drawn me to him. It still does" (*Halflife*, 123). On Wright's translating of Campana, see his interview with Mary Zeppa, "Charles Wright on Eugenio Montale and Dino Campana," *Poet News* October 1985: 1, 8–10, reprinted in *Charles Wright in Conversation*, pp. 29–36.

Yellow

Orig. pub. in *Hearse* 17 (1972): 24.
HF, 42; CM, 35
Pattern: 14

This experiment is a poetic "study" of things yellow. The poet catalogues a score of such things, drawn from a range of categories—natural and artificial, spatial ("distal") and temporal ("what is past"). Some are presented directly, as images without any attendant implication (e.g., the yellow of pencils, straw, grasshopper's wings, sulfur). Others have an emotional register or symbolic import (e.g., "regret," "loneliness," intuition, "death," "the devil's blood"). The catalogue is both public and private: everyone knows what a yellow pencil is, but the color of "amaranth yellow" or the yellow of "the road home" remains undisclosed.

Dog Creek Mainline

Orig. pub. in *Poetry* 120 (July 1972): 212.

HF, 43; CM, 36
Pattern: 6 × 9
Time: 1941
Place: Western North Carolina

    This poem marks Wright's movement away from primarily technical exercises toward what developed into his distinctive subject matter, style, and voice. Writing the poem during the fall of 1971, he came to realize that the story he had to tell came from his own experience. This was a story that began thirty years earlier in the mountains of North Carolina when he was a six-year-old, living at Hiwassee Village in the western tip of the state near the Tennessee and Georgia state lines. Wright's father, an engineer for the Tennessee Valley Authority, moved the family to various dam sites during the poet's early years. He was working on Fontana Dam at the time. Although there is a Hanging Dog Creek that empties into the Hiwassee Lake near Murphy, North Carolina, Dog Creek is a purely imaginary stream. Ducktown and Copper Hill [Copperhill] (l. 38) are to the west of Hiwassee Dam, just across the Tennessee line in Polk County.

    At the beginning of the third section (stanza 7) we get the phrase that is the title Wright's second volume—the "hard freight," largely copper ore and timber, that passed along the railway between Ducktown and Copperhill. But the meaning of the phrase here is that the journey the poet is about to embark on, which will take him back into his past, will be a long, slow, and difficult odyssey. "The contour map of the past," he says, "is the toughest terrain there is" (QN, 18). On this map, Dog Creek is said to be a "mainline," but it turns out to be an "indigent spur," a branch off the main line that rejoins it later on. The poet surely intends for "spur" (Dante's *sprone*) also to mean incentive: Dog Creek and its environs serve to goad the poet to revisit his past in memory, taking him back "cross-tie by cross-tie," like those on the cover photograph of *Hard Freight*. Even a spur can provide an imaginative route for the poet back into childhood—"from Six / To Piled High," meaning from age six until he was grown up.

    Between the "Dog Creek" bookends that frame stanza 1 is a litany of spondees—eleven altogether—that summon up the sights and smells of the Dog Creek. The journey backward begins as a bodily experience—something felt vaguely on the pulse, back of the fingertips, deep in the throat (stanza 2). Mostly what the poet recalls from 1941 are image-fragments: the sky, the Y-shaped streets of Hiwassee Village, five unidentified silhouettes, the trees, the shorebirds, the moths, and the turtles and pike of Lake Hiwassee. The only sounds he hears are the surnames called up by his mind's ear ("The ear, cold cave, is an absence," he says in the penultimate stanza). The staccato of stanza 1 is replaced in section 2 by longer musical phrases, and we begin to see the development of the ingenious descriptions of landscape that will become Wright's signature. The poison swelling in the arm (section 2, stanza 1) is a reference to the blood-poisoning episode that lies behind poem 6 of *Tattoos*, which Wright also describes in *Halflife*, 68: at age six he stepped on a nail, the blood-poison settled in his arm, and hallucination ("tops spin") from high fever ensued.

    The poem concludes with a two-stanza parenthesis that focuses on the body: the poet's own body—his heart, fingers, ear, eye, and tongue have come center stage. The parentheses suggest that Wright is whispering to us about the difficulty of recapturing childhood, returning to the body imagery of stanza 2: hard freight indeed when the "heart is a hieroglyph," the ear "an absence," and "The eye turns in on itself." But what does not fail him is the poetic tongue: "In its slick ceremonies the light / Gathers, and is refracted, and moves / Outward, over the lips, / Over the dry skin of the world." The discovery of light will turn out to be one of the key metaphors of Wright's poetic quest.

1. The Grave of the Right Hand (1970) and Hard Freight (1973)

In an interview with J.D. McClatchy, Wright says that he dates the beginning of his own style from the time of this poem (QN, 104). See also Caseley, 23; Turner; and *Halflife*, 86. In one interview, Wright comments on *Dog Creek Mainline* in the context of his larger project: "I can't say that at that moment, in the fall of 1971, when I wrote *Dog Creek Mainline*, I knew I was going to write a series of trilogies, nine books plus a couple of codas and an introduction that the first one had. But I did know that I was starting on something that was not going to be finished for a while. I knew that it was not going to be a narrative journey; therefore, it can't be like *Piers Plowman* or *The Divine Comedy* or something like that. It was going to have to be separate books where I hoped eventually I would see what form I was working toward, and then once I saw that it would start to coalesce. And that is more or less what happened after I finished the first group of books, *Hard Freight*, *Bloodlines*, and *China Trace*, which became *Country Music*. And I said, 'Oh, this is a trilogy. It moves from here to here. Now, I wonder if I can write another one and then a third one, so that I get a series of pyramids that basically have the same structure but would be, instead of next to each other, superimposed, one on top of the other.' And so, that's what I set out to do" (Suarez, 46).

The third movement of Peter Lieberman's Concerto No. 3 was inspired by the jazz lilt of *Dog Creek Mainline*.

p. 36, ll. 14–15. *its three streets / Y-shaped*. Hiwassee Village had a central street that forked into two other streets.
p. 36, l. 26. *the* should be *The*, as it is in *Hard Freight*.
p. 37, l. 10. *Hard freight*. This is a shipping term, referring to large items of cargo distributed directly to a single location.

Blackwater Mountain

Orig. pub. in *Poetry* 119 (January 1972): 215.
HF, 49; CM, 38
Pattern: 10 × 3
Place: North Carolina
Title: Blackwater Mountain is an imaginary mountain in the vicinity of Sky Valley, North Carolina (see next poem).

This is the third of six three-stanza poems in *Hard Freight*, a pattern that Wright would continue to find congenial. The poet is standing before the lake at Sky Valley, flashlight in hand. A black duck suddenly "explodes" and sets off in the darkness, showing the way to the heavens—the fire that is warming the black moon. This episode is recorded in stanza 3. The first stanza is a recollection in tranquility of the same lake, represented by particularly powerful figures—the green robes of the oak, the husbanding of the light by the lily pads, the light itself flaring like a white disease. Stanza 2 is also a memory, but from an earlier time. The young boy is on a duck-hunting outing with a person identified only as "you" (in actuality James Y. Terry, Jr.), whose approval the young boy seeks. What the poet recalls is his effort to retrieve a duck that Terry had shot and that had disappeared into the "thick brush." For two hours the young boy waded "waist-deep in the lake," trying "Without success or reprieve" to locate the dead bird.

The poem sets up a dialectic between light and darkness. We have, on the one hand, the flares of the last light, the jacklight and flashlight, the stars "flashing like hooks," the glow of the campfire; and on the other, Blackwater Mountain, the encroaching darkness of stanza 1 and the complete darkness of stanza 2, the thicket "as black as death," the black duck, and the black moon. In the end, the light that shineth in darkness wins out. The last five lines— about the explosion of the black duck—derive from Wright's translation of Eugenio Montale's *From a Swiss Lake*: "suddenly a black duck / beats upward on the clotted air from far out on the lake; / he leads the way to a new fire, where he will burn" (*Storm*, 130).

Sky Valley Rider

Orig. pub. in *Skywriting* 3 (September 1973): 4–5.
HF, 46; CM, 39
Pattern: (6 × 6)–3
Place: North Carolina

Before Wright attended Christ's School, a private school in Arden, North Carolina, he spent his fifteenth year at a small (eight students) school, Sky Valley Academy, near Hendersonville, North Carolina. Here's the way Wright describes it: "Sky Valley was ... very Episcopalian, very church-oriented. Mrs. Perry, who ran Sky Valley, was the daughter of Bishop Guerry, the Episcopal bishop of South Carolina, and very much an evangelical. She ran a very tight evangelical ship there at Sky Valley, which settled into me, obviously. It mostly settled into me as something to fight against for the rest of my life, but it's in there. I fight against it, but I wouldn't change it for anything. Obviously it spoke to some part of my nature that I, even at the time, secretly felt was all right and that went begging during the years of my late teens and twenties. But I've come back to it over the last 20 years, and I write about it constantly. All my poems seem to be about the impossibility of salvation" (Clark, 9). In an interview with Michael Chitwood, Wright recounts his time at Sky Valley in some detail (QN, 142–5).

The poem begins with Wright's having returned to Sky Valley, where he had been a student more than twenty years earlier. He finds it that it has not much changed. It's the "same auto-de-fe," meaning that he still senses the imposition the Perrys' rather strict religious code—"evangelical looniness," Wright called it in retrospect (*Halflife*, 109). He had received at Sky Valley what he had never asked for, having been shipped off there by his father, who thought it would be bracing, and his mother, who was impressed by the religious discipline of Anne and Jim Perry (QN, 144–5). The evangelical Anne Perry and her husband had become conscientious objectors during World War II. What Wright received from all of this was "Complacency, blind regret; belief; / Compassion ... / respect." Of these, he has apparently squandered complacency and sloughed off belief. But he has squirreled away compassion and respect in his "camphor box" for a later time.

Section 2 begins with a flashback to the time Wright was at Sky Valley, probably to a Sunday service on what was called the Big Porch, where Mrs. Perry played the "tinkly hymns." One of the hymns, which touched the fifteen-year-old at the time, was about his lost soul, but it has been discarded like the other Sky Valley "goods." "I was put in a landscape," Wright says, remarking about his early life in Appalachia, "and I've been in one ever since. I don't know why that made such an impression on me but it did, and Sky Valley was a continuation of that some years later, and from there it was an easy step into the Italian landscape" (QN, 147). In the last two stanzas of section 2, the poet revisits the hay shed and the orchard at Sky Valley, revealing the features of the landscape that he experienced years earlier and that have remained constant: "Whatever has been, remains." This awareness is reinforced in the final tercet: "The past, wrecked accordion, plays on, its one tune / My song, its one breath my breath." The final phrase—"indivisible cipher"—means that the memory of the past and the experience of the present merge into an eternal code that the poet will spend his entire career trying to decipher and otherwise sing about.

Sex

Orig. pub. *Ploughshares* 1 (December 1972): 1.
HF, 48; CM, 41
Pattern: 4 × 3
Time: 1950s
Place: East Tennessee, near the Virginia state line

This account of a liaison by the banks of the Holston in the back seat of a car is a confession of ignominious failure. The poet, addressing himself as "you," recalls how his attention, oblivious to the natural surroundings, was focused on the "stuck clasp" and "the knees." The objective correlatives of the landscape in stanza 1 prepare us for the poet's failure—the lolling tongue of the river, which is gummy and ill at ease, the declining sneer of the gap, and the chapped lips of the voyeur, darkness. The answer to the groping speaker's cry for "O anything" is, after the rendezvous, "Nothing." The fish and fireflies go about their ordinary business, unaware of the unwinding of the wound and of the fire-tipped fuse, the symbolism of which is only slightly disguised.

p. 41, ll. 1, 3. The Holston River runs through southwest Virginia and east Tennessee. Moccasin Gap is in Virginia.

Northhanger Ridge

Orig. pub. in *Poetry* 122 (August 1973): 252–3.
HF, 51; CM, 42
Pattern: 8 × 6
Time: 1949
Place: Sky Valley Camp, North Carolina

Title: Northhanger Ridge, like Blackwater Mountain, is a purely fictitious name.

The experience recorded here took place during the third of four summers that Wright, a fourteen-year-old in 1949, spent at the Sky Valley camp on Lake Louellen (apparently Llewellyn at an earlier time) in the North Carolina mountains between Hendersonville and Brevard. The boys' camp, about a mile from the music camp for girls at the main compound, was a series of tents and cabins, which the boys themselves helped build during the summers. The experience is recreated for us somewhat obliquely, and some images are purely private (e.g., "dream-wires" in stanza 1 and the twisting and turning "drugged moon" in the last). But this much we learn: the summer was dusty and hellishly hot. The campers trudge off to various religious services, including morning and evening prayers, supervised by their elders, who with their clenched teeth and shrill voices, are determined to get their evangelical message across. The narrative itself is slight. It features a preacher called Father Dog, a stand-in for Father God, who barks his religious message to the docile and uncomprehending young boys. The boys "talk to nothingness" at vespers beneath the crucifix of a sick and wounded Christ. In fact, the whole "page" of the summer memory has been "stripped of its meaning." The evangelical fervor generates a kind of nightmare vision, and the images used to recapture the experience are overwhelmingly harsh, uninviting, and demonic: the elders voices are like "shards of light, / Brittle, unnecessary"; the dark room of the candlelight service "Burns like coal, goes / Ash to the touch, ash to the tongues tip"; and the young boy's nightmares are filled with spiders and skulls. Consolation, redemption, and salvation are the payoff promised by Father Dog, but none of these promises is forthcoming. The "Half-bridge over nothingness" that begins the poem and the "waiting for nothing" that concludes it afford a précis of what Bible Camp meant for the young boy.

Primogeniture

Orig. pub. in *Skywriting*, no. 3 (September 1973): 3; rpt. in *Specimen 73* (Pasadena, CA: Pasadena Museum of Modern Art, 1973), 28.
HF, 54; CM, 44
Pattern: 5 × 3
Time: 1972

    The title of this extraordinary lyric suggests that it represents the state of the poet's soul after the death of his father in 1972. His mother had died eight years earlier. Thus, for the first-born all of the passageways are closed—the doors, the window, the highways, and the waters—except for the chute which slants upward toward heaven and in which the poet finds himself stalled. The last stanza is an invocation to the "Rose of the afterlife" in the face of loss. The Rose is implored to restore the blighted garden and by implication the shattered poet and to devolve (to be passed on to someone else), raise up, rechannel, and hold. The Rose is the Virgin Mary, as in canto 23 of the *Paradiso*, where Beatrice invites Dante to gaze not on her face but on "the Rose in which the Word of God / took on the flesh." The Christian motifs are, of course, displaced in the direction of ordinary experience, but the original or undisplaced form of resurrection in the invocation for the disconsolate body to be raised up is easily recognizable.

Nightdream

Orig. pub. in *Poetry* 122 (August 1973): 249–50.
HF, 55; CM, 45
Pattern: 6 × 6

    This surreal poem springs from the poet's dream about the deaths of his father and mother. The imagery is mostly cold, disengaging, and sinister, marking the dream as a nightmare. Night becomes a panoply, in the sense of both ceremonial grave clothes and a protective covering over the anxieties of the daylight and nighttime visions. In the parenthetical conclusion the Dixieland celebration, with its singing and dancing, contrasts starkly with the dead parents, represented in the dream as sawdust-filled dolls in their coffins.

p. 45, l. 8. *Bob's Valley, Bald Knob.* Bob's Valley is the poet's renaming of Carter's Valley, near Kingsport, Tennessee. Bald Knob is a town in White County, Arkansas, about sixty miles from Little Rock.

p. 45, ll. 11–12. The *Ouachita, Ocoee,* and *Arkansas* are rivers. The Ouachita runs through Arkansas and Louisiana; the Ocoee is a whitewater river in Tennessee; the Arkansas, a major tributary of the Mississippi, has its headwaters in Colorado and runs through Kansas and Oklahoma before entering Arkansas and "sliding" through Little Rock, the home of Wright's father.

Congenital

Orig. pub. in *Poetry* 122 (August 1973): 249.
HF, 58; CM, 47
Pattern: 4 × 3

    Congenital, like a number of poems in *Hard Freight*, puts a great deal of strain on the reader to overcome its obscurity and enter the poet's world. To begin with, "it" in the first line of stanzas 1 and 2 does not attach itself to anything obvious. While it is possible to isolate the syntactic units, even without any punctuation to guide us, the connections between them are tenuous. Semantically, we are confronted with such coinages as "lumescent," "hawk-light," "afterdamp," and "saltlamps." "Lumescent" may refer to the dawning of the light (*lumen*, "light," and-*escent*, beginning to be"), but that works against the nighttime scene (the blue spruce is "night-rinsed"). With such clauses as "the rails / Shinned the saltlamps" and "It ends.... In limp wheels in a wisp of skin" we have entered the world of the altogether private surrealistic image. Stanza 1 does locate us in a particular place. Whatever "it" refers to, "it" begins in the quiet light of the majestic blue spruce. In stanza 2 we move from the natural world, with its imagery of the garden, to the city, or at least to the world of artifice, with its lamps and rails and wheels.

The title suggests that "it" might be related to something the poet has acquired at birth, a notion reinforced both by where "it" ends ("in anatomy") and by the reference to the father in stanza 3. Is it that the poet, who was born on his father's birthday, remains preoccupied with his father's death? If so, perhaps the missing antecedent of "it" in the first line is life, the beginning and end of which the poet charts in the first two stanzas. "It" begins in the Edenic garden of the blue spruce (the site of Wright's birth in Pickwick Dam?) and ends when the saltlamps have gone out, the wheels have become limp, and the body dissipated. The railroad imagery ("rails" in the "afterdamp" and "limp wheels") project the end of a journey.

These efforts at trying to see what the poet sees and understand what he wants us to understand are halting at best. The syntax is too discontinuous, the language often too private, the linkages too indistinct for a coherent reading experience.

But we can say with some assurance that the concluding stanza points to things that the poet has inherited from his father. The poet's hands and searching eyes, his "ever-turning" energy, even his "song" are things that have been congenitally determined. The poem opens with a description of landscape—the garden rather than the city—and Wright's father preferred the former. "He always said," reports Wright, "there was no town he could imagine that he'd rather live inside of than outside of. After hearing that several times, you kind of take on that attitude yourself" (*Halflife*, 148).

Clinchfield Station

Orig. pub. in *Poetry* 122 (August 1973): 251.
HF, 59; CM, 48
Pattern: 4 × 6
Place: East Tennessee
Title: The Clinchfield Station is in Kingsport, Tennessee.

The central metaphor here is the road or the way, and the narrative movement is the traditional one from descent to ascent. Part 1 is about the descent, the Dantean journey that begins in the "underlife" at the bottom of the cosmos, which, as the poet says, alluding to canto 34 of the *Inferno*, begins with the threshold of Hell but, since Dante's story is one of redemption, eventually leads upward to grace and light. Dante gets a glimpse of this as he and Virgil leave Dis, viewing the stars in the final line of the *Inferno*. The poet's ascent—what he calls the "way back"—is not presented in such theological terms. His petition, rather, is to be ferried back to his roots in the landscape of east Tennessee. For him, the "way back is always into the earth," mimicking what Dante says at the conclusion of the *Inferno*: "My guide and I came on that hidden road / to make our way back into the bright world" (canto 34, ll. 133–34; trans. Mandelbaum). Here one encounters the plenitude of the things of the world that are catalogued in the final two stanzas and of which we will see a great deal more in the poems in *Bloodlines*.

* * *

The thirteen poems from *Hard Freight* Wright chose not to include in *Country Music*, along with their original place of publication, are: *Nouns* (*Poetry* 119 [January 1972]: 216), HF, 26; *Definitions*, not previously published, HF, 23; *Emblems* (*Iowa Review* 3 [Spring 1972]: 11), HF, 36; *The Other Side* (*Iowa Review* 3 [Spring 1972]: 10); HF, 38; *Backtrack* (*Ploughshares* 1 [December 1972]: 18; rpt. in *Words* 2 [December 1973–January 1974]: 22), HF, 45; *Victory Garden* (*Poetry* 120 [September 1972]: 215), HF, 50; *Tongues* (*Granite* 4 [Autumn 1972]: 65; rpt. in *Granite* 4 [Autumn 1973]: 68); HF, 53; *Postscript* (*West Coast Poetry Review* 6 [Winter 1972–73]: 5), HF, 57; *Synopsis* (*Crazy Horse* 10 [March 1972]: 45), HF, 60; *Nightletter* (*Poetry* 116 [June 1970]: 186), HF, 63; *Entries* (*Poetry* 116 [June 1970]: 188); HF, 64; *Cherokee*, published as *Formula* in *Seneca Review* 2 (December 1971): 4; HF, 65; *Epithalamion* (*Poetry* 116 [June 1970]: 186), HF, 66.

Chapter 2

Bloodlines (1975)

Dedication: "For Winter Wright," Charles Wright's brother. The photograph of Wright on the cover, staged against a background of a log cabin wall and various rural icons, was taken by Wright's wife Holly. The photo is something of a stunt, as the washtub hanging from the cabin wall easily doubles as a halo, surrounding the somber head of St. Charles of Laguna Beach—an eremite with Ray-Bans and connected to the outside world through the telephone wire above his head.

Bloodlines is a series of autobiographical poems, most of which focus, as the title of the book suggests, on family lineage. The principal bloodlines are those of the poet's parents, Mary Winter Wright and Charles Penzel Wright. The explicitly "father" poems are *Virgo Descending* and *Hardin County*, and the "mother" poems, *Cancer Rising* and *Delta Traveller*. The book begins with a poem in which Wright's grandmother appears in a dream, and it concludes with an image of his sleeping wife and son. The heart of the volume is two long sequences, *Tattoos* and *Skins*. Four of the sections in *Tattoos* also make reference to the poet's mother and father. All of the poems in *Bloodlines* were included in *Country Music*.

Virgo Descending

Orig. pub. in *Ohio Review* 16 (Winter 1975): 18; rpt. in *Cobblestone* August–September 1976: 21. B, 11–12; CM, 51–2
Pattern: 10 × 4

The first poem in *Bloodlines* is a narrative that comes directly from a dream. It begins with the poet's descent into the depths of the earth, where he arrives in an unfinished house being built by his father. Along the poet's journey he encounters first his grandmother and then his aunt, with whom he walks past the closed-door rooms of his father and mother and eventually his aunt's room, almost completed. Before him is his brother's room and behind him his sister's, both unfinished. The structure resembles a large building more than it does a home, what with its large scale and its "Buttresses, winches, block-and-tackle." At the end of the journey the poet, having passed his own half-finished room, arrives in the living room with an open far wall through which streams a radiant light. The poet's father emerges from this light, muttering to himself that he cannot keep the light from his son's room.

The descent into the underworld by Virgo (the astrological sign under which both Wright and his father were born) has parallels to the *nostos* of Odysseus. The meaning of the dream, like that of all dreams, is a riddle. The poet gropes toward its significance: "Home is what you lie in, or hang above, the house / Your father made, or keeps on making, / The dirt you moisten, the sap you push up and nourish." This allegory is related to the fact that the poet's father was in the construction business and was a gardener—a Laertes in his own vineyard. The difference between the poet and his father appears to be this: for the poet, home is never closed off; it is a process rather than a finished product; if it is conceived as a completed structure (the father's vision), then no light can enter. The difference is between a largely material vision of life and a spiritual one, one that opens onto "a radiance / I can't begin to imagine." If the building is finished, then the possibility of enlightenment is foreclosed.

Easter, 1974

Orig. pub. in *Barataria Review* 1, no. 1 (1974): 19.
B, 13; CM, 53
Pattern: 3 × 2

The images in the first tercet are from nature—the climbing rose against the backdrop of twilight and the red stars. Images of the body govern the second tercet—fingernail, eyelash, and bone. In the first tercet nature is said to be "redemptive past pain," which is a hopeful message. But in the second tercet, the possibility of redemption at the Easter season, ten years after the death of the poet's mother, is uncertain: "What opens will close, what hungers is what goes half-full." Still, the hunger for redemption remains.

p. 53, l. 3 *Blood stars.* Red stars, like the alpha star in Cassiopeia.

Cancer Rising

Orig. pub. in *Ohio Review* 16 (Winter 1975): 19.
B, 14–15; CM, 54–5
Pattern: 9 × 4

Virgo Descending is a *katabasis. Cancer Rising*, a poem of death and resurrection, moves in the opposite or upward direction. Wright's mother, who died of bone cancer, is not mentioned explicitly in the poem, but it is difficult not to associate her with the theme of death that runs throughout as a counterpoint to the song of the mockingbird. Cancer (Latin for *crab*) refers also to the zodiac: it is a feminine sign, and the Cancerian character is strongly maternal in her instincts, has a keen imagination, appreciates art and literature, and is often nonverbal, all of which correspond with what we know of Wright's own mother.

"It" in the opening clause is the cancer itself. It begins as a "tiny bump" and then moves inexorably throughout the mother's body. But just as inexorably the song of the mockingbird, beginning deep in its own throat, mimics the course of the disease with its rising and falling scales. After the "down-shift and fall" of the mockingbird's song, it rises (in stanza 3)—toward heaven and with it the mother's corpse—a resurrection of the body. This pattern is repeated in stanza 4: after the tallow and ash, the fire and bone, the haunting song of the mockingbird returns, its "burnt notes" transformed into "an enduring flame." In an earlier poem about the death of his mother—*Homecoming* (GRH, 13)—the death flower is the bell lily, and in part 1 of *Skins* it is the camellia blossoms. Here it is the geranium (l. 24) and the blue "twice-bitten rose" (l. 36). Blue is the triumphant color in the final stanza. The song of the bird rises into the cobalt of the empyrean, and in the final metamorphosis, the blue dove, an image of peace, displaces the mockingbird. The dove's song, like that of the mockingbird's on two earlier occasions (ll. 18, 25), disappears into an ellipsis. We do not hear the dove's song, but we cannot escape its symbolism—renewal of life, deliverance, divine spirit—as if the descending and ascending movements of the poem fulfill an aphorism of Heraclitus: "Immortals become mortals, mortals become immortals; they live in each other's death and die in each other's life" (Fragment 66). The rising movement into the blue and the "enduring flame" also echo the account of Pentecost in the Book of Acts, where the Spirit descends and the Word ascends.

Tattoos

Orig. pub. in *American Poetry Review*, November–December 1973: 34–6.
B, 19–39; CM, 56–76
Pattern: 5 × 3 × 20

Each of the twenty parts of *Tattoos* has the same structure—three five-line stanzas; each has a date at the end, signifying the year in which the experience recorded in each of the numbered parts took place; and each has a note at the end that identifies the actual experience underlying each of the lyrics. The meaning of the title has a number of suggestions—an enduring, indelible inscription, a continuous rhythm, and a visual design or decoration. But the primary meaning for Wright is that the experiences recorded here became permanently imprinted on his psyche. *Tattoos* looks to the past, and these particular experiences remain a part of the poet's consciousness.

Part 1. Wright's note—"Camellias; Mother's Day; St. Paul's Episcopal Church, Kingsport, Tennessee"—links the camellia blossoms on the bush in his backyard at Laguna Beach with two earlier experiences: his serving as an acolyte in St. Paul's Episcopal Church in Kingsport thirty years earlier and the death of his mother. In an interview Wright reports that "The 'little dropped hearts' of the camellia blooms scattered under the huge camellia bush in my backyard in Laguna Beach fifteen years ago started the poem 'Tattoos.' And since 'Tattoos' begat 'Skins,' you could say that those fallen blossoms were the beginning of the entire book, *Bloodlines*, as the other eight poems went in to accentuate or ameliorate the two long central ones. Of course, each one had its own separate trigger, but the initial pull was off the dropped blossoms" (QN, 108). The dropped blossoms, in turn, remind the poet of Mother's Day, the wearing of red and white roses signifying, respectively, living and dead mothers. He remembers the symbolism of this custom from thirty years earlier—when he was an eight-year-old and his mother was alive. But now, in 1973, the consciousness of his mother's death nine years earlier emerges, as the camellias, programmed to drop their little red hearts, fall to the ground as "scales of blood." "So light the light that fires you," says the poet, addressing his mother, and then asks, "Where would you have me return? / What songs would I sing." Wright's mother, who introduced him to Faulkner and other Southern writers, would have liked to be a writer, and she encouraged her son in that direction. His awareness of that lies behind this annunciation of his going forth, which begins here with a return to the past.

Part 2. This poem, which, as Wright's note indicates, is about the death of his father in 1972, opens with his father's body returning to dust, feeding the pin oak and assisted by the linkworm. The "nightflower" is a metaphor, associated in this context with death, and the practically indestructible crabgrass was something Wright's father did battle against for most of his mature life (*Halflife*, 70). The poet both sees and feels his father's spirit turning in the light, which according to the principle of physics announced in the second stanza, is really darkness: "The darkness is only light / That has not yet reached us." The transition to death, as the poet envisions it, was made effortlessly: "You slip it on like a glove. / *Duck soup*, you say. *Duck soup*"—his father's expression when the young Wright didn't understand something, meaning that it was extremely simple (*Halflife*, 70). The final stanza moves from the subterranean world of stanza 1 to the world of air and light: the poet sees the spirit of his father turning in the great wheel of light, "Feeling it change on your changing hands, / Feeling it take. Feeling it."

p. 57, l. 7. *The darkness ... reached us.* "I understand [this] is a physical fact. There is light coming behind all the darkness if it ever gets down" (*Halflife*, 70).

p. 57, l. 12. *Blood Creek.* Wright's poetic renaming of Reedy Creek, which runs through Kingsport, more or less paralleling East Stone Drive, and is near the house on Old Stage Road where he lived.

Part 3. This poem recounts a torch-lit snake-handling ceremony that Wright witnessed outside of Asheville, North Carolina, in 1951. This eerie ritual, believed to have begun with George Hensley in the hills of Tennessee during the early years of the twentieth century and then taken up by other Pentecostal and itinerant preachers, takes its scriptural warrant from Mark 16:15–20 and Luke 10:19. At the beginning of the poem the copperhead is described as altogether lethargic, doubtless a result of the handler's stroking the snake's stomach. In stanza 2 the handler's hand is said to be already "halfway to heaven," not having been bitten. One passage in Mark's gospel reports Jesus as saying, "They [the true believers] shall take up serpents; and if they drink any deadly thing, it shall not hurt them." The belief of the snake handlers was not that they would not be bitten, but that if they were they would survive, provided their faith were strong enough. In stanza 3 the handler (Yellow Shirt) gathers the snake to himself, which initiates a frenzy of handclapping and ecstatic dancing, the copperhead, known for its unusual color and striking pattern, itself apparently having become energized: "hot coil / Grains through the hourglass glint and spring."

p. 58, l. 6. *Dumbbell and hourglass.* The chestnut-colored bands across the back of the copperhead are sometimes described as shaped like an hourglass.

Part 4. This poem recreates scenes from Venice when Wright was a Fulbright lecturer there in 1968. It is a linguistic experiment that strings together a series of images ("I have seen what I have seen") of a city that was built upon "stanchions of joy." The imagery is largely private, but we get a sense of the poet's seeing the city after the manner of Rimbaud—its canals and gardens, its casements and cathedrals, its "radiant underpinning." And Venice is a city of art as well. The poet sees the city as J.M.W. Turner painted it in one of his many oils, and the "footfalls of Tintoretto" are everywhere—in the Scuola di San Rocco, the Palazzo Ducale, and the Gallerie dell'Accademia. The Madonna dell'Orto is sometimes called the "Tintoretto church" because its numerous works by Tintoretto have helped make the church famous. What begins with the drugged Venetian sky ends with all of the ancient structures falling "in a rain of light."

p. 59, l. 2. *White moons, black moons.* After drinking absinthe and smoking hashish in Paris, Rimbaud reported that he saw a succession of black moons and white moons chasing each other (Graham Robb, *Rimbaud* [New York: Norton, 2000], 132).

p. 59, ll. 6–8. *Zuan's canal.* Zuan = the Venetian dialect for Giovanni or John. The reference is to the Rio San Giovanni (San Giovanni Canal).

p. 59, l. 15. *I have seen ... seen.* A line that Pound uses and then repeats in *Canto II* (*Cantos*, 9). The line is sometimes seen as Pound's justification for his obscurity.

Part 5. The experience recorded in this vignette is of an eleven-year-old fainting at the altar. As the sunlight streams through the stained glass at St. Paul's Episcopal Church in Kingsport, Tennessee, the young acolyte keels over. He is "hungering" for real, not spiritual food, because of the practice of not eating before taking communion. The experience is remembered as a descent into a vortex, but the young acolyte is eventually brought back to consciousness by way of the wine from the cup. Like Paul on the road to Damascus, the poet declares: "I am risen, the cup, new sun, at my lips."

The poem is a kind of allegory of Wright's relationship with the Church—from which he received a great deal of religious instruction during his early years. He abandoned the Church after a ten-year struggle, but he could never escape its influence. Having been "raised in a religious atmosphere," he reports, "alters you completely, one way or the other. It's made me what I am and I think it's okay. I can argue against it, but it has given me a sense of spirituality that I prize" (*Halflife*, 74).

Wright on Wright: "I suppose you could say that the Catholic Church is the descendent and heir of the original church, the only and first church; therefore if there is a truth to be found, such a truth would reside there, and not in its tributaries. Being Protestant, one would always stand in the tributarial position and, if one were trying to get back to the original source, the truth, one would always be attempting to go back upstream, against the current, mapping the length of the tributary to its source. So the search is Protestant, since the source just is. But that's not how [W.H. Auden] means it, surely. Surely he meant something more metaphoric, being the good Anglican that he was, a major tributary if there ever was one. And being good Anglicans, metaphorically, we all have to work hard to find the truth, I suppose, which is there for the knowing if you pursue it diligently enough in the right place. The search is, I hope, alive in my work the same way it is alive in my life—the bell that calls me from over the mountain" (QN, 166–7).

p. 60, l. 3. *Falls like Damascus.* The simile derives from the sudden conversion experience of St. Paul on the road to Damascus. Paul falls to the ground in the presence of a great light and is blinded (Acts 22:6–10).

p. 60, l. 15. Wright later identified the one who gave him wine as a Mr. Kent (*Halflife*, 74).

Part 6. This poem records the memory of an hallucination that resulted from the six-year-old Wright having stepped on a nail when he was living in Hiwassee, North Carolina. The ensuing infection resulted in blood-poisoning, which for some reason settled in his arm. He describes the treatment (wet towels) and the symptoms (chalk-white skin, fever, exaggerated heartbeat). The hallucination involves seeing a face at the window—a face he wants to join and so purge himself of his affliction—"burned over, repurified." His desire is to escape from his fever, projected here as a climb up the ten steps of Paradise "Into the high air."

Part 7. This ekphrastic poem is a verbal recreation of Piero della Francesca's *The Resurrection* and the effect that the painting had on the poet when he saw it for the second time, during his Fulbright year—1963—in Borgo Sansepolcro. The best commentary is Wright's own account of his experience of the painting, written in response to a request from someone who, having seen an allusion to Piero in one of his poems, wanted to know about his "association" with the painter:

> Piero della Francesca was the first painter whose work I ever looked at hard, the first painter I ever really thought about. I was in the army in Italy, 1959. March, I think, a friend of mine and I were on a week's leave riding around the country. I had read about Piero in Bernard Berenson's *Painters of the Italian Renaissance* and some glancing references in Ezra Pound. We went to Monterchi, in northeastern Tuscany, just about sundown. Inside the small chapel outside the walls of the town, the Madonna del Parto had been cut out of the wall and was leaning up against it. In preparation for moving the fresco into San Sepolcro (at that time called Borgo Sansepolcro) down the road, and the museum in the Palazzo Communale.... I can't remember where I first saw the *Resurrection*, but it made the greatest initial impression on me that any painting ever has. I guess it was in town [Borgo Sansepolcro], but I don't know if the museum was up and running at that time, March 1959. In any case, I had never seen a stare like that. I later (much later) wrote a poem about it. #7 in a sequence called "Tattoos" in a book called *Bloodlines*, now collected in *Country Music*. The only other direct reference to Piero in my work is in a poem called *With Eddie and Nancy in Arezzo at the Caffe Grande* in a book called *Chickamauga* [NB, 51]. [Piero and his *Madonna del Parto* also make an appearance in *Italian Days* (*WTTT*, 92).] But he and his work have been a constant for me in my life and writing—clear, clean lines, unadorned presentation, the enfolding of landscape into my emotional life, the stare and look that comes from another world and that keeps our own eyes focused, our own feelings reticent but seeping like ground water up through the roots of things.... He is a pleasure to look at, a serious thought to think. I wish I had a few strokes of his edgy and difficult grace. I wish I had that gaze from the *Resurrection*, and saw what it saw. I think I've been trying to find it for the past forty years. The last time I saw that particular painting was in the summer of 1996. I was in San Sepolcro with two other poets, James Tate and Dara Wier. And who should we bump into on our way out of the museum but Tomas Salamun, the Slovenian poet, on his way in. And there we were, four contemporary writers, 504 years after Piero had died,

huddled on the steps of the Palazzo Communale in his home town, hoping that something might rub off and raise us a few inches off the ground. What a guy" ("Piero," in *UP*, 7–8).

The "Nameless, invisible" spirit that spins out of the painting pulls the poet "breath by breath" is an altogether human Christ. Whatever spirituality there is emerges from the eerie, almost deadpan gaze of Christ, which enchants the poet with its luminosity and seems as well to have enchanted the soldiers, who are not so much asleep as in a state of suspended animation. The poet speaks of the pulling force and the ringing tide, which are natural images, referring to the same force that regenerates the trees in the background, which come to life, moving from winter on the left to spring on the right. The demotic hills and trees spell out the hieratic V of Victory, as nature itself is in the process of being resurrected. Transcendence emanating from immanence will become a common theme in Wright's later work.

A reproduction of Piero's *The Resurrection* can be found at http://www.artchive.com/artchive/P/piero/resurrex.jpg.html and a number of other web sites.

Part 8. This poem is a paean to Harold Schimmel's chanting of morning prayers at Positano, a small town on the Amalfi coast in Campania—which was also the setting for *Storm* (CM, 7). Schimmel, a friend of Wright's from his army days and a Hebrew poet, was the one who advised him to read Pound at Lake Garda. Here Schimmel's voice is remembered as resonating across the Lattari Mountains, snapping and drifting with the wind. The prayers originate from the sea, in which Schimmel stands waist deep, holding the Torah. His voice merges with all four of the elements: earth (the mountains), air (the wind), water (the sea), and fire (associated here, as it is throughout the Hebrew Old Testament, with the manifestation of God). The focus is on the body—Schimmel's tongue and lips and his swaying movement ("Reedflow and counter flow"), synchronized with the waves breaking in from the Gulf of Salerno and thus creating a kind of harmonic, hypnotic charm. We are reminded that "chant" and "charm," both of which are associated with sound and rhythm, are etymologically related. Here the chant rises magically to the light of heaven, and everything ends in a fiery apocalyptic brilliance.

p. 63, l. 10. A *yarmulke* is the skull cap worn by orthodox Jews; *tfillin* or *tefflin* are the two small leather boxes containing scriptural passages that Jews wear on their foreheads or arms; and *tallis* is the shawl worn by Jewish men during morning prayers.

Part 9. Wright's note identifies the poem as springing from a 1952 experience of "temporary evangelical certitude." The setting is Christ School in Arden, North Carolina. At the time Wright was a junior at Christ School, which the students sometimes parodied by calling it "Jesus Tech."

The experience is recreated through a series of images, developed in the first two stanzas and recapitulated in the last, that originate from the repeated message of the religious instructors ("Theologians, Interpreters"). The path to be traveled by the young student leads to eternity ("The tracks go on, and go on"), and his certitude comes from the religious map he has been given to chart the way. "Evangelical certitude" turns out to be a solely physical reaction rather than a spiritual awakening. Thus, the experience is recalled in almost completely bodily terms, from the dust-wallowing, the drops dropping, and "scalding starts" in stanza 1 to the ground and scraped fingers and the palm print in stanzas 2 and 3. The young student *sees*, and what he sees is magnified through the eyepiece with its "fixed crosshairs"; and he *hears* the whistles and the intermittent song. He *feels* as well, but what he feels is only corporal. He has no genuine epiphany, which is why the certitude is only temporary.

Part 10. Wright's shorthand for this lyric is "visions of heaven." The date—1973—places the poem near the chronological end of the experiences recorded in *Tattoos* (two other poems in the series, the first and the last, date from 1973, the year the poem was published). The setting is California. The poem begins with a Van Gogh–like scene and concludes with images reminiscent of a medieval tapestry (the unicorn) and of Kafka (the leopard). The "Dichogamous landscape" in these "visions of heaven" is dominated by flora (sunflowers, oleander, hibiscus, moonflowers, smoke trees, spider flowers). The white lady who emerges at the center of the poem is sandwiched between the ominous evil eye, also "flower-like," that stares out from high on the wall, and the vines that strike and recoil in the concluding line. The "found chord" (l. 10) suggests a harmony or interpenetration of the light and darkness, the floral and the human, the red choker and the white parasol, the ordinary and the extraordinary, the unicorn (symbolically a good omen) and the leopard (symbolically menacing). Nevertheless, the atmosphere is as disconcerting as one of Blake's memorable fancies: this is no Eden before the fall.

p. 65, l. 10. *Dichogamous* = having stamens and pistils that mature at different times.
p. 65, l. 14. *The leopard sips at her dish of blood.* Cf. Kafka: "Leopards break into the temple and drink to the dregs what is in the sacrificial pitchers; this is repeated over and over again; finally it can be calculated in advance, and it becomes part of the ceremony" (*Parables and Paradoxes* [New York: Schocken, 1958], no. 20).

Part 11. The experience described here, according to Wright's note, is of an automobile wreck and the ensuing recovery in a Baltimore hospital. In stanza 1, what happened externally—the oily glide, ripsurge, spin, and cracked light—superimposes itself onto the vortex of the poet's psyche: it is his cells that are gliding and his consciousness that is spinning into oblivion. The controlling metaphor for the experience is air travel. The poet loses consciousness during take-off, and the time in the operating room, described with clipped precision, is metaphorically the re-entry. In stanza 3, the poet, equipped with the parachute of life once more, does not sentimentalize the experience. What do we do after having glass shards removed by the surgeon? "We stand fast, friend, we stand fast."

p. 66, l. 8. *glass shards.* Cf. this simile from an early poem: "(And like, in childhood, those bits of glass / Taken into the flesh—which disappear, / Which leave no mark—will these, too, surface / In 25 years or so, / Uncolored, unedged, from our skin?)" (*The Killing*, in GRH, 58). Years later Wright recycles the simile in *College Days*: "Some things move in and dig down // whether you want them to or not. / Like pieces of small glass your body subsumes when you are young, / They exit transformed and easy-edged / Many years later, in middle age, when you least expect them, / And shine like Lot's redemption. / College is like this, a vast, exact, // window of stained glass / That shatters without sound as you pass, / Year after year disappearing, unnoticed and breaking off. / Gone, you think, when you are gone, thank God. But look again. / Already the glass is under your skin, //already the journey's on" (ST, 19–20).

Part 12. This lyric recreates the delighted experience of the ten-year-old schoolboy learning to write cursively by the Palmer method. Although he sees the transcribed words as rolling from his fingers, it is not the process of writing that intrigues him so much as the infinite magic ("mojo and numberless") and the "Sure sleights of hand" that language affords: it can create worlds seen, smelled, and heard. The poet takes great delight in pronouncing the words—"Apple, arrival, railroad, shoe"—and in discovering the drone of their combinations—"A splash of leaves through the windowpanes, / A smell of tar from the streets." Moreover, words provide "Back stairsteps to God," which is the antitype of the Tower of Babel. Thus, instruction in cursive script anticipates what will become the journey of the poet—from a beginning with alpha and an ending someday in the omega of silence.

Part 13. This memory recorded here, the poet tells us in a note, came from his kindergarten years in Corinth, Mississippi. The recollection of the boiler-room setting is vivid; of the masturbating pedophilic janitor, less so. In stanza 3, the young boy is admonished not to tell anyone what has happened, and he apparently has remained silent until the present confession. The poet makes no judgment against the janitor. He feels that the repugnant experience is perhaps an example of a fall from grace from which the janitor's lost soul never recovers.

But he is uncertain and can conclude only that "We give, / And we take it back. We give again ... " What the poet gives, takes back, and gives again is perhaps forgiveness, but the ellipsis at the end trails off into uncertainty, as if there is no way of extricating ourselves from the myth of the eternal return or the Fall or Original Sin.

Part 14. This poem emerged from a dream after Wright had seen Diane Arbus's seven photographs of mentally retarded people. Each of the three vignettes describes one of the photos. The first is without commentary by the poet except for the remark about the shadow and the imperative to call this masked character "Untitled," which was Arbus's title. The second stanza is pure description. The third concludes with a remark about the lisping syllable, a projection, apparently, by the poet that signals the yearning of these masked characters for an identity. The three photographs referred to in the poem are "Untitled (3) 1970-71," "Untitled (7) 1970-71," and "Untitled (4) 1970-71." They can be found in the final series of reproductions in *Dianne Arbus* (Millertown, NY: An Aperture Monograph, 1972), unpaginated. This is a poem of pure pathos, the full effect of which can be felt only with the photos alongside the poem.

p. 69, l. 10. *Nine*. In the third photograph seven of the people are clearly visible. The eighth and ninth are barely captured in the left and right margins of the photo.

Part 15. Wright identifies the subject of this poem as day of his mother's funeral in Kingsport, Tennessee. He was in Rome at the time. The poet's pain is objectified as an electric saw that devastates everything in his mother's bedroom, eventually leaving the house, where it "keeps on cutting," the ellipsis perhaps suggesting that it continues on its way eastward to Rome. It is objectified as well in the "poem" of the dogwood, which is a "poem of pain." The black notches of the dogwood's petals, conventionally associated with the nails of the Crucifixion, here also cause pain, burning in the poet's blood. The dogwood turns out to be a vehicle for the poet to project his grief and sense of loss. Even the feathery fluttering of the petals delivers a farewell.

p. 70, l. 11. *Dogwood*. The grave of Wright's mother, Mary Winter Wright, would later have a dogwood planted on it. In *Apologia Pro Vita Sua* Wright identifies the "winter-weathered dogwood" with the via Dolorosa, punning on his mother's maiden name. See *NB*, 71.

Part 16. This poem recounts the experience of the fifteen-year-old at a strip show in Cherokee, North Carolina. The scene is the county fair, where all is "gloss, gothic, and garrulous." The gawkers pay their fees; the stripper disrobes. Although some leave when her price gets too high, the poet, now aroused, remains transfixed ("staked to *my* tree"). Like the county sheriff, who has been paid off, the teenager remains until the end of the act. In the concluding stanza his flaming id subsides into the insect sounds of the gathering darkness. Here, outside the tent, everything is in stark contrast to the seediness of what has come before.

Part 17. This lyric describes a recurrent dream, first experienced during the poet's college years. The dream has three distinct parts: the poet's ridding himself of the dead moths as, inside his dream, he awakens; the curious encounter with the bride and bridegroom who say to each other, "It's mother again just mother"; and an ascent to the tenth floor of a building where the poet encounters a masked figure named Faceless, who is enjoined to "come back." The elements of the dream remain, by definition, incoherent, though they doubtless are symbolic of certain desires and fixations—catharsis, mother complex, journeys of ascent, encounters with the mysterious Other, and the like.

Part 18. This poem recreates the experience of a visit to the Naxian Lions in Delos Greece, the poet having taken a trip there during his U.S. Army sojourn in Italy. Five of the marble lions, dedicated to Apollo by the Naxians at the end of seventh century B.C.E., have survived.

The remains of three more were mounted on modern bases. To prevent further damage from the wind and sea water, the lions were moved to the Archaeological Museum of Delos in 1999. Images of the lions can be found at http://www.grisel.net/delos_museum.htm.

The first stanza rehearses the voyage to Delos, the "wavefall" and "sealash" piercing the poet's skin as the boat makes its way through the sunlit Cyclades. In contrast, stanza two depicts the bleak, dusty, and bone-dry island. Stanza 3 describes with unadorned accuracy the marble lions themselves. The lions were originally set to guard the sanctuary at Delos, and their open, roaring mouths were apparently intended to inspire divine awe on the part of worshippers. But the poet's own interpretation is that the lions are explaining something—perhaps telling the uncomprehending tourists that they are treading on sacred ground.

Part 19. The subject here is the death of Wright's father. The questions asked by the hemlocks of stanza 1 are answered in stanza 2. The black-draped apple trees signify that "Someone is dead; someone who loved them [the trees] is dead." The glove and the shoe are private emblems, although in *Tattoos*, no. 2, the father slips on the darkness of death like a glove, and there is perhaps some connection between gloves and the father's contracting business and his gardening. The climax of the poem is the son's expression of regret—regret that "anchors" him in the sifting snow. The object of regret remains unspoken (things not done with or said to his father?) in this winter's tale.

Part 20. Wright's note indicates that the final stanza is an adaptation of lines from Eugenio Montale's *Serenata Indiana* (*Indian Serenade*). The stanza parallels closely Wright's later translation: "The octopus that slides / his inky fingers among the reefs / can use you. You belong to him // and don't know it. You *are* him, and think you are yourself" (*Storm*, 29). The note, unlike the other nineteen, does not specify the subject of this dream-like hermetic lyric, which is especially resistant to interpretation.

The "tu" to whom Montale addresses his poem appears to be another version of the shadowy female figures throughout his poems. The "you" in Wright's poem is the poet himself, who is at a turning point. He looks back at where he has been and appears to be ready now to launch himself, bird-like and with the rhythm of his soft voice, into the next phase of his journey.

In adapting Montale's poem, Wright has changed "inky" to "fat." Montale wrote, "Il polipo che insinua / tentacoli d'inchiostro tra gli scogli / può servisi di te," which is a bit more ominous than either the translation or the adaptation. The *polipo* is more like a squid or, as in the Greek root, a cuttle-fish than an octopus. In any event, the poet, still pained by the death of his parents dogging his footsteps, spreads his fingers (stanza 1) like the fingers of the ink-producing and insinuating *polipo* (stanza 3). The suggested identification between the poet and this creature of the sea, mirroring the identification between the poet and the creature of the air in stanza 2, is made explicit in the last line, where the poet concludes the address to himself: "You *are* him, and think yourself yourself."

Hardin County

Orig. pub. in *New Southern Poets*, ed. Guy Owen and Mary C. Williams (Chapel Hill: University of North Carolina Press, 1974), 104.
B, 43–4; CM, 77–8
Pattern: 6 × 5

The poem is dedicated to Wright's father, Charles Penzel Wright, 1904–1972. Wright was born in Hardin County, Tennessee, on his father's birthday, 25 August. His father was a civil engineer, who worked on dam sites for the Tennessee Valley Authority and on the Manhattan Project at Oak Ridge, Tennessee. He later worked in construction for the Eastman Company in Kingsport, where he eventually began his own construction company.

The first two stanzas are addressed directly to the poet's father, whose grief was like a world gone awry—the surreal world of the first stanza. The source of the father's attendant fear and self-pity is not revealed, but its likely cause is the death of his wife. Stanza 3 returns to an earlier time—the light of those first years when he was a child—a time when things were different. Stanza 4 embodies a desire for some radical change, but the desire is not realized: "everything stays the same." The somber and elegiac mood is suddenly abandoned in the final stanza with its announcement of the birth of spring, the poet having now turned away from the private and surreal associations to the reality of what he sees before him, and we are left with a naturalistic description of the landscape, made vivid by the attendant tropes: music, small change, smudge, mansions, and appointments. The final stanza anticipates the recreation of landscape that will mark Wright's later work.

p. 78. Oak Hill. A cemetery in Kingsport, Tennessee

Delta Traveller

Orig. pub. in *Lillabulero* 14 (1974): 170–1.
B, 45–7; CM, 79–81
Pattern: 9 × 8

This elegy is dedicated to Wright's mother, Mary Winter Wright, 1910–1964, who grew up in the Mississippi delta. Wright's own remarks on the poem provide sufficient commentary: "The poem is an elegy to my mother. The first stanza is about me, the other seven are about her, and my relationship to her, or rather to her dying. Filial duty and reaction in stanza 2; how she remains alive in me in stanza 3; how she inhabits her clothes (this life) in stanza 4; my bad dreams in stanza 5; how, in memory, she survives the bone cancer that killed her in stanza 6; how things will devolve to the same thing in stanza 7; as do the dead in stanza 8 and we get them back in temporary reprieve" (*Halflife*, 131).

And, in reply to an interviewer's question about the composition of the poem Wright remarked: "I was in Laguna Beach, California, in a little shack in the backyard of our house in which I used to write. I had written *Tattoos* and *Skins* and I knew I wanted to write a poem about my mother and one about my father. As most of my poems do, *Delta Traveller* probably started with a rhythm rather than a structure. This was at a time when my son was two or three years old, and I had very few stretches of writing time. I would have maybe an hour or so that I could sneak in before I had to help out. That's why the poem came out in those little sections. Each one of them was written at a different time. I know it took somewhere between three weeks and a month. I would work on a section at a time, but what holds the poem together is that it is an elegy. It doesn't go logically from one section to another, nor would I want it to. The skull part was from a dream; the armed lawnchair was actually a chair of my mother's; she had bone cancer, therefore 'bones like paint.' The first part arises from the fact that I was the first child born in this particular hospital and Dr. Hurt was my doctor; the fertility business comes from a *National Geographic* I was reading. The last stanza is about nothing ever being really lost because it stays in the memory and is part of the natural process.... I did have in mind a poem about my mother, but that was not what started it. Something other than the desire to write the poem actually got it going. Perhaps even the word 'quarternight.' It's the sort of word that might get me to hearing a rhythm. I remember I read Andy Adams' *The Story of a Cowboy* [*The Log of a Cowboy*], and there was a cowhand in it named

Fox Quarternight. I thought that was a marvelous name and I may have been saying it to myself and the first line happened, as I was born in the early morning hours in that hospital. (Hence, 'brash tongue on the tongueless ward.') That may have started it all and it flowed from there. I don't really remember but it's a good story and it could be true" (Remnick, 574–5).

p. 80, ll. 24–5. *All this you survive ... a pulse.* Cf. "your gift survived it all ... it [poetry] survives, / A way of happening, a mouth" (W.H Auden, *In Memory of W.B. Yeats*, pt. 2, ll. 1, 9–10).
p. 81, l. 6. *Echo.* The sound of the divine; a "euphemism," as Wright says, "for Whatever's-Out-There" (*Halflife*, 76).

Skins

Orig. pub. in *Poetry* 125 (December 1974): 152–61.
B, 51–70 CM, 82–102
Pattern: 14 × 20

These twenty free-verse "sonnets" are "skins," as opposed to "tattoos," insofar as they have to do with the outer layers rather than the depths of emotional consciousness. The poem as a whole is abstract, conceptual, and hypothetical as opposed to recording actual experiences, mental as opposed to emotional, and external as opposed to internal. Wright describes them as a skin-like "overlay" to *Tattoos* (*Halflife*, 75). He conceived of the twenty parts of *Tattoos* as being connected by the thread of experience. The chief structural feature of *Skins*, on the other hand, is a ladder, a movement upward through the colon that concludes Part 10 and then a movement downward, the poet returning in Part 20 to the point at which he began in Part 1.

The notes at the end of the poem (p. 102)—a list of eighteen topics sandwiched between the beginning and end of the journey at "Point A"—were added when it was published in *Country Music*: they did not accompany the poem when it originally appeared in *Poetry* or when it was reprinted in *Bloodlines*. These brief notes, reproduced at the beginning of each part in what follows, identify the general subject of each of the parts. *Tattoos*, as we have seen, began with the image of the camellias. For the impetus of *Skins*, see Part 1, below. Portions of the notes and commentaries that follow are indebted to Wright's interview at Oberlin College in November 1976, published in *Halflife*, 59–88.

Part 1. Situation, Point A. The impetus for *Skins*, according to Wright (QN, 108), was the abstract statement in lines 2–3: "There comes that moment / When what you are is what you will be." The poem, however, does not focus on this moment, which is as yet not specifiable. The focus rather is on the journey. The poet, *in medias res*, looks back to a receding past and ahead to an uncertain future, representing himself as living in the margins, holding his hands out in supplication, drifting through wherever the "landshed" takes him, and writing "One word at a time." Not unaware of life's practicalities (he counts his money), the pilgrim is nevertheless pulled along by forces outside himself, not (yet) being able to identify "that moment" that defines him. The movement of *Tattoos* was toward the past; *Skins* looks to the future.

Part 2. Beauty. The essence of beauty, according to the poet, is a function of the unknowable mysteries of painting, poetry, and music (ll. 1–5) and of nature (ll. 9–14). In both cases beauty remains hidden in the syntactic gaps and in the "pith and marrow of every root." Beauty contains a sense of the Other that the poet calls "inhuman." This means, on the one hand, "divine," the language of the first six lines—perfection, infinity, salvation, redemption—underwriting this implication. It means, on the other hand "natural": beauty lies in the most interior parts of roots, blooms, rocks, clouds, and seeds. Beauty, then, is both transcendent and immanent. It may be unknowable, but the poet is certain that its sources, at least, are recognizable. Wright will remain committed to this *both/and* aesthetic throughout his career, representing the extraordinary richness of his back yard, Lake Garda, the Montana meadow, and other *loci* where the *genius* resides, and meditating as well on what Vico called the *verum factum*, the realities of the world we make, whether it is the *gnosis* of the Nag Hammadi Library, Abraham von Werdt's wood engravings, the lyrics of the T'ang poets, or the paintings of Piero della Francesca and Giorgio Morandi.

Part 3. Truth. This poem is ostensibly about a photograph of the poet, taken against the background of a glacial slope. The resolution and contrast are imperfect, so that it is difficult to distinguish where the blue escarpment ends and the blue sky begins. It is only "fair print." How the poem is thematically about "truth" is something of a riddle, but it seems to hinge on the Eucharistic imagery in the last five lines. The question is whether the images of ourselves really represent what we are. The poet wants to break down the conventional separation between self and image of self, and in the startling injunction to himself to eat the photograph, we have a projection of ultimate possession. By eating the body and drinking the blood, we identify with Christ, in the Roman Catholic Eucharist; in the Protestant tradition, eating is a symbolic analogy. There are other versions of this metaphor of radical possession: we find it, for example, in Ezekiel's eating of the scrolls, Milton's use of swallowing as a trope for internalizing, and Mark Strand's *Eating Poetry*. In other words, we are what we identify with and thereby possess. The "truth," then, of the poet's identity is a combination of all the images of himself—his pose on the mountain, as well as his sacrifices, greed, and sustenance. Truth is not in a single image: it emerges from all of the images.

p. 84, l. 10. *Take it, eat it, it is your body and blood.* "And as they were eating, Jesus took bread, and blessed it, and brake it, and gave it to the disciples, and said, Take, eat; this is my body. And he took the cup, and gave thanks, and gave it to them, saying, Drink ye all of it; For this is my blood of the new testament, which is shed for many for the remission of sins" (Matthew 26:26–8).

Part 4. Destruction of the universe. This poem begins as an inversion of the creation myth. We are taken through four stages—the structure of the universe (a geometric firmament), God (here, a version of Blake's Nobodaddy), the elements (water, earth, and fire), and seeds (the germ of plant life). Following the ellipsis, which points to the other, unnamed links in the great chain of being, the stars lose their heat, are extinguished, and disappear into oblivion, "Like the corpses of Borneo." Things fall apart, the center cannot hold, and we return to the original geometric structure, though the "dish of sparks," which ignited the process of creation, has now become a death-like "dish of ash."

p. 85, l. 2. *indifferent blue.* Cf. "this dividing and indifferent blue" (Wallace Stevens, *Sunday Morning*, pt. 3, l. 15).

Part 5. Organized religion. This lyric rejects one form of organized religion for another. What the poet cannot swallow and thus moves away from is revealed religion with its "black stone," its God of "the hard breath," and its cloudy theology. What he moves toward is natural religion, represented in what is found in the shallows at the waterfall—an inviting display of the small fauna: the insects explaining themselves, the newts lighting the way with their lanterns, the crayfish opening their doors, and the "drenched wings of sunclusters" (the shine on the water), rising "Like thousands of tiny cathedrals into their new language." Conventional views of God are replaced by a divine immanence, as the wheel—the cycle of nature—arcs downward to the light of landscape. The poem's conclusion is a moment of Wordsworthian sublime.

Part 6. Metamorphosis. This poem recounts the metamorphosis of the mayfly, the oldest of the extant winged insects, from the molting stage of the larva (nymph) through its emergence into its subimago (drying) state and shortly thereafter to its imago (adult) state. The alliterative account of the metamorphosis is zoologically quite accurate. This particular mayfly is female; after "rising out of herself" she "joins" with her mate and drops to "her destiny," which is to lay eggs and start the cycle all over again (the imago is sexually mature)—or to be eaten by a fish or bird. In Ovid, metamorphoses ordinarily involve the changing of human beings into something less than human, illustrating how difficult it is for them to maintain their humanity. In the present poem the play upon "image" and "imago" (adult insect and idealized image of a person) suggests that the Ovidian process might be reversed.

p. 87, l. 2. *instar* = the stage of the mayfly between molts; some mayflies go through as many as fifty instars.

Part 7. Water. This is a paean to what Dante calls "lo gran mar dell' essere" [the great sea of being] (*Paradiso*, 1. 113), "being," in this case, referring to the ceaseless slushing of the tides against the coral shore and the attendant denizens of the deep: starfish, anemone, crab. In the final line the poet addresses the shifting, sluffing sea as "blue mother," identifying her with the goddess of the great sea (*mare*) and with such variations as the *mere* of Grendel's mother. The "blue mother" is, *mutatis mutandis*, Blake's "world"; the "grains of sand" are the "thousands of tiny punctures / Spewing and disappearing."

p. 88, l. 5. *grain of sand*. "To see a World in a Grain of Sand / And Heaven in a Wild Flower / Hold Infinity in the palm of your hand / And Eternity in an hour" (William Blake, *Auguries of Innocence*, ll. 1–4).

Part 8. Water/Earth. This exquisite little lyric begins with the poet about to drift off to sleep on a July afternoon along the shore of Lake Garda, near Verona, Italy. But his somnolent state does not prevent him from recreating the sights and sounds of what is before him. As against the "tedious scarf of sleep," we have a great deal of kinetic energy—the darting lizard, the rising birds, the flashing olive trees, the bees dragging along their pollen, the craning eye of the poppies, and especially the lapping of the lake, captured by three exceptional metaphors. "Small pleasures," the poet announces by way of summary, and then the details of the scene disappear, as in a photograph that is fading out and becoming more and more grainy. The poet wants to dismiss what he has recorded by the "so what" question in the last line, but the poem itself is the only answer to "so what?" that we need. And so we thank the poet for "passing through."

p. 102, l. 8. The broad subject of this second of four poems on the elements is, according to Wright's note, "Water/Earth." In an interview he says that it is "air/earth" (*Halflife*, 75). Air does make its way into the poem, what with the birds rising into the "inveterate blue" and the honeybees dragging "their yellow slumber." So perhaps it should be "Earth/Air/Water."

Part 9. Earth/Fire. Jacob Boehme sees fire as the first principle of life, a magical spirit that does not die. Heraclitus sees fire as central to the process of exchange in a continually transforming universe: "There is exchange of all things for fire and of fire for all things." Charles Wright, in this surrealistic rumination on earth and fire, sees the earth/fire relation as a cycle: we emerge from the earth, experience a fiery interlude, and return to the earth once more. One transcends the cycle by the fire within—"the light of yourself." The image of the "get-away" in the final line is based on an old Montana saying: if the homesteading is not going well, then run away.

Part 10. Aether. Beginning with the alchemical notion of *prima materia*, the poem moves quickly from the archetypal matter to the *quinta essentia*, the fifth substance, known as aether. Aether was said by the ancients to be the substance in the cosmos above the earthly sphere. The poet thus journeys from the alchemist's crucible into the air. He finds his body streaming though the aether among the stars ("radiant archipelagos"), and from the "fabric" of the upper air he is able to abstract one golden thread that will lead him home. The colon that ends the poem leaves us with nothing but blank space, and it marks the top of the ladder in the twenty-poem sequence. Still, the poet has at least "got the jump" on what he must do to get back to Jerusalem, his proper home.

p. 91, ll. 13–14. *golden stitch ... lead you home*. Cf. Blake's promise to the Christians in *Jerusalem*: "I give you the end of a golden string, / Only wind it into a ball, / It will lead you in at Heaven's gate / Built in Jerusalem's wall" (pl. 77).

Part 11. Primitive Magic. The poem records an imaginative journey up the Xingu River to a primitive space in the Amazon rainforest. The scenes depicted in lines 3–8 derive from a television documentary, *The Tribe that Time Forgot*, about a South American Indian tribe, the Arara (Jaguar people). The poet finds that this journey, the first of four explorations of the esoteric arts, is "unworkable," and so he declares that it is better to be lowered into "a round hole in the earth" and "covered with thick feathers." The ascent of the natives' song to the sky (an earlier time of the signs) is trumped by a descent into the earth (a later sign of the times). Solitary confinement, apparently, is to be preferred to primitive ritual in this first of the poems that trace the journey downward.

Part 12. Necromancy. This second of the descent poems centers on the practice of communicating with the spirits of the dead. The ritual of summoning the dead, described in ll. 1–9, comes from *The Grand Grimoire*, first published in French in 1522—a book that Wright had read several years earlier. He draws on the following passage from the chapter entitled "The Magick Secret; or The Art of Speaking with the Dead":

> For this operation it is necessary to attend midnight mass at Christmas and at midnight precisely to have a conversation with the inhabitants of the other world and at the moment that the Priest lifts the Host, bow down and with a frank and severe voice say *Esurgent mortuit et ac me veniut* [the dead rise and come to me]. As soon as you have pronounced these six words it is necessary to go to the cemetery and at the first tomb that meets your eye offer this prayer: "Infernal powers, you who bring the turbid in the universe, abandon your obscure dwelling and retire to the other side of the River Styx".... After this ceremony, which is indispensable to carry out, take a fistful of earth and spread it as one sows grain in a field, saying in a low voice: "He who is in dust awake from his tomb and leave his ashes and answer the questions that I pose him in the name of the Father of all men." Then bend a knee to the ground, turning your eyes to the East and when you see that the doors of the Sun are going to open, arm yourself with the two bones of the dead man that you will put in a cross of Saint Andrew. Then throw them at the first temple or church that offers itself to your eyes. Having well-executed the aforesaid, set out in a western direction and when you have taken 5,900 steps, lay yourself down to sleep on the ground in an elongated position, holding the palms of your hand against your thighs, and your eyes to the sky towards the Moon and in this position, call he or she whom you wish to see, when you see the specter appear, solicit their presence with the following words *Ego sum, te peto, et videre queo* [I am, I desire you, and I am able to see you].

The poet is mystified by what will happen next: Will the dead "sit in their rocking chairs, decayed hands / Explaining the maps you must follow? / Will circles be explicated, the signs shriven?" The pages of *The Grand Grimoire* offer no help. Its author says only that when you have gotten what you want from the spirit, send it away:

> After these words [*Ego sum, te peto, et videre queo*], your eyes will be satisfied to see the object that dearest to you and give you the most pleasurable delight. When you have obtained from the shadow which you have invoked, that which you believe to be to your satisfaction, send it away in this manner: "Return to the kingdom of the elect, I am content with you and your presence." Then picking yourself up, return to the same tomb where you made the first prayer above which you need to make a cross with the end of your blade which you will be holding in your left hand.

The final note sounded by the poet is pure skepticism: he doubts that the spirits can emerge from the land of the dead, the door to which has no knob.

Part 13. Black Magic. This poem recounts the magic ritual of preparing the Hand of Glory, the dried and pickled hand of a man who had been hanged. According to legend, the

Hand of Glory was used by witches and sorcerers to cast a spell over houses. Thus, it was sometimes used as a robber's charm, carried by burglars when they engaged in their thievery. In the macabre process of creating the Hand of Glory, described by the poet in ll. 4–10, the sorcerer would cut off the hand from the fresh corpse of a hanged man, preferably during the eclipse of the moon, and wrap it in a shroud. Afterwards it was pickled for two weeks in an earthenware jar with salt, long peppers, and saltpeter. Next it was either dried in an oven with vervain—an herb said to ward off demons—or laid out to dry in the sun during the dog days of August. It was then made into a kind of candle from the fat of the hanged man, wax, and ponie (apparently dung or perhaps the sesame of Laponie [Lapland]). The candle-fingers could subsequently be lit, and those who saw the burning fingers, it was said, would be frozen in their tracks and rendered speechless. One early account of how to prepare the Hand of Glory is in *Les Secrets Merveilleaux de la Magie Naturelle du Petit Albert Lyons* (1668). (In *Harry Potter and the Chamber of Secrets* Draco Malfoy comes across the Hand of Glory in a pawnshop.)

Part 14. Alchemy. The poet represents the alchemists as filled with incessant talk about anodynes, unguents, and other medicinal potions. The contexts of their talk are the windows of the city's battlements, the river, the primordial light, and "heavy earth." The contexts, then, are a version of the four elements—air, water, fire, earth. The problem is that nothing ever materializes from the alchemists' chatter: "They talk, and nothing appears. They talk and it does not appear," "it" referring to the poetic secret or what Rimbaud calls the *alchemie du verbe*. Thus, the poet can put little stock in this hermetic form of proto-chemistry: unlike Mallarmé, he is not able to see the alchemists as his *nos ancetres*, *nos* referring to his poetic ancestors and those of kindred poets.

Part 15. Allegory. The poet represents himself as returning from down river, where he has encountered a series of images in various mythological and religious traditions said to contain allegorical significance: the all-seeing eye (Rosicrucianism), the seven-caved mountain (the sacred *axis mundi* in the mythology of the native American Mantakas), the serpent nailed on the cross (an image found in Christian, Egyptian, and alchemical traditions), the oak and rose (ubiquitous in legend), and the slaughter of the Innocents (Christian mythology). The catalogue of such allegorical imagery tails off with the ellipsis in line 10, at which point the poet announces that "The Echo is dead." Echo itself has an allegorical meaning. In *Delta Traveller* "the Echo" is "the one transmitter of things: / Transcendent and inescapable." In the present poem the Echo, which is a representation of the divine, is not to be found in conventional allegories but in the "flame, wind, rainwrack / And soil, each a survivor, each one / An heir to the fingerprint." To encounter the Echo we need not revert to the somewhat outmoded and overdetermined symbols of the past. All we need do is open our eyes to the four elements directly in front of us: earth (soil), air (wind), fire (flame), and water (rainwrack). Thus, allegory is rejected, just as the four forms of esoterica (primitive magic, necromancy, black magic, and alchemy) have been. Allegory ordinarily requires a continuous narrative and a specific religious or moral point, neither of which has a central place in Wright's poetic project.

Part 16. Fire. The poet now returns to the four elements. Here he lies down in the flames of his past. Carefully gathering the items to be kindled—the moss, pitch, pine boughs—he adds to these highly combustible materials "All the paraphernalia of past lives": ball bats, blue shoes, headrests, backrests, furniture. He then enters the flames himself in an act of apparent self-immolation. But the fire turns out to be purgatorial, and so the poet rises phoenix-like from the ash, purged, rearranged, recreated, and reinvigorated.

Part 17. Air. The rivers of air, to which the poet has paid little attention heretofore, suddenly startle him and issue in the realization of the final line: "what you take in is seldom what you let out." Previously, the poet had only "filtered and rearranged" the rivers of air, but after his little epiphany, the rivers of air "start to take on / The acid and eye of what's clear": the poet's doors of perception have now been cleansed, so that he can *see* the "milky message of breath on cold mornings." What surprises the poet—the rivers of air that he has played with before—is connected to the metaphorical kernel in numerous languages that identifies breath, air, and wind with spirit.

Part 18. Water. This lyric is carried along by two metaphorical clusters—wearing apparel and mirror—and one central metaphor: light shining off water. The focus, then, is not simply upon the three kinds of water (sea, lakes, river) but also on the reflected light that the poet hopes to find himself moving towards. The sea does not oblige, its "slick confetti" and "surgy retractions / Too slippery and out of place," thus making it into a "wrecked looking-glass." Nor does the "hard glint" of the inland "necklace of lakes," associated here with the bluegrass music of the 1940s: "There's no one to wear [this pendant] now, or hand it down." But the river *can* contain the "shine." The poet refers to the river as an "unwaivering mirror," which displaces the "wrecked looking-glass" of the sea that distorts or parodies representation. The river is "unwaivering" in that it does not relinquish its function of reflection and representation: it does not abandon the "shine," or the illumination the poet wants to move toward. The river is a "speculum," in all of the senses of that word. When the poem is read, we also hear "unwavering," for the shine of the river is resolute, unvacillating, and steady. "Flushed," as descriptive of the river, is also a pun for the river is glowing as well as fresh and vigorous, cleansed as well as abundant and overflowing. The ellipsis at the end signals a tailing off rather than closure, but as the river provides a connection to memory, and as the pilgrim's shoe is intact, the poem's conclusion moves away from irony.

p. 99, l. 6. *wrecked looking-glass.* Cf. Joyce's "cracked looking glass," a phrase Stephen Dedalus takes to be symbolic of Irish art (*Ulysses* [New York: Modern Library, 1946], 8).

p. 99, l. 7. *High Lonesome.* A style of bluegrass music, where a high-pitched, nasal harmony is sung over the main melody. The phrase would become the title of a collection of essays on Wright's work: *High Lonesome: On the Poetry of Charles Wright*, ed. Adam Giannelli (Oberlin, OH: Oberlin College Press, 2006).

Part 19. Earth. The poet confesses that he is not altogether clear about the ascending and descending movements and asks himself whether there is any "other work in this world" besides the going up and the going down. Back on the earth itself, he sees that his meanderings have left little imprint, and he laments the fact that his pilgrimage lacks direction. But what he does not lament is the world of plenitude, the still point of the turning world where the forever growing bounty of the natural world presents itself: "the willow's change / The drift and slip of smoke through the poplar leaves, / The cliff's dance and the wind's shift, / Alone with the owl and the night crawler." Here we have a recapitulation of three of the elements, the fourth being implicit in the underground water that makes possible the "willow's change."

Part 20. Situation, Point A. In the final poem of *Skins* the poet takes stock of his journey, asking what his various encounters with the elements and the esoteric traditions ("those idols of stitched skin") have "come to." In Point A of Part 1 the poet began his quest for the moment that would define him, inching his way along "One word at a time." Here he has arrived back at Point A, still not having found that moment, uncertain about whether anything has changed, and skeptical about a poetic enterprise that has produced only "these sad marks, / Phrases half-parsed, ellipses and scratches across the dirt." He does grant that his pilgrimage has come "to a point," but then he adds "It comes and goes." We are left, then, with a feeling "of the uncertainty of his setting forth," in Yeats's phrase.

p. 101, l. 9. *walking to and from on the earth.* "And the Lord said unto Satan, Whence comest thou? Then Satan answered the Lord, and said, From going to and fro in the earth, and from walking up and down in it" (Job

1:7 and 2:2). The phrase, also used to describe the divine horsemen in Zechariah 1:10, will appear later *The Silent Generation* (NB, 37).

Link Chain

Orig. pub. *Partisan Review* 51, no. 3 (1974): 401–3.
B, 73–5 CM, 103–5
Pattern: 10 × 6
Time: Flashback to 1940s and 1950s
Place: Kingsport, Tennessee, and environs

In the first of six autobiographical vignettes—a chain of early experiences linked by their common locale in east Tennessee—the poet is in Laguna Beach on a Palm Sunday. Seeing the banana leaves triggers a flashback to a time in 1949 when he and his childhood friend, Ed Philbeck, stacked the Palm Sunday fronds for a service at St. Paul's Episcopal Church on Ravine Street (now Road) in Kingsport, Tennessee. The fronds were in the shape of tiny crosses on a background of purple cloth. The accompanying pins were for the congregation to attach the crosses to their clothes. At the eleven o'clock service the young teenager takes a cross and two pins, "One for the cross, and one again for the heart." He apparently intends the latter to be a means of self-abnegation.

Section 2 recreates another scene from the poet's early life, revealing his attachment to the Tennessee landscape. He is on the front seat of a bus headed southwest from Kingsport toward Surgoinsville, Tennessee. Looking at the landscape he determines that this is where, in the language of the gospel tune, he would like to "lay [his] body down." But other places would do as well—under the black cherry tree on the north side of Chestnut Ridge, near Wright's home on Old Stage Road, south of East Stone Drive in east Kingsport, or floating down the river like a leaf. The Holston River snakes along just south of Highway 11-W, but the poet says any river would do. As the old hymn has it, "Lay my body down, / Float my bones in the water of the river." The young boy sees the landscape of east Tennessee as a resting place, eternal or otherwise.

The third vignette recreates the weekend ritual of leaf gathering. The poet and his brother, to whom *Bloodlines* is dedicated, would journey to Moody's Woods to collect oak leaves and then haul them back to the shredder, no doubt on the instructions of their father, who liked to garden. Once shredded, the oak-leaf mulch would then be heaped up over the plants to protect them. The poet concludes by observing that the leaves, "less coarse" now that they have been shredded, will later warm him in the cold room.

The sequence as a whole takes its title from the spondee of the first line in section 3, "link chain," Wright's reversal of the more ordinary "chain link." Compare the variation "hair breath," where we might expect "hair breadth" or "hair's breadth." The entire section moves along spondaically, as befits the two brothers, equally engaged in leaf collecting: the vignette has thirteen spondees altogether. Some point to things recognizable in ordinary experience: "oak mulch" and "drag back." The meaning of others is private: "bone stock," "hair breath," and even "link chain," although the last, along with "circle by circle," reinforces the sense of a communal enterprise, one in which the two brothers are "bound" to the leaf mulch. Given the theme of death that enters sections 2 and 5, "cold room" could well refer to the grave, where unmulched leaves will later provide warmth.

Section 4 records an invocation by the young boy to the Lord of the Anchorite, who, like the Holy Spirit, takes the form of a bird, to gather him up and set him down in his proper place. The scene is a church with its collection box. The boy has his Peter's pence in his pocket.

He senses a connection between dropping the brightly burnished coin in the box and the prayer he offers ("payment").

The setting of section 5 is somewhere above the U.S. highway 19 by-pass, north of Kingsport, toward Gate City, Virginia. The experience recorded is primarily of a consciousness of death. The brooding young boy understands that his identity is connected with this place ("Each root I uncover uncovers me"), but the passing trains and cars reveal to him that each tree he sees "contains my coffin" and that each passing moment brings him, as it will bring the oak trees, closer to his death, represented here by the words of from the burial liturgy, "the earth to the earth again."

We have a thematic repetition in sections 1 and 4, both having to do with experiences in church. Thematically, sections 2 and 4 have to do with death. Section 3 has to do thematically with work (the leaf-mulching ritual). The final section has to do with a remembered ritual of the *danse macabre*. The poet self-consciously recalls the touching bodies and the bouffant hair-do of his partner. He calls her Big Sister, an apparent reference to the beautiful girl often represented in artistic renditions of the Dance of Death. At the end, the beat of the two-step is displaced by the "impending form," recognized in the rhythm of nature. This beat "gathers, it reaches back, it is caught up." All of this is emblematic of the omnipresent possibility of death.

p. 103, l. 3. *Philbeck*. Wright's friend later makes an appearance in *Gate City Breakdown* (*WTTT*, 40).
p. 103. The line space in section 2 between "drag back" and "Up Hog Hill" should be closed.

Bays Mountain Covenant

Orig. pub. *Ohio Review* 16 (Winter 1975): 20.
B, 76; CM, 106
Pattern: 10 × 2
Place: East Tennessee

Title: Bays Mountain is a range that extends from the Long Island on the Holston River in Kingsport, Tennessee, to Blount County, Tennessee, some 115 miles to the southwest. Bays Mountain Park is a nature preserve owned and operated by the city of Kingsport.

This *ars poetica* poem moves from the first-person anaphora of stanza 1, a catalogue of what the poet has been writing about for the past ten years, to a third-person confession in which he admits that he "was suckered by / A foot in the wrong shoe a hat in the wind." He begs the pardon of a "Sir" who is unidentified but who must be a twentieth-century Apollo, and announces that he is now going to turn to the natural landscape for his poetic inspiration. Wright's new covenant is a version of Yeats's *A Coat*. Both poets declare they are discarding the "old embroideries," expecting nothing and offering nothing but the direct and unadorned encounter with the "leaf" and the "swamp log," the Poundian "acorn of crystal at the creek's edge," the "foxglove" and "nightshade." Yeats calls his new enterprise "walking naked"; Wright calls his acceptance.

p. 106, l. 15. *acorn of crystal*. "I have brought the great ball of crystal; / who can lift it? / Can you enter the great acorn of light?" (Ezra Pound, *Canto CXVI*, [*Cantos*, 815]).

Rural Route

Orig. pub. *New Yorker* 50 (9 September 1974): 46; rpt. in *Cobblestone* August–September 1976: 21.
B, 77; CM, 107

2. Bloodlines (1975)

Pattern: 4 × 6
Time: Flashbacks to 1947 and 1973
Place: Kingsport, Tennessee

The final poem of *Bloodlines*—a poem of memory and selfhood—takes place on a night in 1973. The poet's rural route has returned him to the house in Kingsport where he grew up. Wandering into the yard, he takes stock of the trees and bushes surrounding the house, their mysterious codes still unbroken. Then, in a flashback to 1947, he recalls a vision of himself as a twelve-year-old looking "at his face on the windowpane," the windowpane becoming a mirror of the self. Now, twenty-six years later he sees in his mind's eye the same face on the same window, reminiscent of the face in the window in *Tattoos*, no. 6. The face sees nothing exterior to the house, and what it sees inside the house are only the now hollow mementos of an earlier time—"Stuffed birds ... a deer head" and other "small things." It is obvious that the poet suffers some difficulty in accepting this rather unresponsive and disembodied image of himself from an earlier time: he calls this image an "it." It is the same self, but it seems to be altogether Other. He then declares that such visitations of the past are "silly," and yet he recognizes their power continually to call to him. The face remains in the poet's consciousness even after he returns to California. The tale of the face has no moral. It does not offer a signpost toward a destination and does not point to anything to be avoided. It is only a foghorn across the decades, signaling an identity between the poet's twelve-year-old self and his thirty-eight-year-old one. For all the differences between the adolescent and the adult, there is nevertheless a continuity between the two: they are the same person. *Bloodlines* concludes with this same person leaving east Tennessee and returning to his wife and his own bloodline, his sleeping son.

Chapter 3

China Trace (1977)

China Trace contains fifty poems. Wright selected forty-six for *Country Music*, omitting *Scalp Mountain*, *Deep Water*, *Lips*, and *Guilt*. Nineteen of the poems have twelve lines; the remainder range from eleven lines to one. The dust jacket illustration is a detail from *Nine Dragon Scroll* by Ch'en Jung, a painter of the Sung Dynasty, who in this scroll depicts the manifestations of the dragon in the clouds and waves. The book is dedicated to the Wrights' son Luke.

The title obviously points to Wright's interest in things Chinese, particularly the work of the T'ang poets, whose verse attracted him early on. He first became interested in Chinese poetry by way of *Cathay*, Ezra Pound's reworkings of the notes and draft translations that Ernest Fenollosa and his Japanese teachers had made of Rihaku (Tu Fu) and others. Wright was drawn particularly to the way the T'ang poets handled landscape: "One of the great contributions of the T'ang poets is to show us how to get personal emotions out of a real landscape. You transfer it to the landscape and then you get it back. I found that a very *simpatico* way of dealing with the emotional equivalents that one has to come to grips with in a poem and try to handle rather than having them handle you. If you can fix them and maneuver them and make them hard-edged and clear and visual the way the Chinese would, then you find the poet in the landscape and the emotion coming back out of it" (*Halflife*, 132).

"Trace" means a path or trail, as in Natchez Trace (Wright's mother was from Mississippi), so the title suggests that these poems are an effort to follow the path of the T'ang poets by replicating the ways they embodied emotional experience in their representations of landscape. "Trace" also means something that is shadowy, vestigal, or barely perceptible, and as Wright remarked in an interview, he intended the word to carry that connotation as well (*Halflife*, 133).

Wright on Wright: "[E]ach of [the] poems [in *China Trace*] is a chapter in this pilgrim's book ... the journey this fellow starts in his childhood eventually ends up in the heaven of the fixed stars, and he can't get any higher because he doesn't believe—that is, he only believes what he can see. Each of these poems is disparate but is a self-contained chapter; they are referential to each other and to the whole. Each one can be taken out individually, but put in place, in context, they make up this really weird long poem. It has a strange kind of flow-through quality to it" (*QN*, 128–9).

Wright on Wright: "*China Trace* [is] an attempt, or a hope, to write a long poem that is a book of Chinese poems that don't sound like Chinese poems and aren't Chinese poems but are like Chinese poems in the sense that they give you an idea of one man's relationship to the endlessness, the ongoingness, the everlastingness of what's around him, and his relationship to it as he stands in the natural world. I'm trying to talk about things that I don't know anything about, because I haven't been there, in terms of something I do know something about, because I'm standing in the middle of them. This is, of course, hardly an intellectual breakthrough, but it's been workable before.... *China Trace* is ... down to earth, even though it might look more cosmic. That's why there are so many dates, hours of the day, phases of the moon, all of that business where you locate yourself in a particular time and place and are sort of just washed over by the complete everlastingness of it all, that feeling everyone feels, and has felt ever since we stopped beating with sticks on the ground. *China Trace* is a more ambitious book than *Bloodlines* is, as *Bloodlines* was more ambitious than *Hard Freight*. An increase in intensity all down the line. It's also more ambitious in that I'm trying to do all this with everyday objects. At one time I was going to call the book *Quotidiana*, which is the title of one of the poems in the book. The first half was at one time called 'Colophons,' redoings of themes I had tried in the first two books. The second half was to be called 'Medallions' and would take off in the direction in which I hoped to move. They still work in that way, the two sections, but they're not titled anymore. And since it is a book-length poem, they are two halves of the same stick" (*Halflife*, 77–8).

The epigraph to *China Trace* is from T'u Lung's idealized sketch of the travels of the Taoist philosopher Mingliaotse: "I would like to house my spirit within my body, to nourish my virtue by mildness, and to travel in ether by becoming a void. But I cannot do it yet.... And so, being unable to find peace within myself, I made use of the external surroundings to calm my spirit, and being unable to find delight within my heart, I borrowed a landscape to please it. Therefore, strange were my travels." This passage is reproduced as an epilogue for *Country Music*, Wright apparently intending it to stand as both an introduction and a concluding summary for the entire trilogy.

Each of the two numbered sections of *China Trace* contains the same epigraph—from Italo Calvino's *Invisible Cities*:

"On the day when I know all the emblems," Kublai Khan asked Marco," shall I be able to possess my empire, at last?"

And the Venetian answered: "Sire, do not believe it. On that day you will be an emblem among emblems."

Wright repeated the epigraph, he says, not just to be clever but to remind the reader not to forget it and to point to his hope that the fifty poems will be seen as unified parts of the longer poem that is the book (*Halflife*, 80). But the epigraph also calls attention to Wright's conviction that the entire landscape itself is an emblem book, like those of the sixteenth and seventeenth centuries. The poems in *China Trace* are tight, imagistic, extraordinarily condensed, often surreal, and frequently private and elliptical, but they form a narrative movement, or what Wright likes to refer to as the *sottonarrativa* or subnarrative, that begins in childhood and projects itself toward a future death where the poet finds his place in the constellations with at least one foot in heaven.

The pilgrim-poet represents himself in the first person (I, we, us, our) in forty-three of the fifty poems, in the second person once, and in third person twice. In four of the poems (*Sentences*, *Bygones*, and *Depression Before the Solstice*, and *Signature*) the speaker is simply an observing self—an implicit "I." In many of the poems in *China Trace*, however, it is difficult make a sharp separation between the poetic self and everything outside the self. The commonplace dialectic between "I' and "not-I" does not really apply because the self and the other often merge insensibly into each other. The landscape often interpenetrates the inscape. As in the late poetry of Georg Trakl, the poetic self enters into and so becomes a part of what it describes or confronts.

Place and time are often indeterminate in *China Trace*, though specific locations (e.g. Laguna Beach, Montana) are occasionally mentioned, or they can be inferred, and the poems do move through several turns of the calendar. *China Trace* was begun in August, and the early poems move quickly to winter, continuing through early September in part 1, and from October through the following November in part 2.

Childhood

Orig. pub. *New Yorker* 51 (10 March 1975): 101.
CT, 13; CM, 111
Pattern: 5 × 2

    This farewell to childhood, which is likened to a dog that has followed the poet, is a catalogue of the childish things to which he is saying goodbye, including chairs and genuflections, names and faces, the locust husk and clothes. The poet, both of his parents now dead, declares that childhood has now become transparent, so that he is able to see through it into an "Away-From-Here" future. The dog of childhood may well be an incarnation of the Hound of Heaven. Christianity informed the poet's early religious sensibility (his childhood "genuflections"): here he is saying goodbye to the evangelical fervor of his Sky Valley schooling and the Episcopalian catechism of his Kingsport years. The suggestion is that this putting away of childish things, as St. Paul has it, is a necessary condition for the next phase of the journey, which will take him toward "a place / I'm headed for." The destination is revealed in the last poem in *China Trace*, where he arrives in the fixed constellations—the "suit of lights" in the "flat black of the northern Pacific sky."

    The concluding simile, which likens the faces of those from his childhood to "beads from a broken rosary," disappears into an ellipsis. But of course these rosary beads do not disappear, as the memories of childhood will continue to appear through Wright's work. This fact is implicit in the image of the beggar's lice of childhood which, however "Shrunken and drained dry," still cling to his britches leg. They will still be clinging to his britches more than thirty years later in *Littlefoot: A Poem*.

Snow

Orig. pub. *Field* 12 (Spring 1975): 5.
CT, 12; CM, 112
Pattern: 3 × 2

    This poem, says Wright, "sets up what I really believe in the book" (*Halflife*, 81). What he believes in is the Resurrection of his own and other souls into the wind and cloud after they have returned to dust, becoming the "issue" (final result or perhaps progeny) of the upper elements. This is a point of epiphany, where subject and object become identified. *Snow* is an *axis mundi* poem, so there is also a descent involved, represented by the snow, which becomes metaphorically the "white ants" slipping through the "little ribs" of the evergreen branches. This is one example of "things in a fall of a world of fall." The evergreens suggest a Montana landscape, so that the "world of fall" means additionally the world of autumn and an early snowstorm. But the primary meaning is descent—the fall of the body into death. In the familiar narrative pattern of Greek and Christian mythology, the Fall is of course prior the Resurrection, and expulsion prior to recongregation.

    p. 112, l. 1. *dust ... rise.* "We therefore commit his body to the ground; earth to earth, ashes to ashes, dust to dust; in sure and certain hope of the Resurrection" (*Book of Common Prayer*).

Self-Portrait in 2035

Orig. pub. *Field* 12 (Spring 1975): 6.
CT, 15; CM, 113
Pattern: 4–4–1

    This macabre self-portrait is of the dead poet's body, one-hundred years after his birth. The first stanza records the physical process of dissolution. Death is not part of a cosmic structure, what Spinoza called *natura naturata*. It is rather simply part of an organic process—*natura naturans*. The roots and worms have long since invaded the poet's grave, his coffin has rotted away, and his body has been reformed into earth. All that is distinguishable is his bone, shoes, and "dust-dangled" hair, but his bones have been separated from each other, and the laces of his burial shoes have disintegrated. His "face false" is a reversal of the notion of "false face" or mask. All that remains is the antitype or inversion of the mask—the skull itself.

    The first stanza is all present-tense activity: the ruts in the road "recast," "blanket," and "creep up," the process of decay setting up an ironic contrast with what the body had been in the vigor of life. "Becomes" is a pun, the opening clause meaning both that the long decomposed body has come now to be identified with the root from a plant above and that the root shows him to advantage or makes him look good. This second, clearly ironic meaning is reinforced by the repeated word "fine," which is a triple pun, suggesting that all is quite well, that the "recast" body is now only minute particles of dust, and that this is the end to which the body comes (Italian *fine*). In the second stanza all activity has ceased: the stanza is composed completely of noun phrases, the copulas being implicit only. The stanza concludes with a comic understatement: the body is "past pause," to be sure. This mingling of the comic and the tragic creates the grotesque, similar to what we find in, say, Thomas Beddoes or in the *danse macabre*.

    The first injunction in the concluding couplet—"Darkness, erase these lines, forget these words"—is a kind of defense mechanism thrown up against the commonplace anxiety created by the consciousness of death. Darkness has of course failed to heed the imperative. Likewise, the poem ends before the spider can fulfill the command given to it. The one who can recite the poet's "one sin" would be God, God as a spider being a simile found in Nietzsche, Bergman, Indian mythology, and elsewhere, including *Spider Crystal Ascension* (CM, 150).

    The extraordinary music of these ten lines—their alliteration and barking stresses, which owe a debt to the school of Donne and to Hopkins—should not go unremarked.

Morandi

Orig. pub. as *Morandi's Bottles* in *Field* 12 (Spring 1975): 6.
CT, 16; CM, 114
Pattern: 2 × 5

    The images in the first couplet—the tear-shaped vase, the jug, and the porcelain bowl—derive from the paintings of Giorgio Morandi (1890–1964), who painted these same grouped objects scores of times, calling attention to the subtle variations and luminosity of the objects and focusing on the difference in sameness. Wright was attracted to the structure of Morandi's paintings and his handling of space, which the poet remarks is "left to dry." Structure and space are of course poetic principles as well. Morandi's paintings, says the poet, are quiet, still, and not the least histrionic. His vases, tins, bowls, and bottles stand as a "sentry for, and rise from the void." This refers externally to the way Morandi handles negative space. Internally it refers to what Wright calls "negative transcendence" (Spiegelman, 131). In Morandi's landscapes the void is almost always the white space at the bottom of the canvas. In his still lifes it is almost always the unadorned tables on which is objects are placed (the bottom third of the canvas) and the austere backgrounds against which his bottles and vases emerge (the top two-thirds).

The chatty way that each of the couplets begins ("I'm talking about") belies the seriousness of what follows. In the final couplet, for example, we are said to "flash" Morandi's canvases at the darkness, as if they are being shored up against our ruin. The final syntactically ambiguous phrase, followed by the ellipsis, suggests that absence—what is left out—has a visual power on the page, just as it has on the canvas.

Wright on Morandi, from his short essay on the painter: "As Morandi did in his paintings, we should stake our art on the persistence of continuous perception. As Cézanne did as well, we should have a 'tenderness toward the mundane,' a gathering to us of the quotidian. By concentrating on things that are, we can put meaning where it should be—in direct reconstruction, in the picture itself, in the world as it is when we look at it.... Morandi's drawings, toward the end of his life, resemble the poems of certain masters of style: each line tends to be a statement, self-sufficient, self-contained, where no elaboration is needed. The famous bottles and compote dishes begin to be drawn back into the paper, become larger the more they dissemble. It's almost as though they were drawn on the air, that masterly, and in that instant starting to be borne away, the statement having been made, the design now lodged in the memory, tactile and unremovable. Redemptive on the redemptive air. These are Platonic drawings, their form and architecture already seen and palpable, their decisive indications and linear notations traveling like impulses down the arm and out through the pencil. There's ... a landscape from 1960 [the cover of *Country Music*] consisting of a house, a palm tree, the suggestion of a second house, and possibly a third with some intervening trees or shrubbery, apparently all on a slight hillside, which does for his landscapes what the blue drawing [from 1958] does for his mystical still lifes. In both, the windows into the invisible are lit; in both, what is not there is at least as powerful and tactile as what is. If great art tends toward the condition of the primitive, as I believe it does, and toward the mysteries, as I believe it does, then the late drawings tend toward the same condition. They are full of wonder and singularity, lifelines to the unseen" (*Halflife*, 8–9).

For additional appearances of Morandi in Wright's poems, see A *Journal of True Confessions* in WTTT, 143; *Chinese Journal* in WTTT, 199; *Morandi II* in C, 67 (not included in NB); *Still Life with Stick and Word* in NB, 60; *Apologia Pro Vita Sua* in NB, 74; *Basic Dialogue* in NB, 147; *Giorgio Morandi and the Talking Eternity Blues* in NB, 167; *Looking Around* in SHS, 3; and *Homage to Giorgio Morandi* in BY, 60–1. Morandi has inspired other poets. See, for example, the work of Marilena Pasquali, F. Loi and J.-M. Folon in *Tre poeti per Morandi* (Udine: Campanotto, 1996).

p. 114, l. 2. *center bowl*. The porcelain bowl appears in many of Morandi's oils; it is centered in his *Still Life*, 1946, and *Still Life*, 1959.

Dog

Orig. pub. in *American Review*, No. 23 (April 1976): 123.
CT, 17; CM, 115
Pattern: 7–5

Dogs have been sniffing around earlier in Wright's poems. We have already met Father Dog, the evangelical preacher in *Northhanger Ridge* (CM, 42); in *Tattoos*, no. 20, the graves of the poet's parents metaphorically dog his footsteps (CM, 75); and in *Childhood*, dog is a simile for the poet's early years. Among the domesticated creatures Wright favors the dog, the word appearing in his poems seven times more frequently than the word "cat." Other canine titles are *Dog Creek Mainline* (CM, 36–7), *Captain Dog* (CM, 137), *Dog Yoga* (WTTT, 29), *Dog Day Vespers* (WTTT, 32), *Venetian Dog* (NB, 153), and *Appalachia Dog* (ST, 49). The word in these titles—and in the body of other poems—does not always point to a literal dog. Still, "dog" appears frequently enough to call attention to itself. Wright relies on very little of the conventional symbolism associated with dogs (vigilance, faithfulness, companionship, fidelity, and the like). The various dogs take their meaning from their context in the poems.

The "fantailed dog" in the present poem is an apocalyptic creature, identified most clearly perhaps as Sirius, the Dog/God Star. Wright himself reminds us that the spelling of "dog" can be reversed (*Halflife*, 81). Sirius, the brightest star in the Canis Major constellation makes another appearance as the Black Dog in *Called Back* (WTTT, 20). Sirius, the watchmen of the Heavens, represents power and steadfastness. He was a hunter who could also summon others to him: "Everything comes to him," says the poet in his dream-vision of the dog loping in his sleep, and then he repeats the phrase. It is as if the "fantailed dog" is a version of the hound of heaven. But the poet, who realizes that the "fantailed dog" can whistle him down at will, is not yet ready to be summoned into the heavens.

Snapshot

Orig. pub. in *American Review*, No. 24 (April 1976): 123.
CT, 18; CM, 116
Pattern: 3 × 3

In this highly subjective, remote, and dreamlike experience the poet's ghost appears to him through "the great lens of heaven" and then declares that he is wine, sack, and silt. What this might mean is anybody's guess, but we do notice four decidedly different clusters of imagery: photography (snapshot, lens, flash, click), firearms (gun, target, lock-shot, deadeyes), sailing (lanyard, deadeyes, rig), and gallows (hangs, noose, scaffolding). The fear, apparently, is that the poet's own ghost (spirit) will be captured by the lunar camera. This anxiety is hardly relieved by the news that the ghost has slipped through the shroud of the ship's rigging, only to hang like a noose in the wind.

Along with the hermeticism here, we have drama and poetic energy. We have as well the play of sounds on each other. This is not so much the subconscious at work as it is the dream world brought under the control of the conscious imagination. Part of that conscious control is the poet's bringing everything into the domain of the circle—the lunar Os of the first stanza (the lens, the full moon, the target) are mimicked by the ominous Os of the third (the noose, the round mouth, and "O-fire"). Even the deadeye disks and the wine in the glass are examples of this circle imagery.

This poem puts a rather heavy burden on the reader's powers of synthesis. It does not clarify things much to say that this poem illustrates Wright's having come under the influence of the neo-surrealists of the 1960s. However quizzical our response, we realize that there is more to the poem than the free association of dream and the absence of conscious control. Wright, nevertheless, was influenced by the neo-surrealists, a flirtation that was happily short-lived.

p. 116, ll. 5–6. *lanyard ... rig.* A deadeye is a flat disk through which a ship's lanyards pass, securing the ropes that attach to the masthead and the side of the ship.

Indian Summer

Orig. pub. in *Chicago Review* 27 (Summer 1975): 118.
CT, 19; CM, 117
Pattern: 1-1-2-1-3-1
Time: Late October, early November

The poet, watching the frenzy of the snow bees that have been stirred into action by the warmth of Indian summer, concludes that the scene before him, described with such delicacy in lines 1–5, is sufficient. If something else is due him, he will give it back. "And" in line 8 might appear to introduce a fourth item in the series of things to be given back. But the tidy combs of the honeybees, do not belong to the world of purgatorial credits and otherworldly cleansing. Such geometric precision—"my wax in its little box"—is, like the deep daylight and hickory trees, plenitude enough.

p. 117, l. 7. *firedogs* = andirons.
p. 117, l. 9. *sheveled*. Tidy, ordered; the opposite of "disheveled"; Wright's coinage formed by deleting the negative prefix.

Wishes

Orig. pub. in *Ohio Review* 17 (Fall 1975): 21.
CT, 20; CM, 118
Pattern: 4 × 3
Time: Dog Days (late summer)

This is a poem of desire—the poet's desire to escape from his present encumbered situation, from the dreamless heat of the dog days, from the dull daily routines. He can dimly see the other side of the river, but he is unable to write about it, as the vowels have stuck in his throat. He is aware that his pilgrimage must take him through the world of nature ("the dry thread of the leaf, the acorn's root") and that he will be led to the end of his journey by the "blood fly." But at the present he is stuck. Almost any other place else would do—Venice or South Bay.

The poet did have a vision once of the end of the quest—his proper home—but he cannot remember where it was. This means that his wish-fulfillment dream at this particular way station is frustrated. But the vision is saved from being a nightmare by the lights that begin to turn on in the late afternoon in the place he cannot remember, foreshadowing the light of the zodiac into which he is released in the final poem of *China Trace*. Wright never permits the light—and all that it represents throughout his poems—to be completely extinguished.

p. 118., l. 1. *encumbered*. "I was writing [this line] in the mid–1970s when my son was probably four or five years old and I was going crazy with the family business and wanted to be away" (QN, 128).
p. 118, l. 1. *South Bay*. A region in the southwest peninsula of Los Angeles County. *Venice*. A district in west Los Angeles known for its canals, beaches, boardwalk, and Bohemian residential area.

Quotidiana

Orig. pub. in *Chicago Review* 27 (Summer 1975): 119.
CT, 21; CM, 119
Pattern: 4 × 2
Time: Midwinter

Title: Wright at one time contemplated using *Quotidiana* as a title for *China Trace* (*Halflife*, 78).

Like Morandi, Wright repeatedly turns his attention to everyday things. It is sometimes tempting to see the poems in *China Trace* as examples of what Robbe-Grillet called *choisme*, things in themselves as seen through the lens of the camera, devoid of symbolic import or human meaning. But the quotidian for Wright is never simply the physical, which is why he speaks of the "metaphysics of the quotidian" (*QN*, 95; *Halflife*, 97; Farnsworth) and "the metaquotidian landscape" (*NB*, 140). In the present poem the quotidian are the things encountered each winter day—the moss, the grass, the mist, the evening light, the river, the trees, and the alliterative sequences in stanza 2: "salt shoes," "numb nudge," and "sand sieve." But in every instance the commonplace thing is transformed by metaphor, the figure that moves the object toward the metaquotidian. The moss has a "skin" that it retracts; the grass is laced (tied or drawn together; a delicate fabric); the mist is an address (a location; a destination; a formal communication); the late light is a street. Midwinter itself, with it icy necktie and salty shoes, is personified.

The scene described is hardly inviting, what with its frozen river, the absence of other people, and the numbing cold. And yet the poet says *to* midwinter that all of its iciness is what sustains him, or at least enables him to withstand the stasis he currently faces: if the frozen river is writing his biography, midwinter must be providing nothing but blank pages. Still, rather than bearing down on him it bears him up in two senses (helps him to endure, and carries him on an ascent).

At Zero

Orig. pub. in *Ohio Review* 17 (Fall 1975): 21.
CT, 22; CM, 120
Pattern: 2-2-2-1-2
Time: Mid-winter
Place: Iowa

The opening metaphor of the daylight sky's spooning out cream-of-wheat (snow) from its celestial kitchen is not altogether successful: a warm, coagulated cereal works against "at zero." But the imagery of the next two stanzas is precise and revealing: the hunched down shrubs are bibbed and the trees are a wind harp. The imagery of the third stanza (each of these stanzas is a single sentence) is more complicated: "The river lies still, the jeweled drill in its teeth." As Wright has explained, "That's the Iowa River, as I was walking in January one day, or February, and it was frozen and there was a huge flash from the sun off the ice as I was walking by and I saw that. Several colors. Red and green, I think" (*Halflife*, 131). The effect of all of this on the poet comes in the final couplet. He has been assimilated into the bright river with its white teeth and fingernails. The "ground grains" coming off the river's "wheel" appear to be linked to the river-as-drill image. In any case, both the bodily metaphors (teeth, fingernails) and the mechanical ones (tines, drill, wheel) make for an altogether inhospitable scene. In this frigid landscape it is impossible to give nature a human form and meaning.

p. 120, l. 2. *cream-of-wheat*. Wright identifies this as a metaphor for the falling snow (*Halflife*, 145).
p. 120, l. 7. *The river ... teeth*. Cf. "The ice and snow are master jewelers" (Han Yü, *Poems of the Late T'ang*, trans. A.C. Graham [Harmondsworth: Penguin, 1965], 77).

Sentences

Orig. pub. in *New Yorker* 51 (9 February 1976): 102.
CT, 23; CM, 121
Pattern: (3) (5) (3) (1)

What unites the four sentences is the sense of absence and loss and the condition of unbelief. The fish has been absent for a long time, apparently having been decimated by exposure to the wastes (ash) of coal combustion. No "sweet sound" issues from the leaves. The dead are not resurrected. The pavilions of the sky are blank. The voices are lethargic, and they have "great spaces" to cross. Only the trees "take care of their own salvation." The consecrated bread is not ingested: it floats down the river. And heaven is inaccessible: it is a "stray dog" that "eats on the run and keeps moving." These are "sentences" in the sense of grammatical units, but the implication for the poet is that they are also punishments he has to endure or judgments meted out to him. Therefore, at this way-station of the pilgrimage, where everything is dead rather than quick, the prospects of advancing toward a humanized form of nature are dim at best.

Note. With this poem the short rule replaces the asterisk as a section divider, a convention Wright will continue to use.

p. 121, l. 8. *the color of nothing.* Cf. The last lines of Wallace Stevens's *The Snow Man*: "For the listener, who listens in the snow, / And, nothing himself, beholds / Nothing that is not there and the nothing that is."

Death

Orig. pub. in *Chicago Review* 27 (Summer 1975): 118.
CT, 24; CM, 122
Pattern: 2

The "you" addressed by the speaker is death personified, and as the poem is addressed to death, "Darkness" might well be an apostrophe that names "you." "Take" can mean any number of things, but the principal meaning seems to be "accept," though "understand" and "consider from a particular viewpoint" are also possible. For the speaker to accept death as he accepts the rising of the moon means, of course, that he can do nothing to prevent either from occurring. The couplet is not paraphrasable, though its oppositions are infinitely suggestive. The conventional idea that death "takes" us is played off against its reversal. The slowness of the first line is played off against the quicker movement of the second. Death as darkness is played off against the light of the rising moon. The idea of rising is played off against the falling rhythm of the word "rising," a feature that Wright himself has noted (*Halflife*, 49). The commonplace notion in line 1 that the poet can do nothing about either of the natural processes (death and the movement of the moon) is played off against the startling metaphor of line 2 (darkness = black moth). The light burning up in the black moth reverses our common assumption of the moth burning up in the flame, as we have it in, say, Eliot's poem about the black moth, *The Burnt Dancer*. The metaphor is extended by the idea that whatever light there is in life it is burned up in the dark void.

Like Pound's *In a Station of the Metro*, the two halves of the couplet have no copula, thereby forcing us to make the metaphorical connections. One conclusion seems to be that the overcoming of the darkness (death) by light (life), which is the goal of the poet's quest, is at this stage put on hold, as in was in *Sentences* and as it will continue to be in *Next*. Other ideas certainly cluster in the margins. But we must remind ourselves that the poet does not traffic in ideas. "No ideas but in things," as William Carlos Williams put it, a credo echoed by Wallace Stevens: "Not ideas about the thing but the thing itself." It is the effect of the lines on the imaginative eye and ear that is important, and this effect is wholly verbal.

Wright has remarked that he is an admirer of W.S. Merwin (Suarez, 60) and that Merwin is one of the two people in the generation succeeding him that he feels closest to (*Halflife*, 126). H. L. Hix has noted the similarity between *Death* and some lines by Merwin, though the two poems are in what Blake would call a "contrary" relation, *Death* being a two-line antistrophe to the opening four lines of Merwin's *Looking East at Night*: "Death / White hand / The moths fly at in the darkness // I took you for the moon rising" (*The Lice* [New York: Atheneum, 1967], 36).

p. 122, l. 1. In a reply to a questionnaire Wright reports that the first line was originally "You take me as I take the moon rising, darkness," which reverses the meaning completely (*Halflife*, 48). In the questionnaire Wright explains the music of the couplet, which he proceeds to scan, noting a primary stress on "take," "you," "take," "moon," "ris-," Dark-," "moth," and "up," and a secondary stress on "black" and "burns."

Next

Orig. pub. in *Occident* (Spring 1975): 49.
CT, 25; CM, 123
Pattern: 6 × 2
Time: Winter
Place: Iowa

The title entails the notion of sequence, this poem being the subsequent item in the linear chain of the poet's pilgrimage. After *Sentences*, where heaven is always on the run, and *Death*, where the light is burned up in darkness, this portrait of the weary and depressed poet, does not catch us unawares. His problems are several. He is tired of the quotidian things around him, and he is weary of the winter weather. The country of light and good fortune, which he thought he had "signed for," has not materialized. Thus, he wants to lie down in green pastures beside the still waters during an autumn season that is much more congenial and inviting. In such a season, he can drift along with the fall leaves and perhaps discover the country with the lamp he thought he had been promised.

p. 123, l. 6. *penny in each shoe*. The reference is to the "penny loafer," so called because placing a penny behind the instep strap was said to bring good luck.
p. 123, 9. *fallen psalm*. Perhaps a reference to Psalm 6:16: "The lines are fallen unto me in pleasant places."

January

Orig. pub. in *Chicago Review* 27 (Summer 1975): 118.
CT, 26; CM, 124
Pattern: 3 × 2
Time: January
Place: Iowa City

In death or in another life, the rules will have changed, and so the poet will not be able to recognize himself. The sentiment—or perhaps it is a belief—is triggered by the January cold, which produces, as we see in stanza 2, only the slightest activity, and where the only sounds are coughs. The cowering of the grass represents the poet's own emotional state. This is a companion poem to *Quotidiana, At Zero*, and *Next*—each of which reveals that winter is anything but conducive to the poet's imaginative health.

Wright on Wright: "I wrote [*January*] in Iowa City. And it was colder than hell.... I don't know what to say about 'January' except that at the time I wrote it I believed the first stanza very much. I believe it because, in some other life, the face I look on I won't be able to recognize, because it's going to be a leaf or a piece of grass. Or it's going to be a rock or dirt or something. It's not going to be anything I would recognize because it would be insensate" (*Halflife*, 80–1).

This poem appears to be another answering chorus to some lines by W.S. Merwin: "Years from now / someone will come upon a layer of birds / and not know what he is listening for // these are the days / when the beetles hurry through the high grass / hiding pieces of light they have stolen" (*Early One Summer*, in *Migrations: New and Selected Poems* [Port Townsend, WA: Copper Canyon, 2005], 187). See Hix, 5.

1975

Orig. pub. in *American Review* April 1976: 123.
CT, 27; CM, 125
Pattern: 4 × 3

The year 1975 was Wright's fortieth. The Chinese terrestrial calendar takes its names from the twelve animals in the zodiacal cycle. The humorous catalogue of names for the year in stanza 1 is a series of parodies of the Chinese designation for 1975, which was the Year of the Rabbit. This "China trace" turns out to be rather dark humor, the seven names all sounding rather ominous. The poet hopes that his fortieth year will be a turning-point year, but the book that he opens is entitled What I Can Never Know, and what he finds there is a description of the cycle of nature, the lines echoing phrases from Robert Grave's *To Juan at the Winter Solstice* ("Much snow is falling," "water to water"). Graves's poem opens by announcing that "There is one story and one story only." But despite the fact that things in nature (the apricot, fire ant, and weed) seem "raised to a higher power," the poet can only "turn in the wind / Not knowing what sign to make, or where I should kneel." The making of signs and kneeling suggest religious ritual—liturgical acts the poet longs to have knowledge of but about which he remains ignorant. In the fortieth year of *their* wanderings the Israelites are shown the way to the Promised Land. No such deliverance is available to the poet, the impasse he confronts at this point resulting from a failure of knowledge.

Nerval's Mirror

Orig. pub. as a broadside, North Cambridge, MA: The Pomegranate Press, 1975.
CT, 28; CM, 126
Pattern: 3 × 3

The context of this lyric is Gérard de Nerval's *Aurélia*, an autobiographical account of an ascent and descent into primordial worlds of dream and madness. At one point in part 2, Nerval glances in a very tall mirror, and elsewhere he confronts a double figure. In the present lyric the poet contrasts his own situation to that of Nerval, who committed suicide shortly after he published portions of *Aurélia*. At one level, "the call of What's-To-Come" is the call of Nerval's lost lover, Aurélia. At another, it is the descent into hell and death itself. But the poet wants to distance himself from Nerval's oracular madness, announcing that he is "safe" and "well-fed" here in the middle world. So we are not to look for him in "the white night of the Arctic," which echoes the "colored mists of a Norwegian landscape" and the abyss of "the frozen waves of the Baltic" in Nerval's apocalyptic vision (*Selected Writings* [Ann Arbor: University of Michigan Press, 1957], 176). Nerval's mirror, in short, reflects Nerval, not our poet: he may have his "side iced to its side," but he is "floating here" in this world and not in some hypnagogic heaven or hell.

p. 126, l. 2. *the stars.* "I began searching the sky for a star I thought I knew as having some influence on my fate. When I had found it, I went on walking ... towards my destiny, anxious to see the star up to the moment when death would strike me down" (*Aurélia*, in *Selected Writings*, 116; on the stars, see also 120, 122, 133, 134, 159, 160).

p. 126, ll. 1–3. Cf. these lines from de Nerval's *Epitaph*: "He wished to know all things but discovered nothing.... He went away asking: Why did I come" (*Selected Writings*, 249).

Edvard Munch

Orig. pub. in *New Yorker* 53 (4 April 1977): 42.
CT, 29; CM, 127
Pattern: 4-3-4

In this poem Wright pulls us all into the lonely, isolated world of Edvard Munch: we ourselves become characters in the existential drama of his paintings. The windows of our houses and the people all around us we don't know are like those of *Evening on Karl Johan*. Our windraked yards like those in *The Storm*. We stand on the bridge like the anguished character in *The Scream*, "hands to our ears, our mouths open"—or in *Despair* or *Anxiety*. Our shoes are like those of *Four Girls in Årsgårdstrand*. The "flash of the lighthouse" is like the one in *Ibsen with Lighthouse*. The rock coast, where "We can't see," is like the one in *Summer Night*, and the full moon like the one in *The Dance of Life*, where black lines parallel the reflection of the moon on the water. About this painting Munch wrote, "Standing like this—and my eyes looking into your large eyes—in the pale moonlight—do you know—then fine hands tie invisible threads—which are wound around my heart—leading from my eyes—through your large, dark eyes—into your heart—your eyes are so large now—They are so close to me—They are like two huge dark skies." The mood of the poem is one of pathos, irony, and inertia.

p. 127, l. 11. *Notes in a bottle*. This may be a rather veiled reference to Munch's *Self Portrait with a Bottle of Wine*, the bottle being an image of Munch's alcoholism and mirroring the self-alienation of his own portrait.
p. 127, l. 11. *moon*. The full moon can be seen as well in Munch's *Girls of the Pier* and *Summer Night's Dream*.

Bygones

Orig. pub. in *Pocket Pal*. Rochester, NY: Pocket Pal Press, 1975. 28.
CT, 30; CM, 128

In an interview Wright explains that *Bygones* began "as a one-line poem, and then it got longer and then shrank. I thought that I could get one line with a title that made sense" (Remnick, 572). "Bygones" are simply things in the past, but the word also suggests past grievances, as in "let bygones be bygones." If there is a complaint to be made, it would seem to be because the rain has stopped falling on its crystal stems, which ordinarily would require a comma after "falling," not that the rain has stopped falling asleep. Other meanings suggest themselves, depending where we pause in reading the line. If we pause after "stopped," then the participial phrase becomes a metaphor for the cessation. If we pause after "falling," then the adjective phrase describes what happens to the previously falling raindrops. If we pause not at all, then the rain may well have awakened, the somnolent crystal drops having disappeared into a torrent of water.

p. 128, l. 1. *crystal*. The one-liner appears to be a pure image, but crystal may be a metaphor representing pure form, as in Pound's *Cantos* 91 and 92.

Equation

Orig. pub. as a broadside. Cambridge, MA: The Pomegranate Press, 1975.
CT, 31; CM, 129
Pattern: 4 × 3

In this equation the poet is trying to solve for X: the unknown is some misdeed in his past for which he feels guilt and sorrow. Certain names and events from the past are easy to excavate from phone books and photographs, but these have little to do with the interior life. The source of pain lies not on the surface of the body but deeper within. The poet is unable to solve the equation, the cause of his guilt and sorrow being "Something enormous, something too big to see," like the human condition itself.

California Twilight

Orig. pub. in *Marilyn* 1 (Autumn 1975): 23.
CT, 32; CM, 130
Time: July
Place: Laguna Beach
Pattern: 3 × 3

Home alone, the poet records the twilight scene before him in a remarkable three-line display of imagery: "In the green lungs of the willow, fly-worms and lightning bugs / Blood-spot the whips and wings. Blue // Asters become electric against the hedge." Then, as he listens to the sound of the skateboard disappearing down the hill, he wonders "What was it I had in mind." Whatever he had in mind, it certainly was not what appears before him in a startling vision of the last stanza: "Slowly the furred hands of the dead flutter up from their caves." The altogether natural vision of the first two stanzas has been displaced by the supernatural one of line 8, and the poet finds that the pinkish flame (from the lightning bugs? from the sunset?) "is snuffed in [his] mouth." That is, the sudden intrusion of an awareness of death precludes his going back to the colorful scene described with such crisp inventiveness. This is a world of metamorphosis, a world of death-in-life.

p. 130, l. 6. *Oak Street* is in Laguna Beach.

Anniversary

Orig. pub. in *Ohio Review* 7 (Winter 1976): 20.
CT, 33; CM, 131
Pattern: 3-2-2
Time: 5 June 1976
Place: Montana

After the experience of having his sorrowful body "smoothed over" by solitude, which descends from the Montana mountains into the meadow, the poet announces confidently that he will find "the one secret in life that's worth knowing," which the unidentified "you" in the poem is declared to have already found. The "you" is the poet's mother, and the poem is written on the twelfth anniversary of her death, 5 June. The visitation of solitude—personified as dreaming, clothed, and descending into the meadow at dawn like a wind, "bending the grass," is the visitation of his mother's spirit. An ellipsis signals the interruption of this experience. The hem of the garment of solitude has a biblical echo, although the poem reverses the agency that we find in the synoptic Gospels: here it is solitude's hem that does the touching, whereas in the Gospels the woman with her own sorrow (she had been hemorrhaging for twelve years) initiates the touching of Jesus garment. Still, both the poet and the bleeding woman have positioned their bodies to be mended: the woman is miraculously healed, and the poet's sorrows are "smoothed over."

Solitude, which we first encountered in *Tattoos*, where the roots of the camellias are a "remembered solitude," will become a motif Wright turns to time and again in his poetry, appearing more than two-dozen times, almost always in the context of some feature of the landscape and often positively: it is a state of being that is desired and embraced. Solitude is a motif found frequently in the lyrics of such T'ang poets as Han Shan (Cold Mountain), Li Po, Meng Haoran, Wang Wei, and Tu Fu. *Anniversary*, thus, embodies a China trace.

The dropped-down line that concludes the poem is the first example of in *China Trace* of what would become one of Wright's signatures. Here, the empty space both before and above the final words reinforce the sense of remoteness and seclusion. Wright uses the "lowrider" in five subsequent poems in *China Trace*. He later referred to this linear feature as "spatial negation" that creates an "energy of absence" (QN, 173).

12 Lines at Midnight

Orig. pub. in *Ohio Review* 7 (Winter 1976): 20.
CT, 34; CM, 132
Pattern: 3 × 4

In this twelve-line dream-vision the images of the animal with its ear cocked and the hands of the clock monitoring the wind both require two lines, which means that ten items constitute the discontinuous catalogue of surreal midnight sights. The poet senses a hushed emptiness, but within the quiet void there is a great deal of kinetic energy in the setting out and breaking down, the opening up and reaching out, the licking and dragging, the bleeding and tightening. The fragmentary vision is almost completely demonic, like the right triptych of Bosch's *The Garden of Earthly Delights*. The final image of the hands of the clock, one superimposed on the other at 12:00 midnight, reaching outward in their vertical thrust, suggests that this vision is an escape from time. Still, the vision is essentially spatial: it expands to include the four elements and the five senses, but the structure of the sequence of images is otherwise elusive, a function of the idiosyncratic workings of the subconscious. Thus, the poem is a parody of formal structures like those of the twelve-line rondine or the Italian Renaissance madrigal.

Dino Campana

Orig. pub. in *Field* 14 (Spring 1976): 91.
CT, 35; CM, 133
Pattern: 5

Campana was one of the two important Italian influences on Wright early in his career (the other was Eugenio Montale). Wright was attracted to his reputation as a *poète maudit*. Here, the poet announces that after having written a number of "sad tunes," he is now going to step through the door Campana has opened for him. Campana has shown what a poetic pilgrimage should be: he has lit the lamp and laid the table.

Wright on Wright: "If Montale is the 'letter' of the law in Italian poetry in this century, Dino is surely the 'spirit.' The affinity I feel with 'this unique sort of pilgrim' is just that, he is a unique sort of pilgrim. Most of my own work has centered [on] pilgrimages of one sort or another, and I feel a kinship. There is little about his 'lyrics' per se that attract me, and I find there is little to learn from him technically for me at this point [1984]. But his spirit has always moved me, the structure of his longer prose pieces has been a current ersatz model for some 'verse journals' I am trying to write. It was his desperate reaching and yearning for what he felt but couldn't ever write down or understand truly that has always drawn me to him. It still does" (*Halflife* 123).

Invisible Landscape

Orig. pub. in *Field* 14 (Spring 1976): 91.
CT, 37; CM, 134
Pattern: 5-5-2
Time: September
Place: Montana

This is the poet's version of what happens after Genesis 1:5: "God called the light Day, and the darkness he called Night. And there was evening, and there was morning the first day." In the account in Genesis 1 we are presented in an orderly and hierarchical fashion the creation of the four elements, followed by a sequence of created beings, including humankind. In the poet's version of "the first dusk," however, we have a more or less random sequence of things created—clouds, bats, winds, mountains, trees, "wet weather," firmament, and fireweed. Perhaps these things are a bit difficult to make out in the gathering dusk, but they are by no means invisible, so the poem's title is that of a trickster, just like the trickster God in the concluding couplet. In Genesis 1 God is quite satisfied with what he has made, announcing a half-dozen times that "it was good." In the poem, God sneaks into the fireweed, doesn't like what he sees, and moves on. God may be invisible (He's identified with the "lost / Moment"), but the landscape, with its sculling smokeclouds, its fall colors, and its bats jerked through the purple dusk by the "white sound" of their radar, decidedly is not. And while God may grieve over what he sees from the willow herb (fireweed), the poet's vision of this early September evening is cause for celebration.

p. 134, l. 2. *Claw Mountains*. Wright's fictional version of the Cabinet Mountains in northwestern Montana.

Remembering San Zeno

Orig. pub. in *New Yorker* 52 (25 October 1976): 64.
CT, 41; CM, 135
Pattern: 6 × 2
Time: 1 October 1975
Place: The setting is the church of San Zeno Maggiore in Verona, located in the heart of the city on the Piazza dei Signori.

Invisible Landscape concludes the first part of *China Trace*, as the fifty poems were arranged in the separate book. With *Remembering San Zeno*, the first poem in what was originally part 2, we move from the garden to the city, from the spectacle of the Montana landscape to the basilica in Verona—San Zeno Maggiore. This, or someplace like it, is where the poet, who has just turned forty, will be brought, he declares, "After the end." San Zeno, therefore, is projected as an ante-chamber of "the next address," which, with its "Nightfires" that are "beyond the beyond," points to a destination across the Acheron. San Zeno is a stately example of medieval architecture, but the poet sees nothing of the marble lions guarding the entrance, of the sculpted bronze panels on the doors of the western entrance, of the rose window, of the Mantegna triptych of the Virgin and Child. What he experiences, rather, is sepulchral and demonic—"The gloom, like a grease-soaked rag, like a slipped skin / Left in a corner, puddled / In back of the votive stick stands." The flames of the candles, which are "the color of fresh bone," cast a "cold glow," and the people in the cathedral are nondescript automatons—"faces and blank hands." These penitents stare at the poet and move closer to him, somewhat threateningly.

The rose window of San Zeno, about which the poem is silent, is an allegory of the wheel of fortune. The figures on the right of the wheel are being raised up; those on the left are being cast down. The poet's lot, which is projected as "Nightfires," puts him in the company of those on the left. Thus, while the poems in *China Trace* are generally a movement toward some spiritual hope in the future, we begin the second half of the book with an altogether ironic flashback from the poet's Guggenheim year. "San Zeno" is a synecdoche for the Church, but at this way-station in the pilgrim's journey, faith, hope, and charity have been displaced by gloom and doom.

Born Again

Orig. pub. in *Field* 14 (Spring 1976): 92.
CT, 42; CM, 136
Pattern: 6 × 2
Time: 19 October 1975
Place: Laguna Beach

The spiritual rebirth announced in the title is at best only a hope. The wished-for rebirth in the first stanza is in the context of natural religion: the poet yearns to have himself transported into the heavens, "Behind the veneer of light." The time seems to be propitious for a spiritual journey ("walks I will take"): the full moon has projected its pictographs on the flora below.

In stanza 2 we jump cut to rebirth in the context of revealed religion. Ordinarily, being born again is associated with baptism: only through the "water and the spirit," Jesus tells Nicodemus, can he be reborn into the Kingdom of God (John 3:1–5). But here the imagery, deriving from the visions of a cocaine trip, is that of a bizarre Eucharistic ritual: Nothingness administers one of the elements (the wine) and partakes of the other (the bread)—except that in this surreal rite, the poet himself becomes a wafer on the tongue of Nothingness, which appears to be a version of the *deus absconditus*. The object of transubstantiation, then, turns out to become only "bone and regret," and the poet ends up identifying himself with "Breath's waste, the slip-back and failure of What's Past." The wish to be born again has failed; the future hope is erased.

Some of the imagery here is similar to that in *Tattoos*, no. 5, where wine is administered to bring the fainting acolyte back to consciousness. In that poem we also have "the river of heaven," "wafer," "the air," and "waters of nothingness." There the ritual succeeds: "I am risen," the poet declares, and we take the phrase in both its literal and figurative senses. In the present poem, which ends with apostasy, the poet, alas, is not born again. This is the only poem Wright ever wrote while on drugs.

Captain Dog

Orig. pub. in *Field* 14 (Spring 1976): 93.
CT, 44; CM, 137
Pattern: 4–2–3–3

Time: December 1975
Place: Laguna Beach

Wright on Wright: "Captain Dog is what some of my students used to call me about eight years ago. 'Dog' keeps popping up in these poems. 'Captain Dog' is a poem of process, which explains itself and its processes as it goes along. Jump-cut. Jump-cut is what each stanza is doing. There's no logical movement from stanza to stanza. And dog because a dog is a dog. And a Captain Dog is pretty high up in the hierarchy of dogs. There is also the reverse spelling of dog.... I have always been very fond of the phrase Captain Dog, and I like titles with dog in them: *Andalusian Dog, Portrait of the Artist as a Young Dog, Dog Yoga*" (*Halflife*, 81).

This teasing commentary reveals something about the discontinuous form but little about the substance, which has to do with the poet's various emotional states at year-end. In the first stanza, he records the desire to rest his soul momentarily among the clouds, and in the second, he describes the feeling of being unattached to the place where he finds himself. Stanza 3 is about the anxiety of nighttime depression and the breathing exercises aimed at staunching the body's ills. In the final stanza, the poet as dog, though "staked / In the shadow of nothing's hand," appears to have regained some psychic balance: he has asserted his identity, having adapted to the *Angst* he feels, gathered himself together, and moved on.

The insertion of the date at the end is unusual. Perhaps it is intended to mark the poet's fortieth year.

Depression before the Solstice

Orig. pub. in *New Yorker* 52 (21 June 1976): 36.
CT, 45; CM, 138
Pattern: 6 × 2
Time: 17 December 1975

The first stanza describes the sunset of the late December afternoon. The fiery sun is reflected in the windows, but the evening light is "weightless, unclarified," and lying "like despair on the ginger root." Such emotional investment is what Ruskin called the "pathetic fallacy," which is a fallacy only for those for whom scientific accuracy is prior to imaginative representation. In any event, the despairing light suggests that "depression" in the title refers to something other than a meteorological phenomenon (low pressure).

The "Now" of line 5 moves the poem in another direction. It does not mean at the present time. It is simply an introductory signal for the stanza that follows, which takes us back 2000 years in time. As the solstice is only four days away, Christmas, a tribute paid to the ancient festival of the shortest day of the year, will follow in a week.

In stanza 2 the poet recreates the beginning of the journey of the Magi—the "watchers and holy ones" who are setting out on their journey from the east. The Magi have divined the "seal," the secret or hidden knowledge based upon their astrological knowledge. One astronomer believes that in 6 B.C. Jupiter, the regal "star" that conferred kingship, underwent two eclipses before it "stood over where the young child was," as Matthew puts it (Michael Molnar, *The Star of Bethlehem* [New Brunswick, NJ: Rutgers University Press, 1999]). It is the knowledge of this apocryphon or sealed gnosis that the Magi have taped to their sleeves. "Depression," therefore, may take on still a third meaning, the angular distance of a celestial body below the horizon.

"Now" in line 6 provides a fulcrum for the two parts of the poem, balancing what we have in stanza 1—the moon and unclarified light of late afternoon, with its attendant gloom—

with what the Magi have divined in stanza 2—the star of Bethlehem. It is no surprise that on their momentous mission their footprints are filled with sparks. The depression before the solstice has been erased by the flashback to the Incarnation as we move from "Now" to "Then."

Stone Canyon Nocturne

Orig. pub. in *New Yorker* 52 (4 October 1976): 144.
CT, 47; CM, 139
Pattern: 2-3-2-3-2
Place: Los Angeles

Wright on Wright: "*Stone Canyon Nocturne* is a central poem in the book. Stone Canyon is a canyon in Los Angeles. The poem contains things that I believe very deeply. At Stone Canyon, there's a strange physical sensation brought about by extra-bodily substances. There are fossils in the canyon that can come into your hands very easily" (*Halflife*, 83).

This night song, after the apostrophe to the Ancient of Days, contains four movements, focusing respectively on the cold and unresponsive moon, the children existing in the world of Blakean innocence, the flora and fauna of the natural world, and the unresponsive divine Healer.

The Ancient of Days is a biblical name for God, appearing thrice in the Book of Daniel, where it is used in the sense that God's days are past reckoning. Its most familiar visual representation is Blake's hoary father-figure in the frontispiece to *Europe*, stretching out His compass and so symbolizing reason and mathematical order (*natura naturata*). The Ancient of Days is also one of the incarnations of Blake's Urizen, the remote and even cruel first principle of Deism. It is this figure of God, according to the poet, who in a post–Newtonian universe, will not return. Such a conception of God, as an object of belief, is dead. The poet calls the Ancient of Days "old friend," but this is a purely ironic gesture.

Similarly, the empyrean, against which the moon, "like a dead heart," hangs, is no less remote. The moon is conventionally a feminine archetype, an element of *natura naturans* and associated with *yin*, with eros, and, by way of the tides, with the myth of the eternal return. The poet turns all of these conventions on their head. The moon is "cold and unstartable" and "unfaithful." If we assume that *Stone Canyon Nocturne* followed closely on *Depression Before the Solstice*, then the full moon (18 December) would be moving into its waxing phase, reaching its crescent form on Christmas day. As we have seen, the moon is emblematic of other things in *China Trace*, where it appears in ten poems altogether, although one poem, "*Where Moth and Rust Doth Corrupt*," calls attention only to its absence.

With stanza 3 we move down the chain of being into "the other world" of children, that is, the world of play and song, far removed from the abstract world of the Ancient of Days and the uninviting moon. The next step on the ladder takes us into the world of landscape with its swan and fox, its bloodroot and belladonna. If we are to be comforted, our comfort will come from the plentitude natural world, not from the remote deity or from the inaccessible Healer, revolving "through the night wind," who refuses to recognize us.

What then are the things contained in the poem that the poet says he believes very deeply? He believes that there are ideas of God that are not congenial to the human enterprise and that the landscape, especially in mysterious places like Stone Canyon, can provide consolation in the way that the Healer cannot. The Healer, "part eye," can see us in our plight, but like Yahweh before the flood, is saddened by what He sees ("part tear") and so pretends not to recognize his creatures who need healing. The poet believes that the human pilgrimage takes place along an *axis mundi*, an imaginative structure that differentiates between an "up there" and a "down here," between "this world" (Blakean experience) and "the other world" (Blakean innocence), between an exterior and an interior landscape. At this point in his pilgrimage, alas, the poet has made little progress up the ladder: "No one believes in his own life anymore." Still, as Wright says in another context, "I *do* believe in the efficacy of things unseen" (QN, 119).

Reply to Chi K'ang

CT, 48; CM, 140
Pattern: 2–3

Chi K'ang-tzu (223–63) asked this of Confucius about government: "Suppose I were to slay those who have not the Way in order to help those who have the Way, what would you think of it?" Confucius replied, saying, "If you desire what is good, the people will at once be good. The essence of the gentleman is that of wind; the essence of small people is that of grass. And when a wind passes over the grass, it cannot choose but bend" (Confucius, *Analects* 12.19). In short, Confucius counsels Chi K'ang to forget about killing altogether and concentrate on developing an exemplary character. Only then will "those who have the Way" be able to influence "those who do not have the way."

Charles Wright counsels Chi K'ang to abandon *the question* altogether. The grasses (the unprincipled or unenlightened people) can be redeemed by no one, and, moreover, there is no light "at the end of light." There is no political solution by way of governments. The mimosa (the tree outside Wright's window when he was a child) blooms and the grasses bend, regardless of what we do. Still, the poet does at least partially agree with Confucius: whatever changes we desire, they must begin deep within heart and soul. In fact, that is where the roots of light have already begun "to take hold."

Reunion

Orig. pub. in *Marilyn* 2 (Autumn 1976): 32.
CT, 49; CM, 141
Pattern: 3–2

Wright on Wright: "This is the poem I expect to get the most flak about, for that transition in the second stanza, and for that bald statement. I meant the transition to be totally unexpected. This 'I' is the most jarring and wide-gulfed transition in any of the poems. It's the closest I got to 'salvation,' since salvation doesn't exist except through the natural world. In any poem, it's the closest I can get to making a hook-up with my religious background" (*Halflife*, 82–3).

On this particular day the poet does not know what the future holds. The day not only detaches itself from "all the rest up ahead"; it also wants to carry his spirit into the past. In the eternal present, therefore, he finds himself in a state of disarray and confusion. Thus, in a move that seems not to be "totally unexpected" at all, he turns to stocking-taking, asking in the concluding *ars poetica* couplet why he writes poems anyway. And his answer, "to untie myself, to do penance and disappear / Through the upper right hand corner of things, to say grace." The religious suggestions of doing penance and saying grace are obvious—two ways of reuniting with a religious past. Untying himself is a matter of seeking release from being overly anxious about both the future and the past and of finding some Presence in the present. The image he has of himself is that of a static photograph, and his wish is to be free from the stasis of the here and now. The fourth reason given, to disappear into negative space, is more complex, but it is related to the theme of the negating the self that will become more and more insistent in Wright's poems. This is another China trace—the Taoist *wu wei*, a form of quiet contemplation in which things unfold as they will, and the "true purpose of poetry," Wright says, "is to be a contemplation of the divine" (QN, 120). Seventeen years late the poet would write, "We'd like to fly away ourselves, pushed / Or pulled, into or out of our own bodies, // into or out of the sky's mouth. / We'd like to disappear into a windfall of light" (*East of the Blue Ridge, Our Tombs Are in the Dove's Throat*, in NB, 43). And almost thirty years later, returning to line 4 of the poem, Wright would say, "I write, as I said before, to untie myself, to stand clear, / To extricate an absence, / The ultimate hush of language" (*There Is a Balm in Gilead*, in BY, 4).

"Where Moth and Rust Doth Corrupt"

Orig. pub. in *Antaeus* 24 (Winter 1976): 65.
CT, 50; CM, 142
Pattern: 5–5–2

Title: Matthew 6:19–21: "Lay not up for yourselves treasures upon earth, where moth and rust doth corrupt, and where thieves break through and steal. But lay up for yourselves treasures in heaven.... For where your treasure is, there will your heart be also."

Against a particularly empty night skyscape, the poet reflects somewhat despondently on his burned-out life and the oppressive religiosity of his childhood, the ten crosses representing the Episcopalian traditions of his early years in Kingsport, Tennessee, and Sky Valley School in the North Carolina mountains. He instructs the Christian icons to "Lie back and regenerate," but this proves to be difficult, and the ritual from *The Egyptian Book of the Dead* of whispering spells and prayers into the ear of the disembodied deceased so as to insure a joyous afterlife for their souls is not possible: the poet is whispering into a different ear.

He concludes by confessing that he lives in "one world," and as he has "moth and rust" in his arms, the implication is that his treasure should lie in another, spiritual world, one different from that of his childhood Christianity.

p. 142, l. 2. *Baja* = the northernmost state in Mexico. *Prudhomme Bay*. This should be Prudhoe Bay, on the north shore of Alaska.

April

Orig. pub. in *Atlantic Monthly* 239 (April 1977): 45.
CT, 51; CM, 143
Pattern: 6 × 2

This poem is an answer to the previous one, where the laying up of treasures on earth leads to a call for regeneration. In *April* the poet takes stock again, tallying up what his "life has come to," and the sum leads to the knowledge that he should divest, including his name and his identity. He wants none of the "downfall of light in the pine woods, motes in the rush, / Gold leaf through the undergrowth," opting instead to inhabit the deep, where he can be released as a fish, glinting and flashing in the water. The pity of this is that he will no longer be able to cast his eyes on the bee-infested plum tree and the gull "locked like a ghost in the blue attic of heaven." Nor will he be able to feel the gossipy wind as it natters through the damp rooms. The fish-wish turns out, of course, to be only a momentary desire. Wright's poetic gifts lie in his ability to see in the landscape what others of us cannot see and to translate what he sees imaginatively. Because of the riches that lie above the water, it is to our great advantage that the wish remains unfulfilled.

p. 143, l. 5. *stays*. An ambiguous noun: periods of residence, acts of halting, postponements, supports.

Signature

Orig. pub. in *Red Weather* 1 (Fall 1976): 6.
CT, 52; CM, 144
Pattern: 3

The poet's injunction to himself is for his distinctive mark—his signature—to be, not an anticipated ephemeral beauty (the dogwood blossoms), but something substantial, permanent, and firm, rooted in the natural world, like the moss-covered rock. The former is an identity to wait for, and so it produces anxiety. The latter, which has a presence in time and space, can become an identifying characteristic *now*.

Noon

Orig. pub. in *New Yorker* 52 (30 August 1976): 67.
CT, 53; CM, 145
Pattern: 4 x 3

Wright on Wright: "I would like to become the mental landscape that I write about. What I was trying to do in the book [*China Trace*] was to somehow merge the physical and the interior landscapes that we all have in our lives. The closest I've come is the poem called *Noon*, I think. Half the poem is about the physical, the other half is about the probable interior landscape. All the way through this book those are the two things I'm going back and forth with, one against the other. I don't think that the interior landscape is any less real than the exterior landscape" (*Halflife*, 103–4).

The elements of the exterior landscape are "the black bulge of the sky and its belt of stars" in stanza 1, the wind in stanza 2, and the dirt, sucker vines, grass, hollyhocks weeds, and sun in stanza 3. The interior landscape is a composite of the poet's knowledge, desires, and feelings. He knows that he has no answer to the light of the heavens; he knows that he will not be granted what he has asked for; but he also knows that his pilgrimage will eventually lead to his rising from the darkness. The object of his desire is unspecified, but desire is nothing more now than a residue of ashes "Scattered beneath the willow's fall." The phrase "figure of speech" apparently is meant to modify the entire metaphor of the ash of desire, which is a negative or demonic image. Opposed to this is the alliterative phrase "sweet wrists of the rose" in stanza 2, which, for all of its mystery, is a positive or apocalyptic image.

The poem ends on a positive note. The comforting dirt and warm grass are objective correlatives for the poet's interior landscape, and in the solar phenomenon described in the last two lines, which appears to be an eclipse, the shadows serve to afford the poet a clean slate as they begin to exhale the past. This means, in the present context, that he can get on with his journey. In other contexts, the past is a rich repository of poetic material and therefore not something requiring exhalation.

p. 145, l. 11. *tiny horns*. Musical horns.

Going Home

Orig. pub. in *Antaeus* 24 (Winter 1976): 67.
CT, 55; CM, 146
Pattern: 6 × 2
Place: Laguna Beach
Time: Mid-month, more or less

Going Home extends the theme of the "exhalation of the past" in the previous poem. Here the pepper tree in Wright's yard in Laguna Beach, which makes a dozen appearances in his poems, is the trigger that carries him back to the "dirt roads and small towns" and lightning "Strikes in the dry fields" of his Tennessee years. Wright says that the pepper tree was a kind of stand-in for the Southern mimosa tree: "Something about this particular tree outside my window in California reminded me of where I grew up. It became, in a strange way, the mimosa tree that was outside my window when I was a child. That they looked rather alike is probably not incidental. That's why ... it's both the subjective and the objective correlative because it became—not only what started it—it became the continuing grease for the slide" (*Halflife*, 160–1).

The journey backward in time, with its uninviting "dry fields" and "bonesparks," renders the poet immobile: the feet that walk there are nailed. If this is a hangdog month in California, the poet finds the imaginative journey back home to Tennessee no less hangdog. Thus the plea in the second stanza for the eternal spirit (Great Wind) to inspire the poet again.

Of the four elements, earth ("Dirt roads," "dry fields") and fire (lightning "strikes) appear in the first stanza. The other elements are present in stanza 2, but the metaphors of breath and wind dominate. In almost all languages the metaphorical kernel of spirit is wind or air. Wright is drawing on that convention. A "second breath" in the natural world, then, is really a "second birth" in the spiritual one. That what the poet is asking for—to be in-spired and therefore to enter the world of spirit where "everything rises, // unburdened and borne away." This world of spirit becomes in the final line the world of Heraclitean fire. Fire belongs to the metaphorical cluster of light, which, of course, in Wright is the metaphor of metaphors, as it represents the goal of the pilgrimage. In stanza 2 the interior journey back to Tennessee, with the vision of that place that materializes from the pepper tree, is a failed effort to "go home." Thus, what the poet hopes he will be given is a second birth into a new and genuine home.

p. 146, l. 11. *halflife*. In Wright's book of this title, "halflife" refers to prose. Here he seems to be using the word in its scientific sense, the time required for half of the atoms of a radioactive substance disintegrate.
p. 146, l. 12. *everything's fire*. "There is exchange of all things for fire and of fire for all things" (Heraclitus, Fragment 28).

Cloud River

Orig. pub. in *Three Rivers Poetry Journal* 9 (1977): 19.
CT, 56; CM, 147
Pattern: 4 × 2

William Blake's *Songs of Innocence* is the precursor of the hauntingly beautiful image of the unborn children rowing toward the sky's circumference and looking for a place to get born. The poet wants to join the children on their journey down the river of the clouds, rowing toward the circumference. As Blake says elsewhere, "the circumference ... expands going forward to Eternity" (*Jerusalem* 71.8), and in this wish-fulfillment dream, another born-again poem, the poet hopes for an "immense and unspeakable" revelation when he arrives with the unborn children at the circumference. The image of rowing toward the circumference con-

Reply to Lapo Gianni

Orig. pub. in *Iowa Review* 8 (Winter 1977): 39.
CT, 57; CM, 148
Pattern: 2–3–1

Gianni is a somewhat obscure Italian poet (ca. 1250–1328), a contemporary of Dante and one of the members of the Tuscan school of lyric poetry that arose toward the end of the thirteenth century. What Gianni might have said that deserves a reply is uncertain. The poem is apparently an appeal to Gianni to forget about such things as the cult of Eros with its various sublimations of the body-as-garden trope. Gianni should replace the artifice of dreamy troubadour sentiment with a genuine subject matter, such as the twilight scene displaying itself "Outside the window." So should the poet.

p. 148, l. 6. *dog rose*. A deciduous shrub, *rosa canina*. It grows in the spring in Montana.

Thinking of George Trakl

Orig. pub. in *Grove* 3 (Winter 1977): 40.
CT, 58; CM, 149
Pattern: 4–4–2
Time: August
Place: Montana

Autumn moves toward the death of nature, which is an objective correlative of the poet's consciousness of the inevitable moment of our own deaths ("when the time comes"). Trakl's anguished poems are often death-haunted, and, like Wright, Trakl uses natural images to reflect internal moods. One body of memory is already laid out beneath "the ghost light of the stars," the mists of the Montana meadow becoming a shroud, and the night sky becomes a metaphor for God's unfolding hand to call us away. Wright may be "thinking of" Trakl's own poems about the waning of summer, such as *Autumn of the Lonely* and *Decline of Summer*.

Spider Crystal Ascension

Orig. pub. in *Grove* 3 (Winter 1977): 39.
CT, 59; CM, 150
Pattern: 2–1–2
Place: Montana

Wright on Wright: "In one poem, the title, *Spider Crystal Ascension*, is supposed to be ideographic. The title is three separate words that are supposed to give you an idea of what's coming in the whole poem. I did have the idea of compression, which is maybe as close as we can get to the ideogramic method. To compress the language and the thought to such a point that it stops being small and starts to enlarge. I don't quite know how to explain this, but it gets past a certain point, and goes out the other side and gets larger. It expands. Which is to say, rather than writing a lot to get larger and larger, you write less and less. And I don't mean Concrete poetry. I don't mean Imagism, though there is an element of that. Just regular writing, imagery and metaphor, compressed to such an extent that it goes out the other side.

Again, that's one of the reasons I wanted to write very short poems. The black hole might be an example. In the black hole, as I understand it, the gravity is so great that it pulls everything in to such an extent that light cannot escape and has to exit out the other side. And that there is possibly another universe back there. You could take a handful of matter, if it were possible, from a black hole and stand up on your chair and drop it, and it would go right through the earth" (*Halflife*, 79).

Wright on Wright, in response to a question about the changes he made in the poem. "What I did was to get those first two lines and hold onto them for about four days, without knowing what to do with them. I was trying to describe the gigantic movement of the Milky Way through the Montana sky as seen from a place twenty miles from the nearest house, absolutely pitch-black, when the Milky Way is an incredible thing, in the dark of the moon, radiating out, and it really does look like a spider.... I didn't know what to do with it. And then I got that long line—'All morning we wait for the white face to rise from the lake like a tiny star.' That came from the ascent. But that still wasn't enough. I waited another couple of days, and I was walking along thinking about the poem and the phrase 'And when it does...' suddenly came to me. That's my favorite part of the poem. 'And when it does,' what? 'We lie back in our watery hair, and rock.' That's what. You know we're down there too, and one of us is going up.... So those five lines took about eight days, back and forth, back and forth, writing, crossing out, trying to get it to sound right and to say the right thing. I wanted the idea of being electrified up there, so I finally got 'juiced.' Then I still didn't have a title for it, so I decided to take the three biggest words in the poem and put them together" (*Halflife*, 87–8).

Thanks to the poet's explanation, we are able transfer to the mind's eye the figure of the Milky Way as a spider toward which we ascend. The spider is a kind of divine cosmic presence, and "crystal," an image representing refracted radiance, echoes "the great ball of crystal" in Pound's *Canto CXVI*, which for Wright symbolizes "paradisal clarity" (*Halflife*, 16). Our actual ascension into the heavens takes place sometime during the night—in the space following the ellipsis of stanza 1. By line 3 we ourselves have now become part of the Milky Way, though not without some cost to the spider, who has exhausted himself by mending the breaks in the web caused by our having joined the heavenly host. The perspective in the first couplet is from below: we look upward. But as the poet says that line 4 "came from the ascent," the perspective of the concluding couplet is from above: we look down for some evidence that another will be rising to join us. And when a new face does appear from below, "we lie back in our watery hair and rock"—tokens, apparently, of our pleasure at the *anabasis*.

The poet makes us work rather hard to fill in the gaps of this cryptic lyric, and even with his own commentaries the "ideogramic" method makes for a poem that seems overly compressed. But the motif of ascension, which anticipates the final poem in *China Trace*, is clear enough.

Moving On

Orig. pub. in *Greenhouse Review* 3 (Winter 1977): 5.
CT, 60; CM, 151
Pattern: 3–3–1

Wright on Wright, replying in an interviewer's question about the image in the last line of the poem: "[I]t's the image the entire poem works down to. It explains the entire poem. It and the title. It's an emotional construct in that it has serious Christian overtones that are dismissed within the image itself. It has traditional allusions to renewal, rebirth, the source of all energy (the east, the sun, the son), both physical and spiritual. It has a combination Christian and non-Christian vision of the end (the nail and the body that will hang from it). It has the idea that all is a flowing, and so on. I think there are a good many emotional possibilities and values bound up in the image. As for its thematic construction, it does come directly and rapidly out of the argument and construction of the rest of the poem. It's not a surreal and arbitrary addition at the end. The entire poem depends on it, and it depends entirely on the rest of the poem for some of its light. It takes on, gives off, and reflects light, something a good image should do. It both holds the poem together and extends it. And it does its work in just about the length of time it takes to read the image, as it is clear within the context of the poem and clear as to where it wants to move the poem. All the connections happen simultaneously, if you have been paying attention. It makes it possible that not 1 + 2 = 3, but that 3 = 3. There are not parts if the image works correctly. There is only a whole. Naturally, I hope this line is working in such a way" (*Halflife*, 92–3).

Whether this poem achieves the coherence Wright intended is doubtful. It *is* possible to make connections among the various religious images (fleece, fall, flesh made word, wafer of blood, first rocks, nail of the east), but some of the imagery remains too private (wedge of the eyelid down to poison, crack in the porcelain stick) for a completely shared experience to emerge, even for those who have paid attention. The "bright star of the east" would point to the Nativity narrative. Wright changes this to the "bright nail of the east," thereby importing suggestions of the death of Christ and perhaps even the resurrection. Although he is "moving on" in his pilgrimage, what he is ushering his body toward remains uncertain.

Clear Night

Orig. pub. in *New Yorker* 53 (2 May 1977): 123.
CT, 61; CM, 152
Pattern: 4 × 3
Place: Laguna Beach

On this clear night, when the shadows cast by the moon through the deck rails make a piano-key pattern, the poet suddenly assumes the role of the religious ecstatic calling for scourges and various other mortifications of the flesh. "I want to be bruised by God," he asserts, recalling Isaiah 53:5—"But He was wounded for our transgressions, He was bruised for our iniquities: the chastisement of our peace was upon Him; and with His stripes we are healed." The theme of Christian sacrifice is thus introduced. This is followed by two other forms of self-mortification—"I want to be strung up ... stretched"—which extend the theme in the direction of martyrdom, as in sufferings endured, for example, of St. Vincent and St. George or "the eldest" in 4 Maccabees 9:13. The stanza concludes with the poet's wanting "to be entered and picked clean" as if he has chosen the fate of St. Catherine, whose bones were picked by the crows and vultures after she was hoisted on a wheel. As for the desire to be entered, this appears to echo the conclusion of one of John Donne's Holy Sonnets, *Batter My Heart*:: "Except you'enthrall mee, never shall be free, / Nor ever chast, except you ravish mee."

The separation between the anaphora of stanza 2 and the questions asked by the baffled wind and repeated by the castor beans in stanza 3 is the separation between natural and revealed religion. The central stanza is in fact set off against both stanzas 1 and 3. In stanza 1 the routine of the moon's cycle simply repeats what it has been doing *ad infinitum*, and in stanza 3 the engine of the heavens gets cranked up to wheel through another segment of its eternal cycle. Nature goes its way, needing none of the self-denial and self-mortification the poet so forthrightly declares he wants. As Wright says in *Sentences*, "The trees take care of their own salvation," another version of which we have in the next poem.

p. 152, l. 19. *little earrings of death.* Castor beans contain a toxin.

Autumn

Orig. pub. in *American Poetry Review* May–June 1977: 16.
CT, 62; CM, 153
Pattern: 3 × 2
Time: 1 November

"All my poems," Wright has written, "seem to be an ongoing argument with myself about the unlikelihood of salvation" (*Halflife*, 37). What is striking in this poem is the *non sequitur* of the last line. We begin with a description of the golden autumn leaves that "Whisper their sentences through the blue chains of the wind"—a little snapshot of the cycle of the seasons, which has yielded the pod of the carob bean that the poet opens. This is followed by two items directly in front of him (the apples and the quilt) and by one which is distant, "The black clock of the heavens reset in future tense." These are the stars and planets whose future course through the heavens has already been determined.

The *non sequitur* turns out to be only apparent. As already noted (see *Reunion*, above), Wright believes that "salvation doesn't exist except through the natural world" (*Halflife*, 83). Whereas salvation is a complex thing in the Christian scheme of things, in the natural world it is a matter of identifying with the various cyclical processes: the disappearance and return of the sun- and vegetation-gods, the cycle of waking and dreaming, the annual cycle of the seasons (one phase of which we have in stanza 1), the solstitial and lunar cycles of the solar year (the heavenly clock of stanza 2). These patterns are regular, universal, and recognized by everyone, which is one reason for their simplicity, and insofar as the poet possesses and is possessed by the natural cycles, he merges his identity into the larger pattern and so defeats separation and alienation. The sense of regularity is reinforced by the identical syllable count of each stanza—27.

Saint-john's-bread, which is the pod of the carob tree, seems to be set in conscious opposition to the bread which Christ speaks of in St. John's Gospel, the bread of heaven (John 6:32–33)—which is again the difference between natural and revealed religion.

The falling leaves of lines 1–2 are personified as speakers having their own syntax, but in the context of chains Wright may also intend the legal meaning: the consignment by natural law of the leaves to their resting place in the earth.

Sitting at Night on the Front Porch

Orig. pub. in *Vanderbilt Poetry Review* 2, nos. 3–4 (1977): 66.
CT, 63; CM, 154
Pattern: 4-4-2

This poem hinges on the analogy of the car lights below resembling our disappearance into the "great void," as well as the "burning and disappearing" of the poet's mother, who had died more than a dozen years before. Darkness dominates the scene. The poet is sitting on the "dark porch." The car lights disappear as they approach the sea, the prospect below is that of a dark void, and the poet sits alone "sizing the dark." "Sizing," meaning "arranging" or "distributing," contains a hint of taking stock ("sizing up"). In either case, the hope for reunion comes in the final phrase, "saving my mother's seat." When she does turn up, she will have a proper place in her own chair, having emerged from the "great void," which is one form of salvation.

Saturday 6 A.M.

Orig. pub. in *American Poetry Review* May–June 1977: 16.
CT, 64; CM, 155
Pattern: 3 × 2

This little lyric represents a moment of repose before the final poem of *China Trace*. The poet postpones what he has to say, deferring to the wind. Each of the four elements makes its way into the six lines, but the only two with any metaphorical force are the sunlight and the wind. As the sun rises, titling toward the sea, the poet becomes motionless and the wind speaks. We are not told what the wind says, but we are reminded that in a number of Indo-European languages wind, breath, and spirit are the same word. Jesus says to Nicodemus, "The wind bloweth where it listeth, and thou hearest the sound thereof, but canst not tell whence it cometh, and whither it goeth: so is every one that is born of the Spirit" (John 3:8). Here "wind" and "Spirit" are the same word, *pneuma*. A similar cluster of meanings is found in the Hebrew *ruwach*: breath, wind, air, and spirit. And light has its own metaphorical force—enlightenment, recognition, clarity of vision, and the like. Whatever the wind says to the sun-bathed poet, we have the suggestion that it will carry him into the upper world.

Him

Orig. pub. in *Choice* 10 (1977): 258.
CT, 65; CM, 156
Pattern: 2-1-2-1-2

This, the final chapter in the spiritual journey that has been the subnarrative of *China Trace*, is the apotheosis of the poet—his inscription in the fixed stars of "the northern Pacific sky." In the first poem of *China Trace* the poet leaves the home of his childhood. In the last poem, which took five weeks to write, he arrives at another home.

Wright on Wright, in response to an interviewer's question about the identity of "him" here and in the twentieth section of *Tattoos*: "Well, those are two different fellows. 'Hymn' is the other point of the title 'Him,' of course. And that's why it's the last poem in *China Trace*. In that book, 'him' is the character who starts by saying good-bye to his childhood in the first poem and ends up in the sky in the fiftieth poem, which is now the forty-sixth, as I have taken four out for *Country Music*. Each one is concerned with the particular character who most of the time is referred to in the first person but sometimes (twice) in the third person and occasionally in the second person. He progresses from saying good-bye to childhood—because the parents are dead, and when parents die we have to put away childish things and become grown-ups whether we like it or not. And so he moves from there to the heaven of the fixed stars, becoming a constellation, which is as close as he ever gets. ... it does reflect my aspirations of what might happen if there were a heaven, a salvation. That's probably as far as I would go if I were that character, because that's as far as I can see. I would love to believe the world is Platonic, but I think it's Aristotelian" (*Halflife*, 130).

Each of the fifty poems of *China Trace* (forty-six in *Country Music*) is a discrete episode in a journey—a horizontal narrative—that takes the shape of a *nostos* or homecoming. The journey is cyclical, and the completion of the cycle transports the poet to the same point except that now he is on a higher level. In his "suit of lights," he has been "lifted and laid clear." The notion of higher and lower levels means, of course, that another metaphorical structure, that of the *axis mundi* or ladder that runs from the bottom to the top of the cosmos, is operating in the background of these poems. The poet's version of this metaphor is "the star-flowered boundary tree," the boundary being the marker between the higher and lowers worlds. He leaves the lower world, "flies up at the dawn," and is "released," meaning that he has moved into a world of freedom and intensified consciousness. The journey has been stormy, but he can now "sleep through the thunder" and, like the psalmist, lie down beside the still waters, having become, as in the epigraph from Calvino, "the emblem of emblems."

We are reminded, however, before we turn to the next chapter in Wright's poetic odyssey, that *Him*, where the subject is the object and vice versa, is written with a good measure of ironic distance. The poet is observing the character here in the third person, like Joyce's observing his Stephen Dedalus flying upward. The "he" of the poem can both ascend and descend the *axis mundi*. *Him* is a night-time vision and so belongs to the world of dream. When the poet says that he "lies down," we are reminded that while we wake "up" we "fall" to sleep. And the poet will in fact shortly descend to the middle world, the world of the ten thousand things where "the willow bleeds." In the epigraph Mingliaotse says that he would like "to travel in ether" but that he cannot do it yet. The same with Wright, who will replace his "suit of lights" with his walking shorts as he moves toward the second trilogy.

PART II

The Second Trilogy: *The World of the Ten Thousand Things: Poems 1980–1990*

The dust-jacket painting is Paul Cézanne's *Bend in the Road* (1900–1906). *Wright on Wright*: "Cézanne has a way of looking at a landscape that I find particularly innovative, revolutionary, and pleasing to my spirit. He breaks down and reassembles the landscape the way I like to think, when I'm working at my desk, I break down and reassemble what I'm looking at and put it back into a poem to recreate it, to reconstruct it. I like the idea that in fact he is very much of a realist although up close everything looks abstract. But once you get the right perspective, he is showing you just what's out there. I like to think I'm showing you just what's out there, but as I see it. I put these guys [Morandi and Cézanne] on my covers because I would like to get an inch closer to their genius, not because I put myself anywhere near their company" (*QN*, 135).

References to Cézanne or his works appear in other poems by Wright: *Self-Portrait* [4] (*WTTT*, 19), *Journal of English Days* (*WTTT*, 127), *A Journal of True Confessions* (*WTTT*, 143), *A Journal of the Year of the Ox* (*WTTT*, 152), and in the third trilogy, *Apologia Pro Vita Sua* (*NB*, 74), *Back Yard Boogie Woogie* (*NB*, 172).

Chapter 4

The Southern Cross (1981)

Cover art: *St. George and the Princess*, fresco by Antonio Pisanello

The book is dedicated to H.W. Wilkinson, which is the name stenciled on a tin footlocker in Wright's study in which he keeps family papers and mementos. In an interview J.D. McClatchy asked Wright whether the trunk was "a gesture to his past ... a sort of voice-box, a memory and a throat for the past." Wright replied: "Mr. Wilkinson is as mysterious to me as he is to you. His name was on the box when I bought it, and that's all I know about him. *The Southern Cross* was dedicated to the box, actually, ... and not to Mr. Wilkinson per se: he's just a stand-in for a catch-all, if such a thing is possible. A voice-box is a nice way to put it, although it's been more so in the past than it is now.... I guess I thought it was cute, as well, to dedicate a book ostensibly to someone I didn't know. But, as you say, the real gesture was to my past, a way of letting those speak whose voices are too faint to hear. So it's a voice-box in that sense, too; it amplifies the deep and desperate whispers of those who have disappeared into a kind of request for recognition" (QN, 92).

The epigraph, omitted from *The World of the Ten Thousand Things*, is from Dante's *Purgatorio*, canto 21, ll. 130–6. Dante records the scene between Statius and Virgil at the conclusion of the canto:

Già s'inchinava ad abbracciar li piedi
  al mio dottor, ma el li disse: "Frate,
non far, ché tu se' ombra e ombra vedi."
Ed ei surgendo: "Or puoi la quantitate
  comprender de l'amor ch'a te mi scalda,
  quand'io dismento nostra vanitate,
trattando l'ombre come cosa salda."
	[Now he had bent to kiss my teacher's feet,
	  but Virgil told him: "Brother, there's no need—
	you are a shade, a shade is what you see."
	And, rising, he: "Now you can understand
	  how much love burns in me for you, when I
	  forget our insubstantiality,
	treating the shades as one treats solid things."]
	trans. Alan Mandelstam

The four-part division of the poems in *The Southern Cross* was not maintained in *The World of the Ten Thousand Things*. The original volume was framed by the two long poems, *Homage to Paul Cézanne* and the title poem, each constituting a separate part unto themselves. Part 2 included five self-portrait poems alternating with four poems about rebirth. Part 3 contained twenty poems, each of which was a technical experiment Wright set for himself.

Homage to Paul Cézanne

Orig. pub. *New Yorker* 53 (19 December 1977): 36–7; rpt. *Poetry East* 13–14 (Spring–Summer 1984): 66–73, with Wright's comments on the poem (p. 76).
SC, 3–10; WTTT, 3–10

4. The Southern Cross (1981)

Pattern: 128 lines in eight units of sixteen lines each: (6-6-3-1) (4 × 4) (8-8) (2 × 8) (3-3-4-3-3) (3-3-1-5-3-1) (3-2-4-2-3-2) (2-5-2-5-2)

The title calls our attention to the similarity between Cézanne's technique as a painter and Wright's as a poet. Design, composition, and repetition are principles of both painting and poetry. Cézanne's paintings characteristically build up planes of color and small brushstrokes. Color comes center stage in section 4 of the poem, and Cézanne's brushstrokes might be compared to the stanzas laid down on the canvas of the page, sometimes wide (as in the eight-line stanzas) and sometimes narrow (as in the one- and two-line stanzas).

On the impetus for this poem, Wright has said, "I was watching TV one night—I think I was watching the news—it was just getting dark and I looked out into the field through the window in the door, and there were three white pieces of paper just catching the last light. And I wrote down the line, 'In the fading light the dead wear our white shirts to stay warm.' Then I said, well, that's interesting. I put it down, I had supper, and then later on the moon came out, and I watched TV again, and by god those same three pieces of paper were so white that they were picking up the moonlight! And so I went back to the line and rewrote it, 'At night, in the fish-light of the moon, the dead wear our white shirts to stay warm, and litter the fields.' And then the next day I went out to see what they were, and they were sheets of white notebook paper from a kid's notebook. That's why they were so white. It wasn't newspaper or anything. It was blank paper! And so I worked on that particular part of the Cézanne poem for a while and got the first section.... I was doing a lot of looking at Cézanne's paintings, and I'd been thinking about Cézanne a lot at that time.... I thought that certain painterly techniques—which is to say, using stanzas and lines the way painters sometimes use color and form—might be interesting.... So I worked on this poem not knowing how the poem was going to go. I thought it was going to be about ten sections. I knew it was going to be about Cézanne by the time I'd finished the first one. Not about Cézanne himself, but about the process of painting. I knew it was going to be nonlinear. I was going to write sections where each had to do with each other, but not consecutively or linearly.... What I was interested in doing was relaxing the line, using the line more as an overall unit in the poem rather than as a bridge from one part of the poem to the other—as one bridge to another bridge to another bridge. In other words, the lines in the stanza are applied, in a way, rather than narratively leading from one thing to the next" (*Halflife*, 101–3). For a similar explanation see Wright's "Color and Line," *Poetry East*, 13–14 (Spring–Summer 1984): 76

In response to an interviewer's question about whether the dead in *Homage to Paul Cézanne* function as subject matter or formal principle, Wright replied, "[I]t is the subject matter of the poem: it's where I first thought I could juxtapose associational phrases and lines that when put back together, would give a reconstituted, realistic picture. In other words, I was trying to write a realistic poem by nonlinear, nonrealist means. The dead was chosen as a subject matter because that seemed the most tactile abstract thing I could think of, since everyone knows what they are physically, and if you read poems you know what they are metaphysically. I also—used to in the past—write a lot about the dead. Again, it is a kind of informative background to my everyday life. It seemed to be something necessary for me to write out of, or to write against. As Dylan Thomas said, 'You write for the great dead.' You try to write for your betters. If you don't write for your betters you'll be writing for your lessers" (*Halflife*, 155).

Wright typically refers to numbered portions of his poems as "parts" and to divisions separated by a rule as "sections," which is the word he uses in talking about this poem (Spiegelman, 109; *Profile*, 41), even though no number or rule is used to mark the boundaries.

Section 1 (p. 3). The most obvious thing about the dead here is how similar they are to the living. The poet notes more than a dozen things the dead do that are like ordinary human actions: repeat themselves, curl up, lie in our beds, touch us, talk, wait, walk, reach up, give answers, and so on. Some of the activities of the dead seem altogether normal (they wear our shirts to keep warm, they talk in a corner). Other behavior is completely fantastic ("They shuttle their messages through the oat grass," "The reach up from the ice plant," "Their answers rise like rust on the stalks and the spidery leaves"). The concluding line suggests that the intrusion of the dead into our lives is something of a nuisance. Thus, "We rub them off our hands."

Section 2 (p. 4). The dead return each year, and in this section they are shown as becoming more and more sentient. As they "grow less dead," music begins to return to their consciousness, and they "repeat to themselves / ... that song that our fathers sing." The overall sense is that the distance between the living and the dead continues to diminish.

Section 3 (p. 5). In section 1 the world of the dead was largely a vegetable world. In section 2 the dead are associated with the mineral world (the "soiled hands," "the riverbank," the "unreturnable dirt"). In section 3 they belong to the watery world, their story coming incessantly from the "white lips of the sea." The dead inhabit a world of the word, and the story they tell is actually a plea, mimicking Pia's request to Dante in *Purgatorio*, 5:130: "Remember me," and Elpenor's to Odysseus in book 11 of the *Odyssey*, a line that Pound repeats in *Canto I*.

Section 4 (p. 6). The question faced by the poet here is how to represent the dead spatially. Elsewhere in the poem he relies on conventional links between death and the elements, especially fire, wind, and ice, but here he relies on the analogy of painting. We represent the dead with layers of cadmium blue, painting the dead the way Cézanne layered his canvases with a palette knife. The lines on the canvas are both vertical and horizontal, "line by line" referring to a formal process in both painting and poetry.

"And so we come between," says the poet, meaning that we are intermediaries for the dead, building a set of ascending terraces for them. Like the dead, we hang between heaven and earth, and "The dead understand all this, and keep in touch," meaning we have created *ut pictura poesis*. "What we are given in dreams," says the poet in section 8, "we write as blue paint."

Section 5 (p. 7). Here the permanence of the dead is foregrounded. Their presence is both local and universal, immanent and transcendent: their shadows are in the back yard, but they are also a part of the cosmos, sliding into the Milky Way. There is no hint of the dead being reincarnated. Rather, they are re-elemented into the natural world

Section 6 (p. 8). The motif here is the identity between the living and the dead. The dead offer their ministrations and we join them, becoming "what we've longed for." And what we have longed for is to be transformed, only to be told that it's not yet time. The dead have now become the principal actors in this little drama, and it is they who are now offering us consolation.

Section 7 (p. 9). Again, the drama is played out along the *axis mundi*. The dead fall like rain, permeating the earth, but then they "break toward the setting sun." They care little at all for the way we represent them in our verse. What they care about rather is ascension: in the night sky they are beating their drums "Ahead of us," leading the parade into the stars.

Section 8 (p. 10). The focus in the final section is on the rather paltry position of the living vis-à-vis the dead. Even though we look to the heavens and stretch our limbs upward, we remain earthbound. Our words have little effect in interceding on behalf of the dead or speaking for them. All we can do is what the poet has done—write what we are given in dreams in cadmium blue.

About the next nine poems, which form part 2 of *The Southern Cross*, Wright has said: "The first two self-portraits I did (one in *The Grave of the Right Hand* and one in *Hard Freight—Portrait of the Poet in Abraham von Werdt's Dream*) [CM, 18–19] were purely technical exercises. The third (in *China Trace* [*Self-Portrait in 2035*, in CM, 113]) was more serious, and these five, even though originally technically oriented, have come to be the most serious of all, in that I hope they say something about my life, and how I look at it. The second and third ones ... are made up, for the most part, from postcards and photographs that are above my desk. Four has to do with my years in Italy, and five uses rearranged material, in part, from John Donne and Emily Dickinson. All five are separated and punctuated by four longer poems about rebirth, and all nine poems are supposed to work together in the movement of the Bacon paintings [for the Bacon reference, see the commentary for WTTT, 21, below]. *Called Back*, for instance, is supposed to be the least narratively inclined of all the nine poems, each section being more or less independent. The same goes for the last self-portrait. Finally, of course, the poems have no referents but the language, as they have nothing to do contextually with anyone's paintings. They have to do, as I say, with my life, and where and how I live it" (*Profile*, 43–4).

Self-Portrait

Orig. pub. *Seneca Review* 8, no. 2 (December 1977): 36.
SC, 13; WTTT, 11
Pattern: 5 × 3
Place: Laguna Beach

This, the first of the five self-portraits, reveals features of the poet that are only sketches. In his early forties, he is anxious about his achievement, thinking that he will be unmasked as a pretender, though hoping that what is left over from the fire will clear his name. In the meantime, he says, he will continue to "hum to myself and settle my whereabouts," waiting until a fuller portrait emerges. The final stanza is a plea for inspiration, keener perception, protection, and deliverance from "my own words and my certainties."

Mount Caribou at Night

Orig. pub. *Field* 17 (Fall 1977): 86.
SC, 14; WTTT, 12
Pattern: 4 × 6
Place: Northwestern tip of Montana.

Caribou Mountain is in Lincoln County, Montana, located between Blacktail and Caribou Creeks, about four miles, as the crow flies, from Wright's vacation retreat. His cabin there is on a 320-acre tract about five miles south of the Canadian border and about twenty-six miles east of the Idaho state line. It lies just south of the East Fork of the Yaak River and is traversed by Porcupine and Basin Creeks. John McIntire and Jeannette Nolan, Wright's father- and mother-in-law and well-known Hollywood actors, acquired the land for a ranch in 1937. In the 1970s they tried unsuccessfully—testifying at Senate hearings, writing letters, filing appeals—to have the Mt. Henry region protected as a national wilderness area.

The poem is a panegyric to the Yaak River Valley and to several of its early settlers. Three are named: Joseph Walter Smoot (1882–1946), an early homesteader in the valley, who helped build a community center for local residents in 1925; Smoot Creek was named after him. The other two are Sam Runyan (1892–1947) and August Binder (1876–1962), both of whom are buried in the Boyd Cemetery near mile marker 43 on the Yaak River Road in Lincoln County, Montana. The poet speaks to all of the early settlers, now dead, telling them that Smoot, buried under the tamaracks, "still holds the nightfall between his knees."

He then turns his gaze from the earth to the sky. In the flowing heavens, Cassiopeia wheels across the northern sky, causing Andromeda and the Whale (Cetus) to disappear. Hovering over the whole valley is Mt. Caribou, "Massive and on the rise and taking it in. And taking it back / To the future we occupied." The poet imagines that future generations will "walk out / Into the same night and the meadow grass." The early settlers are dead, but the landscape remains alive.

p. 12, l. 23. *cauly hoods*. A caul is the membrane that sometimes covers the head at birth: Wright uses the word again in *The Southern Cross*, 50, to describe the cape over the head and shoulders on the statue of Giordano Bruno.

Self-Portrait

Orig. pub. *Missouri Review* 1 (Spring 1978): 15.
SC, 15; WTTT, 13
Pattern: 5 × 3
Place: Laguna Beach, with a flashback to Venice by way two photographs.

The poet, referring to himself in the third person, gazes at two photographs of himself in the Dorsoduro (southern edge of Venice). The first is on the Trevisan bridge, which crosses the Rio Ognisanti. The second is to the east, on the Campo San Trovaso. Pound lived near the conjunction of the San Trovaso and Ognisanti canals, so the "bridge / To the crystal" seems to be a reference to Pound, the crystal being an important image in the *Cantos* from XCI to CXVI, where Pound asks, "I have brought the great ball of crystal; / who can lift it? / Can you enter the great acorn of light?" (*Cantos*, 815). In his early days in Italy Wright would follow Pound around the streets of Venice and into restaurants (*Halflife*, 63). The images in the third stanza are from postcards. The reindeer are from a postcard from Finland. The image is of course static, but the poet invests it with a sense of life and movement. The images of St. Jerome and St. Augustine are from reproductions of two of the three paintings by Vittore Carpaccio in his cycle on St. Jerome—*Saint Jerome Leading the Lions into the Monastery* and *Vision of St. Augustine*. In the latter, Augustine, surrounded by books, looks up toward the window as he hears the voice of Jerome telling him of his death and ascent to Heaven.

The poem as a whole represents the Italian imprint on Wright's character. He has been "earmarked" by the mystique of Venice/Pound, which contains an "infinite alphabet of his past," "his" referring to both Wright and Pound, their personae merging into a single poetic spirit. For the poet, the "wind will edit him soon enough, / And squander his broken chords," and he will be given some breathing room—lines that seem equally appropriate for Pound, whose "broken chords" will eventually be confirmed. With the Carpaccio paintings we end on not just an Italian note but a religious one as well. Augustine, writing to Jerome on a matter of theology, glances up toward the miraculous light coming through the window, at which point he heard St. Jerome's voice telling him that he had died and was with Christ in heaven.

p. 13, l. 8. *slatch*. The smooth interval between heavy waves, a word Wright would use later in *Returned to the Yaak Cabin ...* in *Appalachia* (NB, 155, l. 13).

p. 13, l. 15. *St. Augustine*. On the legend behind the narrative of the painting, see Helen I. Roberts, "St. Augustine in 'St. Jerome's Study': Carpaccio's Painting and Its Legendary Source," *Art Bulletin* 41, no. 4 [December 1959]: 283–97. The painting is reproduced on the cover of the present volume.

Holy Thursday

Orig. pub. *Antaeus* 30–31 (Spring 1978): 248–9.
SC, 16–18; WTTT, 14–15
Pattern: 10 × 5
Time: Unspecified, except for Thursday
Place: Laguna Beach

Holy Thursday is the English church's celebration of Christ's ascension, thirty-nine days after Easter, a day when, in Blake's time, the children of London were marched to St. Paul's Cathedral for a service. In the first of Blake's *Holy Thursday* poems—from *Songs of Innocence*—the children are portrayed as angelic, and the allusion in Blake's last line, "Then cherish pity, lest you drive an angel from your door," is to Hebrews 13:2, "Be not forgetful to entertain strangers: for thereby some have entertained angels unawares." In the second—from *Songs of Experience*—the ceremony is aligned with the misery and poverty of the children living in an "eternal winter."

Holy Thursday begins with the sounds of the mourning dove, which are joined by five other creatures, all of the flying variety: flies, crows, butterflies, a mosquito, and a mockingbird. These fauna perform their rites against a background of some fourteen species of flora, from the pepper tree in first stanza to the palm tree in the last, establishing themselves against the dirt and rust of the desert-like field. Amid all of this is the poet, who scuffs his shoes in the field dirt and later settles and stands back from the adobe dust. Blake's children are the only thing that make Thursday holy: they alone are associated with canticles, cathedrals, and a "saving grace." They are asleep at the beginning, but by the end they have begun to stir and slide their ladders down in anticipation of a descent. Wright's images of the sleeping children in this surreal poem are closer to those in several of Blake's other *Songs of Innocence: The Chimney-Sweeper, Night, Nurse's Song,* and *A Dream.* Still, the irony of Wright's last stanza is close in its mood to Blake's second *Holy Thursday* song: the second selves of the children begin to stir only to be met with the cadenced "skeletal songs" of the angels.

Self-Portrait

Orig. pub. *Antaeus* 30–31 (Spring 1978): 247.
SC, 19; WTTT, 16
Pattern: 1-4-5-4-1
Place: In the photos, Tennessee and Switzerland

"*The pictures in the air have few visitors,*" wrote Emily Dickinson to her sister-in-law Sue Gilbert—a line that could function as an epigraph for the present poem: the photographs and postcards tacked above the poet's desk have few visitors either. They are visited, one imagines, almost solely by the poet himself. (For a photograph of the pictures above Wright's desk, see p. 75 of *The Other Side of the River.*) There are photographs of the sunset and moonrise, a picture of the Zodiac with arcing lines connecting the stars, and a photograph of Wright's brother—Winter—on a slope at Hiwassee Lake, North Carolina.

The second stanza describes a photo of Winter Wright again, this time atop the Matterhorn. The third stanza is an image of the poet himself in his California home, "Omniscient above the bay" and assuming the pose of one of the subjects in an Edvard Munch painting, holding his left cheek in his palm and noticing a photograph in which the poet Desmond O'Grady is pointing to Wright. The final image is a reproduction of a fourteenth-century

Greek icon, *The Virgin of Tenderness*, from the School of Constantinople. The poet asks the Madonna to point too, just as O'Grady is pointing.

"What I look at," says Wright, "has everything to do with what I think" (QN, 90). Most commonly he looks at the landscape. In the present poem he is once removed from the landscape, looking at its images as reproduced by the camera, or, in the case of the paintings, twice removed (images of images). The movement of this ekphrastic poem is from the cosmos at the beginning to the poetic self, singled out by both O'Grady and the Madonna, at the end.

p. 16, l. 1. *The pictures ... visitors.* From Emily Dickinson, Letter to Sue Gilbert, *Letters*, ed. Thomas H. Johnson, 3 vols. (Cambridge: Belknap Press of Harvard University Press, 1958), 2:339 (letter 194). The letter was written after Dickinson had attended two Sunday services on 26 September 1858.

p. 16, l. 11. *Like Munch.* The Munch painting may be *The Scream*, though there the distraught subject holds his cheeks in both of his palms.

p. 16, l. 14. *O'Grady's finger.* For O'Grady, see *A Journal of True Confessions*, WTTT, 143.

Literature Made out of Other Literature: In James R. Hugunin's comic novella *Something is Crook in Middlebrook* the main character, Art Strewth Middlebrook, is bantering with his friend Al Schmerbauch. Art says, "Or may be the last two people on earth will die at the same instant! Simultaneity .... Yep, and it'll probably be winter on top of the Matterhorn with no one standing there sun-goggled; no one languishing in Munich; the Hiwassee River in Tennessee will be at an all-time low with no one standing on the bank, hands half in pants pockets. No one left to check evidence, receive post cards, paste photos in the family album. Full-color holy cards of Ivana Trump as The Madonna of Tenderness, our Lady of Feints and X's will blow lazily down now-abandoned alleys as peach blossoms follow the moving water" (Oak Park, IL: N.p., 2005), 43. The last clause, a line from Li Po, is taken from Wright's *Portrait of the Artist with Li Po* (WTTT, 34).

Virginia Reel

Orig. pub. *Antaeus* 30–31 (Spring 1978): 245–6.
SC, 20–1; WTTT, 17–18
Pattern: 8 × 5
Time: Spring
Place: Clarke County in northern Virginia, between Winchester and Washington, DC
The poem is dedicated to Mark Strand (see WTTT, 231).

The Virginia Reel is an American country-dance in which couples perform various steps together to the instructions of a caller. There is little in the poem associated with the dance, but there is perhaps a pun in the poet's desire to reel downward in the last stanza when the mysterious hand touches his shoulder and the apple blossoms fishtail to earth. There is also the suggestion of the spool of a motion-picture, in which case the poet can be seen as aiming his camera lens toward the past and producing a kind of documentary about ancestral people and places.

The poem recounts a trip to the ancestral home of the poet's mother in Clarke County, Virginia, returning to a place he has not visited in twenty years. He rehearses the place names, scattered throughout the county and apparently associated with various family members. His Aunt Roberta, his mother's sister, now lives nearby, but all of the other relatives have disappeared from the area. Various memories of the past emerge, including a connection with George Washington's household by way of the poet's great-great-grandfather, and as the poet stands on the porch of the Wickliffe Church, he imagines the spirits of a family servant (Hampton) and his great-grandfather (Jaq) emerging from the cemetery to offer "toasts to our health."

In the final stanza, the poet feels his shoulder touched by a mysterious hand, causing him to confess that he would eventually like to be laid down in this place beside his ancestors, and we conclude with the lovely image of the last apple blossom from the nearby Smithfield orchard falling to earth, "a signal from us to them."

p. 17, l. 3. *suicides*. One of the suicides was Wright's great-grandfather Jaq Powers. See note to p. 18, l. 8, below.
p. 17, l. 11. *great-great-grandfather ...Nelly Custis*. Nelly Custis was one of four children of Martha Washington's son "Jackey" Custis (from her first marriage); a member of George Washington's household.
p. 17, l. 20. Cf. Hamlet's "the thousand natural shocks / That flesh is heir to" (*Hamlet*, 3.1.63–4).
p. 18, l. 1. *Wickliffe Church*. The church began when Frederick Parish was created concurrently with Frederick County in 1738 by an act of the colonial General Assembly of Virginia as an ecclesiastical unit of the Church of England. Cunningham Chapel was the first of three chapels of the parish constructed, probably in 1747, at a location three miles south of present day Berryville. After the original log building was destroyed in the Revolutionary War, it was replaced by the stone structure, The Old Chapel. Some of the original congregation withdrew from Old Chapel, Frederick Parish, to establish a mission at Wickliffe Church, four miles northeast of Berryville in Clarke County, which separated from Old Chapel in 1819; twelve years later a group of members of the Wickliffe congregation, who desired a place to worship closer to the Berryville community, consecrated Grace Church in Berryville. In 1919 the members of Wickliffe joined Grace Church; the historic Wickliffe Church building is now maintained by Grace Church and is used for an annual service.
p. 18, l. 8. *Hampton*. The family servant, an ex-slave. *Jaq*. Jaq Powers, Wright's great-grandfather. When his wife died, he was left with six children, which proved to be too much of a responsibility for him. He committed suicide, at which point Wright's grandmother, Roberta Powers, went to Mississippi to be a governess. There she married John Dawson Winter. Wright's mother, Mary Winter, grew up in Mississippi.
p. 18, l. 16. *Smithfield*. The orchards of Smithfield Farm are on Wickliffe Road to the east of Berryville.

Self-Portrait

Orig. pub. *Quarterly West* 6 (Spring–Summer 1978): 123.
SC, 22; WTTT, 19
Pattern: 3-2-5-3-2
Time: Flashback to the sojourn in Italy in the 1960s
Place: Various Italian sites recalled

The places and things in stanza 1, as Wright says, are those that caught his eye in Italy during his army sojourn there more than twenty years ago. He depicts himself as a latter-day Whitman, "the Great Cataloguer," listing the mountains and valleys, the towns, the paintings, the restaurants, and other features of the landscape that he saw traipsing through Italy. The catalogue concludes with an image of Keats's grave in Rome, above which are resurrected four of Wright's poetic heroes, along with Cézanne, represented here by his *The Black Château*.

Marostica is a small Italian town between Vicenza and Bassano. *Val di Ser* is the Serchio Valley in Tuscany. *Madonna del Ortolo* is a painting by Stephano da Verona in the Museo di Castelvecchio in Verona (and mentioned by Pound in *Canto IV* and *Canto LXXIV* [*Cantos*, 16, 468]). *Bassano del Grappa* is a small town northwest of Venice. *San Giorgio* is an Italian mountain. *Piave* is a river in northern Italy. The church of *San Zeno Maggiore* is in Verona, as is the *Caffè Dante*, located in the heart of the city on the Piazza dei Signori. The ruins of *Catullus'* villa are on a peninsula that extends into *Lake Garda*. *Ponte Pietra* is a bridge across the *Adige* River in Verona. The *Twelve Apostles* is a restaurant built on the ruins of a roman temple near the *Piazza Erbe* in Verona. The grave of *John Keats* is in the Protestant cemetery in Rome.

Wright on Wright, commenting in an interview on the final two lines: "The reason those five [Campana, Rimbaud, Crane, Dickinson, and *The Black Château*] are there is because it was a poem about landscapes. It was a poem enumerating landscapes that I had loved in my life. Then, when it ends on people, they become landscapes that I have loved in my life. Landscapes that have nourished me, landscapes that I have walked through, landscapes that have remained with me. Their works are landscapes. They become objects in my life and not just somebody I read. They become part of the landscapes that mold me into who I am. Now, what I would take from Emily Dickinson, I think, is certainly not her meter or her sound or anything, but it's her way of looking at the unknown.... Emily Dickinson is the closest thing I know to the great hymns of the Southern mountains that I love. White Soul, as it were. And that's because she comes pretty much out of that same period of time, out of those same convictions. Dino Campana, because he is the example of the beautiful mad poet. He really did see visions.... Arthur Rimbaud, because he's one of my favorite poets. I guess you could say I'm drawn to all of them, except Cézanne, because of their sense of the world, and not technique. Cézanne would be technique, and that's why he is "The Black Château" (*Halflife*, 104–5).

Called Back

Orig. pub. *Paris Review* 74 (Fall–Winter 1978): 105.
SC, 23; WTTT, 20
Pattern: 2-4-3-1-5-3-2
Time: Spring, apparently
Place: Laguna Beach

"Called Back" is the epitaph on Emily Dickinson's gravestone in Amherst, the phrase coming from the last letter she wrote—to her cousins—the day before she died: "Little Cousins—Called back. Emily." The poem moves toward the time when the poet himself will be called back: "When the oak tree and the Easter grass have taken my body, / I'll start to count out my days, beginning at one." As life will continue even after death, the implication here is parallel to Northrop Frye's adage that death is not the opposite of life, but the opposite of birth.

The poem establishes a counterpoint between the daylight world of the local flora, where the plenitude of the landscape ("its attendant ecstasies") begins to blossom forth, and the darker, ominous world of the black zodiac, with its Angel of Death and Black Dog and godlike Darkness. In the face of the latter, the poet bows in supplication and offers prayers. What comes from the gestures we are not told, being left only with the image of broken glass beside the highway and the poet's projection of what occurs after death—a version of the myth of the eternal return.

p. 20, l. 3. *octillo*. A desert shrub, also known as candlewood.
p. 20, l. 5. *Juan Quesada*. The artist who had carved a bird from an animal bone.
p. 20, l. 7. *Black Dog*. Sirius, the brightest star in the Canis Major constellation.

Self-Portrait

Orig. pub. *New England Review* 1 (Autumn 1978): 30.
SC, 24; WTTT, 21
Pattern: 5 × 3
Place: Flashback to Murray, Kentucky.

Wright says that this poem "uses rearranged material, in part, from John Donne and Emily Dickinson" (*Profile* 43–4). Dickinson is the presence the poet feels by his side in stanza 1, "the ghost-weight of a past life" he holds in his arms. Her spirit is still waiting to rise. Wright apparently has in mind one or more of Dickinson's resurrection poems. In Poem 621, for example, Dickinson concludes with this "waiting to rise" projection for her and her lover: "Sufficient troth that we shall rise—Deposed—at length, the Grave—/ To that new Marriage, / Justified— Through Calvaries of Love!" And Poem 237 begins with another forecast of resurrection: "I think just how my shape will rise—/ When I shall be '*forgiven*,'—/ Till Hair—and Eyes—and timid Head—/ Are *out of sight*–in Heaven."

The final line of stanza 1 cuts to the present with the poet's declaration that he knows now what he knew at some earlier time when he was lying on his side in Murray, Kentucky—that "she was there, / Asking for nothing." As Dickinson says in Poem 621, "I asked no other thing—/ No other—was denied." The difference now is that she is no longer "heavy as bad luck," so he can "lift her" toward some reunion beyond death.

Stanza 2 brings this mystical union to a quick halt as the evening makes a transition from the previous scene to the present one. The poet now sees that he has betrayed himself by smuggling in what Donne calls "spider love." In Donne's love poem, which is about disillusioned love, the poisonous spider changes everything: "But oh, self-traitor, I do bring / The spider love, which transubstantiates all, / And can convert manna to gall" (*Twickenham Garden*, ll. 5–7). In Wright's appropriation the spider undoes and rearranges, but we understand the effect of such conversion to be the same: the bread of heaven has become gall—a parody of transubstantiation. Thus the poet's appeal to the Angel of Mercy to strip him down, removing the cloak of self-betrayal. Spider love is the demonic version of the mystical union with "her" in stanza 1. Being stripped down and answering to no one leaves the poet with only an exposed ego.

In the final stanza the poet finds a new vision to replace self-betrayal. This is a vision of Blake's Beulah world. The charge to "hold hands" is a plea for a community of souls where "none of us is missing," and this communal vision is a prelude to resurrection, just as the reddening sky is a prelude to the sunrise.

In connection with the five self-portraits, Wright has said, "Francis Bacon has done series of self-portraits (3–4 in a series) in which the image is broken down and distorted a little more in each succeeding picture, all the while retaining the central focus and outline of the picture as a whole and as a composite. If brushstrokes and brushwork can be equated, in this case, with language, and form can still be considered form, then I'm after something like this" (*Profile*, 43).

p. 21, l. 7. *tight dissolve*. A term from the movies, meaning the fading out of one shot as the next one becomes clearer. Wright uses the phrase later in *Jesuit Graves* (NB, 117).

* * *

The poems from *Composition in Grey and Pink* through *New Year's Eve, 1979* formed section III of *The Southern Cross* (the divisions are omitted in *WTTT*). At one time the section had an epigraph from John Cage that derived from a question-and-answer period following a 1971 concert in Irvine, which Wright attended with Donald Justice. Cage was asked, "When you are up there fiddling with your score paper or looking out the window or tapping your finger on the piano, or shifting around on the stool, what are you really doing?" Cage replied, "I'm giving myself instructions and carrying them out." Wright found that interesting enough to try it himself, giving himself instructions for each of the poems in section III and carrying them out (*Halflife*, 143).

Composition in Grey and Pink

Orig. pub. *Ironwood* 6 (Fall 1978): 102.
SC, 27; WTTT, 22
Pattern: 3-3-1-3-1-3
Time: Summer, apparently
Place: Laguna Beach

The instruction that Wright gave himself for this poem was to produce a watercolor in words (*Halflife*, 143). The first three stanzas recreate images of ascent and descent in a grey and pink painting—the flight and fall of the dead souls from the sky, the misty heat of the trees, the butterflies, the late afternoon sunset, the rising rose, the ashes and "trampled garlands." The poem, however, moves beyond the *ut pictura poesis* convention of the first three stanzas. The last three record two wishes—the poet's dream of "an incandescent space // where nothing distinct exists, / And where nothing ends" and then, after the descent of the dogstar, his desire to "sit in a quiet corner / Untied from God." Here the wish-fulfillment dream of being transported to some intensely bright and infinite space is displaced by the quieter and much less spectacular dream of solitary confinement, as it were, removed from both other souls and God. The poem as a whole imitates the process of composing a painting, at least as the poet imagines it might have been composed, beginning with the pink hues of stanza 2 and continuing with the grey of the "ashes."

Laguna Blues

Orig. pub. *Paris Review* 79 (1981): 279.
SC, 28; WTTT, 23
Pattern: 5 × 3
Time: Summer, apparently
Place: Laguna Beach

A hot Saturday afternoon in Laguna Beach finds the poet singing the blues: his instruction to himself was to write a blues poem (*Halflife*, 143), and what he does is to produce a verbal imitation of the musical form. He cannot put his finger on the source of his melancholy, though the "Something" that is "off-key" is more a mental anxiety than an emotional distress. Perhaps it is related to the poet's inability to write, as the pages that are blowing about are either empty (white) or uninscribable (black). The verbal music is nudged along by repeated phrases ("It's Saturday afternoon," "Something's off-key," "lift and fall"), sounds ("kind," "mind," "unkind"; "threads," "heads"), words ("pages," "little," "from," "crows"), and the twelve-syllable refrain—"Whatever it is, it bothers me all the time"—which imitates the standard twelve-bar lyric framework of the blues. All of the other lines, save one, have an odd number of syllables: seven, nine, eleven, thirteen, and fifteen. Externally, things are in a state of flux, with all of the lifting up and falling down, the floating up and gliding down, like the sounds of the blues. The Saturday afternoon is colorless, except for the implied green of the castor beans and pepper plant in line 13. Still, the poet manages a "little dance" as he sings the blues—a two-step of the song and dance man, like a slow drag, perhaps.

p. 23, ll. 5, 10, 15. *it bothers me all the time*. Cf. the lines from Lillian Glinn's *Shreveport Blues*, "he bothers me all the time," and Peetie Wheatstraw's *Last Dime Blues*, "she bothers me all the time." Similar lines appear in numerous blues tunes.

October

Orig. pub. *New Yorker* 55 (8 October 1979): 42.
SC, 29; WTTT, 24
Pattern: 3 × 5

Here Wright's instruction to himself was to write a seasonal poem (*Halflife*, 143–4). The season is obviously autumn, though the description of the landscape is scanty: about the unspecified setting we learn only that it has falling red leaves, slowly drifting clouds, and scattered cornflowers beside a train track, along with the light "falling in great sheets though the trees." As in *Composition in Grey and Pink*, the poet's imagination moves to another level in the second half of the poem, where the motifs of transfiguration, resurrection, and transubstantiation are woven together. These motifs are anticipated by "the nine steps to heaven" in stanza 2—the number of steps in many ancient architectural structures (e.g., stupas and pagodas in places where Buddhism and Hinduism are practiced and the pyramids in Meso-America), which were derived from cosmological myths. One finds the nine steps to heaven in the Caodaism, a Vietnamese religion that synthesizes Taoism, native spiritualism, Christianity, and Islam.

The poet imagines first that the transfiguration will begin in a setting like the present one, with the "almost tangible" sheets of light falling through the trees. Then, after the temperature has dropped further, he projects a resurrection from his "tired body," which will become a "blood-knot of light, / Ready to take the darkness in." The final stanza, with its Eucharist imagery, is introduced by an m-dash and is not connected syntactically to what has come before. It's as if the stanza were the second half of a wish to be transported: "—Or for the wind to come / And carry me, bone by bone, through the sky, / Its wafer a burn on my tongue, // its wine deep forgetfulness." In this version of transubstantiation, which will be initiated by the spirit (wind), the bread (body) becomes fire, and the wine (blood) becomes a mysterious concealment and oblivion.

p. 24, l. 11. *blood-knot*. A knot often used by anglers to join two pieces of nylon filament; also called barrel knot.

Childhood's Body

Orig. pub. *Crazy Horse* 18 (Spring 1979): 32.
SC, 30; WTTT, 25
Pattern: 2-2-3-2-1-3-1

The self-instruction here was "to write a childhood poem unlike any I had done before" (*Halflife*, 144). The poem begins with two metaphors, one spatial and vertical, the other horizontal and temporal. The antecedent of "This," which introduces the first two lines, is the title itself. The child's body with a rope of stars tied to his wrist is an *axis mundi* image, projecting the potential poet's connection with the world of spiritual ascent. The projection of the potential pilgrimage of the child's body comes from the identification of the body and the train.

The poem does not remain in the childhood world after the first two lines. What follows is chiefly what the poet has learned about the poetic vocation: it's not enough to sing and then sing again, it's not enough to "dissemble the alphabet" in the service of personal confession, and it's not enough "to transform the curlicues." What *is* sufficient is that the poet has now discovered a language for the blank tablets before him. His poetic albums will contain the language of landscape, images of which are enclosed within the parentheses of the penultimate stanza. "This," says the poet, "is a lip of snow and a lip of blood," suggesting, among other things, the unity of the natural and the human worlds that will issue from poetic speech.

Driving through Tennessee

Orig. pub. *raccoon* 7 (May 1980): 9; rpt. in *A Millennium Arts Project*, rev. ed. (Washington, DC: National Endowment for the Arts, 1999), 91.

SC, 31; WTTT, 27
Pattern: 5 × 3

For this poem Wright's instruction to himself was "to write a poem that was basically commentary." The commentary turns out to be a rather commonplace observation: the strangeness of what the memory of the past brings back to consciousness. Some memories are what one would expect—parents, places lived, and roads traveled. Other things returning to consciousness are religious figures: Jesus, Stephen Martyr, and St. Paul of the Sword. In repeating a line from Lamentations 3:63—"I am their music"—the poet means that he is the one to memorialize the things recalled from his past. (The context of the passage from Lamentations is quite different from the one we have here: There the biblical writer is lamenting the fact that he is the object of the taunt-songs of Chaldeans, who have destroyed Jerusalem). In singing the song of the unimpeachable ancestors and saints who have come before and of the places of the past, the poet hopes that he himself will be remembered "when the time comes, / For charity's sake."

p. 26, ll. 9–10. For Stephen's martyrdom, see Acts 7. Paul's traditional sword is a symbol both of his eloquence in preaching the Word and of his death.

p. 26, l. 15. *Galeoto.* The Dantean single helmsman or pilot, as in *Inferno* 8.17 (*un sol galeoto*, from *gallea*, galley).

Spring Abstract

Orig. pub. *raccoon* 7 (May 1980): 10.
SC, 32; WTTT, 27
Pattern: 5 × 3
Place: Laguna Beach

For this lyric Wright's cryptic self-instruction was "to write an abstract of a poem that wasn't there" (*Halflife*, 145). This instruction is something of a riddle, and the poem is no less so. The first stanza refers to three of the central elements of poetry: music, language, and image. It's as if Wright has appropriated the Aristotelian scheme: *melos*, *lexis*, and *opsis*, the word lying halfway between the ear and the eye. But each of the three elements is dismissed: the music (*melos*) falls away, and the poet declares that he not interested in either the word (*lexis*) or the image (*opsis*).

The description of the landscape in stanza 2, however, undercuts the position taken in stanza 1, so that the answer to the poet's questions, "What do I care...?" is "A great deal." Stanza 2 is a wonderfully musical description, filled with crisp images, and carried along by nouns and adjectives, which have just been disparaged. Similarly, with the first two lines of stanza 3, after which the poet declares, "One line in the page that heaven and earth make." It is actually two lines, one having to do with the heaven of the full moon and the other with the earthly dew breaking off of the blades of grass. But just as the poem begins to develop some energy, it dissolves: "Meager and rumpled, wrung out, / The poem is ground down from a mumbled joy." So the poem as a completed whole seems not to have been there after all. What we have rather is an "abstract," in the sense not of a lyric summary but of a lyric that has in itself the essential qualities of a more extensive elaboration.

p. 27, l. 9. *Queens of the Night.* Velvety black-maroon tulips.

Landscape with Seated Figure and Olive Trees

Orig. pub. *Shenandoah* 31, no. 4 (1980): 14.
SC, 33; WTTT, 28

Pattern: 5-4-5
Time: Early 1960s
Place: San Ambrogio

The title is, of course, an imitation of the title of a painting. There are numerous artists who have called their paintings *Landscape with Seated Figure*, from Julian Alden Weir and George Inness to Roy Lichtenstein. The seated figure in this particular "landscape" is Ezra Pound, and the description is not of a painting but of a photograph of "the old man" in his garden at San Ambrogio, where Olga Rudge had set up her home in 1924, Pound having settled in nearby Rapallo.

The poem moves from the golden world of the orange blossoms to the silver one of the olive grove until it reaches Pound in stanza 2, who, "Slouched and at ease in the sunfall," is oblivious to everything in the noon-time world around him but the wind—at least as the poet interprets the photograph. As there is a relation between wind and spirit, we are invited to make the connection that we find in Greek, where *pneuma* can mean both "spirit" and "wind." Jesus says "The wind bloweth where it listeth ... so is everyone that is born of the Spirit" (John 3:8). For Pound, "Only the wind matters," which we might translate as "Only the spirit matters." Pound, we recall, was Wright's *spi*ritual in*spi*ration.

Dog Yoga

Orig. pub. *Field* 22 (Spring 1980): 83.
SC, 34; *WTTT*, 29
Pattern: 3-1-2-1-2-1-2-2
Time: Spring
Place: Laguna Beach

Although this poem contains no verbs, various actions and states of being are suggested. The clouds toll their "Mournful cadences," the winds blow "in and out of the open window," the thunder rumbles, the sunlight descends "among the ferns," the eastern sky grows light and the western sky grows dark as the sun extinguishes itself, and so on. Moreover, things repeat themselves, suggesting a myth of the eternal return: "twenty-five years of the same news"; "Year in, year out," the same stories are woven from the dark and the same sounds are whispered by the wind. There are, then, a number of active processes at work. But the absence of explicit verbs helps to establish a general mood of inactivity, a surrendering to gravity so as to reach a state of what the Yoga sutras call "nondoing." The void, which appears in the penultimate line, is not an idea exclusive to Yoga, though it is a part of the vision of Patanjali's *Yoga Sutras* (e.g., 10.1), and in various texts of Tantra Yoga the heart is said to be the locus of the void. The first half of the title is more difficult to explain, even if it is connected somehow to the "noontide's leash." Whether it is worth noting that among the "New Age" movements of the late twentieth century dog yoga studios do exist is uncertain. And in connection with an Eastern religious practice, we are reminded that the backwards version of "Dog" is "God"—a graphical inversion that Wright himself has pointed to: in explaining the meaning of dog in one of his poems, he provided several clues and then added "There is also the reverse spelling of dog" (*Halflife*, 81).

p. 29, l. 13. Cf. Van Gogh to his brother Theo: "But there remains a void in the heart / That nothing will fill" (10 April 1992, Letter 186).

California Spring

Orig. pub. *New Yorker* 56 (23 June 1980): 30.
SC, 35; WTTT, 30
Pattern: 3 × 5
Place: Laguna Beach

The experiment here was to write a poem that "has a verb in every line" (*Halflife*, 143). Each line is a complete, end-stopped syntactic unit. The complex sentences (l. 8 and l. 9) and the compound one (l. 14) have, of course, two verbs. Some of the sentences are literal ("At dawn the dove croons"; "The apricot blossoms scatter across the ice plant"). Some are figurative ("There is a tree which rains down in the field"; "There is a spider that swings back and forth on his thin strings in the heart"). Some are commonplace ("How cold the wind is"). Some are fabulous ("One angel dangles his wing").

Only two of the verbs have objects (l. 3 and l. 13). The rest are either intransitive or copulae, the latter being strung together in ll. 6–10, and the effect of this is to heighten states of being over action. (The comma in l. 11 forces us to insert "cold" after the copula, thus preventing us from reading "is caught" as a passive construction.) There is little sense of the movement that we get with transitivity. The state of being is a kind of lassitude or sluggishness, what with all the hanging and shrinking and drooping and dangling and creaking. Spring is having a difficult time getting untracked. Other than this and the announced grammatical exercise, what holds the poem together is uncertain. We end up with fourteen little snapshots of the California landscape, followed by a quizzical two-word coda—"Nothing forgives." Here a transitive verb is used intransitively as a kind of summary statement: nothing in the cold, sad morning, not even the angel with dangling wing, offers absolution.

p. 30, l. 3. *liquidambar.* Sweet gum tree.

Laguna Dantesca

Orig. pub. *New Yorker* 56 (23 June 1980): 30.
SC, 36; WTTT, 31
Pattern: 2-1-3-2-2-1-2-1

Title: "Dantesca" is an anagram of "A Descant," so that Dantean Laguna is also Laguna Melody or Laguna Musical Theme.

Wright's intent here was "to take images from my favorite poet and use them in my own poem" (*Halflife*, 14). The images from Dante begin with the simile of the "little boat (*navicella*)." Although the *navicella* appears several times in *The Divine Comedy* (*Inferno* 17.100, *Purgatorio* 32.129), Wright almost certainly has in mind the simile that begins the *Purgatorio*: "To course over better waters the little boat of my genius now raises her sails" (*Purgatorio* 1.1–2). The *Paradiso* opens with a reference to Dante's "little bark" (*piccioletta barca*), but there the seagoers have expanded to include Dante's readers; so *Purgatorio* 1, where the poet seeks isolation as he slips across the waters toward the horizon, is the more likely source.

Stanzas 2 and 3 derive, as Wright's note indicates (*WTTT*, 231), from *Paradiso* 3. The woman referred to is Piccarda Donati, the cousin of Dante's wife Gemma and the sister of his friend Forese. Dante receives instruction from her on how to move from the lower to the higher spheres. She is the one who speaks the famous line, *E 'n la sua volantade è nostra pace* ("And His will is our peace," or more familiarly, "In His will is our peace," 3.85). After speaking with Dante, she begins to sing the *Ave Maria* and then vanishes like a weight into the deep waters (3.122–3). At this point Dante's desire turns back toward Beatrice. There are other Dantean images in the poem: the "heaven of the moon" (*del ciel de la luna*) is from *Paradiso* 16.82; the fixed stars are those of the empyrean that appear in the final line of each of the canticles; and the person whose face "rises and falls like a flame" is apparently a reference to the scene where Dante finally encounters Beatrice in *Purgatorio* 32, though it may refer also to the pure radiant light of the Godhead in canto 33, which reveals to Dante the unity of all things. The "big dog" is not Dantean, but it does belong to the fixed stars. It is the constellation Canis Major (greater dog), which contains Sirius, the brightest of the stars as seen from earth.

Wright is on a poetic pilgrimage, the broad contour of which is purgatorial. All pilgrimages are motivated by desire, and desire provides the imaginative thrust of the present poem: the phrase "I want" appears seven times, which perhaps casts a glance at seven terraces of Dante's island-mountain. (The poem has seven lines with an even number of syllables—half of the lines altogether—which an unusually high number of such lines for a Wright poem.) The purgatorial pilgrimage is both a linear progression, moving in time from point A to point B, and a vertical one, ascending and descending along the *axis mundi*. The movement begins horizontally: the poet's desire is to slip toward the horizon, isolated like a little boat upon the waters and moving toward the margins of the world, like Tennyson's Ulysses. Following this is the poet's desire is to descend into the purgatorial waters before finally confronting the Beatrice-like face of enlightenment and then taking his place in the fixed stars, asleep at the foot of Canis Major. The fulfillment of the poet's wish will be his apotheosis.

Dog Day Vespers

Orig. pub. *New Yorker* 56 (23 June 1980): 30.
SC, 37; WTTT, 32
Pattern: 5 × 3
Time: Dog Days (from about July 3 to August 11). The expression is linked to the star Sirius, the brightest star in the sky, known in many mythologies as the Dog Star. In Egyptian myth "dog days" referred to the hot, parched season that followed the rising of Sirius.
Place: Laguna Beach
Title: "Vespers" is a pun, meaning a late afternoon religious service, the sixth of the seven canonical hours of the early evening, or, in the singular, Hesperus or Venus, which "breaks clear" in l. 9. The poem is dedicated to David Young (*WTTT*, 231).

The poem was "an attempt to write a poem at a single sitting without changing anything in it, something I had never done before and haven't done since" (*Halflife*, 143). In order to carry out this charge, the poet has to resort to a flashlight, as the day shifts from sunset to evening and then to nighttime. Sitting on the deck of his Laguna Beach home, he traces the landscape before him. His gaze moves back and forth from the sky and the bay to what is directly in from of him, describing the sunset, the petals of the oleander, the "mantis paws" of the wisteria, and the blue ferns.

p. 32, l. 4. *DeStael* [*de Staël*]. Nicolas de Staël, the Russian abstract artist, whose paintings often contain angular, sail-like shapes, as in his *Agrigente* (1953).
p. 32, l. 14. *stag-stars*. Several constellations are associated with stags. The most familiar is Andromeda.

Portrait of the Artist with Hart Crane

Orig. pub. *Durak* 3 (1979): 41.
SC, 38; WTTT, 33

Pattern: 5 × 3
Time: Late August
Place: Venice

Wright's instruction to himself was to write a poem as a portrait of someone "I could never have been with" (*Halflife*, 144). In his interviews Wright indicates repeatedly that he is a great admirer of Crane. To take one of many examples: "The thing I find interesting about Crane is that he was able to use a highly rhetorical language with the image in a way that I find pleasing. So that the image is not buried under the torrent, nor is the torrent out-dazzled by the image. Somehow it's a nice river running along, and the image is part of the river. It just flows along with it, and they work together" (*Halflife*, 94).

This imaginary encounter with Crane, who died in 1932, begins with a close-up of Crane's face, "pre-moistened and antiseptic, / A little like death on a smooth cloud." It's as if Wright is looking at Walker Evans's photographic portrait of Crane. But we rather abruptly leave Crane, whose face returns only in l. 13. The poet turns instead to a reflection on time, which is triggered by an anxiety about what the future holds for Crane's work. Will it be only a "watery light" rather than radiance? The inexorable tick-tock of time, the poet goes on to say, is the great destroyer: each night slept and day lived moves us closer to death. This heightens the poet's anxiety about his own work—about not being able, after some weeks, to complete his own poem because of the instability of language. There is, as a consequence, a great divide between the radiance of the sun and that of his own verse.

p. 33, l. 5. *pergola*. A trellis or arbor.

Portrait of the Artist with Li Po

Orig. pub. *Durak* 3 (1979): 40.
SC, 39; WTTT, 34
Pattern: 5 × 3
Time: October

This is the second portrait of someone "I could never have been with" (*Halflife*, 144), and it is the first of many appearances that Li Po (701–62), the great poet of the T'ang Dynasty, will make in Wright's poems. In the first stanza Wright imagines Li Po's burial mound, but the state of death is not anything that the wandering Li Po ever wrote about. Nor did Li Po ever say "anything about the life after death." His vision, rather, was focused on the world of the ten thousand things. Wright is obviously attracted to the ebullient, carefree spirit of Li Po—one who sometimes launched his poems into the world by floating them downstream. As a kind of tribute to his master, Wright inscribes a line in his notebook from Li Po's *Talk in the Mountains*, and as night comes on, he turns his attention to the gathering darkness and imagines the western movement of the stars.

The poem concludes with a riddle about the distance between the two subjects of this portrait—the T'ang poet who died some twelve centuries ago and the living Charles Wright: "The distance between the dead and the living // is more than a heartbeat and a breath." As death collapses all categories of space and time, we might have expected the poet to say, "is *no* more than a heartbeat and a breath." That is, when the breath leaves the living, then the category of distance is irrelevant: all the dead form a large company without distinction. What then is the "more" that makes for the distance between the two? It must be their different attitudes toward death and the hereafter.

p. 34, l. 2. *small mound*. Legend has it that the drunken Li Po died by falling into the river and drowning, after seeing the reflection of the moon there and trying to embrace it.

p. 34, l. 1. *high heavenly priest of the white lake.* The epithet given to Li Po in Robert Sward's poem *Li Po*, in *Four Incarnations, New & Selected Poems, 1957-1991* (Minneapolis: Coffee House Press, 1991).

p. 34, l. 8. *paper boats.* According to Frederick Turner, Tu Fu would also "compose his poetry, fold it into little paper boats, and float it down a stream" ("Space and Time in Chinese Verse," in *Time, Science, and Society in China and the West*, ed. Julius Thomas Fraser [Amherst: University of Massachusetts Press, 1986], 248).

p. 34, l. 12. "You ask me, 'Why dwell among green mountains?' / I laugh in silence; my soul is quiet. // Peach blossom follows the moving water; / Here is a heaven and earth, beyond the world of men" (Li Po, *Talk in the Mountains*). In Arthur Cooper's translation: "They ask me where's the sense / on jasper mountains? / I laugh and don't reply, / in heart's own quiet: // Peach petals float their streams / away in secret / To other skies and earths / than those of mortals" (*In the Mountains: A Reply to the Vulgar*, in *Li Po and Tu Fu* [Harmondsworth: Penguin, 1973], 115).

p. 34, l. 15 *river of heaven.* A conventional metaphor for the Milky Way in both Eastern (Japanese, Chinese, Indian) and Western traditions. Li Po uses the phrase in *Drinking Alone under Moonlight*.

The Monastery at Vršac

Orig. pub. *Field* 22 (Spring 1980): 82.
SC, 40; WTTT, 35
Pattern: 2-1-4-2-1-3-1
Place: Vršac, northern Serbia, at the Mesic Monastery

Wright remarks that the assignment he set for himself in this poem was "to end the poem with a big statement and then to comment on that statement" (*Halflife*, 144). The poet and his unidentified companion have visited the fifteenth-century Orthodox monastery. They retire to the monastery grounds, where they discover that the late afternoon atmosphere is shrouded by an "awful" stillness. Except for the nuns, all is solitude. The "big statement" that issues from the experience comes in the penultimate stanza: time is the great destroyer, a theme we have already encountered in *Portrait of the Artist with Hart Crane*. Time and the summer rains "erode our hearts // and carry our lives away." This reflection on the inevitability of death has been initiated not just by the awful stillness but by previous "signals" of mortality; the visit to the bishop's grave and the eddying dust. Each year, says the poet, we sink "another inch into the earth." The *comment* on the "big statement" is simply a plea for mercy for those "who have learned to preach but not to pray." Supplication rather than sermonizing is the proper attitude.

Dead Color

Orig. pub. *Water Table* 1 (Fall 1980): 41.
SC, 41; WTTT, 36
Pattern: 4-2-4-2-1-1

Title: A dead color is a dull or cheerless color or one without a gloss, but Wright may take the phrase from Cézanne's account of how he got such bright colors. Ambroise Vollard records this conversation:

> When I saw Degas again, he happened to have a box of pastels in his hand, and was spreading them out on a board in front of the window. Seeing me watching him:
> —I take all the color out of them that I can, by putting them in the sun.
> —But what do you use, then to get colors of such brightness?
> —Dead color, Monsieur.

Cézanne is referring to the painting's undercoat, though the technique was not original with him. Dutch painters of the seventeenth and eighteenth centuries applied dead colors to their canvases as one of the initial steps in painting still lifes and portraits.

Although this is a poem, Wright says, that has "no point of reference" (*Halflife*, 144), it does contain several biblical echoes and a phrase from Cézanne. Too, the final line refers to the windows of Paradise (*Halflife*, 145), which makes the nighttime heavens a point of reference—an apocalyptic point, as it turns out. The poet is in a state of watchful expectation, waiting to hear a voice from the clouds or see a face appear from the water. On both counts his wishes are not fulfilled, so he turns his attention to what lies before him—the aphids in the lemon trees and the ant on the possum's skull—at the same time aware that above him "starpieces dip in their yellow scarves toward their black desire." It's at this point that the epiphany occurs—a vision of the "rapturous windows" of Paradise.

p. 36, l. 4. *no voice comes on the wind*. An echo of Job's condition before the voice from the whirlwind.
p. 36, l. 5. Cf. "By the waters of Babylon we sit down and weep" (Psalm 137.1). *Har* = Hebrew for hill or mount.
p. 36, l. 6. *face of the deep*. Genesis 1:2, Job 38:30.
p. 36, l. 14. *Windows, rapturous windows!* The line has been picked up by a popular folk duo, Harrod and Funk, in their song *When I'll Fly Away*: "When I fly away, I will be unbound. / When I fly away, I'm nowhere to be found. / Windows, rapturous windows, blue, infinite blue."

Hawaii Dantesca

Orig. pub. *New Yorker* 56 (29 September 1980): 50.
SC, 42; WTTT, 37
Pattern: 2–3–1–3–1–2–1–2–1
Time: Autumn

In the series of exercises Wright posed for himself for the twenty poems in part III of *The Southern Cross*, this is the second one in which he takes images from Dante and uses them for his own purposes. The chief image, as Wright's note indicates (*WTTT*, 231), is from *Purgatorio* 1: "This solitary island, all around / its very base, there where the breakers pound, / bears rushes on its soft and muddy ground. // There is no other plant that lives below: / no plant with leaves or plant that, as it grows, / hardens and breaks beneath the waves' harsh blows" (ll. 100–5, trans. Allen Mandelstam). At the end of this canto Virgil, at the instruction of Cato, girds Dante with the reeds of humility to protect him from pride, the source of all the deadly sins. The reeds replenish themselves as they are plucked. As in *Laguna Dantesca*, other images are rooted in Dante: the descent under the earth, the angels' wings, the stork simile, and the untying of the knot (*Paradiso* 28).

The poet reads the white Hawaiian flowers as metaphors for the dead, and he sees the broken shadows of the missing above the sugar cane. But nobody is attentive to these features of the landscape, save the poet, who exhibits his attentiveness to nature's plenitude in stanza 4. He is also very self-conscious about death. In addition to the dead and the missing we have his declaration that "Soon it will be time for the long walk under the earth toward the sea"— that is, to enter the realm of the dead. Thus, the desire to return to his childhood by way of a photograph of himself at age three, and the desire to prepare himself by assembling his means of poetic production: "Time to gather the fire in its quartz bowl." Like *Laguna Dantesca* this is a poem of desire, the desire in this case taking the form of three hopes. First is the hope that the white-winged angel (a reference to the angel who pilots the ship in *Purgatorio* 2) will arrive, and, second, the hope that she will not come until some distant time: "I hope the island of reeds is as far away as I think it is" (ferry me away from the Inferno, but not yet). Third, the poet hopes that he will be forgiven if the knot he ties is the wrong one, which is an allusion to Beatrice's reference to the knot in *Paradiso* 28.58. There she wonders if Dante's fingers are fit to untie the problem (knot) of the relation of the spiritual and the natural world, which is the relation lying behind Wright's entire pilgrimage.

Ars Poetica

Orig. pub. *Antaeus* 40–41 (Spring 1981): 406.
SC, 43; WTTT, 38
Pattern: 1–3–1–3–1–2–2–1
Time: Winter
Place: Laguna Beach

Any number of Wright's poems can be considered *ars poeticae*. This is the first of three with that title he has (so far) written. In the present poem the nature and function of poetry is first of all a matter of place. "I like it back here," says the poet, meaning in the writing "room" of his garden, where he is in direct contact with all the elements of the landscape, as opposed to the world out "there." He is better "here" than "there" because when he is writing his identity as a human being is most fully realized. "I am more myself when I'm writing," Wright told an interviewer, "than when I'm out doing daily things. Somehow my job is to bring what's here, there. My business is the metaphysics of the quotidian" (Rubin, 28).

In order to conduct this business the poet calls down the spirits from above and attends to the "voices rising out of the ground." "What will it satisfy?" and "this business I waste my heart on" are both self-deprecating and ironic asides, suggesting that in this serious business of "the metaphysics of the quotidian" the poet should never be overly confident that he has achieved a perfected form. Otherwise, there would be no reason to keep on writing, and the concluding line—"And nothing stops that"—makes it emphatically clear that not writing is not an option.

Bar Giamaica, 1959–60

Orig. pub. *New Yorker* 56 (12 January 1981): 36.
SC, 44; WTTT, 39
Pattern: 4–1–1–2–2–1–4
Place: Milan

The poet's self-instruction was "to make a photograph I wish I had taken, by substituting my friends for some unknown people in someone else's photograph of a place I used to frequent" (*Halflife*, 144). Wright has provided a fairly complete commentary on the poem in *Halflife*, explaining how in leafing through a book by the Italian photographer Ugo Mulas (1928–73) he recognized a photo of a bar he had frequented in 1959–60. The people in the photo, taken six years earlier, reminded Wright of the people he had known in Verona and Milan who often frequented the bar with him. Saddened that he had no photo of his friends, "I decided to take Ugo's picture and replace the people in it with the people I'd known.... The poem is almost an exact replica, descriptively, of the photograph, only the names have been added—all real names—to give me the photograph I'd never been able to take.... Even the two unknown passersby, the metal *caffe* tables and the river gravel in the courtyard are included" (*Halflife*, 52). Wright has a similar but briefer commentary on the poem in Zawacki, 29.

The thirteen friends named in ll. 1–10, some of whom were members of Wright's army unit, are Grace Pecchiar, a friend from Trieste; Ingrid Tuktens; Arnie Goldstein; Chuck Borsuk; Dick Venezia; Yola Andreis; Susan Williams; Elena Rocchio; Winfrid Thorp, a chief warrant officer; Harold Schimmel, a poet, who had majored in English at Cornell; Jim Gates; Carl Glass; Peter Hobart, an art history major from Yale; and George Schneeman, a painter. Some of these friends make appearances elsewhere in Wright's poetry: Goldstein, Venezia,

Gates, and Pecchiar in *Italian Days*; Goldstein and Thorp in *Scar Tissue II*; Thorp, Hobart, Schimmel and Schneeman in *Littlefoot*, part, 31; Tuktens in *Lines on Seeing a Photograph for the First Time in Thirty Year*; and Schimmel in *Tattoos*, part 8.

For a reproduction of Mulas's photo, *Bar Giamaica, 1953-54*, see http://www.ugomulas.org/index.cgi?action=view&idramo=1107773031&lang=eng

Gate City Breakdown

Orig. pub. *Poetry Northwest* 21 (Summer 1980): 26; rpt. as an Iron Mountain Press broadside, 1985.
SC, 45; WTTT, 40
Pattern: 4-6-4
Time: December 1953
Place: Gate City, Virginia, not far across the state line from Kingsport, Tennessee. The bridge crossing the North Fork of the Holston River was doubtless on "back road" 224, about three miles from Gate City.

Wright recalls an incident from the Christmas holidays after his first semester at Davidson College. His instruction to himself was "to do something I had done before, deliberately retrograde either in manner or location" (*Halflife*, 144). The something done before was an escapade with childhood friends. He and three of his chums make a moonshine run across the state line from Kingsport, Tennessee, to Gate City, Virginia. The opening simile, likening the adventure to finding a seam of hard coal, reveals that the young men's goal was not so much the whiskey itself as the excitement of an adventure they had fantasized about. On the way back, they are chased by the sheriff, but they manage to escape because of the ineffectiveness of the roadblocks ("breakdown"). In the penultimate couplet the poet provides another "breakdown" (analysis), dismissing the memory of this little episode as "ridiculous, and full of self-love." But at the same time we are asked to remember him skidding around the curves and outrunning the sheriff's patrol car. Now that the experience has been writ in ink, it *has* become part of the "dust" left by the poet.

The title echoes Bennie Moten's blues song, *Kansas City Breakdown* (1928) and Jonathan Cain's 1970s rock album, *Windy City Breakdown*.

New Year's Eve, 1979

Orig. pub. *Iowa Review* 11 (Spring–Summer 1980): 216.
SC, 46; WTTT, 41
Pattern: 5-3-4-2
Place: Laguna Beach

This poem was written at Laguna Beach during the time that the three-day annual meeting of the Modern Language Association was being held in San Francisco (December 27–31 1979). The introspective observations of the first stanza (the self is continuous; we are always indebted to others) are more or less commonplaces. Stanza 2, where Wright addresses himself by using his own name (something has done on three other occasions in his poems), is a series of three unanswerable questions. How these two stanzas function in relation to each other is not apparent, though they do embody motifs that are omnipresent in Wright's poetry: the self, the past, the dead. But Wright cuts to the chase in stanzas 3 and 4, which center on the hermit crabs, and these creatures stand in sharp contrast to the speaker's observations and queries in the first two stanzas. Scuttling across the floor of the sea, far removed from the light above, "What matters to them is what comes up from below, and from out there / In the deep water." They are concerned only with their immediate environment—the oceanic netherworld. They "quarter and spin" in a kind of vortex, an *axis mundi* archetype. The *axis mundi* reaches down to the demonic world: we have death by water, but water is also life-giving. The poem, then, is not a demonic *nekyia* but a creative descent. And insofar as the hermit crabs are concerned with what "comes up," the suggestion is that there can be a creative ascent as well.

The Southern Cross

Orig. pub. *Paris Review* 80 (Summer 1981): 165–79.
SC, 49–65; WTTT, 42–55
Pattern: Variable: 286 lines: (1–2–2–1) (2–3–1–3) (2–3–2) (1 × 3) (5–2–3–3) (3–6–3) (2–1–3) (3 × 3) (8) (5) (12 × 4) (3–1) (6) (6) (3 × 3) (14–1) (3–4–3–3–4) (2–7–7–7–3–2) (4) (4–4–4–4–1) (1–12–1) (7 × 2) (3–4–3) (4) (1–10–1)
Times: April, with flashbacks to August 1935 (Pickwick, Tennessee), 1936 (Knoxville, Tennessee), 1941 (Hiwassee Village, North Carolina), 1953 (Arden, North Carolina), Winter 1959 (Milan), April 1961 (Lake Garda), April 1961 (Verona), December 1962 (Kingsport, Tennessee), November 1964 (Rome), 1969 (Venice), unspecified dates (Laguna Beach; Lincoln County, Montana; Ischia, Gulf of Naples; Seville). In an interview, Wright calls this a six-month poem: "I wrote for six months and that was the 'structure' of the poem (guided a bit by me, of course, toward the end, and ending)" (Spiegelman, 118).
Places: Laguna Beach with flashbacks to North Carolina, Tennessee, Italy, Spain, Greece, Montana

The poem is dedicated to Mark Jarman (WTTT, 231), who told Wright it was time for him to write a long poem. Its twenty-five sections are of variable length, ranging from four to forty-eight lines. Its dominant theme is the vicissitudes of memory.

Wright on Wright: "Anyone's autobiography, at least in his own eyes, is made up of a string of luminous moments, numinous moments. It's a necklace we spend our lives assembling. That's what *The Southern Cross* is about, saying some of those beads. But that 'I' isn't I anymore. It's someone else, the character who plays me, someone who's a better actor than I could ever be. I'm just the writer. Someone else is starring in my part. I remember him just well enough to try to write about him. A case of the negative sublime. I guess art's always after the fact. The real is imaginary, or imagined. Reconstitution, reconstruction, representation is all we're left with. Autobiography becomes biography in the end" (QN, 107).

Section 1 (p. 42). Three things are said to "divine" us, "to divine" meaning to discover us by divination or to prophesy something about us: the night music, the Southern Cross constellation, and the sunrise. The poet's gaze is entirely upward, and each of the three "things" is remote: we "never touch them," the night music produces "black sounds," the constellation is as distant as a kite (the Southern Cross is actually the smallest of the constellations), and the sunrise is an "empty sleeve." There is perhaps some story line that would connect us to the nighttime and daylight empyrean, but the poet can discover no trace of it.

Section 2 (p. 42). The poet records several memories from his childhood. The first—the memory of a lake and curtains blowing in and out of the windows—comes from his first year in Knoxville. Since few of us can remember experiences from our first year, this memory is doubtless triggered by a photograph of the one-year-old Wright "spraying the dead grass with a hose." The images of the six-year-old in his brown suit (from his Hiwassee Village years) and the eighteen-year-old in his white shoes (from his Christ School years) seem also to come from photographs. Such memories tumble over each other, "overlay after overlay," so that the poet is uncertain about what actually presents itself to consciousness: "And then it's not. And I'm not and they're not." Thus, he is not able to extract any meaning from the memories.

Section 3 (pp. 42–3). Wright's birthday, August 25 (also his father's birthday), put him under the sign of Virgo. Here he projects his doom (death?) as occurring under the "cold stars of the Virgin" (Virgo). This section begins on a downbeat, with its doom and woe and dark spring morning. But it concludes with an affirmation about the sweetness of the past, an affirmation that Wright himself found somewhat problematic: "Even when I wrote that [the last two lines of section 3] I said, 'Look, is this really true?' I mean what about World War II, what about Hitler, what about the Holocaust, they're not very sweet. I've always written about being young. And one's youth, one's past, is always, unless you had a terribly unfortunate time, something you look back on with a certain amount of pleasure, a certain amount of nostalgia. I equivocate somewhat on that statement because it isn't entirely true, but in my case it's certainly been more true than not, so I left it there" (QN, 149).

Section 4 (p. 43). Section 1 moved from nighttime to sunrise. This brief section, which is almost pure description, moves from daytime to night. The ocean, likened to brooding self-absorption and regret, is an objective correlative for the poet's own emotional state.

Section 5 (pp. 43–4). What focuses this springtime Italian memory, which doubtless goes back to the poet's visits to Lake Garda in 1959–60, is the movement of the wind, water, and clouds: the wind fishtails the olive trees, the sunset ebbs and flows, the clouds troll across the hills, and the lake laps at the shore. Punta San Viglio is the point jutting into the lake, like an eagle's head, about two miles west of the town of Garda on the eastern shore; Sirmio (Sermione) is the peninsula that extends for about three miles into the southern part of the lake; and Bardolino is a town just south of Garda on the lake's eastern shore. The waters have a story to tell—"a ghostly litany"—about the unburdening of guilt. The story of the clouds, trolling the western sunset, is about the search for unresurrected bodies. The ceremonial prayer (litany) of the waters is "ghostly" in several senses: spectral, spiritual, and in the context of dead bodies perhaps even fearful.

Section 6 (p. 44). The poet's memory takes him back to the River Adige in Verona twenty years earlier. He recalls that Dante and Can Grande had stood where he stood, on the banks of the river near the Sant'Anastasia church in the northeastern tip of the old city. As a river of "sighs and forgetfulness," the Adige may appear first to be a modern-day composite of the Acheron and Lethe. But it is neither: rather than sighs, it bears gifts, and rather than forgetfulness, it is a spur to remembering. Centuries before, so goes the legend, Catullus had sat in the same place. The setting is a sacred place, as even God had spoken "in the rocks." The lyric focuses chiefly on the light: the secret light that Campana had seen, the glint of the moon on the water, the flaring cypress trees in the Giusti Gardens across the river to the east, and now, in April 1961, "a different light" doing "the same things on a different water."

p. 44, l. 2 *the secret light Campana saw*. The reference is to the general visionary quality of Campana's work, which became increasingly hallucinatory and eerie.

p. 44, l. 5. *Dante*. After being exiled from Florence, Dante was given refuge in Verona by Bartolomeo della Scala. His son, Can Grande ("Big Dog") della Scala (1291–1329), lord of Verona, was the greatest member of the pro-imperial, or Ghibelline, family that ruled Verona from 1277 to 1387. Dante's famous theory of polysemous meaning is set down in a well-known letter to Can Grande della Scalla.

p. 44, l. 6. *S. Anastasia*. Verona's largest church, a cavernous Gothic structure on the piazza Sant'Anastasia.

p. 44, l. 8. *Giusti Gardens*. Renaissance gardens of the Palazzo Giusti, which remain true to their original designs more than four-hundred years later. They lie east of Sant'Anastasia across the Adige River.

p. 44, l. 9. *Catullus*. Catullus was born in Verona ca. 84 B.C.

Section 7 (p. 44). The memory recorded here is of the poet's father and mother. Though they had died some years before (Wright's father in 1972 and his mother in 1964), they and their voices and the things they once owned drift "like smoke through the living room," continuing to haunt him.

Section 8 (p. 45). "Thinking of Dante," the poet begins to feel that he is growing wings, and so puts himself in the place of Dante, who speaks of his own wing feathers as guiding him to lofty heights under the compassionate tutelage of Beatrice (*Paradiso* 25.49–50). Thinking of Dante also spurs a recollection of three characters from *The Divine Comedy*: La Pia, the shade in canto 5 of the *Purgatorio* who asks Dante not to forget him when he gets back to earth; Charles Martel, the young prince Dante meets in cantos 8 and 9 of the *Paradiso*—depicted as a loving friend and genuinely concerned about the well-being of society; and Cacciaguida, Dante's great-great-grandfather, who figures in the central episode of the *Paradiso*, cantos 15–18. Finally, thinking of Dante causes the poet to reflect on the realm of the dead ("the other side") and the "other side of the other side," which is "the great flower of Paradise"—the celestial rose swirling with angels that Dante finally sees that the end of the *Paradiso*.

Section 9 (p. 45). The setting here is the California seacoast, where the poet has gone with some unidentified friends. As the wind arises, the sea deals him a hand of five blank cards. So he turns his attention to a half-dozen of the ten thousand things that constitute what he calls "the truth": the pelicans, the green afternoon, the malingering gulls, the shadow of an airplane, an island in the distance, and the orange smog. The curious image of the beachgoers staying briefly on the shadow-cross cast by the airplane seems vaguely symbolic. It is, in any event, out of sync with the mood of the rest of the vignette, which is quiet contemplation.

Section 10 (p. 45). This five-line lyric is an homage to the Big Dipper, which, the poet says, has followed him throughout life and continues to ladle out its blessing of black water. But if it has followed him, he has also followed it, and the poem could serve as a kind of foreshadowing epigraph for books that will follow: *Black Zodiac*, its daytime companion *Negative Blue*, and *North American Bear*, where the seven "tin stars" of Ursa Major will play a central role. Wright is forever gazing at the heavens for signs of what is beyond space (the infinite) and time (the eternal).

Section 11 (pp. 46–7). The date of this section—about a visit to Venice—is 1969, when Wright was teaching at the University of Padua. Venice is a *genius loci* for Wright, and the present section, along with section 12, glances back to the Venice of *Tattoos*, no. 4, and foreshadows several later Venetian poems, especially *Venexia I* and *Venexia II* (*NB*, 65–6). The poet begins and ends by announcing things that are difficult to remember: the sounds of the canal, the way the winds moved, the reflection of light from the canal, and the look of the snow on the church roof. But this is a tongue-in-cheek remark, because what follows in each case is a succession of vivid memories, each of the things said to be dim in the poet's memory being described in characteristically glowing detail. In fact, the things half forgotten emerge more clearly than the half dozen things the poet does remember: himself at various places in Venice, "the way Pound walked across San Marco," the time that James Tate visited, and the Venetian floods. In each of these latter cases the recreation of the memory is brief and presented with little detail. The point of the irony seems to be that those things more difficult to remember require greater efforts at recreation or greater concentration in rummaging through the recesses memory to bring them to consciousness. In any event, stanzas 1, 2, and 4 provide strong evidence to deny the claim of things "hard to recall."

p. 46, l. 5. *Toio's*. A Venetian restaurant, now (alas) called Toni's.
p. 46, ll. 8–12. *Zattere*. Bank in the south of Venice, facing the Giudecca Canal. The Rio Ogni Santi is south of the

San Trovaso Church on the Dorsoduro (southern edge) of Venice. The Church of San Sebastiano is also in the Dorsoduro, to the west.

p. 47, l. 4. *Pound.* When in Venice during his army tour, Wright would occasionally see Pound walking along the Zattere or in the Piazza San Marco. In the *Cantos* Pound mentions the view from his first room in Venice: "Well, my window ... looked out on the Squero where Ogni Santi ... meets San Trovaso ... things have ends and beginnings." From that room he wrote his first book of poems, *A Lume Spento* (Canto LXXVI).

p. 47, l. 6. *Tate.* Wright's friend, the poet James Tate, who visited him in 1969.

p. 47, l. 6. *Palazzo Guggenheim.* The restored mansion in the eastern Dorsoduro that housed the Peggy Guggenheim art collection.

p. 47, l. 9. *da Montin.* A restaurant in the Dorsoduro.

p. 47, l. 11. *Torcello.* An island north of Venice.

p. 47, l. 17. *San Gregorio.* A church in Venice dating from the ninth century.

p. 47, l. 18. *San Trovaso.* A *squero* or gondola repair shop on the Rio San Trovaso, southwest of the Accademia Gallery.

Section 12 (pp. 47–8). These four lines are a Venetian afterthought. Sandwiched between the abstract aphorisms of lines 1 and 4, Venice is said to "lie like silk // at the end of the sea and the night sky, / Albescent under the moon," a perspective on the city that comes from an eye in the sky, as it were. Silence will of course "have the last word," but not before the poet tries out his silk simile. The concluding aphorism is a poetic counterpart of Whitehead's riddling account of interpenetration, where he argues that everything is everywhere at once: "In a certain sense everything is everywhere at all times. For every location involves an aspect of itself in every other location. Thus every spatio-temporal standpoint mirrors the world" (*Science and the Modern World* [New York: Macmillan, 1929], 133).

Section 13 (p. 48). Sitting above the ocean in Laguna Beach, the poet's gaze is fastened on the golden orioles as they "stitch and weave" their golden threads into the "grey cloth of daylight," along with the falling crows, which appear to be like the "black notes" of a musical score—an image Wright returns to in *There Is a Balm in Gilead* (BY, 4). The fog weighs down the morning, though it eventually lifts, providing a view of the gleaming palm trees.

Section 14 (p. 48). This is another interlude on memory. An "otherness inside us," which is an awareness of the past, is the spur to memory. We cannot reach down and touch it. Still, we continue to pray to the past and embrace it, even though we can never remember enough.

p. 48, l. 10. *Anytime, Anywhere.* The macho motto of the U.S. Marines.

Section 15 (pp. 48–9). The site of these three tercets is the poet's deck in Laguna Beach. The mood, one of gloomy discontent, is projected onto Friday, "with its sack of bad dreams," "handful of ashes," and "postcards of melancholy." And the one word on the page of the sea below is "despair." The poet presents himself as lighting one match after the other, searching for something in the "black air." This effort seems to be rather futile, but still, as a metaphor for the poet's pilgrimage, it represents his dogged determination not to abandon his quest for some light in the darkness.

Section 16 (p. 49). This is a flashback to the time Wright was a Fulbright student (1963–65) when he visited Ischia, a volcanic island in the Tyrrhenian Sea, at the northern end of the Gulf of Naples. His exact location ("here") is unspecified, but it is the town of Forio d'Ischia, where he has a view of the sea and of the houses at Sant'Angelo on the southern coast of the island, as well as a volcano, apparently Monte Epemo, which marks the highest point of the island. He reports hearing a story from Nicola, who was a local man married to an American painter, about the migration of the doves from Africa and the local planting of crops. But the landscape, he concludes, was always the best part, and the description of that landscape is the best part of this free-verse "sonnet" with its coda.

Section 17 (pp. 49–50). "Places," says the poet in the first and last stanzas, "swim up" in the memory "and sink back." Three places swim up in this lyric: Seville on an Easter morning, Milan and its Brera Palace on a rainy winter day, and the Greek isles (Hydra and Mykonos).

All three were places Wright visited in 1959. The poem has no central focus, because the point is that what returns to us in memory is random and momentary, like a daydream.

Section 18 (pp. 50–1). "Rome," says the poet, "was never like that," "that" referring to the point in the previous section about memories becoming more and more indistinct with the passing of time. And yet, as it turns out Rome *was* like that, for while Wright does catalogue a series of things remembered when he was studying at the University of Rome in 1964 on a Fulbright grant, he also records, as he did in section 11, a list of things forgotten: the names of streets and shops, the colors at sundown, the smells of the stairway, the slant of light through the windows. But among the things remembered—the hanging boar in the butcher shop at Christmas, the flower paintings at Jack Zajac's apartment, the holy days—two images are recalled with bright and exacting detail. Both have to do, appropriately, with memorials: Bruno's mournful statue on the Campo dei Fiori at the beginning and the tombstones of the English Cemetery at the end.

p. 50, ll. 15–18. *Regina Coeli ... Bruno*. The Regina Coeli is a prison near the Tiber, off the Via della Lungara in the Trasteverre section of Rome. The Lungotevere runs along either side of the Tiber, about a half-mile northwest of the Pantheon. In the Campo dei Fiori, about five-hundred yards south of the Pantheon, stands a bronze statue of Giordano Bruno, marking the spot where he was burned alive in 1600, having been condemned to death by the Inquisition. For an image of the statue, see http://www.romeartlover.it/Vasi28.html or the fifteenth image at http://www.bridgeandtunnelclub.com/bigmap/outoftown/italy/lazio/rome/campodeifiori/index.htm

p. 51, l. 2. *Via Giulia*. A street that runs parallel to the Tiber for close to a mile before the bend in the Tiber.

p. 51, l. 6. *Piazza del Biscione*. A piazza adjacent to the Campo dei Fiori. The Palazzo Pio faces onto this little square.

p. 51, l. 13. *Zajac's place*. The apartment of the prominent Santa Cruz artist Jack Zajac.

p. 51, l. 14. *Days of the Dead*. November 1 and November 2, the Catholic holy days of All Saints' and All Souls' days.

p. 51, ll. 16–17. *Keats ... Someone's son*. Keats and Shelley are buried in the English (or Protestant) Cemetery in Rome. The sons of Goethe and von Humboldt are also buried in the cemetery.

Section 19 (p. 51). In this quatrain, time is the great destroyer, depicted here as lowering its dead body into the water and as responsible for the "petals of wreckage in everything." But out of time's landscape comes the "resurrection of the word," which is the poem you are holding in your hand. The *topos* is a familiar convention: we die and nature dies annually, but the poetic word lives on.

Section 20 (p. 52). The poet observes the processes of nature that are played out before him—the spider inching its way across the porch of the Montana cabin and the creeks descending through the "great meadow." The night before he had watched "the bullbats / Diving out of the yellow sky." These movements against the landscape seem to be motivated by an entelechy the poet only half understands or understands not at all. Nature goes about its business: "the spider has got her instructions / And carries them out." The contrast is between the observed, which "knows just what to do," and the observer, who is mystified by what he sees before him.

p. 52, l. 1. *cabin*. The cabin was—and still is—located on the property then owned by Wright's in-laws, Hollywood actors John McIntire and Jeanette Nolan, a 320-acre tract in Lincoln County in the northwestern tip of Montana.

p. 52, l. 4. *two creeks*. Basin and Porcupine Creeks traverse the Lincoln County property.

Section 21 (pp. 52–3). This is the poet's fourth take on the difficulty of remembering (see sections 11, 14, and 18). He begins by saying, "I can't remember enough" and concludes by confessing, "I'll never be able to [remember enough]." The twelve intervening lines, however, reveal, as in section 11, that the announced failure of memory is greatly exaggerated. While there are obviously many things the poet cannot recall, the recollections of the Kingsport hills and the other details of the Tennessee landscape, as well as of the poet's leaving home, once again are etched with a verbal energy that serves, as the philosophers would say, to deny the antecedent.

p. 53, l. 4. *Carter's Valley.* East of Kingsport, Tennessee, traversed by Carter's Valley Road.
p. 53, l. 7. *11W.* A U.S. highway that runs through Kingsport, where it is called East Stone Drive.

Section 22 (p. 53). This is the second flashback to the wilderness area of northwestern Montana. The entire poem is metaphorically fresh description, save for the final two lines, where, once again, the poet observes that everything before him on this hot July Sunday is inscribed with an élan vital: "Everything has its work, // everything written down / In the secondhand grace of solitude and tall trees...." This grace, unlike the firsthand grace reserved for human beings, is known or experienced only indirectly. The religious language of the last stanza hints at an underlying religious ritual: nature is called to prayer by the wind, morning is decked out in its vestments, the lilacs begin to bleed, and the "last of the dog roses offers itself."

Section 23 (p. 54). As we move from July to August, the poet depicts the landscape (both objective and, in the second stanza, subjective) in imagery that is oral ("licks," "mouth," "lips") as well as aural ("little fugues," "faint notes of piano music"). The stasis of the sleeping ferns is counterbalanced by the movement of the leaping toads. The scene is depicted without commentary, though the middle stanza seems to be a kind of wish-fulfillment reverie in which the poetic voice is on the threshold of opening itself up.

Section 24 (p. 54). Wind, the poet declares in this quatrain, animates everything—our past, present, and future lives and "all we look on." We are reminded again that wind is a metonym for spirit, as in Jesus' remark to Nicodemus in John 3:8, "The wind bloweth where it listeth ... so is everyone that is born of the Spirit." In the Gospel of John, as remarked earlier, the Greek *pneuma* is used for both wind and spirit. Too, the wind in the Montana "garden," which we have visited in sections 20, 22, and 23, is not unlike the wind (symbolically the spirit) that enters the *hortus conclusus* in Song of Songs 4: 12–16. If everything we see is "windfall," then the fruits of the garden are all around us, but "windfall" also carries with it the sense of grace or an unexpected gift.

p. 54, l. 12. *Windblown ... go away.* Cf. Job 1:21: "Naked I came from my mother's womb, And naked I shall return there"

Section 25 (pp. 54–5). The final section returns to beginnings—Wright's place of birth in Pickwick Dam, Tennessee, where his father was an engineer for a TVA dam project. Wright's family moved from Pickwick Dam when he was about six months old, and he has never returned. But he feels that there is some imprint in the landscape of that place that defines him and is waiting to be rediscovered. Someday, he says, he will find out the "landscape that keeps my imprint" and "enter my old outline as though for the first time," like the dead who are revealed as themselves in *Homage to Paul Cézanne* (p. 4, l. 7).

Because he was too young, the poet can never remember the city, which was actually a very small town (today it has only about 400 people). But it is nevertheless projected as an ideal city in his imagination, "its walls the color of pure light." This is a version of Pound's city of Dioce, "whose terraces are the color of stars" (*Canto LXXIV*). Other parallels suggest themselves: the vast circuit of the city in the pure heavenly light of *Paradiso* 33 and the divine light of the city in Revelations 21. This is where the poet would like to lie down, as he comes to the conclusion of the title poem and of the volume.

p. 54, l. 20. *August heat of 1935.* Wright was born on August 25, 1935.

CHAPTER 5

The Other Side of the River *(1984)*

Cover art: Untitled image by Czech photographer Joseph Sudek.

Lost Bodies

Orig. pub. *Field* 24 (Spring 1981): 48–52.
OSR, 3–6; *WTTT*, 59–62
Pattern: (2–1–2–2–2–1–2) (3–3–1–2–1) (3–2–1–3–1) (3–4–3) (6–2–2) (3–3–1–3) (4–1–2–3)
Time: Flashbacks to 1947 and early 1960s
Place: Kingsport, Tennessee, and Lake Garda, Italy

Lost Bodies, when set beside the poem that follows, *Lost Souls*, reminds us of the conventional *Dialogus inter corpus et animam* that goes back to Anglo Saxon times (e.g., *Soul and Body* in the Vercelli and Exeter Books), is omnipresent in medieval poetry, and continues in the well-known body and soul dialogues of Marvell and Yeats. A modern variation of the debate is Wallace Stevens's *Sunday Morning*.

Section 1 (p. 59). The poem begins by setting up an opposition between two recollections, one of the landscape of an Italian town, Torri del Benaco, on the eastern side of Lake Garda, near Verona, and the other of a concrete cross in Kingsport, Tennessee, advising all onlookers to "get right with God" for "Jesus is coming soon." The latter pricks the poet's conscience a bit, thinking that if he had his life to live over, he would opt for medieval Christianity, in which case he would "thoroughly purge his own floor." Here the poet is alluding to the prophecy of John the Baptist that Christ the winnower "will thoroughly purge his floor, and will gather the wheat into his garner; but the chaff he will burn with fire unquenchable" (Luke 3:17). Luke had just said that Christ "shall baptize you with the Holy Spirit and with fire." Accordingly, in his description of the landscape of Torri del Benaco, Wright begins with the image of fire and concludes with the image of wind (spirit).

"Something's for sure in the clouds," says the poet, "but it's not for me." This something is the promise of spirit and fire that in the New Testament account is fulfilled at Pentecost. The poet seems to be not much interested in the doctrine of all this, but he clearly is interested in the fire and wind of the landscape, which are metonyms for a kind of natural religion. Paul makes a distinction between the *soma psychikon*, the natural man, and the *soma pneumatikon*, the spiritual man (1 Corinthians 2:14–15). In the present poem the lost body is that of the *soma psychikon*. The fire of the cypresses, the light on the water, and the wind rushing through the almond trees belong to the vision of the *soma pneumatikon*.

The remainder of the poem alternates between memories of the Italian landscape and scenes from Kingsport.

Section 2 (pp. 59–60). In the medieval dialogues of the soul and the body the body is ordinarily devalued, according to the doctrine that held the body to be the container of our bestial impulses. In this section the opposition is between the Get-Right-with-God cross and "everything Jesus promised," on the one hand, and, on the other, the recollection of the story of crude sex in the back seat of the Buick told to the twelve-year-old Wright by Harold Shipley. This is the body devalued, not in the interest of elevating the soul, but only to heighten pure lust of the *soma psychikon*. "What can you say to that?" asks the poet. Well, not much, except that the two men in the Buick belong to the chaff that will be burned "with fire unquenchable." Small wonder that the five senses of the twelve-year-old had to count off the rosary beads.

Section 3 (p. 60). The poet returns to the memory of Torri del Benaco (section 1), a place he says he remembers poorly. But he remembers it well enough to mark it as a place of Edenic beauty, which is a perfect place for a lost body—a place where the *soma pneumatikon* would feel quite at home. The "garden" will reappear in section 6.

p. 60, l. 12. *Saló*. A town directly west of Torri del Benaco, on the western shore of Lake Garda.

Section 4 (pp. 60–61). Wright will later refer to himself as a "God-fearing agnostic" (ST, 16). This section contains the germ of that confession. On the one hand, the poet knows that he has to commit himself to something ("sign your name"), and yet, on the other hand, he cannot bring himself to affirm a resurrection after death: "When you die, you fall down, // you don't rise up / ... into the everlasting." That is exhibit A in the album of lost bodies. Nor can he affirm an identity with Jesus: "a piece of his heart is not a piece of your heart, / Sweet Jesus, and never will be." The concluding line reminds us that each day is a cycle of sleeping, into which we "fall" at night, and waking, into which we "rise" in the morning—a cycle that will repeat itself until death takes us.

Section 5 (p. 61). The poet takes us back to the scene of the seamy episode recorded in section 2. Fleenor's Cabins, Harold Shipley, and the two men in the Buick have disappeared into the past as "lost bodies." The concrete cross, however, is still there, though it has sunk "deeper into the red clay." But it is the enduring cross that calls up a momentary vision of "that luminous nameless body whose flesh takes on / The mottoes we say we live by"—that is, the body of Christ. This, again, is the *soma pneumatikon*.

Section 6 (pp. 61–2). The poet's memory calls him back to Italy one last time, this time to Sermione, the peninsula that extends for about three miles into the southern part of the Lake Garda, and to Gardone and Desenzano, towns on the western and southwestern shores of the lake. The clearest memory is of a garden outside the town of Garda. This is a vegetable garden, but the poem has already taken on an allegorical slant, so that to deny that garden is also Garden is to rely on what Blake called the "Corporeal Understanding."

Section 7 (p. 62). The final section, which finds the poet's skepticism tempered, begins with a biblical allusion to the "glorious body" of Philippians: "Who shall change our vile body, that it may be fashioned like unto his glorious body, according to the working whereby he is able even to subdue all things unto himself" (3:21). And, the poet asks, why not accept this view of the spiritual body (*some pneumatikon*), a body that is no longer lost? The syntax of ll. 3–4 seems confused, but the sense appears to be this: the alternative to the glorious body would be to yield to the workings of the principalities and powers "to subdue the celestial flesh." And when the "mighty working" takes over, the garden turns brown and dies. In the final lines the poet awakens from his reveries, brought back into the present of chain saws and diesel rigs.

Lost Souls

Orig. pub. *Field* 24 (Spring 1981): 53–6.
OSR, 7–10; WTTT, 63–6
Pattern: (4) (3-1-3-1) (3-3-3-1) (5-4-1) (10-8) (4-2-4) (10)
Time: Flashbacks from childhood and early life: 1951, 1953, 1957, 1964, 1972
Places: Kingsport, Nashville, and Utah

Section 1 (p. 63). The opening quatrain depicts the body rising from the darkness of sleep with its dream-memory into the daylight world, where ordinary memory takes over. The "you" who effects the raising up from the depths of sleep and who unshutters the blind eye is not identified, but is apparently the natural force that controls the cycle of sleeping and waking. "You" is what causes the poet to remember, and sections 3–7 contain a series of memories from a twenty-one year period, beginning in 1951, when the poet was 16.

p. 63, ll. 1–3. These lines appear to allude to several verses in Matthew 6. The "bad eye" is a version of what Matthew calls the "evil eye" (6:21) in the KJV, but the meaning of *ponēros* (bad) in this verse from the Sermon on the Mount seems to be physical (diseased or blind) rather than ethical (wicked). The immediately preceding verses in the Sermon on the Mount have to do with the difference between earthly and heavenly treasures, with its metaphors of "moth and rust," which corrupt the former but not the latter. Wright's "dust and moth" appears to echo Matthew's phrase.

Section 2 (p. 63). As a child, the poet dismissed the dream-world, assuming that it had nothing to do with him. But now that he has put away childish things, he sees otherwise: just as his father had to come to terms with the dreams he wrote out, so must the poet, offering his dreams to us as readers in order to "summon the spirits and set the body to music." This final line of the section has a Yeatsian ring, reminiscent of the final stanza of *Among School Children*, where Yeats says that images are "presences" symbolizing heavenly glory and where, with "the body swayed to music," we cannot tell the dancer from the dance.

Section 3 (pp. 63–4). The memory of his father takes the poet back to the time of his father's death (1972). At the "laying out" of his father's body, he encounters a person whose name he did not remember. This man, as it turned out, was George Vaughan ("One of the kindest men I have ever known"). An employee of Wright's father, he had taught the sixteen-year-old how to use a jackhammer on one of his father's construction sites, and had befriended him in other ways: "He took my hand when my hand needed taking."

p. 63, ll. 13 ff. Wright's father (1904–72) worked in construction after serving as a TVA engineer—first with the Eastman Construction Company in Kingsport, Tennessee, and then with the company he founded.

Section 4 (p. 64). This memory is from 1957, the summer after Wright graduated from college. He recounts the time in Nashville when he and a group of five friends used straws to suck gin from the "heart of a watermelon." And he recalls the comment of the host—the cousin of Agnes Donaldson—after the watermelon had yielded up its spirits: "What a life ... Jesus ... what a life." The irony of this remark is clear enough, coming as it does from a "lost soul."

Section 5 (pp. 64–5). This memory is from the summer after Wright graduated from high school when he worked as a reporter for the Kingsport *Times-News*. The job entailed checking the police blotter each evening for stories about local drunks, accidents, and petty crimes. This particular evening he wanders over to the "drunk tank" at the local jail, "The world and its disregard in the palm of my hand." What he recalls are the smells and "the desperate grey faces" of the local farmers who have been hauled in for drunkenness—"the residue of all our illuminations and unnamed lives."

For an amusing account of Wright's two-month stint with the Kingsport *Times-News*, see QN, 12–18.

Section 6 (p. 65). The poet glances at the photos of himself on the wall and at the shelf of magazines, presumably containing his published poems, and asks whether these tokens from his past all add up to anything. Does what happened to one in the past relate to what one is today? Does one's account of memories really represent accurately what happened? The poet, of course, recognizes that all autobiographical reflection is in some respects fictional. As he says in his essay "Miseducation of the Poet," "But *the way it was, what it was like*, is something we make up, something we reconstruct and reinvent to suit our purposes" (QN, 5). In the same essay he speaks of the mythical quality that results when we try to reconstruct a particular place in our past—a place "that is so 'other' it has stopped belonging to us and who we were and has become a zone, a region south of the past that lies at the end of a mythic expanse of light, and which we more often talk of and then turn away from than journey through" (QN, 11).

In the present section the poet is not willing to go quite that far. The episode he records about his chasing the pintail duck as a sixteen-year-old in the company of his childhood friends remains with him as a permanent memory because it is something he cares about. That is his answer to the "so what" question.

Section 7 (pp. 65–6). The opening quotation from Blake's poem refers to the weak-willed sexuality of the timid Thel, who can never move out of her fantasy world of unborn innocence. Wright changes the context of the "little curtain of flesh" entirely. His curtain is one drawn back and then opening onto the memory of his mother's death in 1964. He was in Rome as a Fulbright student at the time and because of travel complications was unable to return for her funeral. He imagines the eight years his father spent as a widower in "the cave of cold air." The final half-line, from the familiar hymn, serves as a benediction for these two "lost" souls, in the sense not of defeated or hopeless but of no longer present. The "*still small voice of calm*" also expresses a desire for the tranquil voice of God to quiet the maniacal honking in the Roman streets below.

p. 65, l. 23. *Blake*. "Why a little curtain of flesh on the bed of our desire?" (William Blake, *The Book of Thel*, pl. 6, l. 20).

p. 66, l. 1. *Wasatch Range*. A mountain range in Utah. Wright was at the University of Utah at the time.

p. 66, l. 8. *O still small voice of calm*. The last line of the hymn *Dear Lord and Father of Mankind*; the music is by Frederick C. Maker, and the lyrics come from a long narrative poem by John Greenleaf Whittier, *The Brewing of Soma*.

Lonesome Pine Special

OSR, 11–18; WTTT, 67–74
Pattern: (7) (7–3–7–5) (12) (10–9) (15) (15) (6–19–13–2) (1–14) (18) (14)
Time: Flashbacks to 1950s
Place: Settings of the separate sections: eastern Kentucky, east Tennessee, Idaho, New River (Virginia/North Carolina), northwestern Montana, eastern North Carolina/South Carolina, northwestern Montana, Sam's Gap (North Carolina–Tennessee state line), northwestern Montana, Henderson County, N.C.

Title: From a song by the Carter Family, recorded in Memphis in 1930. The first stanza: "I was walking out this morning with rambling on my mind / I am going to catch that special train for lonesome pine / You can hear the whistle blowing as she's coming down the line / That's the train I catch this morning just to ease my troubling mind." The songs of the Carter family have especially influenced Wright's later poetry. See "A.P. and E.D." in *Halflife*, 53–5.

We ramble with the poet as he traverses in memory nine roads he has traveled—those described in each of the first nine sections: U.S. 25E, U.S. 23 in Virginia, Idaho 75, U.S. 52,

5. The Other Side of the River (1984)

County Road 508, U.S. 176, U.S. 23 in North Carolina, and Solo Joe Road in Montana. These are the roads that linked Wright to worlds elsewhere. The tenth section is about an imaginary North Carolina road.

Section 1 (p. 67). The focus here in on an idyllic landscape along a curve on U.S. 25E near Barbourville, northwest of the Cumberland Gap between Middlesboro and Corbin, Kentucky. "How pleasant it must be to live" in this bottomland, muses the poet.

Section 2 (pp. 67–8). In the poet's youth, the considerable traffic back and forth between Kingsport, Tennessee, and Big Stone Gap, Virginia, about forty miles across the state line on U.S. 23, included the bootlegging expeditions of a local golf-playing character named Lone. "[S]licker than owl oil," Old Lone, with his sideways swing, was legendary for hustling his way around the golf course, and he continued to sell his moonshine even after the Moose Lodge began to offer whiskey legally.

Section 3 (p. 68). On this journey up highway up U.S. 75, north of Twin Falls, Idaho, and just south of the Sawtooth National Recreation Area, no one but the poet seems to be aware of Ezra Pound's birthplace in Hailey or, ten miles further north, of Hemingway's tombstone. The trip was no doubt undertaken as a homage to two very different American stylists much admired by Wright.

Section 4 (p. 69). This trip along U.S. 52 across the New River near the Virginia–North Carolina state line produces a stunning description of the landscape along the riverbank and issues in a Wordwsworthian reflection on the mysterious way the memory imprints such scenes on our consciousness: "What is it inside the imagination that keeps surprising us / At odd moments // when something is given back / We didn't know we had / In solitude, spontaneously, and with great joy?"

Section 5 (pp. 69–70). The trip here is along Lincoln County road 508 in northwest Montana. This secondary road, also known as Yaak Road, traces an S-shaped route from the junction with U.S. 2 northwest of Troy, Montana, to the junction with secondary road 567 at the Yaak River. In this homesteading backcountry, the poet launches downstream the wooden floats that he has whittled—a symbolic gesture "To carry my sins away." Two of the early settlers of this wilderness we have met in *Mount Caribou at Night*: Sam Runyan (1892–1947) and August Binder (1876–1962), both buried in the Boyd Cemetery near mile marker 43 on the Yaak River Road. The wooden chips eventually float past Binder's cabin and over the waterfalls. "[N]ext year," along with the ellipsis at the end, suggests that the ritual will be enacted again.

Section 6 (p. 70). This excursion finds the poet driving south down the curvy Saluda Grade between two small towns in North Carolina just north of the South Carolina border. The grade of this steep road is close to 6 percent in some places. As he descends into South Carolina, the kudzu ascends everywhere, threatening to envelope the entire landscape. The poet's description might seem an exaggeration to those unfamiliar with this scrambling perennial vine, but kudzu can in fact grow as much as sixty feet in a season and ascend to heights of more than one-hundred feet.

Section 7 (pp. 70–2). This travelogue, which takes us along U.S. 2 in northwestern Montana, begins with Yoshida Kenkō's maxim, an Eastern version of Stevens' principle that "Death is the mother of beauty" (*Sunday Morning*, pt. 5, l. 3, p. 6, l. 13). On the indissoluble connection between beauty and its perishability, Kenkō wrote, "If man were never to fade away like the dews of Adashino, never to vanish like the smoke over Toribeyama, but lingered on forever in this world, how things would lose their power to move us! The most precious thing in life is its uncertainty" (*Essays in Idleness*, trans. Donald Keene [New York: Columbia University Press, 1998], 7). The poet affirms the truth of this observation as it applies not to death itself but to the disappearance of scenes in memory.

The poet's excursion takes him west from Kalispell, a town in Flathead County, southwest of the Wright property in Lincoln County. U.S. Highway 2 runs east-west between Kalispell and Libby, near the Idaho border. From Highway 2 he exits onto the dirt back-roads near the small town of Kila, recounting a tale about one of the early trappers, and eventually arrives at a mining area known as Hog Heaven. Here the poet's descriptive powers shift into high gear, as he takes us through the landscape toward an abandoned cabin, an image of loneliness and emptiness but "oddly beautiful in its desolation / And attitude." The concluding reflections confirm Kenkō's epigram: beauty remains even after the inhabitants of this place have long disappeared.

p. 71, l. 10. *Flathead Mine.* The Flathead mine, the principal mine in the area described, is located about thirty-five miles by road southwest of Kalispell and forty miles northwest of Polson. During the late 1930s and 1940s it was one of the largest silver producers in the Pacific Northwest.

p. 71, l. 15. *Hog Heaven country.* A mining district located in Flathead County west of Flathead Lake.

Section 8 (pp. 72–3). Returning once again to U.S. Highway 23, this time on its southern extension at the North Carolina–Tennessee state line, the poet relives a near encounter with death, when his car skidded toward a precipice at Sam's Gap. He now shifts into low gear once again, as he had done earlier to back out of his predicament, announcing that "grace" was both the cause of his brush with death and his salvation. Wright will occasionally alter a commonplace with a witty reversal, as in the opening line: "There is so little to say, and so much time to say it in." Compare the droll reversal of a later line: "Don't just do something, sit there" (*SHS*, 79).

Section 9 (p. 73). Jump-cut to Montana and Solo Joe Road, off state Highway 508. Solo Joe Road is a "good road," an affirmation twice made, but this section has less to do with the road than Solo Joe Perrault himself, a hermit who lived at the mouth of the Solo Joe Creek for twenty-five years. He was a placer miner, as well as one of the first barbers in Troy, Montana, cutting hair there in 1894 and 1895. The focus is on the mythology that has grown up around this early prospector, dead now for more than fifty years (he died in 1925)—a mythology substantial enough for him to be remembered on a memorial plaque.

p. 73, l. 5. *Mt. Henry.* About three-and-a-half miles, as the crow flies, southwest of the Wright property; named for Henry Wegner, a 1906 homesteader on the East Fork of the Yaak River.

p. 73, l. 15. *placer-mine.* The mining of minerals from alluvial deposits in stream beds.

Section 10 (pp. 73–4). The final road in this chronicle of past journeys is an imaginary one, a narrow logging road that the poet would like to discover in Henderson County, North Carolina, somewhere near the Sky Valley school he attended in the early 1950s and above Lake Llewellyn (now "Louellen"). This is the place where Wright has said that he "came into consciousness" (*QN*, 162). The imaginary road is the "road in, which is always longer than the road out." Were the poet to find it, he would follow it as it descends downhill and disappears. The imagery of the last two lines suggests a *nekyia*, a descent into the underworld where the pilgrim receives the instructions necessary to continue his journey.

p. 74, l. 1. The Pinnacle and Mt. Anne [Ann] are in the Sky Lake vicinity of Henderson County.

Two Stories

Orig. pub. *Antioch Review* 40 (Spring 1982): 180–2.
OSR, 19–22; WTTT, 75–7
Pattern: (10) (5) (1–27) (10) (6) (4–2–4)
Time: Flashbacks, 1946–47
Place: Laguna Beach, with flashbacks to Tennessee

The two stories in this six-section poem are sandwiched between two non-narrative sections at the beginning and two at the end. The story of the sleepwalking poet and the bear on Mt. Leconte (section 3) is incredible, but we have the poet's sworn testimony that it is true. The story of the rattlesnake (section 4) is no less incredible, though the poet cannot attest with certainty that it really occurred.

p. 75, l. 20. *Mt. LeConte*. An imposing mountain (5693 feet) in the Great Smoky Mountains National Park, southeast of Gatlinburg, Tennessee

Section 1 (p. 75). The lights of Laguna Beach, seen from the deck above, remind the poet of the lights of Kingsport thirty-five years before—when he was an eleven-year-old. Then, he imagined them as shore lights, "As something inside me listened with all its weight / For the sea-surge and the sea-change." This foreshadows the poet's career. The line echoes Ariel's song about the profound transformation of Ferdinand in *The Tempest*: "Nothing of him that doth fade / But doth suffer a sea-change / Into something rich and strange" (1.2.403).

Section 2 (p. 75). In this meditation on the past the poet reverses the usual notion that the past makes an imprint on us. Here, we make an imprint on it, leaving our fingerprints along its wall. As the imprints are like fossils, the implication is that they can be excavated.

Sections 3 and 4 (pp. 75–7). The two stories of the title, just mentioned.

Section 5 (p. 77). The complaint here is directed at discontinuity, which "sends us apart and keeps us there in a dread." The rear-view mirror image at the end explains the nature of this dread. The implication is that the present never really exists, that the future is unknown, and that all we've got is a mirror onto the past which continues to recede. We back into an unknown future with our eyes fastened onto the only thing we can know—the things that have come before. Yet these things become more discontinuous as time's winged chariot hurries along.

Section 6 (p. 77). This rather woeful conclusion is about writer's block, the fading of poetic powers ("embolisms"), and the approach of death ("the end of the road"), the noisy world out there still barking away with its distractions. The poet more or less resigns himself to transferring his problems to someone or something else, and so he says farewell to Miss Sweeney, the poetic incarnation of his fifth-grade teacher, Miss Watkins. Just as the ocean rocks back and forth, so in the next life the poet will rock back and forth from heel to toe, performing a meaninglessly repetitive little dance.

p. 77, l. 15. *embolisms*. The primary reference appears to be to the poet's own work—his verbal interpolations—but in the context of poetic anxiety there is also the suggestion of prayers.

The Other Side of the River

Orig. pub. *New Yorker* 58 (5 April 1982): 46–7.
OSR, 23–6; WTTT, 78–81
Pattern: (4-4-1) (3-14-3) (2-1-2) (7-7-6) (2) (3-5-6)
Time: Spring (Easter)
Place: Laguna Beach, with flashback to South Carolina, North Carolina (1950–51), and Monterey Bay (1958)

Title: In an interview with Willard Spiegelman, Wright remarked, "In Kingsport (Tennessee) where I grew up, the state line was on the other side of the Holston River, just a little out of town. Virginia was the state. Enlightenment is like that, just across the line on the other side of the river" (Spiegelman, 115). Here we have both the literal and the figurative meanings for "the other side," a phrase that appears with some regularity in Wright's poetry. The title of one of the poems in *Hard Freight* is *The Other Side*, and Wright speaks of "the other side of the sky" in *Homage to X*. In *The Southern Cross* he writes, "Thinking of Dante is thinking about the other side / And the other side of the other side," and the phrase will continue to crop up in later poems: "no one could answer back from the other side" (*Italian Days*), "the other side of the sky" (*To Giacomo Leopardi in the Sky*), "other side of the light" (*A Journal of English Days*), "on the other side" (*A Journal of One Significant Landscape*), "on the other side" (*Opus Posthumous*), "supplicant whispers for the other side" (*Appalachian Book of the Dead III*), "the other side" (*Spring Storm*), "the other side" (*American Twilight*), "things of the other side" (*River Run*), "other side of our lives" (*Body and Soul*), "look for us soon on the other side" (*Buffalo Yoga*), "past midnight's the other side" (*Buffalo Yoga*), and "deep light on the other side" (*Littlefoot*).

The "other side" echoes throughout both the Bible and African-American spirituals as the site of the Promised Land or other sacred space: Elijah is transported to heaven by a whirlwind after crossing over the Jordan, and John the Baptist engages in his christening rites on the other side of the Jordan. So when the poet says in section 5 that he wants to sit on the river bank and peer across at the "face of whatever, / the whatever that's waiting for me," he is looking into a time and space beyond ordinary reality—a Promised Land. The crossing to the other side of the Red Sea by the Israelites was an escape from slavery; the passage to the other side of the Jordan recorded in Joshua 3–5 was an entrance into new land, physical as well as spiritual.

Section 1 (p. 78). On this rainy Easter day the landscape, with its burdened palm trees and dark puddles and with nothing rising "more than halfway out of itself," portends very little hope for either a seasonal or a spiritual rebirth. True, the little mouths of the flower open themselves to receive the rain, but there is no sense that that has anything to do with the Easter season. Wetness is all in what the poet calls in the first line of the next section "spring's disgrace."

Section 2 (pp. 78–9). Here the flashback of the hunting trip of the poet and his brother Winter is sandwiched between two tongue-in-cheek comments on metaphor. In the first tercet, we are told that "There is no metaphor for the spring's disgrace," "spring's disgrace" being of course a metaphor itself. This is followed by a simile ("rose leaves look like bronze dove hearts") and then by another metaphor (the preening trees), such proud primping being a discredit to the Easter moment. The final tercet actually contains no metaphor, though the force of the violet blossoms of the periwinkle as "deep bruises" is not diminished by its being a simile. In the account of the hunting story itself, the description of the landscape relies on four metaphors and three similes, which rather deflates the claim that "There is no metaphor for any of this."

p. 78, l. 14. *Garnett*. A small town west of Charleston near the Georgia state line.

Section 3 (p. 79). This is a meditation on the manifestation and disappearance of "Something infinite" in all the "harmonies and structures" that link us to the past. Here the metaphors are musical (harmonies) and architectural (structures, narrowing the surfaces). It is important that the sky be properly fitted in, for the infinite, though fleeting, lies not just behind the surface reality but behind the heavens as well—another version of the immanent/transcendent dialectic.

Section 4 (pp. 79–80). Looking at the night sky, the poet is transported back to 1950, when he was a student at Sky Valley School in Henderson County, North Carolina—the place of his imaginary journey in section 10 of *Lonesome Pine Special*. His assignment is to repair the fire tower on Mt. Anne [Ann] in the Sky Lake area of Henderson County. High above the school he looks down upon Lake Llewellyn (now Louellen) below. He observes that the present nights are like those long ones he experienced as a fifteen-year-old and that they are "increasingly difficult to describe." Moreover time is running out. But the metaphor of the present sky as a "silvery alphabet of the sea" hardly needs improvement. Nor does the description of the "after reflection" of Lake Llewellyn and environs: "Aluminum glare in the sponged dark, / Lightning bugs everywhere, // the plump stars / Dangling and falling near on their black strings." Years later, in *Scar Tissue II* (ST, 41), Wright briefly revisits the firetower.

Section 5 (p. 80). This couplet is the only section that relates directly, as already said, to the motif of "the other side of the river."

Section 6 (pp. 80–1). The final section returns to the theme of the disappearance of things in memory: "There comes a point when everything starts to dust away / More quickly than it appears, // when what we have to comfort the dark / Is just that dust, and just its going away." In the scene that follows the poet is transported to a time in 1958 when he was at the Presidio's Army Language School, Monterey, California, studying Italian. He remembers the sunset over Monterey Bay, the immediacy of which was a numinous experience. In the concluding stanza, he returns to the present, now a *sunny* Easter day, summing up his experience of remembering by borrowing a line from *A Short Life of Trouble*, a traditional bluegrass tune sung by Flatt and Scruggs and numerous others. In the song a "short life of trouble" is the fate of a boy with a broken heart. In the poem, it is "remembering what I did do, and what I didn't do."

Homage to Claude Lorrain

Orig. pub. *The Reaper* 4 (1982): 31.
OSR, 29; WTTT, 82
Pattern: 8–4–8
Time: Flashback to 1959
Place: Flashback to Verona

The setting of this exquisite lyric is Wright's three-room apartment in central Verona, where he lived in 1959–60—via Anzia n. 3, several hundred meters northwest of the River Adige. He begins with a description of a half-remembered Lorrain print, framed above his bed, of a ship foundering in a tempest. In the final stanza, the poet situates himself between the "sea fires" of the Lorrain print and the "curled sheets" of the River Adige, completing the metaphorical cluster of the first stanza: he is burning on his swivel stool like the flaming waves in Lorrain's print and then, as he imagines his future, he projects the hope that his life, "unsigned and rigged for the deeps," may one day fit into the metaphoric frame.

p. 82, ll. 1–3. *print ... drawing.* This appears to be Lorrain's etching *Ship Foundering in Storm*, but there are other candidates: his chalk and ink drawings *A Ship in a Storm* (1638) and *Storm at Sea* (1630), or his pen and ink drawing with the same title (1643–44).

Mantova

Orig. pub. *The Reaper* 4 (1982): 30.
OSR, 30; WTTT, 83
Pattern: 5–7–5–1–2
Time: 1959

The setting is the Palazzo Ducale in Mantova, a town on the Mincio River, which discharges Lake Garda at its southern tip. The poet recalls seeing the frescoes of Mantegna (ca. 1421–1506) on the palace walls on a rainy day in 1960. He also recalls a bizarre dream he had of a lavish banquet where, as in Swift's *A Modest Proposal*, the menu consists of roasted children. This eerie vision disappears in favor of a vertiginous description of the watery landscape, both above and below, and we're left with two rhetorical questions ("Words, but who can remember? // What words does the sky know, or the clouds know?"). What the poet does remember are Giulio Romano's frescoes at his architectural masterpiece, the Palazzo del Tè, a summer residence designed and decorated by Giulio for Duke Federico Gonzaga. Giulio (1492–1546), the greatest of Raphael's pupils, settled in Mantova in 1524. The lion's at the riverbank are from the frescoes at the Palazzo del Tè.

Driving to Passalacqua, 1960

Orig. pub. *Ploughshares* 31 (Fall 1983): 31.
OSR, 31; WTTT, 84
Pattern: 2 × 10
Place: Verona

Wright's note indicates that "Passalacqua" refers to "Caserma Passalacqua, Headquarters SETAF (Southern European Task Force), Verona, Italy," the site of his army unit. SETAF was activated in 1955 at Camp Darby near Livorno. Shortly afterward, it moved its headquarters to Caserma Passalacqua in Verona. Troop strength reached 10,000, and USASETAF was formally established with a U.S.-Italian agreement. In 1959, following President Dwight Eisenhower's visit to Rome, U.S. troop strength was cut in half, equipment from disbanded U.S. units was turned over to Italy, and Italian Army personnel were assigned to the SETAF general staff to assist with binational responsibilities.

The first stanza describes the daily route of Wright from his apartment at Via Anzia n. 3 to Caserma Passalacqua, which is in the Veronetta section of Verona, just east of the Adige between Ponte Navi and Ponte Aleardi. The southern limit of the Caserma is the old Roman wall in that part of the city. The course of Wright's morning drive was around the bend of the Adige from Via Anzani and then south past San Fermo Maggiore, a red-and-white striped Romanesque and Gothic church. From there he apparently turned east on Via S. Francesco and then south on Viale della Università to the main entrance of Caserma Passalacqua with its "spiked fence." Arriving for daily duty, the poet appears at roll call, reads his mail, and discovers that two people in his unit, Ed DiCenzo and Joe Lucciola, have headed off on assignment.

The morning sunlight flashing here and there on the Adige reminds the poet of the Phlegethon (Gk. "flaming"), and so he likens his crossing the Adige to Dante's crossing the Phlegethon, a river of boiling blood, in Canto 11 of the *Inferno*. "All day the river burned by my desk," the poet concludes, "as I sailed my boats down its licks for a foot or so." One hears an echo of Dante's little boat in *Purgatorio* I and *Paradiso* II.

p. 84, l. 2. *Santa Maria dell'Ortolo*. Wright appears to have misremembered the name. He has conflated Santa Maria in Organo, a church east of the Adige on the drive south along the river past the Ponte Pietra, and the Madonna dell'Ortolo, a church in Venice.

p. 84, l. 6. *Catullus off to my left*. This is a reference to "VALERI" (Catullus' middle name) carved in one of the stone seats of the Teatro Romano.

p. 84, l. 15. *bivio*. Crossroads.

Three Poems of Departure

Orig. pub. as *Four Poems of Departure* in *Antaeus* 47 (Autumn 1982): 16–17; no. 3 not included in OSR or WTTT. Rpt. *as Four Poems of Departure*. Portland, OR: Trace Editions, 1983.
OSR, 34–40; WTTT, 85–93
Pattern: (7) (5 × 2) (5 × 2)
Time: July, August
Place: Yaak Valley, Montana

Three Poems of Departure interrupts a sequence of four "Italian" poems, just as *Three Poems for the New Year* will do a few pages later. The scene is the front porch of Wright's Montana County cabin in late summer. "Departure" has three referents. First of all, summer is departing, signaled by the grass turning bronze and the aspen leaves waving goodbye. Second, someone somewhere has departed this life, signaled by the inconsolable mourning. And third, the departure of the pilgrim-poet himself is imminent, signaled by his throwing a handful of dirt into the wind. He prepares to set off for the next stage in his quest for a sacred place.

The departure in the second poem is a hike through the wilderness that takes the poet up toward the summit of a mountain and then down the other side. "Us" apparently refers to the poet and his wife: the meadow of their Montana property, he says, "surrounds us on three sides." Darkness approaches. The sun has already set on his wife, back at the cabin, and it will soon set on him as he moves down a western slope, miles away from where she presently is. His destination is not specified: he says only that he leaves. But the ascent and descent motif, which is omnipresent in Wright's poetry, has symbolic overtones, suggesting that this literal departure is also a figurative one.

The departure in the third poem is from Montana to "the desert," meaning back to Laguna Beach by way of the California deserts. It is the 28th of August, and there is a touch of fall in the air. The night before departing the poet and his wife survey the heavens.

The motif of departure, along with the descriptions of the landscape in all three poems, is reminiscent of the poets of the T'ang dynasty.

p. 85, l. 1. *cabin*. See note to p. 52, l. 1. See also *Mt. Caribou at Night*, WTTT, 12.
p. 86, l. 9. *Betelgeuse*. One of the two bright stars that dominate Orion, also called Alpha Orionis.
p. 86, l. 10. *pony stars*. A reference perhaps to some of the lesser stars in Pegasus or some other constellation.

Italian Days

Orig. pub. *New Yorker* 59 (6 February 1984): 50–1.
OSR, 34–40; WTTT, 87–93
Pattern: 1. (5–7–7–6–6–7–7–5) 2. (10 × 5) 3. (7 × 7 + 1)
Time: 1959
Place: Verona and environs, Ferrara, Vicenza, Milan, Rome, and elsewhere in Italy

This poem traces the poet's exploratory excursions throughout Italy during his first year of army duty in Verona. In part 1 he first recalls a weekend trip to Ferrara, with its wide streets, where he saw a painting by Cosimo Tura in the museum, and an earlier weekend trip, where he had a brush with death when the helicopter engine malfunctioned on a flight to Merano, a town in the Trentino Alto Adige region of northern Italy. The helicopter ride described here is north from Verona to Merano across the Val d'Adige, returning south across Trento in Trentino Alto Adige, then across the town of Schio, northeast of Verona, before arriving back at Caserma Passalacqua. This close encounter introduces the theme of death, which becomes a center of attention of the poem.

We then jump-cut to Ferrara, Rimini, and Ravena, with its basilica, S. Apollinare in Classe. The poet calls Ravena "western Byzantium" because of its extraordinary mosaics, especially in the basilica. Back in Verona, he describes a walk through town after everyone has emptied out of the Caffè Dante. His procession is northeast toward the S. Anastasia Church and the Hotel Due Torri (on the Piazza Anastasis), then northwest toward the Duomo, Verona's cathedral, just south of the loop in the Adige, and finally northeast again over the Ponte Pietra, where he encounters a beggar. The city sights are contrasted with the natural cycle in the mountains to the north, where "Snow has been leaving its same message / For thousands of years // on the bark of the cedar trees." Part 1 concludes with an observation about the power of this natural cycle ("the comings and goings in this world"), the suggestion being that the poet's wanderings out from his home base in Verona and his ambling through the city itself are a part of this process. The poet returns to "the comings and goings in this world" in the final stanza of part 3.

p. 87, l. 2. *Cosimo Tura*. An Italian painter of the Ferrarese school (ca. 1430–1495). His *Annunciation* in the Museo del Duomo in Ferrara is the painting referred to. A reproduction can be found at http://gallery.euroweb.hu/html/t/tura/

p. 87, l. 2. *Miss d'Este*. Isabella d'Este (1475–1539) presided over the splendid court of Mantua (which included Raphael, Mantegna, and Romano). Her sister Beatrice (1475–97) was the duchess of Milan, another magnificent court (which included Corregio, Castiglione, and da Vinci).

p. 88, l. 6. *Non si taglia la pasta*. One doesn't cut one's pasta.

p. 88, l. 14–15. *Modugno*. Domenico Modugno (1928–94), an Italian singer, popular in the U.S. in the 1950s, largely because of his *Nel blu Dipinto di blu*, better known as *Volare*, and his 1954 hit, *Ciao, Ciao, Bambina*.

p. 88, l. 15. *Via Mazzini*. Now perhaps Verona's most famous street, running from the Piazza Erbe to the Piazza Bra.

p. 88, l. 18. *Caffè Dante*. On the Piazza dei Signori.

p. 88, l. 19. *Can Grande*. Can Francesco della Scala, the greatest member of the illustrious Scaliger family in Verona. Among the guests of his court was the exiled Dante. His tomb, with an equestrian statue, is alongside the other elaborate Gothic shrines to the Scaligeri that surround S. Maria Antica.

p. 89, l. 1. *Dolomites*. Mountains in Veneto Region (province of Belluno) and in the Trentino Alto Adige Region (provinces of Trento and Bolzano).

Part 2 recounts a weekend adventures in Vicenza and other nearby towns (Soave, Asolo, Padova) in the Veneto with army friends (Arnie Goldstein and Dick Venezia) and a woman from Trieste, Grace Pecchiar. Venezia, referred to as "Lord of the Bees," seems to be the ring leader of the bar-hopping, hot-handed trio—"Always looking for the event, //not knowing that we were it." On one Sunday excursion to Milan and Certosa, they end up in the studio of Roberto Scuderi, who would be dead within a year. Reliving the experience of the climb to Scuderi's room and of the painter's calling his name, the poet remembers the treatment of light in Scuderi's paintings. The reverie about the painter grains out and then turns blank, but the light of Milan remains—"Light like a sheet of paper / Everywhere, flat and unwrinkled and unreturnable."

p. 89, l. 6. *Palladio*. Andrea, the leading architect of his time in sixteenth-century Veneto. His hometown of Vicenza contains the greatest concentration of his buildings.

p. 89, l. 9. *Venezia*. Dick Venezia, also appears in the imagined Ugo Mulas photograph in *Bar Giamaica, 1959-60* (*WTTT*, 39).

p. 89, l. 19. *Vincentine*. Dick Venezia.

p. 89, l. 21. *Grace*. Grace Pecchiar, a woman from Trieste, who was also inserted into the Mulas photograph in *Bar Giamaica, 1959-60* (*WTTT*, 39).

p. 90, l. 6. *Trattoria La Brera*. A fictional restaurant.

p. 90, l. 7. *Scuderi*. Roberto Scuderi, Wright's artist friend who was accidentally electrocuted in 1961 at age 27.

p. 89, ll. 23–4. *Soave ... Euganean Hills*. *Soave*: a walled village near Vicenza, known for its wines. *Asolo*: another walled town, forty miles northwest of Venice at the foothills of the Dolomites (Italian Alps). *Padua* (Padova): a city in the Veneto, about halfway between Venice and Verona. The *Euganean Hills* are south of Padova.

p. 90, last l. *dopoguerra* = postwar period

Part 3 opens with a self-interrogation: when death comes, "What will your question be ... And what will it profit you?" No such questions crossed the poet's mind when he was bivouacked outside of Marostica in the foothills north of Vicenza: "What eschatology of desire // could move us in those days. / What new episiotomy of the word?" Later, outside of San Gimingano in Tuscany, perhaps at a cemetery or at the San Vivaldo monastery and church, the poet realizes "that no one could ever last for good, / That no one could answer back from the other side." Still, he has learned how to speak to the voices of the past.

Consciousness of death naturally makes an impact on the poet as he descends into the catacombs in Rome. The travelogue continues as he resurrects memories of Siena, Monterchi, Verona, Bassano (here in the company of two friends, Jim Gates and Tom Fucile), and Sommacampagna. Stanza 6, which returns to Roberto Scuderi and the helicopter incident, opens with two verb phases in which the auxiliary is not attached to a main verb ("Scuderi did ... helicopter did"). The free associations here provide no answer to the question, "Did what?" But they do throw the emphasis back on death, reinforced by the image of Monte Grappa as a "Ghost hat on the head of northern Italy." In counterpoint to death are the images of the *Madonna del Parto* in Monterchi, her pregnant belly containing the Word, and the image of the creation of life in the Edenic scene from the bronze doors of San Zeno Maggiore in Verona. These images of birth anticipate the light, orchard blossoms, and other springtime icons of the final stanza, blotting out the ominous threads of death that have been haunting the poem. Thus the upbeat conclusion: "What gifts there are are all here, in this world."

p. 91, l. 15. *Marostica*. A medieval town, surrounded by the ancient walls of its castles.
p. 91, l. 23. *San Gimignano*. A medieval village in Tuscany, south of Florence.
p. 92, l. 2. *Via Cassia*. One of the major northern roads to and from Rome.
p. 92, l. 11. *Pinacoteca*. The Pinacoteca Nazionale, located in the fourteenth-century Palazzo Buonsignori, contains an extensive collection of thirteenth- to sixteenth-century Sienese paintings.
p. 92, l. 13. Piero della Francesca's *Madonna del Parto* (Madonna of Childbirth), a detached fresco, in the Chapel of the cemetery in Monterchi (Arezzo). The figure of this Madonna, the protector of pregnant women, with her austere expression and her heaviness with child, stands out against the damask canopy, held open at the sides by two angels. The sacred and ritual nature of the image is further emphasized by the fact that the angels are drawn from the same cartoon, repeated in mirror likeness. For an image of the *Madonna del Parto*, see http://www.artchive.com/artchive/P/piero/delparto.jpg.html
p. 92, l. 17. *Borso*. Borso d'Este (1413–71), Duke of Ferrara and Duke of Modena. The Zattere is the bank in the south of Venice, facing the Giudecca Canal.
p. 92, l. 19. *San Zeno's doors*. The forty-eight panels of great bronze doors of the basilica San Zeno Maggiore depict scenes from the Bible and the life of San Zeno, an African who became Verona's first bishop in 362. For an image of the Adam and Eve scene, in the upper panels of the left door, see http://ruskin.ashmus.ox.ac.uk/catalogue/cat_page.php?id=WA.RS.REF.071.
p. 92, l. 20. *Jim Gates and Tom Fucile*. Wright's army friends.
p. 92, l. 21. *Bassano ... Monte Grappa*. Bassano, about 21 miles northeast of Vicenza, sits by the River Brenta with Monte Grappa in the background. In World War II Monte Grappa was the refuge of the local partisan brigades that had organized to fight the occupying Nazi forces.
p. 92, l. 23. *Sommacampagna*. A small town in the Veneto region of northern Italy, about four miles southwest of Verona.
p. 93, l. 3. *Riva*. A small town on the northern tip of Lake Garda.
p. 93, l. 4. *Like Blake*. As in any number of William Blake's engravings (e.g., the frontispiece of *Europe*).

Three Poems for the New Year

Orig. pub. as *Four Poems of the New Year* in *Antaeus* 47 (Autumn 1982): 16–17; no. 3 not included in OSR.
OSR, 41–3; WTTT, 94–5
Pattern: 1. (4–3–3–1) 2. (5–1–5) 3. (5–1–4–1)
Time: January 1982
Place: Laguna Beach

These are companion poems to *Three Poems of Departure*, which come between, once again, four "Italian" poems, though the mood of these three is much more melancholy. In the first the poet confesses three times that he has "nothing to say" about the landscape. This notion of futility becomes the central theme. The poet may try to console himself, but he knows that such consolation is vanity, and he has "sung in vain" for the previous year. The metaphorical kernel here is emptiness, like the *hebel* (vapor) which the preacher in Ecclesiastes attributes to all things (*vanitas* in Jerome's Latin Vulgate). Of course, in denying that he has anything to say, the poet does make several affirmations (e.g., "the sky tilts / Toward the absolute," and he lives "at the edge / Of the black boundary"). Still, the pilgrimage has moved only "from the dark to the dark," and we conclude with the distressing observation that the dull monotony of the cicada's song is "true advice."

The second poem is a winter's tale in which the poet awakens in middle age (he is 47) into a dream world. He sees himself as an abandoned Rimbaud, the *poète maudit* much admired by Wright. The snow, fogged window, and vanishing scarf are objective correlatives for feelings of absence, obstacles to vision, and disappearance.

The focus of the third poem, which finds the poet looking over the landscape all day in solitude, is on unfilled desire. The nagging "ache for fame"—the "ache for anything" is unfulfilled, leaving only "a thick dust and a weariness in the heart."

The three poems offer a rather gloomy new year's prospect for the disconsolate poet.

p. 94, l. 4. *my coming in and my going out*. The phrase is biblical, appearing in Acts 9:28, Deuteronomy 28:6, and most familiarly in Psalm 121:8.

p. 95, l. 7. *deserts and caravans*. After wandering across France and crossing the Alps, Rimbaud abandoned poetry and became an explorer, joining desert caravans. In the context of snow, the imagery may derive from the "snow deserts" in Rimbaud's *Genie* (the final prose poem in *Illuminations*) and from the departing caravans in the Alps in *After the Flood* (the first prose poem in *Illuminations*).

Roma I

Orig. pub. *Paris Review* 25 (Winter 1983): 92.
OSR, 44–5; WTTT, 96
Pattern: 7 × 3
Time: October 1963

During Wright's "first year" as a Fulbright student in Rome (1963), the city appeared to him from his balcony as an abstract watercolor, each season having a distinctive "local color." The parenthetical vignettes of stanza 2 are memories of seeing a famous film star and a more famous movie director in front of a restaurant and a plaque honoring a Polish patriot whose name the poet has forgotten. In stanza 3 Wright appropriates the motif of Pound's *Rome*, applying it to his own situation. Pound's poem is a translation of Joachim du Bellay's translation of Janus Vitalis Panormitanus' *De Roma*. Pound's poem begins, "O thou new comer who seek'st Rome in Rome / And find'st in Rome no thing thou canst call Roman / Arches worn old and palaces made common, / Rome's name alone within these walls keeps home" (*Personae* [New York: New Directions, 1990], 39). Wright depicts himself as a bird, flying into Rome and pecking at the seed of its riches—"The form inside the form inside." What is common for Pound—the ancient arches and palaces—becomes for Wright the obelisk and the stone boat. Pound's sonnet concludes with the paradox of the temporal and the timeless: "That which stands firm in thee [Rome] Time batters down, / And that which fleeteth doth outrun swift time." In Wright this becomes "The smell of a dozen dinners is borne up / On exhaust fumes, // timeless, somehow, and vaguely reassuring."

p. 96, l. 2. *Via del Babuino*. One of Rome's most central and magnificent streets, running from the Spanish Steps to Piazza del Popolo.

p. 96, l. 8. *Ristorante Bolognese*. Located on Via Boldrini, no. 1.

p. 96, l. 9. *Monica Vitti and Michelangelo Antonioni.* Film star and famous movie director.
p. 96, l. 11. *Polish patriot.* This is Henryk Sienkiewicz, patriot and author of *Quo Vadis*, who is honored by a plaque on the façade of the Hotel Inghilterra on Via del Corso, which intersects with Via del Babuino at the Piazza del Popolo.

Roma II

Orig. pub. *Paris Review* 25 (Winter 1983): 93
OSR, 46; WTTT, 97
Pattern: 7 × 3
Time: 1964

This poem arises from Wright's second year in Rome as a Fulbright student, 1964, the year his mother died. Its subject matter is emptiness—the desolation experienced from his mother's death but more generally the sense of nonbeing that will become a common theme in Wright's poetry. "[E]mptiness," says the poet in the third stanza, "is the beginning of all things." The idea, which relates to patience, restraint, simplicity, and lack of desire, has a number of congeners: the Nothing of Stevens and Heidegger, the *deus absconditis* of *The Cloud of Unknowing*, the abyss of Boehme's *Urgrund*, the presence of absence, the Negative Capability of Keats, the spirit of darkness in St. John of the Cross, the self-negation (*kenosis*) of the Incarnation in Philippians 12:7, the ascesis of the spiritual life, the "way down" of Heraclitus, and Eliot's vacancy. In addition, there are the Eastern forms in the *shunyata* of the Mahayana Buddhists, and *wu wei* of Lao-Tzu's *Tao Te Ching*.

The second stanza opens with a plain-spoken declaration: "The poem is a self-portrait // always, no matter what mask / You take off and put back on." The metaphors here are from painting and drama. The former trope links with the "mother's miniature" of the first stanza, the sketches of the Irish poets in the second, and the azure-gowned masters in the third, which is a description of Carpaccio's *Funeral of St. Jerome*. Jerome's body, surrounded by the "masters" officiating at the funeral, is laid down, like the poet's mother in stanza 1. The latter metaphor—of the persona or mask—connects with the theme of emptiness: the self-portrait is a "mouthful of air."

p. 97, ll. 1–2. *mother's miniature ... next year.* Wright's mother had died in 1964. Wright's next or second year in Rome as a Fulbright student was 1964.
p. 97, l. 3. *church building.* A building owned by the Catholic Church.
p. 97, l. 3. *Campo dei Fiori.* See note to p. 50, ll. 15–18, p. 113, above.
p. 97, l. 12. *Pollarolla.* A restaurant.
p. 97, ll. 21–2. *masters stand ... above their heads.* For a reproduction of Carpaccio's *The Funeral of St. Jerome*, see http://www.abcgallery.com/C/carpaccio/carpaccio7.html

Homage to Cesare Pavese

Orig. pub. as *Omaggio a Pavese* in *Agni Review* 17 (1982): 5; rpt. in *Agni* 56 (2002): 429.
OSR, 47; WTTT, 98
Pattern: 5 × 4

Wright's note: "'Verrà la morte e avrà i tuoi occhi,' 'La terra e la morte,' *Il mestiere di vivere*" (WTTT, 231).

The first line is a translation of the first line of Cesare Pavese's *Verrà la morte e avrà i tuoi occhi*, a poem that was famous in Italy, Wright reports, when he was there in the late 1950s (QN, 129). "Your eyes" are those of the woman Pavese is said to have killed himself over, Constance Dowling, an American actress he had met in Rome. The manuscript for *Death Will*

Come and Will Wear Your Eyes was found in his desk. The poem—no. 13 in this manuscript—was written a few months before Pavese's suicide in 1950, in the course of a tumultuous love affair with Dowling. Wright's borrowings can be seen in this translation of the first three lines of Pavese's poem by Marco Sonzogni and David Wheatley: "Death will come and will wear your eyes—/ the death that is with us / from morning to evening, sleepless."

In addition to using the first line at the beginning of stanzas 1 and 3, Wright draws on the language and imagery of other texts by Pavese. Stanza 3 is an improvisation on certain phrases from *La terra e la morte*: "At nightfall the countryman's gesture falls silent. / You are the great fatigue, and the night deep enough to give it peace. / You're secret as rock or grass or earth. / You thrash about in yourself like the sea. / The word doesn't exist that could possess you or hold you back.... You cannot speak in words; no one's word reaches you" (from Pavese's *Death and the Earth*, trans. Alan Williamson, in *American Poetry Review* September–October 1997).

Stanza 4 derives from the final entries in Pavese's diary, *Il mestiere di vivere*, written shortly before his suicide: "This is the balance sheet of an unfinished year." "Names do not matter." "One nail drives out another. But four nails make a cross" (*The Business of Living: Diaries 1935-1950*, trans. A.E. Murch [London: Quartet Books, 1980], 350, 349). Wright says in an interview that "four nails make a cross" is the only thing in the last stanza from Pavese (QN, 130), but there are obviously several other passages from Pavese he has woven into this stanza.

Pavese's projection of his death and of Dowling's reaction to it is recreated by Wright as a myth of unrelieved pathos. The final entries in Pavese's diaries hint that the cause of his suicide might have been not simply unrequited love but also political disillusionment, but in Wright's poem the suicide is laid at the feet of "you": "Woman is as woman does." This is the metaphorical darkness with its "black heart and its black hands" that lays Pavese down.

Part of Wright's project during his Fulbright year in Rome was to translate Pavese. He ended up devoting most of his energies to Montale, a more interesting poet for him, but he nevertheless greatly admired Pavese. Thus, the "homage."

Cyropexy

Orig. pub. *raccoon* 14 (January 1984): 11–13.
OSR, 51–3; WTTT, 99–101
Pattern: 3-3-3-3-3-4-5-4-4-5-4-3
Time: Flashback to 1981
Place: Laguna Beach

Wright on Wright: "A cryopexy is an operation on the eye to repair a tear in the retina; it's a freezing process. I had it done to me, to my eye, back in 1981. After they do it, they don't let you do anything for about ten days to two weeks except watch television. That's the only thing you can do because you never move your eyes when you watch television. You can't read, you can't walk around, you can't do anything, you can *just watch TV*. Or you can sit out on the front porch of your house if you live in California and look up at the sky and write a poem about light, which is what this is. The entire poem is about the effects of light coming into the eye.... I would try to visualize and make as concrete as possible what was going on with the blood spots as they moved across the surface of the eye and as the sunlight came in" (QN, 130–31).

The poem is twelve visualizations of these moving blood-spots. The effect of the light manifests itself primarily as movement, structure (charts, layers, espaliers, tracery, ladders, folds) and color (some twenty shades of the spectrum are catalogued).

T'ang Notebook

Orig. pub. *New Yorker* 59, no. 5 (21 March 1983): 40.
OSR, 54–6; WTTT, 102–4
Pattern: 5–3–2–2–3–3–4–4–7–5–3–3
Place: Laguna Beach

Wright on Wright: "I feel a great affinity, a great closeness to the poets of the T'ang Dynasty and their poems, as do many people, because they are wonderful poems. But there's something about landscape particularly. My poems are mostly landscapes, both interior and exterior, and sometimes projected interiors. Psycho-transference of one landscape to a different kind of landscape. One of the great contributions of the T'ang poets is to show us how to get personal emotions out of a real landscape. You transfer it to the landscape and then you get it back. I found that a very *simpatico* way of dealing with the emotional equivalents that one has to come to grips with in a poem and try to handle rather than having them handle you. If you can fix them and maneuver them and make them hard-edged and clear and visual the way the Chinese would, then you find the poet in the landscape and the emotion coming back out of it. This appealed to me tremendously and I have tried that, I think, all the way through my work" (*Halflife*, 132–3).

The present poem is an example of Wright's making the T'ang poets his own, his appropriation coming from *Three Hundred Poems of the T'ang Dynasty*, trans. Xuzhou Ding (Taipei: Wu Chou Chu Pan Shê, 1973). (The page numbers in what follows are to this edition.) Some of the language of Tu Fu's *Seeing Li Po in a Dream II* makes its way into section 9 ("heavenly net"[330]) and section 10 ("The fears that are borne on a little boat"[330]); of Ts'ên Ts'an's *A Song of White Snow in Farewell to Field-Clerk Wu Going Home* in section 10 ("The north wind rolls the white grasses and breaks them"[278]); and of Tu Fu's *A Night Abroad* in section 10 ("A light wind is rippling at the grassy shore" [310]). The "Lady of Light" in section 9 may have been picked up from Tu Fu's *Thoughts of Old Time I* (320). Other borrowings are more extensive, as in the following examples:

Section 1. "The fine clouds have opened and the River of Stars is gone, /A clear wind blows across the sky, and the moon widens its wave ... But so sad is this song of yours and so bitter your voice.... Stop your song, I beg you, and listen to mine, / A song that is utterly different from yours.... They might punish me with lashes in the dust of the street" (Han Yu, *On the Festival of the Moon to Sub-Official Zhang*, 44).

Section 2. "How gladly I would seek a mountain / If I had enough means to live as a recluse! / For I turn at last from serving the State / To the Eastern Woods Temple and to you, my master.... Like ashes of gold in a cinnamon-flame" (Meng Hao-jan, *From Ch'in Country to the Buddhist Priest Yuan*, 228).

Section 3. "That constellation, with its seven high stars, //is lifting its sword in the midnight" (Mêng Hao-jan, *General Kê-shu*, 236).

Section 4. "O pilgrim of fame, O seeker of profit, / Why not remain here and lengthen your days?" (Ts'uêi Hao, *Passing through Hua-Yin*, 294). "But I look toward home, and the twilight grows dark / With a mist of grief on the river waves" (Ts'uêi Hao, *The Yellow Crane Terrace*, 294).

Section 5. "The low wet clouds move faster than you do / Along the wall toward the cold moon" (Ts'uêi T'u, *A Solitary Wildgoose*, 298). "All night I ask what time it is" (Tu Fu, *A Night-Vigil in the Left Court of the Palace*, 304).

Section 6. "Stories of passion make sweet dust, / Calm water, grasses unconcerned. / At sunset, when birds cry in the wind, / Petals are falling like a girl's robe long ago" (Tu Mu, *The Garden of the Golden Valley*, 368).

Section 8. "The moon goes down behind a ruined fort, / Leaving star-clusters above an old gate.... / There are shivering birds and withering grasses, / Whichever way I turn my face" (Ssŭ-k'ung Shu, *To a Friend Bound North after the Rebellion*, 276).

Section 11. "When the mind is exalted, the body is lightened / And feels as if it could float in the wind" (Wêi Ying-wu, *Entertaining Literary Men in My Official Residence on a Rainy Day*, 426). "I hear the bell tolling between me and sleep" (Wêi Ying-wu, *Mooring at Twilight in Yû-yi District*, 430).

Section 12. "Over the wide river-lands flies an egret. / Can you guess why I sail, like an ancient wise lover, / Through the misty Five Lakes, forgetting words?" (Wên T'ing-yun, *Near the Li-Chou Ferry*, 436). "Wildgeese fly down to an island of white weeds" (Wêi Ying-wu, *Mooring at Twilight in Yû-yi District*, 430).

Section 7, about the poet's discovering a spider and a bird settling in for the night, contains no allusions to or quotations from the T'ang poets. Otherwise, Wright has improvised on the language of ten T'ang poets, appropriating their language of landscape by a process he calls "psycho-transference."

p. 102, l. 10. *dog* = Canis Major, the Great Dog, containing Sirius, the dog star.

Arkansas Traveller

Orig. pub. *New Yorker* 60, no. 1 (27 February 1984): 46–7.
OSR, 59–62; WTTT, 105–7
Pattern: 10–25–3–14–13–5
Time: Flashback to 1945
Place: Arkansas

In section 1 (p. 105) the description of the people on an Arkansas River sandbar is from a photograph of Wright's grandfather, Moorehead Wright (1872–1945), and others. Wright refers to his grandfather later as "my look-alike" (p. 107, l. 2). The people in the photo are described against an imagined backdrop of a vesper choir of frogs (the basses) and insects (the sopranos) that emerge from "the vaulted gum trees into the stained glass of the sky."

Section 2 (pp. 105–6) contrasts a 1952 scene from Wright's time at Christ School, an Episcopal boarding school where he completed his last two years of high school, with a scene from ninety-five years earlier when his great-grandfather arrived in Arkansas. In the first scene Wright recalls the words of a drunken classmate, sixteen-year-old Ellison Smythe, who had awakened in "the back seat of an Oldsmobile 88" to ask, "Where are we?"

Charles F. Penzel (1840–1906), from whom Wright takes his middle name, is the "Arkansas traveler." A descendant of minor Bohemian nobility, he had emigrated—also at age sixteen—from "the archduchy of Upper Austria," soon after found himself fighting for the Confederacy in the Civil War, was wounded at the Battle of Chickamauga, twice captured and imprisoned at Rock Island, a swampy island on the Mississippi. The passages in italics and some of the other material about Penzel in this section are drawn from his letters about the move to Arkansas in the mid-nineteenth century and from his obituary. (Charles F. Penzel later appears in Wright's *My Own Little Civil War*, in BY, 65).

Charles F. Penzel also asks, in effect, the same question asked by Ellison Smythe, "Where are we?" The passage from Penzel's letter indicates that he is not convinced that being sent to Arkansas "was such a great blessing."

p. 105, l. 12. *Ellison Smythe*. A classmate of Wright's at Christ School, Arden, North Carolina. They were both coaches of the "Brat" football team, the level below junior varsity, and they both graduated in 1953. Wright has taken a bit of poetic license with the surname, which was Smyth. For Wright's own account of his years at Christ School, see *QN*, 4–10.

p. 106, l. 13. *began his career*. After the Civil War, Charles F. Penzel returned to Little Rock, where he founded Little Rock's German National Bank and later held a position with the Guaranty Trust Company in Little Rock. He owned a grocery company, served as president of the Exchange National Bank and as the chairman of the board of trustees of Arkansas College (now Lyon) from 1899 to 1901. As a trustee, he contributed financially to the college, making several donations to cover salary shortfalls and other debts. During the national bank crisis of 1883 Penzel was among those who carried a large amount of gold and cash into the First National Bank to prove the solvency of the bank and thus to prevent depositors and speculators from withdrawing their funds.

Section 3 (p. 106). Each of the end-stopped lines in this tercet appears to be entirely discontinuous with the others. Still, the suggestion is that religious beliefs (as in the miracle of the first line) are "intricate catechisms of desire" only—longings that are not fulfilled by studying the night-time landscape, where the stars plunge "down the wrong side of the sky."

Section 4 (pp. 106–7). Here we return to the "Arkansas traveller," this time the young Wright on his summer visits to his grandparents' home Little Rock where he recalls the daily monk-like rituals that gave evidence of his childhood and the night-time ritual of trying to count the fireflies after the lights were turned off. These trips occurred before 1945, the year his grandfather died. The concluding two lines are presumably his grandfather's advice about the importance of devotion, in the sense of fidelity, affection, and loyalty. The grandfather, Moorehead Wright, was also an "Arkansas traveller," having migrated to Arkansas from North Carolina.

p. 107, l. 2. *my grandfather*. Moorehead Wright (1872–1945) was president of the Union Trust Company of Little Rock.

Section 5 (p. 107). The story of young Wright's summer sojourn in Little Rock continues with the account of rising early to play golf with his grandfather and of going to sleep on the porch in the evening, the frog and insect sounds humming in his ears.

Section 6 (p. 107). The concluding section is a commentary on the poet's having resurrected through memory his grandparents Wright and his great-grandfather Penzel: "To speak of the dead is to make them live again." This is an act of devotion. But then the poet unties himself from his past, letting "it rise away from me like a balloon" until it becomes small and then disappears altogether. He has revisited these Arkansas travellers through memory, brought them to life, and then released himself from them. Having untied the knots that have attached him to the past, he is now free to move on.

To Giacomo Leopardi in the Sky

Orig. pub. *Field* 28 (Spring 1983): 40–4.
OSR, 63–7; WTTT, 108–12
Pattern: Variable (14 stanzas—2 ll. to 12 ll.)
Time: July–August
Place: California, Montana

This poem is a one-way conversation with Leopardi (1798–1837), the great nineteenth-century poet, philosopher, and scholar, who is addressed familiarly in the second person. The conversation is continued over the course of almost a month (July 17–August 15), beginning on the deck of Wright's house in Laguna Beach and concluding at his Montana cabin under the shadow of Mt. Caribou. Leopardi is "on the other side of the sky," sometimes "hiding behind the noon light," sometimes visible through the clouds, sometimes floating behind the stars. While he is occasionally glimpsed (the poet speaks of seeing his face), Leopardi's location is indeterminate: he may even be administering the Eucharist in another solar system: "if you housel elsewhere a different sun." Leopardi, who represents the spirit of poetry, is Wright's soul mate: "You make me bitter for being so much like you." Leopardi's desire was to escape "from the grief of being here" into the immense spaces of the cosmos, and yet at the same time, the poet projects onto his hero an affection for the world of the ten thousand things: "You'd like it on this side, I think." Thus, we have a desire for spiritual communion ("It's the mind ... / That bears us up and shines a light in our eyes") and at the same time an unwillingness to abandon the plenitude of the physical world.

The main thrust of the poem is Wright's desire to communicate with his Italian precursor. The poem begins and ends with injunctions about communication: "Listen to what these words say, from one who remembers you" and "Think of me now and then." Communication is the means of cementing a community together, and one of the central symbols of community is communion—an icon of unity. The reference to the Eucharist in section 1 becomes a primary metaphor for the union between Wright and Leopardi. Wright in fact uses the metaphor in his reply to an interviewer about the poem: "When I talk to Giacomo Leopardi, for example, it's more of a way of paying tribute to him as a writer, and what his writings have meant to me. Not too much feedback, either, as you might expect. I suppose there is some sense of retrieval going on in other cases, dredging the waters of memory, as it were, for those I once actually knew, as opposed to someone whom I only admired but never knew. But poetry has always been, on one level, a communion with the dead, hasn't it? One often writes to impress them, to sing to them, to let them know you're around, if nothing else. Besides, as I said once before, they've got all the answers, don't they? Poetry so often rises out of previous poetry, rather like new vegetation out of old vegetation, enriched and informed by what's dead. So in that way, we're always in a constant communion, eucharistically, with the dead" (QN, 170).

As for making poetry out of other poetry, Wright embeds various passages from Leopardi's poems into nine of the fourteen sections. "[Y]ou're part of my parts of speech," writes the poet. The borrowings, translations, and mistranslations, which flow in and out of Wright's speculations and descriptions of the landscape, are in the notes that follow.

p. 108, ll. 1–6. *If you are become ... remembers you.* "If you are one of those / eternal ideas, refused the vesture / of bodily form by eternal wisdom, / along with the submission / of the pains of life foredoomed in fragile frames; / or if your home is in another earth / mid the supernal whirl of countless worlds, / illumined by a nearby star more splendent / than the sun, and if you breathe a kinder ether; / from down here where our years are ominous / and brief, receive this hymn from an unknown adorer" (Giacomo Leopardi, *To His Lady*, in *Poems*, trans. Jean-Pierre Barricelli [New York: Las Americas Publishing Co., 1963], 67).

p. 108, ll. 8–15. *Looking out ... sure water.* "This lonely knoll was ever dear to me / and this hedgerow that hides from view / so large a part of the remote horizon. / But as I sit and gaze my thought conceives / interminable spaces lying beyond / and supernatural silences / and profoundest calm, until my heart / almost becomes dismayed. And as I hear / the wind come rustling through these leaves, / I find myself comparing to this voice / that infinite silence: and I recall eternity / and all the ages that are dead / and the living presence and its sounds. And so / in this immensity my thought is drowned: / and in this sea is foundering sweet to me" (Giacomo Leopardi, *The Infinite*, ibid., 35).

p. 108, ll. 16–19. *Whenever I see you ... so much like you.* "Now I shall praise it ever, when I see you / floating through the clouds, or when, / serene sovereign of the ethereal fields / you look down on this mournful human site. / You will often see me wander through the woods / and by the verdant banks, mute and solitary, / or sit upon the grass, content enough, / if only heart and breath be left for me to sigh" (Giacomo Leopardi, *The Solitary Life*, ibid., 49).

p. 108, l. 20. *You make me bitter ... like you.* "Alas, how similar / your manner is to mine! ... so close a kin to youth, / bitter sigh of our autumnal days" (Giacomo Leopardi, *The Solitary Thrush*, ibid., 87).

p. 109, l. 1. *picture.* The 1959 photograph is of the Pietra bridge over the River Adige.

p. 109, l. 4. *What purpose ... my course?* "tell me: what purpose / has my brief drifting, / or your immortal course" (Giacomo Leopardi, *Night Song of a Wandering Asian Shepherd*, ibid., 95).

p. 109, l. 5–7. *You try to erase ... your sighs.* "Forever rest. You throbbed / enough. There is no thing at all that can be worth / your stirrings, nor is earth in any way deserving / of your sighs" (Giacomo Leopardi, *To Himself*, ibid., 115).

p. 109, l. 8. *Never to see ... joy.* "Never to see the light, / I think, were best" (Giacomo Leopardi, *On an Ancient Sepulchral Bas-Relief*, ibid., 125).
p. 109, l. 10–12. *I know ... waits for you.* "If you are one of those / eternal ideas, refused the vesture / of bodily form by eternal wisdom ... from down here where our years are ominous / and brief, receive this hymn from an unknown adorer" (Giacomo Leopardi, *To His Lady*, ibid., 67).
p. 110, ll. 5–6. *So frail ... paradise.* "but if one discord tone / assails the ear / such paradise that moment turns to naught. / O human nature, how / if frail and vile throughout, / if dust and shade, can you feel with such loftiness" (Giacomo Leopardi, *On the Portrait of a Fair Lady*, ibid., 135).
p. 110, l. 13. *Noon ... sky.* "... you will not long remain / thus orphaned, for soon on the other side / you will see the sky / with dawning rise of morn grow nearly white" (Giacomo Leopardi, *The Setting of the Moon*, ibid., 139).
p. 111, l. 6. *Teresa.* Countess Teresa Malvezzi di Medici, who was the object of Leopardi's affection until he forced a break.
p. 111, ll. 16–19. *You did ... wrong flesh.* "How many imaginings, and mad ones too, / your bright mien and your companion stars / more than once engendered in my thoughts, / when quiet on the greensward I would sit, / to pass the time of evening watching / the sky ... / What boundless thoughts, what gentle dreams the sight / of that far sea aroused within me, / and those blue mountains I discern from here, / which I thought to cross some day, divining / my future life in mystic worlds and mystic bliss! / Ignorant of my fate, how many times / I should have exchanged most willingly / this barren, sorry life of mine for death" (Giacomo Leopardi, *Memories*, in *Poems*, 73).
p. 111, l. 23. *And 1,700 miles.* Scene change from California to Montana.
Wright's note (*WTTT*, 231): "*Giacomo Leopardi*, tr. Jean-Pierre Barricelli: Las Americas Publishing Co., 1963: 'L'Infinito' [*The Infinite*], 'La vita solitaria' [*The Solitary Life*], 'Alla sua donna' [*To His Lady*], 'Le ricordanze' [*Memories*], 'Il passero solitario' [*The Solitary Thrush*], 'Canto notturno d'un pastore errante nell'Asia' [*Night Song of a Wandering Asian Shepherd*], 'A se stesso' [*To Himself*], 'Sopra un basso rilievo antico sepolcrale' [*On an Ancient Sepulchral Bas-Relief*], 'Sopra il ritratto di una bella donna' [*On the Portrait of a Fair Lady*], 'Il tramonto della luna' [*The Setting of the Moon*].

Looking at Pictures

Orig. pub. *Illuminations* 1 (Spring 1983): 4–5; rpt. in *Poetry East* 13–14 (Spring–Summer 1984): 74–5), with Wright's comments on the poem, p. 76.
OSR, 68–9; WTTT, 113–14
Pattern: 4–6–5–5–3–5–3–3–5–4
Place: Charlottesville study

The poet has come to his room to look once again at the photographs and reproductions of paintings that he has pinned to the wall on both sides of the room. They represent, he says, "all I've thought most beautiful / In the natural world." Some of the images, however, are from the artificial world: the calligraphy of the Koran, the tambourine of Fra Angelico's angel, Marc Rothko's *Red Ochre Black on Red*, St. George's banner, Cézanne's *Château Noir*, and the Cycladic flute player. The poet would like to become one with the images before him, entering their "tired bodies." The Rothko painting, for example, rouses the poet's desire to sink through the canvas "flat on my back / Endlessly down into nothingness." But he postpones that disappearance indefinitely, because he has other images to catalogue. There are twenty-one altogether, and they speak only to the eye. He cannot hear the music of the angel's tambourine or the speech of the fathers in riding boots or Gabriel's annunciation to Mary.

The process of moving from one image to another is "synaptical": the poet jumps from image to image, and whatever connections there are between them are left hanging in the gap. "Art," says Wright, "tends toward the certainty of making connections. The artist's job is to keep things apart, allowing the synapses to speak" (*Profile*, 48). Wright does, however, deduce one principle from having re-viewed the images on his walls: as we walk "in cadence into the past," "We stare at the backs of our own heads continually." This means that as we journey backward, we discover ourselves in what we see in front of us. And most of what the poet sees is religious in its subject matter: St Francis (twice), the Virgin Mary (twice), the Koran, the expulsion from paradise, Fra Angelico's *Angel Playing a Tambourine*, the Pope's hunting party, St. George, the devouring devil, the Annunciation, St. Anne, and Ignatius Loyola.

For a reproduction of some of the images above the poet's writing desk, see the "note" on p. 75 of OSR.

p. 113, ll. 7–8. *Verse of Light.* "God is the light of heaven and earth: the similitude of his light is as a niche in a wall, wherein a lamp is placed, and the lamp enclosed in a case of glass; the glass appears as it were a shining star. It is lighted with the oil of a blessed tree, an olive neither of the east, nor of the west; it wanted little but that the oil thereof would give light, although no fire touched it. This is light added unto light: God will direct unto his light whom he pleaseth. God propoundeth parables unto men; for God knoweth all things" (Koran, Surîh 24:35, trans. George Sale).

p. 114, l. 14. *suicides.* See note to p. 18, l. 8, above. In Wright's case, only one of his great-grandfathers committed suicide.

California Dreaming

Orig. pub. *Paris Review* 25 (Winter 1983): 88–91.
OSR, 70–3; WTTT, 115–18
Pattern: 5–6–6–11–12–8–7–10–5
Time: October–December
Place: Laguna Beach

Title: *California Dreaming* is the title of a pop song released by The Mamas and the Poppas in 1965. It has also appeared on albums by The Beach Boys and a number of other recording artists.

In 1988 Wright said to an interviewer, "Not long ago I was trying to do a Glenn Gould fugue-like little poem and I had somebody humming in it, just like Glenn Gould does in all his recordings" (Clark, 13). Although the word "hum" appears in Wright's poetry as early as 1972, his only published poem that has "someone humming" in it is *California Dreaming*. This is apparently the poem referred to. In any event, it does have a fugue-like structure insofar as it has a statement and exposition of a single subject or theme (light) and an answer to the subject (the poet's ambivalent feelings about the place in which he finds himself).

Light, with all of its symbolic connotations, is a recurrent theme in Wright's poetry. Here it is a central image in each of the eight sections that lead up to the goodbye to California in the coda:

1. The "net of splendor" (L. *splendere*, to shine). "We shine in our distant chambers, we are golden."
2. The "October sun"; "the Sunday prayer-light"; the "slow sparks of the west"
3. The "ridge of lights"
4. The "little rainfall of light"; the "shining" honey bee wrapped in the spider's web
5. The "gold lamé of the moon"
6. The "Sunflick" of morning; "We rise and fall like the sun"
7. The "Sun like a Valium disc"
8. The "setting sun"; "Christmas lights"

As a counterpoint or "answer" to the subject are various expressions of the poet's alienation, disappointment, and bewilderment. In section 1 he feels separated ("We are not brethren") and disaffected ("We are another nation"). His "shining" is projected into some future time and place. In section 2 he senses that the "idea of God" is on the other side of the drugged Pacific: his body is "Rinsed in the Sunday prayer-light, draining away / Into the undercoating and slow sparks of the west." In section 3, he expresses his disillusionment with the ridge lights he has been staring at for six years, and the environment (the "fallen" clouds and the hot Santa Ana winds) is disheartening and unpleasant. In section 4, the imitative counterpoint is the poet's anxious suspicion that there may be no anagogic meaning and "no ladder to Paradise // but the smooth handholds of the rib cage." The "answer" to light in section 5 is the direct self-judgment, "I ... wonder just what in the hell I'm doing out here / So many thousands of miles away from what I know best." In section 6, it is the inability to answer the question "how we should live our lives in this world"; in section 7, the absence of a genuine Muse; and in 8, the inability to be part of an authentic community.

Wright left California for Virginia in 1983, and *California Dreaming*, published the same year, is his farewell song to Laguna Beach. The speaker in the popular song finds himself on a dreary winter day longing for southern California where he would be "safe and warm." The coda of the poem, however, inverts this wish: the California world is falling away from the poet—"taken away by the wind to forgetfulness." If people are always dreaming of California, the poet is not one of them. He strikes out for a commonwealth *on the other side* of the country where he can write about what he knows best. And this, as he says in section 5, "is the little thing. / It sits on the far side of the simile, // the like that's like the like." The California landscape is an imitation of an imitation, twice removed from the Platonic Idea.

p. 116, l. 13. *Marine base*. The El Toro Marine Corps Air Station, twelve miles northeast of Laguna Beach.

p. 116, ll. 19–20. *Point Conception and Avalon*. Point Conception: the "Cape of California" where the coast turns from east/west to north/south at the northernmost tip of the Santa Barbara Channel. Avalon: a picturesque town on Catalina Island in Los Angeles County.

CHAPTER 6

Zone Journals (1988) and Xionia (1990)

Zone Journals

Cover art: Detail from an untitled diptych by Cy Twombly (1981).

"[A] zone, a region south of the past that lies at the mythic expanse of light, and which we more often talk of and then turn away from than journey through" (*Quarter Notes*, 11).

Wright on Wright: "*Zone Journals* is about sacred places. Sacred places, language and landscape, and how they coexist in each other, and speak for, and to, each other. The two primary sacred places in the book are the Long Island of the Holston River in Kingsport, Tennessee, where I grew up, sacred ceremonial ground of the Cherokee nation, and northern Italy, especially the Veneto region, where I first began writing poems. The center, the exact center of the *Journals*, takes place during a two-month period spent in a farmhouse outside Padua in the summer of 1985, with my family and Mark Strand and his family. The center of the center, as it were, is a description of a room of Renaissance frescoes in the Palazzo Schifanoia in Ferrara. They depict the tripartite levels of existence—everyday life, allegorical life, and ideal life. It's a concept that appeals to me" (QN, 97).

Wright on Wright, in response to an interviewer's question about whether the poems in *Zone Journals* were not more expansive and relaxed that his earlier sequences: "I think so. They are verse journals, remember, and are greatly concerned with line as well as story line. They are, I suppose, in as loose a form as I can work with and still work in lines. As opposed to sentences, I mean. One of the purposes of the journals was to work with a line that was pushed as hard as I could push it toward prose, conversational in tone but with the rhythmic concentration of what we call poetry. The journals' very nature, by definition, makes them more explicit. They are more didactic than other poems, perhaps, and more emotionally open. One tends to speak one's mind more nakedly in journals. One tends to say what is really troubling one's sleep. At the same time, of course, they *are* poems, with all a poem's avoidances and exclusions. Still, the word 'journal' is operative, and allows more quotidiana in, and the speculations such dailiness leads to" (QN, 106).

Yard Journal

Orig. pub. in *Five Journals* (New York: Red Ozier Press, 1986). Also reproduced in an artist book by David Freed, along with six color etchings; 10 x 12 x ¾-inch format; edition: 30. ZJ, 3–5; WTTT, 121–3
Pattern: 10 x 6

6. Zone Journals (1988) and Xionia (1990)

Time: Spring
Place: Charlottesville

Yard Journal continues Wright's longstanding reflection on the relation of the visible world, the world of the ten thousand things, to the invisible one. The dialectic of the seen and the unseen is one of the many oppositions omnipresent in his poems: the "minute particular" and the cosmos, dark and light, subject and object, the human and the divine, life and death, *mythos* and *dianoia*, presence and absence, emptiness and plenitude, *katabasis* and *anabasis*, the abstract and the concrete, the relative and the absolute, stasis and movement, the ephemeral and the enduring, among numerous others. In the present poem the dialectic is between both the excluded and the included and the visible and the invisible. What is visible and included are all the striking images of the rainy afternoon world in section 1 and those perceived in the deep dusk of section 2. But one image is excluded: "Somewhere out there an image is biding its time, / Burning like Abraham in the cold, swept // expanses of heaven, / Waiting to take me in and complete my equation."

This anticipates the reflection on exclusion at the center of the poem: "Exclusion's the secret: what's missing is what appears / Most visible to the eye: // the more luminous anything is, / The more it subtracts what's around it, / Peeling away the burned skin of the world // making the unseen seen." The idea that what is excluded is "Most visible to the eye" is counter-intuitive: ordinarily we would say that excluding things makes them invisible. But the lines that follow reveal that the paradox is a matter of what Wright calls elsewhere "spatial negation" and "negative transcendence." Spatial negation is what we find in painters like Morandi and Mondrian, "a sort of white hole that has a kinetic draw to it that the lines of the poem float on and resist" (QN, 173). But it is more than simply the empty spaces created by the lines on the page, which in the journal form tend to become more expansive. The luminous unseen has metaphysical import. As Wright replied to an interviewer, "Keeping things apart, leaving things out, blank canvas, blank page spaces, not quite completing what is obvious, completing what is not obvious, the idea of knowing what comes next and then declining to say it, or fill it in, determination to keep the circle from touching—one works, as I once said, in the synapse, in the electric field between what is and what isn't, between the beginning and the beginning. It's not so much a desire to keep things tentative as one to keep things from touching, from becoming complete and becoming final. One wants to feel the kinetics, the possibilities, always the what's-left-to-do. If you know what it is, and you know where it goes, the longer you can keep it out, the deeper it will go once you put it in. Exile's the ultimate synapse—from there you can go anywhere. Cézanne, Matisse, Morandi, and Mondrian— negative transcendence, what you take out is stronger than what you put in. There are no Gods, there are only saints" (Spiegelman, 121). This, as Wright says in *Yard Journal*, is the "architecture of absence." Subtraction, as he writes in a later poem, drawing on Lao Tzu, leads to wisdom (*A Journal of One Significant Landscape*, in WTTT, 198), which, like love in section 2, is another of those abstractions that matter.

The *via negativa* requires descent, and the Dante simile that animates the final section embodies a wish to mount the bumblebee and go down into the "underlight" and the "pit / At the end of every road."

p. 122, ll. 21–3. The simile here derives from canto 17 of Dante's *Inferno*, at the beginning of which Geryon, the monster, lands on the brink of the abyss, his tail hanging over the side. His face is that of an innocent man, but his body is half-reptile, half-hairy beast, with a scorpion's stinger at the end of his tail. After encountering the usurers, Virgil and Dante mount Geryon, who takes them to the bottom of the pit near the eighth circle of hell (Malebolge), where in the first *bolgia* of circle 8 they begin to encounter the initial company of sinners who have committed fraud.

A Journal of English Days

Orig. pub. *Field*, 30 (Spring 1984): 5–15; rpt. in *Five Journals*.
ZJ, 6–18; WTTT, 124–34
Pattern: "September" 10-8-6; "October" 6-4-4-5-6-11-11-11-14-4-14-4-4; "November" 6-2-4-2-4-3-5-5-5-10-8-6-3-3-5-5-5-5-5; "December" 7-7-10
Time: September–December 1983
Place: England

In most of Wright's poetry from the mid-1970s on, his descriptions of the external landscape are balanced by reflections that come from the inner life—psychological, philosophical, and religious speculations or meditations that are most often triggered by the exterior landscape. In the present poem the latter are almost completely absent. There is a brief digression on the difference between spirit and flesh in part 1 (p. 125), the observation that "Nothing is ever finished" in part 2 (p. 127), and the brief excursus on homesickness and the even briefer one on desire and loneliness in part 3 (pp. 13, 132), but otherwise the interior "landscape" gives way almost completely to the exterior.

The poem originates from a four-month trip to England in 1983. Outside of excursions to Warwickshire, the Lake Country, Oxfordshire, Surrey, and West Sussex, the walking tour takes place in London. Here and there the tour becomes a memorial walk, as Wright recalls the birth- or death-days of Sir Philip Sidney (p. 126), Paul Cézanne (p. 127), Ezra Pound (p. 128), and John Keats (p. 129). The poet also records a half-dozen sounds he hears during the four months, but the journal is almost completely a recreation of what he sees, done with typically inimitable originality.

Part 1. September (pp. 124–5). The travelogue begins on Kensington Church Walk at St. Mary Abbots, a Victorian Gothic church, serving the parish of Kensington. While a funeral is going on inside, the poet seats himself on a bench and wonders what it must have been like years before when Ezra Pound left Venice for London in 1908, the year that saw the publication of his *A Lume Spento* and *A Quinzaine for this Yule*. Pound, who lived for a time near Kensington and Church Walk, had "a dead galaxy / Set to go off in crystal inside his head." This is a foreshadowing of the crystal image that would eventually enter the *Cantos*–from "the Great Crystal" of *Canto XCI* through "the great ball of crystal" of *Canto CXVI*. In section 2 the poet returns of St. Mary Abbots a week later to find someone meditating on the bench he had earlier occupied. The late September day is invested with a mystical aura, leading him to conclude that the "difference between the spirit and the flesh / is finite"—an example of what he will later call "the immanence of infinitude" (CM, 211).

p. 124, l. 12. *Ancient Lights*. In English property law, the right of a building or house owner to the light received from and through his windows.

Part 2. October (pp. 125–9). Here the scene shifts to Warwick Castle, on the banks of the Avon in Warwickshire, more particularly to its St. Mary chapel and the dungeon below. Here lie the tombs of Fulke Greville, the Elizabethan poet, dramatist, and statesman, and others, who are not really his "kinsmen" but various Earls of Warwick: Thomas Beauchamp, Robert Dudley, Richard Beauchamp, et al. Fulke Greville, friend of Queen Elizabeth I and Sir Philip Sidney, had been presented the dilapidated Warwick Castle in 1604. Wright notes punningly that that for centuries now Fulke Greville, sealed up in his stone tomb, has had his "passions heeled." Later in the day the poet emerges from the castle dungeon, the rainy day offering a strange consolation after he has seen the instruments of torture below, and he has the curious experience of the castle having slightly risen and settled again.

Section 2 finds the poet back in the Kensington and Chelsea borough of London—in

Lennox Gardens—where during the late rainy afternoon he has a vision of Charon poling his way across the Thames. He returns to Lennox Gardens on October 17, Sir Philip Sidney's birthday, and watches nightfall approach. In section 3, five days later, at a place unspecified but apparently in Kensington, the colors and patterns of the leaves remind the poet of Cézanne, whose death-day it happens to be. This association, along with the moon that has appeared but which Cézanne "never painted," triggers the memory of a trip in 1968 to Puyricard, where Cézanne had a studio. Cézanne, he concludes, "made us see differently."

The amble in section 4 appears to begin in the Lennox Gardens area. The direction is generally north and slightly west through Knightsbridge, across Kensington Road (the "main road") into Hyde Park and, past the Brompton Oratory, then to the Serpentine. On the return, the poet goes west into Kensington Gardens, ending up in a "chestnut and beech grove." Unwilling to retrace his steps, he is reminded that it is Pound's birthday and recalls Pound's remark about the English mind being "cold soup" and about his recollection (in *Canto LXXX*) of old friends and Christmas in the country. The "late grass green neon" may cast a glance at the "grass-blade" and the "green elegance" at the end of *Canto LXXX*, where Pound also mentions the Serpentine, the curved pond in Hyde Park near Kensington.

Section 5 begins the next day (Halloween) with Hopkins's judgment that Keats was too possessed by a dreamer's sense of fairyland luxuriousness, but the poet counters, "what other early interest / Can one assume" if he was born, as Keats was, on Halloween? The closing imagery is from the account of Keats's close friend Charles Brown, who reported that in Rome on 3 February 1820 he saw Keats cough up blood. He advised Keats to go to bed, at which point Keats asked for a candle. After looking at the drop of blood, he said, "I know the colour of that blood;—it is arterial blood;—I cannot be deceived in that colour;—that drop of blood is my death-warrant;—I must die" (Charles Armitage Brown, *The Life of John Keats*, ed. by Dorothy Hyde Bodurtha and Willard Bissell Pope [London: Oxford University Press, 1937], 64). Keats died twenty days later in the arms of his painter-friend Joseph Severn.

p. 125, l. 21. *Who was friend ... Sidney*. Fulke Greville's tomb is inscribed with the epitaph he composed for himself: "Folk Grevill Servant to Queene Elizabeth Conceller to King James Frend to Sir Philip Sidney. Trophaeum Peccati." Fulke Greville, Lord Brooke (1554–1628) was a statesman, man of affairs, patron of letters, a poet, and biographer of Sidney during the reign of Elizabeth I. He was murdered by his servant Ralph Haywood, who thought he had been omitted from his master's will.

p. 126, l 3. For images of the rib-caged and lung-like torture devices, see http://good-times.webshots.com/photo/ 2013949620080491467fzGrhY and http://good-times.webshots.com/photo/2712989910080491467OBpUqg

p. 126, l. 17. Charon required payment of a coin from the dead before he ferried them across the Acheron.

p. 126, l. 22. *Sir Philip*. Sir Philip Sidney died in 1586 at age 32. He had been in the Netherlands participating in a skirmish against the Spanish at Zutphen, where he was wounded in the thigh by a musket blast. He died twenty-two days later.

p. 127, l. 20. *Godfrey*. David Godfrey, Canadian novelist, with whom Wright stayed on his trip to France. Godfrey, and ardent nationalist, won the Governor-General's Award for his novel *The New Ancestors*. With Denis Lee he founded House of Anansi Press, the publisher of Wright's *The Dream Animal* (1968).

p. 128, l. 4. *Oratory*. The Brompton Oratory, the first new Roman Catholic Church to be built in London after the Reformation, is just to the east of the Victoria and Albert Museum.

p. 129, ll. 3–4. *Pisa ... dead friends*. In 1943 Pound was arrested by the U.S. Army, charged with treason for his radio broadcasts, and imprisoned in Pisa in a metal cage, where he was exposed to the elements for six months. For Pound's memories of old friends and Christmases, see *Canto LXXX* (*Cantos*, 535).

p. 129, ll. 10–13. *Hopkins ... active thought*. "Since I last wrote I have reread Keats a little and the force of your criticism on him struck me more than it did. It is impossible not to feel with weariness how his verse is at every turn abandoning itself to an unmanly and enervating luxury. It appears to me that he had something like 'O for a life of impressions instead of thoughts.' ... He lived in mythology and fairyland the life of a dreamer" (Gerard Manley Hopkins, letter to Coventry Patmore, 6 May 1886, in *A Hopkins Reader*, ed. John Pick [New York: Oxford University Press, 1953], 166.

Part 3. November (pp. 129–33). An excursion to the Lake District is introduced by a phrase from one of Wordsworth's Lucy poems, *She Was a Phantom of Delight* (l. 24), in which the connection between Lucy as "Woman" and "Spirit" is, for Wordsworth, blurred. This is followed by a brief reflection on the difficulty of specifying the "line" that separates both states of human consciousness and those in the flux of the natural world. We are then transported to the megalith at Castlerigg, near Keswick in the heart of the Lake District. The stone circle there, consisting of thirty-eight un-hewn boulders of variable sizes and shapes, goes back five millennia. For the poet, Castlerigg is a sacred place ("Mouth-mark of the invisible"), where the air becomes "ecclesiastical smoke" and where, again, the lines that demark features of the landscape are "untraceable." In section 2 the excursion continues to Steeple Aston, a village outside Oxford, and the poet records a snippet from a local leaf-burner in a Norman churchyard, where Delia Johnson is buried. Winter approaches.

In section 3 we return to the Chelsea Embankment in London, where the colors remind the poet of a Whistler painting—"orange, / Tamarind, apricot // jade of the slate slip of the river." A remarkable description of the Thames follows. Section 4 returns us to where our tour began, at the Kensington Church Walk, and the poet declares his homesickness, except that "home" is an indeterminate place or time, unseen, unheard, and unremembered. The November sky is here and there like a Constable painting (the third artist called on to supply a figure for the landscape). In section 5 we accompany the poet on a Sunday train ride through southern England, where the damp landscape, joyless sounds of the trains, and the desolate faces of the people produce little but melancholy.

p. 130, l. 8. *silver Y moths*. So called because of a noticeable "Y" on each wing.
p. 130, l. 11. *Helvellyn and Thirlmere*. A mountain (3250 ft.) and lake in the Cumbrian Lake District.
p. 130, l. 20. *Steeple Aston*. A village outside of Oxford.
p. 131, l. 3. *God Knows His Own*. The epitaph on Delia Johnson's tomb.
p. 133, l. 4. *Redhill ... Haywards Heath*. Redhill is a town in Surrey. Haywards Heath is a town in the center of the Mid Sussex district in the county of West Sussex.

Part 4. December (pp. 133-4). December emerges from the landscape, affecting the poem's most extensive meditation: "How sweet to think that Nature is solvency, //that something empirically true / Lies just under the dead leaves / That will make us anchorites in the dark / Chambers of some celestial perpetuity—// nice to think that, / Given the bleak alternative, / Though it hasn't proved so before, // and won't now / No matter what things we scrape aside—/ God is an abstract noun." But perhaps God is a concrete noun: it is nice to believe that beneath the surface of the landscape's dead leaves we might, after our own deaths, retire to a life of religious seclusion in the chambers of some eternal heaven. This is an article of faith and hope, not something to be confirmed or disconfirmed by empirical proof. The "bleak alternative" is, of course, that death ends all.

The poem's coda is a flashback to the time of the poem's beginning. The poet and his wife are looking across the courtyard of the Victoria and Albert Museum at the bronze statue of the Buddha, and, staring at the Buddha, the poet has something like an out-of-body experience in which the "skin" of the world has become weightless. He observes that the process is an "emptying," like a balloon that is expelling all of its air, but it is occurring somewhere else. This is an example of what the Buddhists call *shunyata* (Sanskrit for "void" or "emptiness"). Another analogue is in what the author of the Book of Ecclesiastes says at the beginning of his long sermon: "vanity of vanities; all is vanity." He means that everything is full of emptiness, and "emptiness," as noted in the commentary for *Three Poems for the New Year*, is the root meaning of *vanitas*. The general movement here is katabatic: the leaves are falling on the Buddha, and the "world's skin" is "down drifting down / Through the faint hiss of eternity." We have, then, a kind of descent into the void. The imagery of the final three lines is too surreal to translate, but as the final accent falls on the "Buddha's eye," this is a moment of vision.

p. 134, l. 7. *Bronze Buddha*. This twenty-foot-high sculpture has been displayed in many different locations in the Victoria and Albert other than the courtyard. Presently it is on long-term loan to a Buddhist temple in Birmingham, England.

March Journal

Orig. pub. *Field* 31 (Fall 1984): 89–91; rpt. in *Five Journals*.
ZJ, 19–21; WTTT, 135–7
Pattern: 4-4-4-2-7-6-1-4-2-5-5-5-1
Place: Charlottesville

Wright on Wright: "Since part of the scaffolding of the *Journals* is process itself, and ideas about that process, I've been able, from time to time, to work those ideas into the texts themselves. It's especially apparent in March Journal" (QN, 110–11).

Ideas about three kinds of process are at work in the poem: the process of history or time, the process of nature, and the process of poetic art. The process of history is present in the allusions to the end of history—the Rapture (section 1) and eschatology (section 7).

The poet asks at the beginning, "What will we do?" when, after the Rapture, everyone has disappeared "Into the black hole of Somewhere Else"—Wright's version of the bottomless pit in Revelation 20:1. "After the first death is the second," says the poet, following the eschatological vision of the author of Revelation (20:15). But rather than a lake of fire (20:14) and a new heaven and a new earth (21:1), the poet sees the earth simply as a "turbulent rest, // a different bed," and the "little fire in the afterglow" is only an occasion "to warm your hands." Similarly, toward the end of the poem the poet asks, with a glance at T.S. Eliot, "How can we ... say that all quartets are eschatological" when we are confronted with the wonders of the natural cycle right before our eyes? This is a version of what some New Testament theologians call "realized eschatology," which dismisses theories of transhistorical phenomena and the end of time and in favor of the lasting legacy of the here and now.

The processes of nature are recreated in the "second wind" passage of section 3, in section 5, and in the first part of section 7, each of which presents the landscape as a site of dynamic energy. Nature as process is even implicit in the first part of section 3, with its recounting of the dissection of dogfish by Wright's son Luke.

The process of the poetic is presented in the four even-numbered sections. These brief (one- and two-line) interludes amount to a poetic testament about lineation, rhythm, structure, and form. The poetic line should be clear, clean, sharp, and incisive (section 2). Poetic rhythm should repeat and expand on the cadences from "the roots of the world," which are the patterns of sound present in the legacy of nature (section 3). Structure should resolve what Coleridge calls "opposite and discordant qualities," "[i]ts parts tight but the whole loose // and endlessly repetitious" (section 6). And, finally, form, because changeable, is finite, though in casting "an undestroyable hush over all things," it moves in the direction of the infinite and eternal (section 8).

p. 135, l. 16. *Power Putty*. A flexible silicone rubber that can be squeezed, stretched, and pulled for the purpose of strengthening the muscles in the fingers and hand.

A Journal of True Confessions

Orig. pub. *Verse* 3 (1985): 14–15; rpt. in *Five Journals*.
ZJ, 22–31; WTTT, 138–46
Pattern: Nine parts, indicated by dates: 15 July 1984 (4 × 6); 6 August 1984 (10 × 2); 25 August

1984 (8 × 3); 9 September 1984 (4–5–4); 25 September 1984 (4–4–5–4–4–3); 5 October 1984 (5–5–3); 19 October 1984 (8 × 3); 20 October 1984 (10 × 2); 3 November 1984 (8 × 3)
Time: Dated sections: July–November 1984, with flashbacks to Italy (1963)
Place: Puget Sound and the Strait of Juan de Faca; Laguna Beach, California; Prato, Tuscany; aboard ship in the Aegean Sea, out of Piraeus, Greece; Charlottesville; Rome

This poem, along with *March Journal* and *Night Journal*, was written during the time of Wright's holding an NEA grant. He calls A *Journal of True Confessions*, five months in the making, the "centerpiece" of *Zone Journals* (A *Millennium Arts Project*, rev. ed. [Washington, D.C.: National Endowment for the Arts, 1999], 90). Wright has said on several occasions that the one work in particular that influenced his own writing was St. Augustine's *Confessions* ("Book"; Davis, 191). The "true confessions" in the present poem are not a disclosure of shortcomings. Wright is using the word in its more general sense of autobiography as self-examination and self-revelation. Here we have eight episodes, some exterior, others interior, in Wright's *livre de bonne foy*.

Part 1. 15 July 1984 (pp. 138–9). The first vignette is set in the waters of the Pacific northwest near the Canadian border. Here Wright, who had been in Port Townsend, Washington, for the summer, is on a salmon fishing trip with two of his friends, Ray and Mark (Raymond Carver and Mark Strand). Their small boat bobs in and out among the larger fishing vessels. The excursion begins at daybreak and ends as darkness approaches in the Strait of Juan de Fuca, a strait connecting Puget Sound and the Pacific Ocean. The drifting and trolling and waiting throughout the day create the sense of a leisurely venture, but at the same time the account, carried along by fifteen present participles, is filled with a great deal of kinetic energy.

Part 2. 6 August 1984 (pp. 139–40). The poet has returned to Laguna Beach, where he lived and "lolled" for seventeen years, having left California for Virginia the year before. His poetic goal during this time was to try "to get the description right," and what he learned was something about presence in absence—"that what you see // both is and is not there, / The unseen bulking in from the edges of all things, / Changing the frame with its nothingness." He also learned about the importance of subtraction—that everything unessential to his verse had to be pared away. He learned, in other words, not to overwrite, but to "underlook." The last six lines of this section are evidence that the poet learned his lesson well: the nothingness in the frame of the description, once the turkey buzzards have made their exit, is "something quite small / And indistinct and palpable as a stain // of saint light on a choir stall." This anagrammatic saint-stain is an example of presence in absence.

Part 3. 25 August 1984 (pp. 140–1). This flashback is to 1960, the second year of Wright's army tour in Italy. On his forty-ninth birthday he and his army friend George Mancini are in Florence as the sun sets over Prato, a Tuscan town just to the north of Florence. Mancini is prattling about his writing ability, and then, as the sun sinks, he wishes Wright a happy birthday. The scene then changes to a cruise with Mancini on the Aegean six months later. The captain has his arm around the poet, who shortly ducks out, apparently because of the captain's approach, and returns to his room, where he and Mancini drink stingers.

Stanza 3 returns to the present, Wright's 1984 birthday. The poet stares at the night sky and reflects on his past and future: the experience in Italy was the starting point of his poetic career and it remains the starting point, and the future ("what's-to-come") remains as well, though now it is writ large ("What's-to-Come").

p. 140, l. 3. *stinger.* Typically, whiskey and soda, but drinks made from brandy, crème de menthe, and sometimes vodka are also called stingers.
p. 140, l. 10. *dog days, indeed, Fortunatus.* "Yes, these are the dog-days, Fortunatus" (W.H. Auden, *Under Sirius*, l. 1).

p. 140, l. 12. *Tell Laura I Love Her.* A popular teenage song of the 1960s.
p. 140, l. 16. *Piraeus.* A city south of Athens.
p. 140, l. 17. *Ungaretti.* Giuseppe Ungaretti (1888–1970), Italian poet, founder of the Hermetic movement. In this line Wright reverses his usual practice of putting the words of others in italics. "What?" is Mancini's question.
p. 140, l. 20. *called to horn.* Summoned.

Part 4. 9 September 1984 (p. 141). The scene changes to the Charlottesville back yard, where the poet is attentive to the sunlight and wind, and later, in the familiar and now darkened dwarf orchard, to the fruit trees, which "seem etched like a Dürer woodcut against the sky, / The odd fruit // burined in bas-relief." He expresses the hope that he can find the right words, and then enjoins his readers, in an echo of Whitman, to keep their ears open. Whitman says, in fourteen syllables, "If you want me again, look for me under your boot-soles" (*Song of Myself*, pt. 52, l. 10). Wright says, in thirteen syllables, "If you want to hear me, you'll have to listen again."

p. 141, l. 12. This is a seventeen-syllable *single* line: "through with joy" should be indented, as it is in ZJ.

Part 5. 25 September 1984 (pp. 141–2). "It's all such a matter of abstracts," says the poet in these stanzas of indeterminate setting, the abstracts being love, affection, and light in the first stanza and the poetic line in the sixth. The characteristics of the line are identified by still more abstractions: "special," "self-contained," "firm," and "intimate." The final features of the line are less abstract: it will be as precisely cut as a wood engraving ("carved") and free of all bombast ("as though whispered into the ear").

Between stanzas 1 and 6 is a *bricolage* of passages from the Book of Revelation, Ovid's *Metamorphoses*, and Dino Campana's *Orphic Songs*. The first comes from the salutation and inaugural vision of John of Patmos's *apokalypsis*: "Behold, he cometh with clouds; and every eye shall see him, and they [also] which pierced him: and all kindreds of the earth shall wail because of him" (Revelation 1:7). "Jesus Christ, who is the faithful witness, and the first begotten of the dead" (Revelation 1:5). "And his feet like unto fine brass, as if they burned in a furnace; and his voice as the sound of many waters" (Revelation 1:15).

This is followed by a description of the night sky, which is as dark as that blackness into which Pluto and his horse-drawn chariot descended after he had abducted Persephone and galloped down into Tartarus (*Metamorphoses*, bk. 5). Here Ovid's "world below" is used as a metaphor to account for the night sky's blackness. The Campana borrowing comes from Wright's own translation:

> Monte Filetto, 25 September—A nightingale sings in the limbs of the walnut tree. The hill is too beautiful against the too-blue sky. The river sings its own sweet selfsame song as best it can. It's been an hour now that I've watched the space below and the road halfway up the hill that leads there. Up here the hawks live. The fine summer rain patterned a fine tune on the walnut leaves. But the leaves of the acacia tree dear to the night submitted without a sound like a green shadow. The blue opens up between these two trees. The walnut stands in front of my room's window. At night it seems to gather all of the darkness up and curve its shadowy melody of leaves like a harvest of songs about its milky round and almost human trunk: the acacia knows how to outline itself like an illusion of smoke. The stars were pirouetting on the deserted hilltop. No one is coming down the street. I like to watch the empty countryside with its scattered trees from my balcony, the soul of solitude beaten out by the wind. Today when the wind and the whole landscape were so sweet after the rain I thought of the young ladies in de Maupassant and Jammes their pale oval faces inclined over the tapestries and engravings full of memories. The river takes up its lullaby again. I walk away. I look back at the window once more: the slope is a little golden painting among the quick cries of the hawks." (Dino Campana, *Orphic Songs*, trans. Charles Wright [Oberlin College: Field Translation Series 9, 1984], 65–6)

Wright leaves it to us to make connections among these texts. The three passages all have to do with the upper world: Christ coming in the clouds, the Ovidian darkness of the night sky, and Campana's romantic reverie about the "too-blue" and later the night sky. For Campana the upper world is not the "other world," but Wright's simile for the circling hawks—"lost angels against the painted paradise"—invests Campana's basically mimetic passage with an aura of religious myth.

Part 6. 5 October 1984 (pp. 142–3). The October landscape prompts the poet to reflect on the use of the line by the "great painters"—Morandi, Picasso, Cézanne, and Rothko, though Rothko's line "was no line at all," the transcendent fields of color of his late signature style embodying an empty melancholy, like the multiform "fields" of the Locust Avenue sky and the grass of the backyard.

p. 143, l. 8. *Locust Avenue*. Wright's home is on Locust Avenue in Charlottesville.

Part 7. 19 October 1984 (pp. 143–4). The poet recalls a discussion in Rome he had had nineteen years earlier with Desmond O'Grady, Irish poet and translator who had spent a number of years abroad in Rome and elsewhere. O'Grady had asked Wright where the cadence or measure was in his poetry, and Wright now explains that he has never ceased looking for it, cataloguing the places in the landscape he has sought it out—in the "musical shape of the afternoon," "the slice of sunlight," the flight of the mockingbird, in the angle of the afternoon light (an echo of Dickinson here), and in the "uncut grass" (an echo of Whitman). But, the poet confesses, however much we might have tried to get the measure right, "our lines seem such sad notes for the most part." Thus, he moves from "line" to "life," praying in a direct and passionate outburst to St. Francis Xavier, the great propagator of Christianity, to "hear my heart, / Give my life meaning, heal me and take me in." Here we have a confession in Augustine's sense. Augustine repeatedly asks the Lord to behold his heart, and twice in book 10 of the *Confessions* he prays for healing.

p. 143, l. 10. *Born one day later*. O'Grady was actually born two days later than Wright—27 August 1935.
p. 143, l. 12. *via dei Giubbonari*. The neighborhood where Wright lived during the second year of his Fulbright study.
p. 143, l. 16. *Largo*. The Largo Argentina, a square, with four Republican temples, to the east of the Campo dei Fiori.

Part 8. 20 October 1984 (pp. 144–5). The poet recounts two stories about Leonardo da Vinci, both from Giorgio Vasari's *Lives of the Artists*. As for the first story, which is filtered through Freud's retelling, the poet wonders what the release and descent of the wax figurines might have meant for those members of the "amber menagerie" itself. But the point of retelling both stories is found in the last two lines: both celebrate *homo lundens* and *homo faber*, along with the combination of beauty and fear that issue from the productions of each.

p. 144, ll. 10–14. *Freud*. "There (in Rome) he got a soft lump of wax, and made very delicate animals out of it, filled with air; when he blew into them they flew around, and when the air ran out they fell to the ground" (Sigmund Freud, drawing on Giorgio Vasari's account, in "Leonardo da Vinci and the Memory of His Childhood," in *The Freud Reader*, ed. Peter Gay [New York: Norton, 1989], 476).
p. 144, l. 15. *Like Li Po's poems downriver, downwind*. Cf. *Portrait of the Artist as Li Po*: "He [Li Po] would write his verses and float them, / Like paper boats, downstream // just to watch them drift away (*WTTT*, 34).
p. 144, l. 20–p. 145, l. 5. *Giorgio Vasari ... beauty and fear*. "When Leo was made Pope, Lionardo went to Rome with Duke Giuliano de' Medici, and knowing the Pope to be fond of philosophy, especially alchemy, he used to make little animals of a wax paste, which as he walked along he would fill with wind by blowing into them, and so make them fly in the air, until the wind being exhausted, they dropped to the ground. The vinedresser of the Belvedere having found a very strange lizard, Lionardo made some wings of the scales of other lizards and fastened them on its back with a mixture of quicksilver, so that they trembled when it walked; and having made for it eyes, horns, and a beard, he tamed it and kept it in a box, but all his friends to whom he showed it used to run away from fear" (Giorgio Vasari, "Lionardo da Vinci," *Lives of the Artists*, par. 18). Vasari will become a not infrequent source for Wright. See *A Journal of True Confessions* (*WTTT*, 144), *A Journal of One Significant Landscape* (*WTTT*, 195, 197), *To the Egyptian Mummy in the Etruscan Museum at Cortona* (*NB*, 49), and *Lives of the Artists* (*NB*, 114).

Part 9. 3 November 1984 (pp. 145–6). It is difficult for the poet to distinguish between form and function in the late fall landscape. In this final confession, he speaks about things unseen, about a song devolving into a vague "something," about an equally vague and vacant "what-comes-out," and about "nothing on everything." If these things could be specified, then the function of the landscape might emerge. But against these hazy abstractions, the poet offers at the beginning one of his typically fresh and precise descriptions of the fruit trees, tomato skins, and sweet woodruff, and, at the end, of the wind in the dogwood trees, with their "flamingoing berries and cupped leaves," along with the "odd stains / And melodramatic stutterings" of the yard, with its "crisp leftovers, // and gulled blooms in the rhododendrons, / Veneer, like hard wax, of nothing on everything." For the final note sounded here, Wright has Heidegger, who declaimed that "Nothing befalls on everything," on his side.

Night Journal

Orig. pub. *Field* 31 (Fall 1984): 92–4.
ZJ, 32–4; WTTT, 147–9
Pattern: 5–5–5–10–10–5–5–5

The opening poem by Issa (1763–1827), a Japanese haiku poet of the Edo period (1600–1868), is an elegy written on the first anniversary of the death of his daughter Sato from smallpox. The dew suggests the fragility and impermanence of life, and yet ... perhaps there is something beyond the grief and transience—and yet ... perhaps there is some consolation in the beauty of the dew-covered world. "Few words" indeed—only seven. Issa's haiku serves to announce the theme of the remaining seven stanzas—words.

The three words that "contain // all we know for sure of the next life" are "world of dew." The assertion moves in two directions. Our knowledge of the next life is as ephemeral as the dew, which comes and goes, "and yet," like Issa, we hold out for something permanent beyond what passes away. Or perhaps the three words are those following the colon—"Close your eyes"—in which case all we know for certain of the next life is a dark nothingness.

In stanza 3 the poet's words, which should be the black figure against the white ground of the page, "disappear when held up to the light," so that he sees only empty space, as in an over-exposed photograph. In stanza 4 the world of the ten thousand things cries out "Precisely nothing" because the words are not available, drying "behind the tongue" like "embolic sunsets." Similarly in stanzas 5 and 6, words drift away "to the nothingness / Behind them ... trailing their dark identities" and are without destinations, "like blown kisses ... swallowed by ghosts." And in stanza 7, we are told that the atonal, unsyncopated bird songs have no accompanying words.

The usual convention in lyrics about life and language, such as in Shakespeare's sonnets, is that while we are mortal, the language that has captured our thoughts and feelings is not. Here Wright reverses the convention, concluding that "Words, like all things, are caught in their finitude. / They start here they finish here / No matter how high they rise." The inability of words to do their proper job is a familiar theme in Wright's poems. In the present poem we have a variation on that theme, with the attendant irony that the poet's words—387 of them—have not disappeared into nothingness, thus providing another response to what follows Issa's "And yet."

p. 147, ll. 17–20. As indicated in the introduction, these lines owe a debt to Annie Dillard: "The Chinese say that we live in a world of ten thousand things. Each of the ten thousand cries out to us precisely nothing.... You empty yourself and wait, listening. After a time you hear it: there is nothing there. There is nothing but those things only.... You feel the world's word as a tension, a hum, a single chorused note everywhere the same. This is it: this hum is the silence" (*Teaching a Stone to Talk* [New York: Harper & Row, 1983], 69, 72).

A Journal of the Year of the Ox

Orig. pub. in a limited edition of 150 copies by The Windover Press (Iowa City: University of Iowa, 1988). Portions had appeared in the *New Yorker* 62, no. 36 (27 October 1986): 40, and *New Yorker* 62, no. 24 (4 August 1986): 26–7.

ZJ, 37–84; WTTT, 150–90

Pattern: Variable. This 950-line poem has a vaguely Dantean scheme: thirty-three dated parts, some of them having multiple sections (e.g., 20 January, five sections; 9 July, eight sections; 25 July, six sections; and 3 August, 6 sections). Each of the parts is introduced by an m-dash and concludes with a date.

Time: 20 January–25 December 1985

Place: The first part is set on the Long Island of the Holston and in Italy and Charlottesville, foreshadowing the chief locales of the rest of the poem. Twenty-two of the remaining parts are set in Charlottesville, three on the Long Island of the Holston, four in Italy, one in Amherst, Massachusetts, one in Clarke County, Virginia, and one of indeterminate location (the four-line interlude dated 9 May 1985).

Title: In the Chinese calendar, 1985 is the Year of the Ox.

Wright on Wright: "Disconnection and association ... seem to be linked with the short poem—with the obvious exception of *The Cantos*, of course—and one thinks of Dr. Williams and Company. It was interesting to me to try it in longer reaches—not interminably, like *The Cantos*—and I've made several attempts at that since I saw it emerge in *China Trace*. The first time was in *Homage to Paul Cezanne*, and it was fairly short and crude. Eight overlays, each different, hoping to form one consistent picture. In *The Southern Cross* it got a bit more sophisticated, but it was in *A Journal of the Year of the Ox* that it became what I had hoped it might. The structural elements—the four entries about the Cherokees and the Long Island of the Holston, and the long sojourn in northern Italy—of 'sacred places,' as well as the natural one of the four seasons, plus the visits to the two great American medieval writers, Poe and Dickinson, and the two great Italian ones, Petrarch and Dante, et cetera, all combine to both hide and expose the story line, which is, like most story lines, circular. It deals with circumference, as Emily said her business was. It's mine, too, the outer boundary. In its way, Ox is a longer poem than the whole book *China Trace*, though probably not as vertical" (QN, 115–16).

Part 1. 30 January 1985. Section 1 (pp. 150–1) finds the poet, at the beginning of the new year, stepping back to take stock of his pilgrimage. He discovers little to encourage himself: he remembers less and less, "everything bright falls away," and knowledge of what he should be doing is uncertain. His mood is melancholic, and he asks for pity in "his going up and his going down." The bleak January landscape reinforces the poet's despondency. What he particularly wants to recall is the story of the Cherokees on the Long Island of the Holston, but his knowledge of this chapter of local history is slight: even though he used to drive across the island on his way to play golf, "Nobody tells you anything." The Long Island of the Holston, a Cherokee island at the junction of the North and South Forks of the Holston River, was an important objective in the colonial battles with the Cherokees that began in the middle of the eighteenth century. The poet feels the ghost-like presence of Dragging Canoe, a Cherokee leader and warrior of the Chickamauga (ca. 1732–92), who was adamant in his resistance to the sale of Cherokee lands to whites.

Section 2 (p. 151) is a brief interlude about something that remains hidden from us, like the history of the Cherokees, but that nevertheless mysteriously affects us: it "sifts us the same, / Scores us and alters us utterly: / From somewhere inside and somewhere outside, it smooths [*sic*] us down."

6. Zone Journals (1988) and Xionia (1990)

In section 3 (pp. 151–2) what memory brings to consciousness is far removed from Cherokee history. The poet is taken back to the final days of his army service with 163rd Military Intelligence Battalion at Caserma Passalacqua in Verona. The section opens with Indaco, a major in Wright's unit, making a joke about intelligence activity: Indaco takes a Sandeman sherry figurine from his paper bag, slides it along the bar, and says to Wright, "Here's your Spook," meaning that this is his spy. The Sandeman figurine, manufactured in one of the dozens of ceramics factories in Nove, twenty minutes north of Vicenza, was a cloaked figure with a brimmed hat that actually looked something like a spy. Rather than the usual send-off, Major Indaco and another officer let Wright know they are glad he is leaving. This attitude springs apparently from certain "small failures" on Wright's part—the losing of an intelligence document, something he accidentally burned, his long hair, and the like. This memory merges into one about art—Wright's nightly readings in Bernard Berenson's volumes on the art of the Italian Renaissance and discussions about art with two fellow officers, Peter Hobart and George Schneeman. All three of the naive young Americans, trying to adjust to the Italian environment, were "hungering after righteousness," like the blessed in the Sermon on the Mount (Matthew 5:6).

Section 4 (p. 152) is another interlude, a single quatrain as in section 2. (All of the stanzas in part 1 are quatrains: the stanzaic pattern is [4 × 6] [4] [4 × 6] [4] [4 × 6].) Here we have a brief meditation on form, spurred apparently by the memory of the discussions of art, in which the young officers were "luminous in [their] ignorance." "Form comes from form," says the poet, repeating the scientific and artistic commonplace. Forms in nature are produced by other forms, not from matter or force or spontaneous generation; similarly, art comes from other art. Still, a certain mystery attends the notion of form, which is open-ended, fluid, and unavailable to sight or touch. These ineffable qualities glance back to that "grace beyond the reach of art," alluding to Pope's *Essay on Criticism*, in section 3.

Section 5 (p. 152–3) returns to the present. If the attempt to recapture the past through memory has yielded little (section 1), the brutally frigid landscape of the Charlottesville yard yields even less. Wright is forever trying to pry meaning from the landscape, but this January, "with its quartz teeth / And fingernails // that wears us away," is especially recalcitrant: "And today I remember nothing. / The sky is a wrung-out China blue // and hides no meaning. / The trees have a pewter tinge and hide no meanings. / All of it hustles over me like a wind // and reminds me of nothing." No human presence arises from the landscape: nobody is here and everybody is not here. The entire section focuses on negative presence: "nobody" is repeated four times. The bitter cold, eroding "us away / Into an afterthought," is an objective correlative for the poet's bleak internal state. But the dropped-line of the final quatrain signals a slight reversal. Two possibilities enter the poet's consciousness as antidotes to the sense of absence that otherwise prevails. What emerges from the frozen midwinter scene might be a "glint" or one of glittering "absences who lips at the end of understanding," in which case the poet has some hope that the sense of nothingness may not be altogether negative. And in the climax of this section we have an image of the pursed lips of absence, ready to receive a kiss, suggesting that the various absences are to be embraced.

p. 150, l. 4. *his going up and going down.* Cf. "And the Lord said unto Satan, Whence comest thou? Then Satan answered the Lord, and said, From going to and fro in the earth, and from walking up and down in it" (Job 1:7, 2:2).
p. 150, l. 7. *keening.* Lamenting.
p. 150, l. 9. *everything bright falls away.* Cf. Thomas Nashe's well-known line, "Brightness falls from the air" (*Summer's Last Will and Testament*, l. 17).
p. 152, ll. 7–8. The allusion is to Alexander Pope's "And snatch a grace beyond the reach of art" (*Essay on Criticism*, l. 152).

p. 152, l. 8. *Berenson's*. Bernard Berenson (1865–1959) was a celebrated American art critic and connoisseur of Venetian, Florentine, and other painters of the Italian Renaissance.

p. 152, l. 9. *Hobart and Schneeman*. Peter Hobart (an art history major from Yale) and George Schneeman (a painter), members of Wright's Army group in Verona, the 430th CIC Detachment for security on military installations. Schneeman is today best known for his collaborative work with poets, his interest in collaboration having been sparked by his observations of Giotto's painting while in Italy. Hobart, the youngest member of the third generation of Hobart Brothers, an industrial company, later chaired the International Sculpture Center and has made numerous documentary films on modern art.

Part 2. 30 January 1985. The two scenes here (p. 154), one at evening and the other the next morning, both have to do with diminishment. "How does one deal," asks the poet, "with what is always falling away?"—a version of the question asked in part 1 (p. 150, l. 9). In the first octave, the focus is on the disappearing light as sunset begins to coagulate and clot into darkness. These lines are powered by exceptional tropes: the clouds as a dissolving Mannerist painting, the birds that "swoop and climb" beyond the picture frame, the gathering of light by the house across the street, the clouds as blood, and the streetlights as praying mantises.

In the second octave we move, night having come and gone, from the diminishing light above to the diminished trees below. As for the answer to the question about how to deal with what always diminishes before our eyes, the grass knows, says the poet, but the grass of course remains mute. The poet feigns ignorance: like the grass, he also knows. The things that fall away—the light and the leaves—always come back, and if the poet knows anything, he knows that he is intimately connected with this cyclic, natural narrative. And so he "deals with" what is forever disappearing in the same way that he always has, by representing the landscape as a glorious and mysterious process, moving through its various phases of tragic descent, comic resurrection, ironic alienation, and romantic triumph.

p. 154, l. 6. *Munch house*. A house on Locust Avenue in Charlottesville that looks like a house in one of Edvard Munch's paintings. The house is also mentioned in *Reading Rorty and Paul Celan One Morning in Early June* (NB, 10).

Part 3. 7 February 1985 (p. 154–5). The poet opens with an abstract lyrical flourish on the imperceptible. We ourselves, he asserts, are surrogates for the "unseen" and the "invisible," and the background of our lives is not language but the blank spaces surrounding language. The unknown is what defines us. Winter, the poet continues in stanza 2, is as abstract as these conjectures on the invisible and unknown. This may be true if winter is characterized only conceptually, "as flat planes and slashes." But winter is also decidedly concrete, as the poet's description of its sights and sounds immediately proceeds to reveal. The worm's-back simile for the mountains, the hallelujah metaphor for the trees and telephone poles, the humming of black notes with their attendant stone simile—all these evocative figures give lie to the winter-is-abstract thesis. What *is* abstract is the "stillness of form" that lies behind what presents itself to the poet's eye and ear. This form is "the center of everything," a version of the aphorism that God is a circle of which the centre is everywhere and the circumference nowhere.

Part 4. 13 February 1985 (p. 155). The speechless rain in the first stanza becomes a metaphor for the youthful desire for oblivion in stanza 2. The theme of both stanzas is disguised identity and disappearance. In stanza 1 the rain is disguised in a white cloak that slips off the shoulders of the wind, to which it has nothing to say. Nor does it signal or gesture to what has carried it along. The repetition of "nothing" reinforces the theme that this natural phenomenon is without intent: the raindrops disappear aimlessly into nothing. A similar disappearance is what we yearned for in our youth: though unique, like each of the raindrops, we wanted to fade into our surroundings so as not to call attention to ourselves.

6. Zone Journals (1988) and Xionia (1990)

Part 5. 25 February 1985 (pp. 155–6). This part is a variation on the theme of disappearance. In the Part 4 the rain disappeared into nothingness and the young people wished to disappear into oblivion. Part 5 is an Ovidian metamorphosis: we become wintry features of the natural world, slipping *into* the landscape "One, one and by one." The poet repeats this phrase five times, which suggests that this identification of the human and the natural is an inexorably continuing process. The refrain echoes Pound's line about the return of the gods "one, and by one" (*The Return*, l. 5). There are no gods in this winter interlude: it is only "we" who long to return and to announce "*Here I am, here I am ... I'm back.*" The chances of our being recognized, however, are remote: our own identities are swallowed up by the "ruin" of winter, with its frozen buds and snapping branches and icy tree limbs. We are, thus, identified with the landscape, and our pleas to be recognized as selves distinct from that landscape go for naught. In Ovid, human beings find it very difficult to maintain their humanity, the metamorphoses often involving the some form of flora or fauna. In part 5 we have a similar slippage.

Part 6. 9 March 1985 (pp. 156–7). The stutter of "fever and ooze" that begins and ends this nine-line lyric is an annunciation of the first stirrings of spring. The evidences of its heat (fever) and slow leakage (ooze) begin to be felt beneath the earth and through the threshold to the underworld—"Deep in the hidden undersprings" and "down the secret valleys and dark draws." Evidence of the beginnings of seasonal change comes from things seen and felt, but also from things heard—the singing moss and the wagging tongues.

Part 7. 27 March 1985 (pp. 157–8). The poet recalls a time in March 1959 when he was sitting in a park just north of the Santa Anastasia near the Ponte Pietra, looking across the River Adige toward the Teatro Romano. As the river throws up its spray onto the poet, he recalls that the word "VALERI," Catullus' middle name, was carved in the left wing of a bench at the Teatro Romano, a detail that appears also in *Driving to Passalacqua*, 1960 (*WTTT*, 84). The facts of Catullus' life are sketchy, but we do know that he came from Verona, and he, or at least his family, had a house in Sirmione, a town on Lake Garda. The ruins of a Roman villa, known for centuries as "Grotte di Catullo," lie at the tip of Sirmione. On numerous occasions Wright has described his first encounter with Pound's poetry on the Sirmione peninsula in the very ruins of what is said to have been Catullus' villa. Thus, the experience described here must have been almost coincident with the epiphany Wright had in 1959 that led him to poetry. In any event, Catullus, along with Pound, is associated with the *genius loci* of Verona, and the poet tries to imagine "What it must have been like to be him."

The next stanza jump-cuts to a romantic reverie about a woman he once saw at sunrise while sitting on his bench. Here he merges his own vision with that of Catullus' epithalamium, incorporating a good deal of the imagery from Catullus' poem: "see how the torches shake their tresses," "the marriage veil," "wearing on thy snow-white foot the yellow shoe," "golden feet," and so on (Poem 61, in *Catullus Tibullus Pervigilium Veneris*, trans. F.W. Cornish. [Cambridge, MA: Harvard University Press, 1962], 69–85). Beauty and desire are the thematic foci here, and, as Wright will later say (part 16), "Nothing's so beautiful as the memory of it." Such romantic interludes are infrequent in Wright's poetry.

Part 8. 9 April 1985 (p. 158). As the seasonal cycle progresses into spring, the poet's eye catches the blossoming limbs of the crab-apple tree against the western sky and the rosebud with "its Tiffany limbs." This vision of plenitude is suddenly reversed, as everything descends into a dark vortex—"the not no image can cut." This aural pun means both that no image, like the ones just used to describe the riot of spring's colors, can stand against the Nothing of the dark abyss, and that no image can cut the mysterious "knot" of vacancy.

Part 9. 16 April 1985 (pp. 158–60). In this second of four parts devoted to the Cherokee sacred place, the Long Island of the Holston, the poet begins with a precise topographical description of the Holston River and then moves to an eighteenth-century account of a voyage down the river from Kingsport to Nashville by Colonel John Donelson. As Wright's note (p. 232) indicates, much of the material here is indebted to a special issue of the *Iron Mountain Review* devoted to the Holston River. The first ten lines, for example, are drawn from Edgar Bingham's "Landscape of the Holston," *Iron Mountain Review* 1, no. 2 (Winter 1984): 19. Bingham writes: "The Holston River system drains the Great Valley of Southwest Virginia and Upper East Tennessee. Its easternmost feeder streams, the Watauga and South Holston, gather their waters from the slopes of the Old Appalachians, with the former flowing through the deep water gaps in the Stone and Iron Mountains.... Other streams associated with the Holston follow courses that coincide with the structural alignment of this ridge and valley province—essentially a trellis pattern." Bingham also speaks of the "broad regional uplift" and the changing of the water gaps to "wind gaps," and he writes, "The sandstone-capped Clinch Mountain forms a western wall directly overlooking the Holston. A complex of crystalline uplands define the eastern margins of the Great Valley, with the Great Smoky and Unaka systems dominant south of the Watauga River."

The material on Donelson (p. 150, ll. 21–3, p. 159, l. 18–p. 160, l. 11) derives from *Journal of a Voyage, Intended by God's Permission, in the Good Boat Adventure, from Fort Patrick Henry on Holston River, to the French Salt Springs on Cumberland River, Kept by John Donelson*, in J. G. M. Ramsey, *The Annals of Tennessee to the End of the Eighteenth Century* (Philadelphia: Lippincott, Grambo, and Co., 1853), 197–202. Selections from Donelson's *Journal* are reprinted in *Iron Mountain Review* 1, no. 2 (Winter 1984): 15–18, and the quotations in italics on p. 159, along with some of the surrounding lines, come from the following passages in the *Journal*.

> [A]s soon as the Indians discovered his situation they turned their whole attention to him, and kept up a most galling fire at his boat.... Mrs. Jennings ... and the negro woman, succeeded in unloading the boat, but chiefly by the exertions of Mrs. Jennings, who got out of the boat and shoved her off, but was near falling a victim to her own intrepidity on account of the boat starting so suddenly as soon as loosened from the rock. Upon examination, he appears to have made a wonderful escape, for his boat is pierced in numberless places with bullets. It is to be remarked, that Mrs. Peyton, who was the night before delivered of an infant, which was unfortunately killed upon the hurry and confusion consequent upon such a disaster, assisted them, being frequently exposed to wet and cold then and afterwards, and that her health appears to be good at this time, and I think and hope she will do well. Their clothes were very much cut with bullets, especially Mrs. Jennings's (Donelson's entry of 10 March 1780, *Journal*, rpt. in *Iron Mountain Review*, 16–17)
>
> After we had passed the town, the Indians having now collected to a considerable number, observing his helpless situation, singled off from the rest of the fleet, intercepted him and killed and took prisoners the whole crew, to the great grief of the whole company, uncertain how soon they might share the same fate; their cries were distinctly heard by those boats in the rear. (Donelson's entry of 8 March 1780, *Journal*, rpt. in *Iron Mountain Review*, 16)
>
> We still perceived them marching down the river in considerable bodies, keeping pace with us until the Cumberland Mountain withdrew them from our sight, when we were in hopes we had escaped them. We were now arrived at the place called the Whirl or Suck, where the river is compressed within less than half its common width above, by the Cumberland Mountain, which juts in on both sides. (Donelson's *Journal*, ibid.)
>
> Monday, 27th [1780]. Set out again; killed a swan, which was very delicious.... Tuesday, 28th. Set out very early this morning; killed some buffalo. (Donelson's *Journal*, ibid., 18)

In part 1 of the poem (p. 151) the focus was on disappearance of the sacred ground of the Cherokees. Here the focus begins with the struggles and sufferings endured by the white voyagers as they attempt to survive the dangers of the river and the attacks of the Cherokees, but

6. Zone Journals (1988) and Xionia (1990)   153

it concludes with a lament about the disappearance of the Cherokee Nation. We are enjoined to imagine the Cherokees' having to surrender their Long Island—"The ground that everyone walked on, // all the magic of water, / Wind in the trees, sunlight, all the magic of water."

p. 159, ll. 5–7. *Leonardo da Vinci ... to come.* "In rivers, the water that you touch is the last of what has passed and the first of that which comes: so with time present." Leonardo's lines are quoted as an epigraph to section V of Jeff Daniel Marion's "By the Banks of the Holston," *Iron Mountain Review* 1, no. 2 (Winter 1984): 10.

p. 159, ll. 8–9. *The Cherokee ... French Broad.* "From this point [the confluence of the Ohio to the mouth of the Little Tennessee] to the mouth of the French Broad, it was called Cootla, and from there to the mouth of the Watauga, and perhaps to its source in Virginia, the Holston was known to the Indians as the Hogoheegee" (J.G.M. Ramsey, *The Annals of Tennessee*, quoted as an epigraph to section II of Jeff Daniel Marion's "By the Banks of the Holston," 4–5).

Part 10. 27 April 1985 (pp. 160–1). In this second of three journal entries for April, the month itself becomes the subject. Lines 9–11 are borrowed from Folgóre da San Gimignano, who wrote a series of *corone* in which he gives his readers a gift for each of the months. For April, he gives a flowering countryside with, among other delights, fountains, female companions, and song and dance. Then, he says, in the lines picked up by Wright, "And around about there will be many gardens, and everyone will be stretched out at ease there, each will worship and bow with reverence to that gentle one to whom I have given the crown of precious stones, the finest that Prester John or the King of Babylon has" (*The Penguin Book of Italian Verse*, ed. George Kay [Harmondsworth: Penguin, 1965], 72). The *people* enjoying the delights of Folgóre's garden are changed by Wright to *April*: it is the month itself that is stretched out and that rises and bows. The description in both cases is altogether contrary to Eliot's "the cruelest month."

This zone of the seasonal cycle is, however, otherwise disquieting. It reflects a "fatal quiet" of the underworld; its butterflies flutter in "a dark confusion"; its flowers are clenched; its scents climb "like desperation"; its sky is choked; and it is edgy—all of which serve as antitypes to the April of gentleness and pastoral ease that we have in Folgóre. And Folgóre's pleasant vision, sandwiched between the initial unsettling scene and the gloomy coda—"April, // dank, unseasonable winter of the dead"—is erased altogether.

p. 160, l. 12. *mirror-slide.* That is, the underworld reflection of April, a demonic parody of Folgóre's April.

Part 11. 6 May 1985 (pp. 161–2). The poet recounts a winter pilgrimage some ten years earlier to the Emily Dickinson homestead in Amherst, Massachusetts, where he stood in the cupola with two poet friends, JT (James Tate) and Joe Langland. The cupola afforded Dickinson views of The Evergreens, Amherst College, the town, and the Pelham Hills to the east. After Tate and Langland have left, Wright, surveying the scene below and beyond, looks out upon what Dickinson saw—the railroad, the streets, the house of Austin and Sue (Dickinson's older brother and his wife), and the orchard. He almost expects an epiphany—something coming up "through my feet like electric fire" or even a visitation from Dickinson herself—but nothing extraordinary occurs. As a certain slant of light angles through the window, he thinks he hears a voice from a "wren-like" figure in the evergreens, but that turns out to be imaginary as well. His reverie is interrupted by voices from downstairs calling his name, but only after the sunlight, momentarily mesmerizing him inside a crystal vortex and seeming to portend a recognition of some kind, turns out to be only sunlight.

p. 161, l. 3. Both Tate and Langland were teachers at the University of Massachusetts, Amherst.

p. 161, l. 18. *1862.* The year Emily Dickinson began her correspondence with Thomas Wentworth Higginson. After this time she resisted the efforts of her friends to have her works published; 1862 was also a period of great stress for Dickinson: her friend Charles Wadsworth had moved to San Francisco, and Samuel Bowles, also a friend, was suffering ill health in Europe.

p. 161, l. 22. *wren-like, sherry-eyed figure.* In July 1962 Dickinson wrote to T.W. Higginson, in reply to his request for a portrait, "I had no portrait now, but am small, like the Wren, and my Hair is bold, like the Chestnut Bur—

and my eyes, like the Sherry in the Glass, that the Guest leaves" (*The Letters of Emily Dickinson*, ed. Thomas H. Johnson [Cambridge, MA: The Belknap Press of Harvard University Press, 1958], 268).

Part 12. 9 May 1985 (p. 162). With the rhetorical question at the end of this quatrain, the poet affirms Marsilio Ficino's neo–Platonic view of the Absolute. In his treatise on love, Ficino writes: "[I]n the same way that the Mind, just born and formless, is turned by Love toward God and is formed, so also the World Soul turns itself toward the Mind and God, from which it was born.... [T]here are three worlds, and three chaoses. In all of them finally, Love accompanies chaos, precedes the world, wakens the sleeping, lights the dark, gives life to the dead, gives form to the formless, perfects the imperfect" (Marsilio Ficino, *De Amore*, trans. Sears Jayne [Woodstock, CT: Spring Publications, 1985], 129). "Greater praises than these," Ficino adds, "can hardly be expressed or conceived." Wright's version of this is "What better good can be spoken of?"

In *Thinking of Marsilio Ficino at the First Hint of Autumn* (SHS, 61), Wright later declares that Ficino was probably right about the Absolute, referring to the Renaissance philosopher's general outlook on the transcendent. In his *Platonic Theology* Ficino ordinarily uses the term "absolute" to modify something separated from matter, like grace, the soul, and the Celestial Mind. In the present context, this something is Love—a metonym for the Absolute.

Part 13. 15 May 1985 (pp. 162–3). In mid–May the poet finds himself watching the movement of the clouds and the "constellations of sunlight" moving through the leaves of the peach trees. He is lying in a bed of clover where he sees "bees like golden earrings / Dangling and locked fast" to the white heads of the clover. He proclaims that "The world is an ampersand," meaning that the ten thousand things of the world are conjoined. And then he reflects that the wind will eventually take the clouds and the light "to that point / where all things meet." This is the point of an eternal now, Wright's version of Eliot's "still point of the turning world" where the divine and human intersect and where, in this world of the ampersand, all things are linked.

This is a theme that will be repeated in Wright's poems. In *Sky Diving*, the final poem in *Negative Blue* the he writes, "I've talked about one thing for thirty years, // and said it time and again, / Wind like big sticks in the trees—/ I mean the still, small point at the point where all things meet; / I mean the form that moves the sun and the other stars" (201). In the final poem of *Chickamauga* this still point is the intersection of "the edge of the landscape and the absolute" (NB, 67). In the final poem of *Black Zodiac* it is the intersection of emptiness and plenitude. In the final poem of *Appalachia* it is the balance between the "burning heart" and the "burning feather of truth" (NB, 190). The "form that moves the sun and other stars" is an echo of the final line of Dante's *Paradiso*: *l'amor che move il sole e l'altre stelle*. Wright's "form" and Dante's "love" amount to the same thing: they are both metaphors for God.

p. 162, l. 18. *God's third face*. The Holy Spirit.

Part 14. 23 May 1985 (pp. 163–4). This is the poem's second homage to a fellow poet. It represents Wright's effort to connect with the spirit of Poe, who was a student at the University of Virginia in 1826. West Range at the University of Virginia is a row of dormitories. Over the door of Poe's room 13, which was renovated in the 1950s to look almost exactly like it did when Poe was a student, is a bronze plaque with the inscription "*Domus parva magni poetae*" ("Small home of a great poet"). Wright thinks that the label "great poet" does not really apply to Poe, whose poems he had first read in 1957, when he was stationed at Ft. Holabird, Maryland, shortly after he had been commissioned as an army officer. Still, he hopes to call up Poe's spirit, which he does successfully, taking some inexplicable pleasure in the success of his little conjuring ritual.

p. 163, l. 12. *Magni Poetae which I don't believe*. But cf. Wright's remark, quoted in the headnote above, about "the two great American medieval writers, Poe and Dickinson" (QN, 116).
p. 163, l. 24. *BOQ*. Bachelor Officers' Quarters.

Part 15. 12 June 1985 (pp. 164–5). This is an interlude on music, more particularly on the impossibility of trying to imitate the pure, invisible language of music in the language of poetry. Even musicians, like the trio across the street and, years before, the horn player in Verona, fail, for music is of the spheres. The music of part 15 itself is, nonetheless, quite striking, as is the clothing imagery of the first stanza.

p. 165, l. 8. *smorzando ... andante*. *Smorzando* ("dying") is a directive to perform a certain passage of a composition with the sound suddenly dying away; *andante* ("walking"), to perform in a moderately slow pace.

Part 16. 9 July 1985 (pp. 165–9). The scene changes to Cá Paruta, a villa on the western slope of the Eugenean Hills which Wright and Mark Strand rented for part of the summer of 1985. The climax of part 16 comes in the last section, where the figure of Dante materializes in the garden, calls the poet "Brother," and proceeds to tell him that nothing has changed in the last six centuries. He then enjoins the poet to "concentrate, listen hard, / Look into the nature of all things." The poet finds this advice to be something of a letdown ("Not exactly transplendent"), and his looking to the nature of things in the remainder of the section turns up ordinary sights and sounds, the descriptions of which are hardly memorable: the wind in the trees, the car radio, the children's chants, and the whining motor scooter.

The descriptions that precede the final section are, however, anything but commonplace. Section 1 (pp. 165) is an exceptionally rich recreation of the north wind. Section 4 (pp. 166–7), the sound and sense of the poet's experience of the early evening light, are equally compelling. Alongside these landscape passages are two reflective sections, meditations on the self: section 2 (p. 166), the anxious self and its little allegories of Grief, Despair, and Death; and section 6 (p. 168), the uncertain, shifting self that is *both/and* and *neither/nor*.

p. 167, l. 2. *my son and friend*. Luke Wright and Mark Strand.
p. 168, l. 18. *Madonna*. Mount Madonna, visible from the Villa Cá Patuta and hovering over the surrounding landscape as a presiding presence, makes seven appearances in the Cá Paruta poems.
p. 168, ll. 21–2. The voices turning in the wind and orbiting the two poets recall the sinners in Canto 5 of the *Inferno*, who are borne around the third circle by a tempest.
p. 169, l. 6. *Berici Mountains*. A small volcanic cluster of mountains south of Vicenza.
p. 169, l. 12. *extantsy*. Wright's coinage, a back-formation from "extant," referring to the continuing sound of the voices, expanding centrifugally, that he had heard in the presence of Dante's ghost.

Part 17. 25 July 1985 (pp. 169–73). This part begins with scenes from the Eugenean Hills—the trucks from the stone quarries, the monasteries on the surrounding peaks, the sounds outside the villa—leading up to an artistic representation of "scenes from everyday life" in section 4. The scenes referred to here (pp. 170–2) are from the fresco cycle *Salon of the Months*, painted by Francesco del Cossa and others (chiefly Cosimo Tura and Ercole de' Roberti), in the Schifanoia Palace to celebrate the investiture of Borso d'Este as the Duke of Ferrara in 1471 by Pope Paul II. Borso had earlier been made Duke of Modena by the Emperor Frederick III. The frescoes are in three bands along the four walls of the salon, beginning with *January* on the south wall and continuing counterclockwise through December on the west wall. The allegorical scenes in the top fasciae have to do with the triumph of Roman divinities—Minerva, Venus, Mercury, et al. The center fasciae, narrower bands than those above and below, contain the twelve signs of the zodiac. Each sign has associated with it three deacons or deans, one on each side of the sign and one above it. In the bottom panel are sumptuously decorated scenes from the life of the city at the time.

Wright's eye focuses on at least seventeen scenes from the fresco, verbally recreating images from both the top and bottom scenes, as well as to the middle fascia—"such a narrow meaningful strip." (The note to p. 170, ll. 17 ff. below identifies these images.) He then asks himself what it all means, which is a rather tall order as the poem involves images from Roman mythology (band one), astrological symbolism (band two), and imaginative recreations of contemporary courtly life and practical labor (band three). Moreover, like the calendar illustrations that appear in northern European art, each of the Roman deities, each of the signs of the zodiac, and each of the scenes of daily life is related to a particular month. Is the fresco, asks the poet, an allegorical representation of our own lives? A commentary on them? Does it point to meanings that lie outside the pictures? Is it no more than a decoration to amuse the bored ladies of the court? Were Cossa, Tura, and de' Roberti revealing things they didn't intend? Is what might have begun as contemporary storytelling about the duke and his court only fantasy? The fresco is a hermeneutical puzzle for the poet, who leaves the questions unanswered.

The last two sections are implicit allegories. The first is about the postponement of the redemption of the earth by heaven: the sky behind Mount Madonna is a "medieval ring of Paradise ... blue of redemption / Against which, in the vine rows, // the green hugs the ground hard," but the sky is not yet ready to gather the earth up. In the second allegory the scythe of Alfredo, the weed cutter, swings "Inexorably as a visitation, or some event / The afternoon's about to become the reoccasion of." The reoccasion turns out to be, in Wright's free association, the visitation of St. Catherine of Alexandria, a fourth-century Christian who, according to legend, converted a number of pagan wise men who were subsequently martyred. She herself was sentenced to be killed by means of a wheel set with spikes or razors. When she was placed upon its rim, her bonds were miraculously loosened, the wheel broke, and the spikes flew off, killing the onlookers. She was eventually beheaded, calling down blessings on all who should remember her, and was subsequently transported to heaven. (Carpaccio's tempera of St. Catherine is in the Museo di Castelvecchio in Verona.)

p. 170, l. 15. *Madonna's tongue.* The peak of Mount Madonna. See n. to p. 168, l. 18, above.

p. 170, ll. 17 ff. The list that follows identifies the month, the fascia, and the plate in Wright's source, Ranieri Varese, *Il Palazzo di Schifanoia* (Bologna: Grafica Editoriale s.r.l, 1983). If no plate is listed, then Wright's source is Varese's commentary. Readers can find reproductions of the frescoes also at http://www.abcgallery.com/I/italy/cossa.html and http://www.wga.hu/html/c/cossa/schifano/index.html.

p. 171, l. 3. *Borso ... jester Scoccola.* April, bottom fascia, pl. 17

p. 171, l. 4. *Borso receiving ... hawking.* August, bottom fascia

p. 171, l. 5. *Or listening ... knees.* June, bottom fascia

p. 171, l. 6. *Or giving ... his due.* March, bottom fascia, pl. 8

p. 171, ll. 7–11. *Borso d'Este ... archway.* March, bottom fascia, pl. 7

p. 171, l. 12. *A child ... right.* March, bottom fascia, pl. 8

p. 171, l. 12. *a monkey ... leg.* March, bottom fascia, pl. 7.

p. 171, ll. 15–16. *At the tip ... teeth.* July, center fascia, panel 3, pl. 2 and pl. 23.

p. 171, l. 17. *At the lion's ... celestial tree.* July, center fascia, panel 2, pl. 2 and pl. 23.

p. 171, ll. 19–21. *And musician ... heaven.* September, center fascia, pl. 29

p. 171, ll. 23–p. 172, l. 3. *Up there ... finery.* This appears to be a composite of several sections of the top fascia (pl. 2 and pls. 9–10)

p. 172, l. 4. *Love ... trace.* April, top fascia, pl. 9

p. 172, l. 5. *Cybele ... Corybants.* July, top fascia, pl. 23.

p. 172, l. 6. *Apollo, Medusa's blood.* May, top fascia, pl. 18.

p. 172, l. 6. *Attis in expiation.* July, top fascia, pl. 23.

p. 172, l. 15. *Virgo ... heel.* August, top and center fasciae, pl. 25.

p. 172, ll. 16–17. *And turreting ... tear of light.* This appears to describe the ideal city in the background of *March, The Triumph of Minerva,* top fascia, pl. 3 and pl. 4

Part 18. 3 August 1985 (pp. 173–77). The final Cá Paruta entry begins with a visit by the poet to the village Arquá Petrarca, where Petrarch lived, southwest of Padova (Padua), his house now containing a permanent exhibition of Petrarchan works and memorabilia. In the fourteenth century, Francesco the Elder gave Petrarch a strip of land at Arquà in the Euganean hills, where the ageing poet built a little cottage. Because the view was so beautiful, he decided to spend the last years of his life there. Wright names some of the more famous visitors to Arquá who signed the guestbook, now under glass: Count Giustino Valmarana, an eighteenth-century scholar, theater enthusiast, and patron of Tiepolo; Rilke; and the King of Abyssinia.

The poet takes us on a tour of the museum, cluttered up with "everything one would hope would not be put forth / In evidence on Petrarch's behalf," and after recreating the landscape that Petrarch would more or less have seen, he tries to imagine what the house would have looked like before history damaged it. The poet then writes his name in the dirt and knocks twice as he leaves, just as he had done on leaving Poe's student quarters, with the hope that good luck might attend him or that Petrarch's spirit might be summoned.

p. 174, l. 4. *Laura*. The idealized woman of Petrarch's *Rimes*.
p. 174, l. 26. *Victor Emmanuel II*. In 1861, Victor Emmanuel II assumed the title of King of Italy, becoming the first king of a united Italy, a title he held until his death in 1878.

The remaining sections are a series of extraordinarily evocative vignettes of Cá Paruta and its environs:

Section 2 (p. 175). Back in his room the poet recounts the invasion of his quarters by a butterfly, a wasp, and a bumblebee; two leave; only the wasp remains, searching the dark crevices for a landing place.

Section 3 (p. 175). Here the emphasis is on stasis—the windless and cloudless midsummer. The "blood stills" and the vendor's cry "hangs like a sheet in the dry air." The opening image of Mount Madonna, with its metaphor-simile combination, is as fresh and astonishing as it is ingenious.

Section 4 (p. 176). The poet is curious about the meaning of St. Augustine's dictum, "whatever is, is good" (*Confessions*, bk. 7, par. 17). He wonders whether it refers to the "paracletic nature of things," that is, the view that all creation, even that which "rusts and decays," is revelatory in a spiritual sense. If this is what Augustine meant, then the voices that are disappearing from the garden would be paracletic.

Section 5 (p. 176). The poet imagines that in the emerging nightfall "the towers and deep dish" (apparently the "radar stations" of part 17 [p. 170, l. 3]) and Mount Madonna itself are calling the stars ("children" and "little ones") out of the sky, and he then makes a connection between the great river of heaven (the Milky Way) and "the great river of language." Each of us is a word, and, like the stars, the word also belongs to the myth of eternal return. It will "come back / To its true work." Therefore, the imperative: "concentrate, listen hard," which was the instruction he was given by Dante in part 16.

Section 6 (pp. 176–7). In the concluding section, the poet follows Dante's injunction. In the darkness of the lower garden at Cá Paruta, he encounters only the book of silence, and although he understands nothing, he does not despair. He keeps on turning the pages: "somewhere in here, I know, is my word." Thus ends the Italian sojourn.

Part 19. 20 August 1985. On this August day, licked clean by the sun, the poet complains that he cannot remember his youth, represented as a "seam of red silt." All he can unearth is "a handful of dust." The imagery here echoes that in the second stanza of part 1 of *The Waste Land*, where we have the beating sun, the red rock, and the narrator's saying, "I will show you fear in a handful of dust." The scene in Wright is not so bleak as the parched desert and "stony rubbish" in Eliot.

p. 178, l. 1 *handful of dust*. The phrase also appears in Donne's "Devotion IV (*Devotions on Emergent Occasions* and Tennyson's *Maud* (2.5.1.241). Conrad's uses it in both *Youth* and *The Return*, and it is the title of an Evelyn Waugh novel.

Part 20. 25–29 August 1985 (pp. 178–9). On his fiftieth birthday—25 August 1985—the poet leaves Winchester, Virginia, on a rainy morning and crosses the Shenandoah River, driving south to Clarke County, the area where his mother's ancestors had lived. He had made a pilgrimage to the same place seven years before (see *Virginia Reel* above, *WTTT*, 17–18). He reflects on his ancestors' having left the area, as he himself proceeds to do on this trip, the Clarke County landscape disappearing behind him. The rain, cold wind, and lowering sky are reason enough for leaving this place of his mother's family, "A weight so sure and so fixed." And yet an elegiac mood pervades the poet's distancing himself, literally and figuratively, from this ancestral home: "What makes us leave what we love best?" He knows that something important is disappearing—he calls it "the dream"—and he knows as well that what disappears is the vision of "the abiding earth" that makes life endurable. And yet this vision is momentary, ephemeral, and easily erased, like all those things in the catalogue of similes in the last five lines.

p. 179, l. 17. *Castleman's Ferry*. Near Berryville in Clarke County, Virginia, on the Shenandoah River.

Part 21. 5 September 1985 (pp. 179–80). As autumn attempts to get its engine started, the poet speculates about things hidden, spurred by what Augustine conjectured about matter and spirit, good and evil, time and memory. Augustine said that "Time is memory," but for the poet the remembrance of things past proves to be difficult because time remains hidden, just "As the sentence hides in the ink, // as cancer hides in the smoke, / As dark hides in the light."

p. 180, ll. 2–3. "For the Almighty God, Who, as even the heathen acknowledge, has supreme power over all things, being Himself supremely good, would never permit the existence of anything evil among His works, if He were not so omnipotent and good that He can bring good even out of evil. For what is that which we call evil but the absence of good? (Augustine, *The Enchiridion; Addressed to Laurentius; Being a Treatise on Faith, Hope and Love.*, trans. J. F. Shaw [New York: Christian Literature Publishing Co., 1886], chap. 11). On the impasse between matter and spirit, which Augustine calls "contraries," see *Enchiridion*, chap. 14.

p. 180, l. 10. *Time is memory*. Saint Augustine, *Confessions*, trans. R.S. Pine-Coffin (Harmondsworth: Penguin, 1961), 276 (bk. 11, chap. 27).

Part 22. 15 September 1985 (pp. 180–81). Here Wright presents the third chapter in the saga of the defeated Cherokees, introduced in part 1 and continued in part 9. He begins with an account of Dragging Canoe and Abraham (Ooskiah), Cherokee war chiefs who, at the instigation of the British, planned to attack the western settlers near the Long Island of the Holston (now Sullivan County, Tennessee) and at Watauga. The settlers had been warned, and so a militia had been gathered under command of Captain James Thompson, who lived on the island. On 20 July 1776 Thompson's militia defeated Dragging Canoe and his forces in the Battle of Island Flats. Abraham was driven back the next day at Watauga.

The poet then presents one account of the defeat of the "Cherokee's mystic Nation," drawn from Thompson's own account: "There were streams of blood every way; and it was generally thought there was never so much execution done in so short a time on the frontiers. Never did troops fight with greater calmness that ours did. The Indians attacked us with the greatest fury imaginable, and made the most vigorous efforts to surround us. Our spies really deserved the greatest applause. We took a great deal of plunder and many guns, and had only four men greatly wounded. The rest of the troops are in high spirits and eager for another engagement. We have the greatest reason to believe they are pouring in great numbers on us, and beg the assistance of our friends" (James Thompson, et al., "Account of the Battle Fought on the 20th of July, 1776" in J.G.M. Ramsey, *The Annals of Tennessee to the End of the Eighteenth Century* [Charleston: John Russell, 1853], 154). The poet judges this to be nothing but "Exaggeration and rhetoric," but he does grant that this sad episode in Tennessee history began "the inevitable exodus, // Tsali and the Trail of Tears."

p. 181, l. 15. *Tsali*. The Cherokee hero martyred in connection with the infamous Trail of Tears, when thousands of Cherokee were rounded up for forced removal to Oklahoma. The historical record is unclear, but Tsali appears either to have been executed by his own people or to have willingly sacrificed his life so that some of his people could remain in their mountain country. Whatever the facts, Tsali became a symbol of Cherokee resistance to oppression.

Part 23. 29 September 1985 (pp. 181–2). We move from history and politics to landscape. The opening line from *The Cloud of Unknowing* announces one of Wright's central tenets: "*Attention is the natural prayer of the soul.*" His mentor in this regard is Dante, who remains the great exemplar of "absolute attention" (*Halflife*, 178). The four five-line zones of attention in the present lyric move from light to silence. The opening description of daylight is extraordinary in its evocative imagery and music: "Sunday in all the windows, // the slow snow of daylight / Flaking the holly tree and the hedge panes / As it disappears in the odd milk teeth / The grass has bared, both lips back // in the cool suck of dusk." The poet takes us next to the interior landscape behind the eye, where the prayer wheels turn the parts of speech in an imaginative universe of whiteness. From the butterflies of stanza 3, which also reveal the poet's absolute attention, we progress to the nighttime of silence, interrupted only by the wind's "Shuffling the decks of the orchard leaves." This remarkable lyric is an example of what Wright calls in another context the "imaginary, mythical, still, brightly lit center of attention at the heart of the universe" (*Halflife*, 128–9). His power of expression is much more heightened here, where the subjects emerge from the dwarf orchard, than in reflecting on the fate of the Cherokees.

p. 181, l. 16. *Attention ... soul.* Paul Celan underlined this passage by the French philosopher Malebranche in Walter Benjamin's essay on Kafka. See Philippe Lacoue-Labarthe, *Poetry as Experience*, trans. Andrea Tarnowski (Stanford: Stanford University Press, 1999), 64. The original source is from *Cloud of Unknowing*, chap. 4, par. 11. In the translation by Clifton Wolters: "So pay great attention to this marvellous work of grace within your soul" (*The Cloud of Unknowing and Other Works* [Harmondsworth: Penguin, 1978], 65).

Part 24. 4 October 1985 (pp. 812–3). The landscape seems especially recalcitrant in revealing its secrets. For the poet, the grammar of early October never moves beyond the phonological level—except for one syntactic category: the apostrophes of the weather. Otherwise, it is the syllables, vowels, consonants, sibilants, and gutturals that want to "break out in speech and tell us something." But this something never manages to get itself uttered, and in the final two lines whatever letters the bird repeats remain a secret. Revelation, if it is to come, will require morphemes and syntax.

Part 25. 12 October 1985 (pp. 183–4). The opening commonplaces about truth and beauty could have been extracted from a primer on metaphysics and a textbook on aesthetics. They seem not to be related to what immediately follows, but defining by negation (X is absence of Y) does connect with the theme of emptiness introduced in the final lines. What follows in the description of the scene before the poet is a sense of diminishment: the jay is stuffed and immobile, the light diluted, and the cloud is like a slowly extended bass note. The world of plenitude that we find so often in Wright has been replaced by a world of diminution. But this is a world he identifies with: "The disillusioned and twice-lapsed, the fallen-away, / Become my constituency.... Are those I would be among, / The called, the bruised by God ... the shorn and weakened." Wright has said before that he wants "to be bruised by God" (CM, 152), echoing the well-known prophecy in Isaiah (53:5). At the beginning of his Galilean ministry Jesus declared that he would set free "them that are bruised" (Luke 4:18), and the poet takes some comfort in being part of this community of the bruised: "There is no loneliness where the body is. / There is no Pyrrhic degeneration of the soul there." At this point the poet takes stock of the winking and flashing of the scene before him, but both the poem and his own name turn out to be written on glass, which is "The emptiness that form takes, the form of emptiness." In this poetic syllogism, then, truth and beauty are—to return to the opening abstractions—defined by absence.

p. 184, l. 22. *The heart is a spondee*. The double thump of the heartbeat is underwritten by the spondees strung throughout the poem: "pear tree," "light-slant," "deep weight," "fluffed up," "bass note," "sunlight," "twice-lapsed," "die back," "soul there," "noon's glare," "wind spurts," "form takes," "ash leaves," "three birds," and "dead oak."

Part 26. 22 October 1985 (pp. 184–5). This lyric continues the body and soul dialectic of part 25. Here the soul is initially absent—a vacancy that has "come to rest" beside the body. Or so it seems in the poet's "as if" world. The poet predicts, however, that the soul will rejuvenate itself tomorrow when the rains come. Then it will take its proper place in the "center of things." Throughout, the Indian summer landscape is a subjective correlative for the sense of absence felt by the poet. He experiences not the dark night of the soul but the "chill luminance" of the body, and what the "landscape illuminates" is, again, not plenitude but "extraction."

Part 27. 29 October 1985 (pp. 185–6). The setting here is the Charlottesville front yard with its backdrop of the brilliant October leaves ("maples kick in their afterburners," "Autumn firestorm in the trees"). It's Sunday, which prompts a series of religious metaphors: the seasonal catechism, the rosary of the dogwood berries, the *Kyrie eleison* zithering above the power lines. But our journey is purgatorial, and the "after*burners*" in the opening line of stanza 2 provide a segue to the allusions to Dante's *Purgatorio* that follow. It is we who are subject to purgation. Those of us with our eyes sewn shut are contemporary versions of the penitents purging themselves of envy in canto 13 of the *Purgatorio*; those of us bearing rocks upon our backs alludes to the stony weights carried by the proud in canto 11; and as we escape the flames of Antepurgatory, we encounter the angel's sword, an allusion to canto 9, where the angel at the gate inscribes Dante's brow with the mark of the seven sins. Hope, which has been abandoned at the entrance to hell, is a purgatorial virtue. Thus, the poet hopes that our foreheads might be cleansed of the inscription of the sevens sins, and he hopes as well that the way up the purgatorial mount is different from the descent into the inferno.

For Wright purgatory is what Keats called a journey through the "vale of soul-making"—a pilgrimage that, if hope is fulfilled, will issue in an emancipated vision. Purgatory is not an otherworldly place but a decidedly immanent progression through life in the present, which is the focus of the second volume in each of the first two trilogies (*Bloodlines* and *The Other Side of the River*) and will become the focus of *Black Zodiac*, the second volume of the third trilogy. Purgatory, says Wright, is "the richest of all of those three books [*Inferno, Purgatorio, Paradiso*] in that it is a combination of scraping the inferno off your shoes and having your eyes on the prize at the same time" (Suarez, 56–7). The central purgatorial images are fire, the natural form of which in this lyric is the "firestorm" of the October leaves, and the ladder or spiraling stairway. The refining fire relates to how we are to live in this life, and the purgatorial way leads upward toward freedom, perfection, and original innocence at the top of the spiraling mountain or ladder. Dante is understandably the chief purgatorial source for Wright. The Dantean purgatorial progression leads from *quid agas* (the moral level in the polysemous medieval scheme) to *quo tendas* (the spiritual or anagogical level). Thus, while the purgatorial progression is a journey through life, it is a journey of ascent. In the present poem the way up is the object of hope.

p. 185, l. 15. *Kyrie eleison*. Lord, have mercy.

Part 28. 11 November 1985 (p. 186). This triptych begins with a declaration of a singular interest: "I have no interest in anything // but the color of leaves." But of course this interest is not exclusive, as the color of blood and the color of breath are also offered as objects of solitary interest. Even within each of the three stanzas what the poet goes on to describe belies what he initially avows. In stanza 1, we move from an interest in the golden leaves of late autumn to the Byzantium simile. The Byzantine world moves us backward in time, bringing with it suggestions of a golden age or an ideal vision, like that depicted by Yeats. In the third stanza, we move from an interest in the color of breath into a green-world vision of the kind we find, say, in Shakespeare's comedies. Sandwiched between these golden and green worlds is the world of black blood and of the dark waters "beneath the self." This is a demonic parody of both the golden world of Byzantine artifice and the green world which represents the beginning of life ("Alpha of everything"), the imminent revival of the year, and the triumph of life over death. Behind the three stanzas is an implicit progression of the natural cycle—from the gold of autumn through the darkness of winter to the rejuvenation of spring. Moreover, the "jade / Calvary of the begotten sigh" evokes the conclusion of the Passion story, and with it the idea that death precedes resurrection. Thus, while the beginning of each stanza is a stark and restricted declaration of interest in a color, the movement in each stanza is centrifugal—a movement outward to a broad historical cycle (from Byzantium to Calvary) and an inclusive natural one (from autumn to spring).

Part 29. 20 November 1985 (pp. 186–7). The poet records three dreams, the first two of which are anxiety dreams. In the first he reads a text about his bitter and anxious heart. In the second his identity is completely erased as he disappears into the light. In the final dream he shows slides of religious subjects—the Resurrection (Piero della Francesca's fresco, perhaps), intercessory prayers, the Sorrows of the Virgin, the Assumption of John the Evangelist (Giotto's painting, perhaps). What we have of the slide-show dream (it apparently continues beyond the ellipsis) appears to be a wish-fulfillment for the transport of the soul after death: it begins with Resurrection and ends with Assumption.

The poet insists that the self revealed from his dream world is not his persona, a mask of bitterness and anxiety, but his genuine melancholic state, and he repeats the text read in the first dream. He then returns to the waking world of mid–November, where, after the experience of the dream world, the ordinary activities of his neighbor and his son seem "otherworldly." What is actually otherworldly is the content of the dreams that have just been recounted. What happens in both the world of the dream and the world after death is, the poet says, "important," even though we have no knowledge of either. Thus, the conclusion about the mystery of nothingness.

Part 30. 28 November 1985 (pp. 187–8). This is a confession that turns into a brief *apologia pro vita sua*. It begins with the poet's announcement that all his life he has "stood in desire," the objects of this desire being what he has loved—"what you can't think" and "what may be gotten and held." What one can't think could be the infinite and eternal—what Keats says "teases us out of thought"—or else things seen and heard and felt on the pulse in solitude. The poet asks to be left alone in his dark world, echoing Job ("Now therefore be content, look upon me [6:28].... Let me alone, for my days are vanity" [7:16]). The darkness provides food full enough "and more precious than time." This is a world cleared of all detritus. The emphasis is on what is indivisible, whole, contained, and concise. "The shorter the word," says the poet, "the more it serves the work of the spirit." One such word is "love." Later Wright will use a similar, longer word, "affection," which he says is "the absolute // everything rises to" (*Apologia Pro Vita Sua*, in NB, 84).

p. 188, l. 1. In *Zone Journals*, the last half of this line is dropped down.

Part 31. 5 December 1985 (pp. 188–9). On a rainy day at the end of November the poet returns to the sad chapter of Cherokee history he has visited three times before (parts 1, 9, and 22). He stands across the river from the Long Island of the Holston, once a Cherokee sacred ground and burial site. Earlier in the day he had crossed a footbridge to an island in the Holston where he found an inscription of a block of marble recording two dates: the year that the Cherokees were forced by treaty to relinquish the Island and the year that the City of Kingsport had returned 3.61 acres of the Island to the eastern Cherokee tribes—170 years later. The poet makes no comment on this latter act, but it is clear he sees it as an empty gesture. However benevolent the intent in returning a small portion of the two-square-mile Island to the Cherokees, the current state of the Island does nothing to repair the desecration of what had been a holy space for more than ten thousand years. What was once sacred ground is now the site of a coal gasification plant of the Tennessee Eastman Company, the burial sites have been bulldozed, chain-link and barbed-wire fences cut across the island, and trash has accumulated along its banks. The rain does nothing to wash away the sins of the past or the specter of industrial clutter now strewn across the Island.

p. 188, l. 12. *Tennessee Eastman Corporation*. Tennessee Eastman, a Fortune 500 company, had produced a wide range of chemical products in Kingsport since the 1920s. It also used the Long Island of the Holston as a fuel-supply yard for its nearby acetate plant. Eastman, incidentally, was one of the worst polluters in the region, indeed in the nation.

p. 188, l. 13. *Bays Mountain*. A range that extends from the Long Island of the Holston River in Kingsport to Blount County, Tennessee, some 115 miles to the southwest. A few miles from downtown Kingsport and at the northeastern end of the ridge lies Bays Mountain Park.

Part 32. 12 December 1985 (p. 189). As the year-end approaches, the poet records his impression of the dove-colored sky, followed by an anecdote about his effort the following night to find Halley's comet with his son's telescope. He is unsuccessful, but not to worry, because "An ordered and measured affection is virtuous / In its clean cause // however it comes close in this life. / Nothing else moves toward us out of the stars." The comet has become a metaphor for the light from the heavens which seeks in its orderly and precise way to send us on earth a signal, even though in this life the light may not get close to us.

p. 189, l. 20. *Halley's comet*. The famous comet would make its closest approach to the sun on its present 76-year orbit about two months later—on 9 February 1986. The comet was much less visible than it had been in 1910.

Part 33. 25 December 1985. The opening lines come from the anguished lament of the psalmist, who feels he has been abandoned by God (Psalm 22:14). The psalm begins with the question asked by Jesus at his death: "My God, my God, why hast though forsaken me?" The psalmist is mocked by his enemies, who are represented as dogs and other animal predators. The mood is not unlike that at the beginning of *A Journal of the Year of the Ox*, with its melancholic sense of absence. In such a situation, the poet asks rhetorically, Who wouldn't want his body to be delivered? The question then becomes, Is the life of contemplation worth anything, and, if so, how far down can one descend into the dark night of the soul?

The winter backdrop is not conducive to reversing the poet's plight, and yet in the last lines a ray of hope emerges: "the cold / Hung light a lantern against the dark // burn of a syllable: / I roll it around on my tongue, I warm its edges...." The suggestion is that there is enough warmth and light for the poet to continue his pilgrimage beyond the final ellipsis. More syllables, once they have been warmed to the core, will emerge from the poet's tongue.

While Wright's poetic pilgrimage is a purgatorial narrative along an east-west axis, it is also a journey up and down the *axis mundi*. How far down into the abyss of nothingness, he asks, can one go before there is a recognition and a reversal? The question is not answered here, but the syllables on the poet's tongue are beginning to warm up, so, again, the suggestion is that he still hopes for a spiritual enlightenment that lies somewhere down the road or up the ladder.

Wright on Wright: "A *Journal of the Year of the Ox* would be more like an aircraft carrier—many small lyrics riding on its superstructure. How's that for an outrageous linkage? Of course the Ox poem had to finish at the end of December, 1985, as one of its structures was the length of the year. But what went in, and what ended it, was very open. When I thought, or felt, the circle had almost been completed, I stopped" (*QN*, 109–10).

Light Journal

Orig. pub. *Gettysburg Review* 1, no. 1 (Winter 1988): 31.
ZJ, 87–8; WTTT, 191–2
Pattern: (5) (4–1) (3) (5)
Time: Memory of Greece, 1959

The four sections of this poem are held together by the motif of light. In section 1, the prime word ("Let there be light" [Genesis 1:3]) is part of two complex noun phrases, neither of which has a predicate. The imagery is pathological. In the first phrase, it is the poet, apparently, who speaks the word "light" and then vanishes into the body's circulatory system. In the second phrase, light moves up through the body until it arrives finally at the heart, the place of "the inarticulation of desire." The process described sounds almost like a medical procedure that tracks light through the veins and arteries. In any event, it is impossible to say what follows the ellipsis, since nothing is asserted about the speaking and vanishing, on the one hand, or the "Trip and thump of light," on the other.

Sections 2 and 3 are quotations from poems. The first (ll. 6–9) is from some lines Wright wrote twenty-six years earlier about the light and water of the Grecian landscape. He was not certain what he meant by the lines, but he stands by them. The second (ll. 11–13) is a translation of Salvatore Quasimodo's three line poem *Ed è subito sera*: "Ognuno sta solo sul cuor della terra / trafitto da un raggio de sole: / ed è subito sera." The phrase "Everyone stands by himself" can mean "stands alone" or "stands beside his other identities" or even "upholds himself."

In section 4 the poet notes the oddness of the three things just recorded that have persisted in his memory, but he realizes that while many of the things that defined his self twenty-six years earlier are different from those that define him today, there is still an identity with all of his personalities from birth to the present: "someone I was once has stayed / Stopped in the columns of light / Through S. Zeno's doors, // trying to take the next step and break clear...."

Light is an apocalyptic metaphor for Wright, representing the epiphany or enlightenment at the end of the journey. Light can pierce us, as Quasimodo says, freezing us in a moment of time, but we can be released from that moment and move toward the next stage of illumination. Except for the "prime word" these four sections would be discontinuous fragments.

p. 191, l. 13. The last line of Quasimodo's poem, *Ed è subito sera*, later became the title of his most widely read book (1942).
p. 192, l. 5. S. Zeno. The church of San Zeno Maggiore in Verona.

A Journal of One Significant Landscape

ZJ, 89–95; WTTT, 193–8
Pattern: (4 × 4) (4) (4 × 4) (4) (4 × 4) (4) (4 × 4) (4) (4 × 4) (4) (4 × 4)
Time: April–late September
Place: Charlottesville

A certain ambiguity attends the word "one" in the title. The pronoun could be used for emphasis, as in "That was *one* terrific book." Or it may point simply to a particular landscape among others that are significant. As it turns out, the poem recreates in the sixteen-line, odd-numbered sections an assortment of landscapes over a six-month period. These focus on the flora of the back yard and "down-country" and the sky above. Images from both middle earth and the upper world appear in all of the odd-numbered sections. Artificial structures only occasionally come under the poet's watchful eye (the board fence in section 3, the house and barn of section 7, and the dome of the Florence cathedral in section 9). The four-line, even-numbered sections are meditations on "exhilaration and sadness" (section 2), truth and beauty by way of Lao Tzu (section 4), the difficulty of seeing what is on "the other side" (section 6), the word of God by way of Ruysbroeck (section 8), and the mystery of the "diamond zones" and colors in painting (section 10).

The poem as a whole is what Claude Lévi-Strauss in *The Savage Mind* calls a *bricolage*, materials drawn from a "heterogeneous repertoire" of "whatever is at hand," some of which is "the remains of previous constructions" (Chicago: University of Chicago Press, 1966, 16–17). The heterogeneous repertoire here includes Rilke's *Letters on Cézanne*, Vasari's *Lives of the Artists*, St. John of Ruysbroeck's *Spiritual Espousals*, the *Tao Te Ching*, and John Clare's *Natural History*.

The sister arts of painting and music suffuse the poem. Wright has been reading Vasari, and so Cimabue is called on for a simile in section 5, and anecdotes about Brunelleschi and Uccello are recorded in section 9. Remarks about vanishing points and Cézanne's "diamond zones" appear in section 10, gilded calligraphy in section 5, photographic processes in section 7, and partially erased parchment in section 11. The poet's ear is attuned to the music of the landscape as well: the quince hums (section 1), the wind whispers (section 3), the apples and pears buzz (section 5), the grass moans and the birds plink (section 7), the weeds exhale and the pines echo (section 11). The epigraph for all of these descriptions of the landscape might well have been the quotation from John Clare that Wright reproduces in section 7: "I put down these memorandums of my affections." Memory, according to Clare, is secondary to life, which is primary (or "principal"). And yet life is but a shadow of memory ("the soul of time").

The reader is aware too of the religious themes introduced by the poet with the help of Lao Tzu (sections 4 and 11), Ruysbroeck (section 8), Brunelleschi (section 9). The poet speaks of sainthood (section 1), absolution and imminent radiance (section 3). The Ruysbroeck quotation might also be taken as an epigraph for the whole. God speaks the "deep / Unfathomable word" to us, says Ruysbroeck, the quotation tailing off into an ellipsis. Had Wright continued the quotation, we would learn that the unfathomable word is the imperative "See." Images of the landscape, which are a function of seeing, dominate the poem. The descriptive scenes alternate with philosophical meditations on the impossibility of searching for happiness, internal radiance as the goal of the poet's effort, the failure of truth, beauty, and goodness by themselves to define the poetic enterprise, the poet's regret about wasting his time yet his continuing to abide in the face of the "idea of emptiness." Section 9—on Brunelleschi and Uccello—presents little vignettes from Vasari's *Lives* without commentary, yet it is difficult not to see them as allegories of the poet's pilgrimage. With Uccello he keeps his eyes fastened on the four elements, and with Brunelleschi he piles stone on stone in his climb toward Paradise.

p. 195, l. 1. *Truthful words*. Wright is quoting from D.C. Lau's translation of chap. 81 of the *Tao Te Ching*.
p. 195, l. 7. The reference here is to Cimabue's *Crucifixion* in San Francesco at Pisa, described by Vasari as "with several angels who are weeping and holding in their hands a few words written above his [Christ's] head" (Giorgio Vasari, "Life of Cimabue," *Lives of the Artists*, trans. George Bull [Harmondsworth: Penguin, 1965], 1:54).
p. 196, ll. 15–16. *John Clare*. "I feel anxious to insert these memorandums of my affections as Memory though a sec-

ondary is the soul of time & life the principal but its shadow" [from the entry in John Clare's *Journal* dated 3 June 1825, in *The Natural History Prose Writings of John Clare*, ed. Margaret Grainger [New York: Oxford University Press, 1984], 247.) Edward Hirsch uses the same variation as Wright—"I put down these memorandums of my affections"—as the opening line of his poem *Memorandums* (*The Night Parade and Other Poems* [New York: Knopf, 1989], 3).

pp. 196–7, ll. 19–22. *For the Heavenly Father ... nothing else.* The lines from St. John of Ruysbroeck (1293–1382), Dutch mystic, come from his *Spiritual Espousals*: "Our heavenly Father wishes us to see, for he is the Father of light (cf. Jas. 1:17). Accordingly, in the hidden depths of our spirit he eternally, ceaselessly, and without intermediary utters a single fathomless word, and only that word. In this word he gives utterance to himself and all things. This word ... is none other than 'See'" (*The Spiritual Espousals and Other Works*, trans. James A. Wiseman [New York: Paulist Press, 1985], 146 [bk. 3, pt. 1]). Wright's translation is the same as that in Annie Dillard's *Pilgrim at Tinker Creek* (New York: HarperCollins, 1985, 266).

p. 197, ll.3–7. *Thus stone ... Paradise.* "As stone upon stone, course upon course, endlessly I raised, / So pace by pace ascending higher, I returned to heaven"—lines added by Giovanbattista Strozzi to Brunelleschi's epitaph in Santa Maria del Fiore (Giorgio Vasari, "Filippo Brunelleschi," *Lives of the Artists*, 1:173).

p. 197, ll. 11–18. *Paolo Uccello ... he'd call out.* "Paolo decorated the vaulting of the Peruzzi in fresco with triangular sections in perspective, and in the angles of the corner he painted the four elements, representing each by an appropriate animal: a mole for earth, a fish for water, a salamander for fire, and for air the chameleon, which lives on air and assumes any colour.... He left a daughter, who had some knowledge of drawing, and a wife who told people that Paolo used to stay up all night in his study, trying to work out the vanishing points of his perspective, and that when she called him to come to be he would say, 'Oh, what a lovely thing this perspective is!'" (Giorgio Vasari, "Paolo Uccello," *Lives of the Artists*, 1:102, 104).

p. 197, l. 20. *diamond zones.* In one of his letters Paul Cézanne says that colors were to him "numinous essences" beyond which he knew nothing and that "the diamond zones of God" remained white (qtd. by Heinrich Wiegand Petzet in his "Foreword" to Ranier Maria Rilke's *Letters on Cézanne* [New York: Fromm International, 1985], xxiv).

p. 198, ll. 4–6. *As the master said ... subtract.* The reference is to chap. 48 of the *Tao Te Ching*: "In the pursuit of learning one knows more every day; in the pursuit of the way one does less every day. One does less and less until one does nothing at all, and when one does nothing at all there is nothing that is undone" (trans. D.C. Lau); "The student learns by daily increment. / The Way is gained by daily loss, / Loss upon loss until / At last comes rest. / By letting go it all gets done; / The world is won by those who let it go! / But when you try and try, / The world is then beyond the winning" (trans. R.B. Blakney).

Chinese Journal

Orig. pub. *Gettysburg Review* 1, no. 1 (Winter 1988): 32.
ZJ, 96–7; WTTT, 199–200
Pattern: 4-4-4-2-4
Time: Autumn
Place: Charlottesville

The five sections of this poem seek to replicate the vision of Giorgio Morandi, in whose repeated drawings of bottles less is more, and the hard-edged, clear vision of the Chinese poets. About the Chinese poets Wright has said, as already noted, "One of the great contributions of the T'ang poets is to show us how to get personal emotions out of a real landscape. You transfer it to the landscape and then you get it back" (*Halflife*, 132). This transfer is apparent in the static aggression of the spike plants in section 2 and the longing of the Pothos plant in section 3. It is sufficient, the poet concludes, to find the right word. Throughout is the refrain of the motifs of absence and stasis: the spaces in Morandi's bottles, the stillness of bristly spike plants, the nothingness on which the stems of the Pothos plant dangle, and the sense of rest after the falling of the leaves and water. This is a world in a grain of sand.

p. 199, ll. 1–4. *Morandi*. See the commentary on *Morandi*, CM, 114.

Night Journal II

ZJ, 98; WTTT, 201
Pattern: 6 × 3

Time: Winter
Place: Charlottesville

The first *Night Journal* poem (*WTTT*, 147–9) foregrounded the ephemeral quality of words as they disappear into nothingness. The present poem is a variation on the same theme. Here the soundless speech of the *spiritus mundi* (the "breath of What's-Out-There") implode "into articulation ... for the unbecome." The phonemes of the *spiritus mundi*, trailing along the ground, thus issue in nothing. Similarly with the poet: "I'd say what it says: nothing with all its verities / Gone to the ground and hiding." Although he is unable to answer this spiritual What's-To-Come, he feels rather at home in the *Urgrund* of the hidden god, as he longs for silence in solitude. This dark night of the soul is what Wright elsewhere calls "negative transcendence" (Turner; Spiegelman, 121).

  p. 201, l. 6. *unbecome.* According to the Buddha, the Unbecome is Nirvana (*The Tibetan Book of the Dead*, ed. W.Y. Evans-Wentz [Oxford: Oxford University Press, 2000], 68); in Angelus Silesius it is the Godhead (1.29).

Xionia (1990)

Xionia orig. pub. in an edition of 250 copies at The Windhover Press, University of Iowa, 1990.

The title is a play on "Zion," the Old Testament mountain that came to stand for Jerusalem and by extension to the entire Promised Land. "Xionia" (or "Zionia"), thus, represents the end of the movement toward which the journals point. It also has a private meaning—the Victorian house in Charlottesville where Wright lives and where he wrote the poems in *Xionia*. The previous owners had named the house "Ionia." Wright and his wife decided to prefix the name with an "X."

Silent Journal

Xionia, 11; *WTTT*, 205
Pattern: 5
Time: Winter
Place: Charlottesville

Landscape, as Wright repeatedly reveals, has its own language. Here the language is the inaudible snow that "continues to fall." This metaphor slides into a simile: the back yard is "like a book of snow / That holds nothing and that nothing holds." The simile in turn slides back into metaphor: the book of snow is an "Immaculate text" that is prescient and true, though not overly so. The precursor here is Wallace Stevens's *The Snow Man*: "...For the listener, who listens in the snow, / And, nothing himself, beholds / Nothing that is not there and the nothing that is" (ll. 13–15).

  p. 205, l. 3. The dropped-down line should be extended to the right. In *Xionia* the line is properly formatted.

Bicoastal Journal

Xionia, 12–13; *WTTT*, 206–7
Pattern: (7 × 2) (5 × 2) (7 × 2)
Time: January
Place: California, Charlottesville

The two coasts are sun-lit California, with its jacaranda and eucalyptus, and chilly Virginia, with its oaks and pines, laurel and maple. The constant element on both coasts is water.

The California landscape of section 1 is saturated with moisture, even after the rains cease. In section 3 the poet gazes upward into the undulating needles of the pines, which he projects as the rippling current of a "sea wash." This triggers his desire to be elsewhere—in an elemental world where he is identified with water and fire. Water, ordinarily a lower-world archetype lying beneath the vegetable world, is conventionally associated with dissolution and death, but here it is an image of an apocalyptic wish-fulfillment. If not "hugging" and "licking" the natural world, then the poet would like to be "memory, touching the undersides / Of all I ever touched once in the natural world."

Each of these projected journeys is a concrete instance of the power of contemplation embodied in section 2, by way of Richard of St. Victor. Richard says, "Contemplation, in free flight, circles around with marvelous quickness wherever impulse moves it. Thinking crawls; meditation marches and often runs; contemplation flies around everywhere and when it wishes suspends itself in the heights" (Richard of St. Victor, *The Twelve Patriarchs, The Mystical Ark, Book Three of the Trinity*, trans. Grover A. Zinn [New York: Paulist Press, 1979], 155). Richard doesn't say so, but contemplation can also descend into the depths, as in the journey of the poet in section 3. In Richard's formulation, contemplation can be either imaginative or rational in various combinations, or it can be "beyond" both. "There are," he says, in a passage that Wright reproduces almost verbatim, "six kinds of contemplation in themselves, and within each there are many divisions. The first is in imagination and according to imagination only. The second is in imagination and according to reason. The third is in reason and according to imagination. The fourth is in reason and according to reason. The fifth is above but not beyond reason. The sixth is above reason and seems to be beyond reason" (ibid., 161). Richard has no name for what lies beyond reason, but he is clearly referring to some anagogic state—a world, as Yeats says, "out of nature." Here the poet cannot confront the "absolute" directly, but its murmur can "retoggle" him and thus switch the apocalyptic circuit back on.

Saturday Morning Journal

Xionia, 14; *WTTT*, 208
Pattern: 2-5-5

This journal entry finds the poet singing the Saturday morning blues: nature provides no answers; form is dissolving, and inaccessibility is (punningly) "in the wind." The reason for this bleak state of affairs is that "There is a twice-remove in the light." In the Platonic scheme of things, this means that whatever light the poet sees is an imitation of an imitation, and so is two steps removed from the genuinely real world of Ideas, as the California landscape was in *California Dreaming* (*WTTT*, 115–18). This twice-removed world has "been translated into a new language," about which the poet understands nothing.. He thus stands clueless before the "local objects." The landscape reveals a "false weather," like the shadows on the wall of the Plato's cave. The landscape has some innate quality ("the inborn"), but the poet is baffled by the "new language" of the world before him.

December Journal

Xionia, 15–17; *WTTT*, 209-11
Pattern: (9 × 2) (5 × 2) (10 × 2) (4 × 2)
Place: Charlottesville

This is another of Wright's versions of the dialogue between the body and the soul—between the corporeal or material world and the spiritual one. The first two lines set the terms of the debate. In the fuller passage from "Of True Religion," which Wright paraphrases, Augustine declares, "It is sin which deceives souls, when they seek something that is true but abandon or neglect truth. They love the works of the artificer more than the artificer or his art, and are punished by falling into the error of expecting to find the artificer and his art in his works, and when they cannot do so they think that the works are both the art and the artificer. God is not offered to the corporeal senses, and transcends even the mind" (Augustine, "Of True Religion," sec. 36, par. 67, in *Augustine: Earlier Writings*, trans. John H.S. Burleigh [Philadelphia: Westminster Press, 1953], 259). Here the opposition is between the objective things of this world (works), which are available to the senses, and the skill (art) of the creator (divine artificer), which is not. Wright then adds a line from later in Augustine's treatise: "Nothing is good if it can be better" (ibid., sec. 41, par. 78; p. 265). But the poet, glancing at the oaks and cedar before him, is unwilling to grant that this is the case. The cedar for him suffers no imperfection, being a true example of its species, and moreover it "ghosts a unity beyond its single member," meaning that it fits perfectly into the genus of trees. Thus, the poet is not prepared to reject the significance of the visible world. What he does reject is the hierarchical dualism in Augustine's theology.

For Wright the visible world is never the material world only. The tree is always a surrogate for something else, even though it might be "the blank / The far side of the last equation." The difference between Wright and Augustine is that Wright does not believe in any kind of absolute separation between subject and object, the material and the spiritual, the human and the divine. They interpenetrate. "[W]e carry this world with us," he says, "wherever we go, / Even into the next one." "[T]he word," he says, echoing Eliot, is "inside the word."

To be sure, the things of this world "fall away," but the "utmost" is always contained in the least. Augustine says that when we love the things of the world, we fall away from truth, our affection for the world being therefore wasted (section 3). But Wright cannot abandon his affection for the landscape, and while we may never be able to live up to the affection we feel—that disposition of the heart Wright (re)turns to time and again—we must nevertheless continue to love even those things we can't understand. Affection, he will later say, is "the absolute // everything rises to" (*Apologia Pro Vita Sua*, in *NB*, 84). What Wright opposes finally to Augustine's separation of body and soul is captured perfectly in the extraordinary phrase of the last stanza, "the immanence of infinitude / In whatever our hands touch." "The other world is here," he adds, "just under our fingertips." This is Wright's version of Blake's holding "Infinity in the palm of your hand / And Eternity in an Hour" (*Auguries of Innocence*, ll. 3–4). It is also a poetic version of what Christian theology calls the Incarnation.

p. 209, l. 16. *the word inside the word*. Cf. T.S. Eliot: "Signs are taken for wonders. 'We would see a sign!' / The word within a word" (Gerontion, l. 18)

p. 210, l. 1. *Pollocked*. That is, the colors of the December landscape are like a Jackson Pollock painting.

p. 210, ll. 4–5. *Entangled ... next one*. "He [the corporeal creature] does not know that he is still entangled in the lust of the eye, and that he is carrying this world with him in his endeavor to go beyond it" (Augustine, *Of True Religion*, sec. 29, par. 40; p. 244).

p. 210, l. 7. *Everything's beautiful ... due order*. Cf. Augustine: "A line of poetry is beautiful in its own way though no two syllables can be spoken at the same time. The second cannot be spoken until the first is finished. So in due order the end of the line is reached" (ibid., sec. 21, par, 42; p. 245).

p. 210, l. 10. *integer vitae*. Blameless in life; innocent. Cf. Thomas Campion: "The man of life upright, / Whose guiltless heart is free / From all dishonest deeds, / Or thought of vanity.... / He only can behold / With unaffrighted eyes / The horrors of the deep / And terrors of the skies" (*Integer Vitae*, ll. 1–4, 13–16, an imitation of Horace, Ode, 1.22).

p. 210, l. 15. *that spells my name right*. An aural pun.

p. 210, l. 19. *How are we ... fall away*. "So long as a thing is a matter of fun and games, we know that it arouses laughter when it counterfeits truth. But when we love such things we fall away from truth" ("Of True Religion," sec. 49, par. 95; p. 274).

A Journal of Three Questions

Xionia, 18; *WTTT*, 212
Pattern: 4–3–1
Place: Charlottesville

Beginning with an observation about the bees atop the junkweed blooms, the poet quickly turns his attention to the ants descending the stems of the plant into the darkness around "the roots of the wheat grass and the violets." Then we have four selections taken from *Tian Wen: A Chinese Book of Origins* (trans. Stephen Field [New York: New Directions, 1986]. "Tian Wen" means "heaven asks" or "heaven's questions," or perhaps "questions about heaven." It is a collection of 186 poetic passages, mostly in the form of two-line questions. These are Wright's borrowings:

> The beginning of the end, / How was it recognized? (no. 95)
> From light until dark / Is a pass of how many miles? (no. 16)
> When dark and bright were obscured, / Who could distinguish? (no. 3)
> Mean creatures are the bees and ants. / Why is their power pervasive? (no. 174)

The "six-pointed junkweed" has a parallel to the "nine-jointed calamus" in couplet no. 51 of the *Tian Wen*, "prehensile darkness" perhaps owes something to "the darkest dark" of no. 5, and no. 6 is a riddle about "the root."

The *Tian Wen* contains a great deal of mythological and legendary material, now shrouded in the mystery of the past. Its questions seem not to have been posed as riddles, for they have no answers—at least any that we can determine now. Various theories have been advanced about origin and function of the *Tian Wen*—a catechism for shamans, a story-teller's prompt book, and a debate exercise for Chinese dialecticians, among others (see Field's introduction, xi–xvii). But for its latter-day uses, we can be certain of one: the "Book of Origins" provided material for making a poem. The poem begins and ends with ants and bees, but Wright has changed couplet 174 of the *Tian Wen* from a question into an affirmation.

Georg Trakl Journal

Xionia, 19–20; *WTTT*, 213–14
Pattern: 9 × 4
Time: June 21
Place: Charlottesville

Wright has remarked that one of his three favorite poets is Trakl, the other two being Rimbaud and Hart Crane: "It's their passion I love. They are great 'I' poets, whatever persona they use" (*Profile*, 46). In both Wright and Trakl the landscape speaks vividly, and both poets write often of solitude and silence. "I wish to walk near the forest edge," Trakl writes, "a man of silence, from whose speechless hands sank a sun of hair" (*Revelation and Decline*, in *Poems* [Athens, Ohio: Mundus Artium Press, 1973], 171). There is a connection as well in the images both poets call on, though in different contexts. In this poem they are thorns, stars, wounded mouths, things crystalline, toads, pine trees, and roses. The theme of decline runs throughout Trakl's poems, and *Georg Trakl Journal* is about the decline of the poet's powers: "Last year, and the year before, // the landscape spoke to me / Wherever I turned," but now on the first day of summer, the "Fricatives and labials," the vowels and consonants, so abundantly present before, have disappeared. Only silence remains, and the poem concludes with a declaration of muteness: "Nothing says anything // Nothing says nothing."

But as is so often the case in Wright's poems, stanzas 1, 3, and 4 undercut the announcement of writer's block in stanza 2. The poet in fact does not remain silent. His description of the bodies gliding through the dwarf orchard, the arbor vitae, the stars above the ash trees, and the "Haloes of crystal thorns" parachuting out of the sky reveal anything but a diminution of linguistic energy. In the last stanza, with its cluster of religious tropes (nun, crosses, haloes, cloistered, vows) we have a dazzling example, not of nothing saying anything, but of something saying everything. The effect, then, is characteristically ironic: the poet's actions belie his lament about loss.

p. 213, l. 9. *St. Thomas*. The words of Thomas the Apostle: "Except I shall see in his hands the print of the nails, and put my finger into the place of the nails, and put my hand into his side, I will not believe" (John 20:25). Cf. Trakl's "The hand of St. Thomas touches the wound" (*Poems*, 45).

Primitive Journal

Orig. pub. *New Republic* 198 (25 April 1988): 36.
Xionia, 21; *WTTT*, 215
Pattern: 5 × 2
Time: April
Place: Charlottesville

The "weight of afternoon" in this poem about the poet's feelings of heaviness, weariness, and oppressiveness reminds us of Emily Dickinson's *There's a Certain Slant of Light*. Dickinson's "imperial affliction" and "heavenly hurt" parallel Wright's "weariness ... oppressive as purity." In *Primitive Journal* the heaviness felt in the external world of stanza 1 is projected as internal weariness in stanza 2, echoing the "internal difference" caused by Dickinson's "slant of light." In both poems, in other words, the objective becomes subjective. The journal entry is primitive not so much in the sense of archaic as in the sense of basic, original, and instinctual ("beyond our knowing").

Language Journal

Xionia, 22–5; *WTTT*, 216–19
Pattern: (10 × 2) (10 × 2) (10 × 2) (10) (10)
Time: February–March
Place: Charlottesville, with flashback to Umbria

This poem is a critique of the theory of language of the so-called Language Poets, a movement that began in the 1970s, taking its cues from Gertrude Stein, Louis Zufoksky, the Black Mountain poets and others, and marrying itself to certain postmodern tenets, such as the indeterminacy of meaning, the centrality of the reader, and the priority of language to all other poetic concerns. Wright has remarked elsewhere that because the Language Poets eschew meaning and purpose he sees their work as reaching a dead end (Clark). In the opening paragraph of *Halflife*, Wright says, "Poems are put together with words, not Language. Word by word. Theory comes after the fact, it is not the fact. The line is a fact, it is not a theory" (3). This remark, he told an interviewer, was "aimed at Language Poetries and their attendant pedantries. A side-swipe on the way to, I hope, a larger truth—which is that poetry, if not Platonic, is surely numinous. And luminous. And exists outside the realm of theory. And prior to it, not successive. No Deconstruction first, then deconstructed poems (Language Poetry). No Post-Structuralism then de—as it were—structured poems (Language Poetry)" (Caseley, 24). While Wright is attracted to the emphasis on sound one finds in a Language Poet like

Michael Palmer, he nevertheless judges the movement as a whole as producing "junk" (Clark). In the poem Wright's appraisal of the Language Poets' enterprise, which appears explicitly in section 2 and implicitly in the rest of the poem, is less blunt. In section 2, which is sprinkled with phrases drawn from Douglas Messerli's introduction to *"Language" Poetries*, Wright simply says of the Language theorists' contentions, "I don't think so," adding that the proper verb for describing the poet's function is "reconstruct, not deconstruct."

The poem begins on a late February afternoon in Charlottesville and ends a month later, with a flashback of a remembered trip through Umbria sometime earlier (section 3). The unlikely trio at the beginning of section 1 (St. Jerome, Han Shan, and Paul of Thebes), who would "feel at ease" in the present scene, set the tone for the religious imagery that flows through this section: the "Light of martyrs and solitaries," the leaves like golden and blood-stained reliquaries, "the expiation of held breath," even the "radiance" of the Locust Avenue joggers on this Sunday afternoon. The Language Poets claim that "Nothing means anything" (p. 217, l. 7), but in section 1 the poet reveals that the landscape is invested with a surplus of meaning, from the celebration of the saints who dance their way back into the avenue of light to the poet's awareness of the despair that lies just below the surface of the baroque landscape. The poet's language successfully captures the numinous qualities of this landscape.

Similarly in section 2, the poet affirms, as against the Language Poets, that there is a "vertical axis / Of meaning" contained in the beads of water on the oak tree. This is a meaning that points to something beyond morphemes and syllables. It points to "the music of what's real, / The plainsong of being"—which the poet aims to reconstruct.

"What I remember is how / I remember it," says the poet about the "*Umbria mistica*" of section 3. Umbria is best known as the birthplace of Saint Francis of Assisi, and that, along with a religious tradition, earned the region the name "Umbria mistica." The landscape with its Umbrian light, a silver haze that hangs over the gentle curves of the Perugian countryside, contributes to the mystical aura. The road from Spello to Collepino, both small villages, girdles the southeastern flank of Mount Subasio. The direction of the trip described is northeast from Spello to Collepino and then over Mount Subasio in a counterclockwise direction down the hairpins to the "sanctuary"—the Basilica of San Francesco d'Assisi at the western base of the mountain. The memory of the ascetic landscape leads to reflections about both the pain and pleasure of guilt, self-denial, and deprivation, and this in turn to reflections on the connections between the concrete and the abstract. Abstractions such as "self" and "lies," which are "Inside the centricity of surface," are deeper and more substantial than language, however difficult it is for us to "put our finger on" them. They remain hidden yet discoverable, just as the word "lies" is hidden in the word "lines."

Language, the poet affirms in section 4, is an instrumental value, not a final one. It is a means of truth-telling, and the story it tells in late March (section 5) is not comic, but ironic.

p. 216, ll. 4–5. *Jerome.* St. Jerome (ca. 340–420), Christian apologist and translator of the Bible from the Hebrew and Greek into Latin. *Cold Mountain.* A Chinese poet of the T'ang dynasty, ca. 7th–9th centuries, also known as Han Shan. *Paul of Thebes.* An ascetic (ca. 230–341), traditionally regarded as the first Christian hermit. During his own stay in a desert in Syria, Jerome wrote the story of Paul's life.
p. 217, l. 1. *Maybe the theorists ... from language.* "The poets in this anthology have all foregrounded language itself as the project of their writing. For these poets, language is not something that *explains* or *translates* experience, but is the source of experience" (Douglas Messerli, "Introduction," *"Language" Poetries: An Anthology*, ed. Messerli [New York: New Directions, 1987], 2).
p. 217, ll. 7–10. *Nothing means ... slip of phrase ... transformation of adverb ... phoneme.* "The poets in this collection ask for a reading in which meaning, whether understood as curative or entertainment, is not self-contained ... but is inseparable from the language in process—the transformation of phoneme into word, the association of one word to the next, the slip of phrase against phrase...." (ibid., 3).
p. 217, l. 16. *along the vertical axis.* "[Bruce] Andrews [one of the Language Poetry theorists] argues consistently for

sense emerging from an 'interplay on the surface' of the poem rather than along a 'vertical axis' in which meaning takes place largely 'below the plane, out of sight, or earshot'" (ibid., 4).

p. 217, l. 20. *The sound of one hand clapping.* "What is the sound of one hand clapping?" is an ancient Zen koan.

p. 218, l. 12. The Language Poets, as Messerli points out in the introduction to his anthology (note to p. 217, l. 1, above), seek to "explode" the idea of the self (6–7).

p. 218, l. 17. *Raggio verde.* Green flash, an atmospheric phenomenon that is seen as a faint green beam of light visible in the Italian west on the top of the sun's disk at dawn or at sunset.

Primitive Journal II

Xionia, 26; *WTTT*, 220
Pattern: 2-3-2-3
Time: September
Place: Charlottesville

The September weather cleverly repeats itself across than landscape polyphonically, from the "fugue" of the dry conditions to the "psaltery of the sunlight." The musical tropes lead up to a plea, once again, for affection, a grace that lies beyond wisdom. True affection, declares the poet, should be the object of our prayers. The conclusion turns on a distinction between charity and affection, both of which are forms of love. Affection is a matter of devotedly adoring the natural world; as grace, it is a beneficence freely given. Charity, which cannot "touch" affection, is apparently for Wright a matter of compassion toward others, in the Pauline sense. This journal is "primitive" insofar as it calls on the primal form of language (music) to engage the relation of the primal virtues to the landscape.

May Journal

Xionia, 27–8; *WTTT*, 221–2
Pattern: 9 × 4
Place: Charlottesville

Notes from the provinces, says the poet, usually begin with a weather report and then go on to speak of the effects of the weather on the heart or soul. This note from Charlottesville—the poem—follows the first part of the convention but not the second. An ordinary note might observe, for example, that the new life bursting forth on this May afternoon signals an end to the wintry depression of the soul or lifts the heart from its icy doldrums. But the poet's note has nothing of that. The opening convention may be ordinary, but there is nothing ordinary in the poet's own weather report about the golden broom of sunlight, the "floor of being" like a crystal ... the landscape half shines through," and the flashing tulips. The weather report shows everything to be brilliantly lit, and the poet extends his description by locating the "word as world" halfway between the eye ("Image as image") and the ear ("note of music").

The weather report contains no message, but in stanza 3 the poet does speculate on the meaning of what he sees before him. The issue is whether or not the visible world we inhabit, as opposed to the Utopian world we desire, is Paradise. Is Paradise what was described in the weather report of stanza 1? Or is that simply an illusion, "a trompe l'oeil" that only gives the impression of a genuine Paradise? The poet says the he once read about this in a book, and the book may well have contained Wallace Stevens's *Sunday Morning*, where the speaker, who is also living in "an old chaos of the sun," asks, "And shall the earth / Seem all of paradise that we shall know?" The conventional view of Genesis is that with the Fall we got kicked out of Paradise, our proper home, and that our journey through this life is an effort to get back home. The poet appears to agree with the view that the landscape before him is only an illusion of Paradise. In any event, he does concur that Paradise is still lost and that whatever shelter we have from the stormy blast, it is not, as the hymn has it, "our eternal home." "[S]helter is not transcendence," he declares, adding that "I haven't found it [the paradisal shelter] back here in the dwarf orchard."

In stanza 4 the poet's circle of speculation expands outward. What is it that has triggered the questions about Paradise and transcendence in the first place? He cannot answer the questions he poses in the last stanza, but the assumptions underlying the questions reveal that he affirms something like the myth of the eternal return—the universal story in which certain events of creative and religious significance continue to be reenacted. One such story is the movement from death to life that we call the comic and romantic vision. Such a vision elevates the speechlessness of ecstasy over the muteness of verisimilitude. It is as if "the sirens had something to say to us after all," what they had to say, which was more important than their melody, being the promise of knowledge, a quickened spirit, and even wisdom. Such is the end to which a daily weather report can lead.

p. 222, ll. 4. *Someone.* A purely fictional character

Vesper Journal

Xionia, 29; *WTTT*, 222
Pattern: 4 × 2
Time: Late spring
Place: Charlottesville

The first quatrain notes the last two things that cross the poet's field of vision in the twilight of the lower orchard—the grackles and dogwood petals—and the last thing he hears—the doves' moans. The description is presented with little rhetorical ornament, the only figurative flourish being the petals-as-skirts simile.

The second quatrain speculates about the place of the human voice in the world just described. The answer seems to be that it has very little place, because "language, always, is just language." But language has the power to be more than just itself, always moving out from its ostensible referents to a wider world of meaning. Even in the present poem, which seems to be straightforward semantically, we may wonder whether "old friend" is an appositive or an apostrophe and whether "last things," in the context of the end of the day, carries an eschatological intimation.

A Journal of Southern Rivers

Orig. pub. New Yorker 64, no. 20 (4 July 1988): 28–9.
Xionia, 30–33; *WTTT*, 224–6
Pattern: (6 × 2) (2) (6 × 2) (2) (6 × 2) (2) (6 × 2) (2)
Time: July–September 1987
Place: Yaak Valley, Montana

In a life-changing experience that occurred twenty-eight years earlier, Wright had read Pound's *Blandula, Tenulla, Vagula* (Pleasant, Tender, Evanescent) at Sirmione on Lake Garda near Verona, Italy. He dates the beginning of his poetic career from that moment in March 1959. The title is a variation on Hadrian's address to his soul on his deathbed, "Animula, vagula, blandula" ("little soul, evanescent, pleasant"). Pound's poem begins, "What hast thou, O my soul, with paradise? / Will we not rather, when our freedom's won, / Get us to some clear place wherein the sun / Lets drift in on us through the olive leaves / A liquid glory?" Pound's first question refers to the conventional view of paradise as otherworldly. In his second question paradise is an earthly paradise, a paradise of the here and now, which is what both Pound and Wright affirm. Pound said that "the essence of religion is the *present tense*" (*Selected Prose, 1909-1965*, ed. William Cookson [New York: New Directions, 1975], 70), and for him Paradise was also in the present tense, not some construct projected into the future or beyond death. He called this latter a "painted paradise at the end of it" (Canto LXXIV, in *Cantos*, 456), an image that Wright picks up in stanza 2, opposing the "painted and paralyzed" Paradise to the "liquid glory" of the earthly one, which comes from "Love of the physical world." "Let the wind speak / that is paradise," Pound wrote in his *Notes for Canto CXVII et seq.* (*Cantos*, 822), and Wright concurs. It is the question about the soul in the earthly Paradise that "has never changed."

In an interview with J.D. McClatchy, Wright provides what amounts to a gloss on the idea of Paradise in the first two stanzas of the poem: "The textures of the world are an outline of the infinite. Stevens said, or at least I seem to remember that he said, the thing seen becomes the thing unseen. He also said that the reverse way was impossible. Roethke wrote that all finite things reveal infinitude [*A Far Field*, pt. 4, l. 13]. What we have, and all we will have, is here in the earthly paradise. How to wring music from it, how to squeeze the light out of it, is, as it has always been, the only true question. I'd say that to love the visible things in the visible world is to love their apokatastatic [restored] outline in the invisible next" (QN, 120).

Attention to the "liquid glory" of the things of this world means attention to the "isness of everything" (section 2) or Heidegger's "Being" (section 3). Such attention produces the "awe and astonishment" by which "we regain ourselves in the world" (section 3). Wright's universe is not a hierarchical one, where the separation between the immanent and the transcendent is absolute, but an interpenetrating one—a universe in which the entire cosmos can be reflected in a drop of dew. The context of the drop of dew passage from Dogen Zenji in section 4 is enlightenment: "Gaining enlightenment is like the moon reflected on the water. The moon doesn't get wet. The water isn't broken. Although its light is broad and great, the moon is reflected even in a puddle an inch wide. The whole moon and the whole sky are reflected in one dewdrop on the grass" (*Shobogenzo*, vol. 1, trans. G. Nishijima and C. Cross [London: Windbell Publishers, 1996], 36). Dogen Zenji goes on to say, "Enlightenment does not divide you, just as the moon does not break the water. You cannot hinder enlightenment, just as a drop of water does not hinder the moon in the sky. The depth of the drop is the height of the moon. Each reflection, however long of short its duration, manifests the vastness of the dewdrop, and realizes the limitlessness of the moonlight in the sky" (ibid.).

This is an Eastern version of the interpenetrating view of the cosmos that we find in Wordsworth and Blake, where our perception of the eternal world comes from the ordinary things of this one. Wright says, "We walk with one foot in each world" (section 2). At the end of the famous Simplon Pass episode of *The Prelude* Wordsworth writes, "The unfettered clouds and region of the Heavens, / Tumult and peace, the darkness and the light—/ Were all like workings of one mind, the features / Of the same face, blossoms upon one tree; / Characters of the great Apocalypse, / The types and symbols of Eternity" (bk. 6, ll. 635-40). For Blake the "types and symbols of Eternity" are likewise to be found in the unexceptional things of the natural world: "To see a World in a Grain of Sand / And a Heaven in a Wild Flower, / Hold Infinity in the palm of your hand / And Eternity in an hour" (*Auguries of Innocence*, ll. 104). In *December Journal* Wright characterized such vision as the "immanence of infinitude" and in the present poem as the "single spirit that lies at the root of all things" (section 5).

The poem moves from early July to September, and during this time the poet has passed another birthday—his fifty-second. He wonders how many chances are still left to get it right (section 5) and whether he can really trust his words (section 6). But the first stanza of section 7 about the coming storm should allay his fears—it does ours—about the power of words to do their proper job. So in spite of his anxieties, underwritten by the interrogative mood in the last half of the poem, Wright returns to the affirmation with which he began: "What lasts is what you start with," which is both Pound's line about Paradise and the southern rivers of Wright's early life.

p. 225, ll. 6–10. *If being ... no other.* The reference is to Martin Heidegger's various statements in *Being and Time* that the question of being relates to the totality of existence in this world. He says, for example, "Being is always the Being of an entity" (trans. John Macquarrie and Edward Robinson [New York: Harper & Row, 1962], 29).
p. 225, l. 15. *selva illuminata.* illuminated forest.
p. 225, l. 21. *to face all and not shirk.* Wright has said that this was an actual injunction he received (personal communication).

China Journal

Orig. pub. *New Yorker* 64, no. 32 (26 September 1988): 46.
Xionia, 34; *WTTT,* 227
Pattern: (3) (3) (2) (4)
Time: 1988

These four stanzas, each identified by a place-name, originated from Wright's trip to China in 1988. His note on p. 232 to Giacomo Prampolini's translation *Poesia Cinese* refers not to specific borrowings from those poems but simply to his effort to imitate the concision and concrete imagery of the Chinese poets.

p. 227, l. 5. *Chengdu.* The capital of the Sichuan province.
p. 227, l. 8. *Jialing River.* A tributary of the Yangtze.
p. 227, l. 9. *the power that moves what moves.* Wright's note: "'Takushanshan': Lakota Sioux" (*WTTT,* 232). Takushanshan (also Takushkanshkan, Takuskanskan) is the chief of Lakota gods. His name means "something that moves" or "the moving god"; thus, he is seen as the sacred air or breath of life and spirit.
p. 227, l. 10. *great river.* The Buddha actually overlooks the confluence of three rivers, the Minjiang, the Dadu, and the Qingyi.
p. 227, l. 11. *Leshan.* The city of Leshan in the Sichuan province is the site of the Great Buddha (seventy-one meters high), which was carved over a ninety-year period during the T'ang dynasty. Wright spoke in Leshan at the Fourth Sino-American Writer's Conference, April 1988.
p. 227, l. 16. *Xi'an.* The site of one of the most significant archeological discoveries of the twentieth century. The reference to the "emperor's men" is to the terra cotta warriors and horses unearthed about a mile east of Emperor Qin Shi Huang's Mausoleum, Lintong County, Shaanxi province. More than 7,000 pottery items have been unearthed.

Local Journal

Orig. pub. *New Yorker* 64, no. 41 (28 November 1988): 38–9.
Xionia, 35–7; *WTTT,* 228–9
Pattern: (7–4–1–7) (1–6–1–4–1–6)
Time: November–December
Place: Charlottesville, James River

The drama of the year's end is winding down—from the "afterpiece" of November's "commedia dell'arte" to the "denouement" of December. All the world's a stage: the clouds rearrange themselves against its "backdrop," and Expiation, who should be center stage in this morality play, is dozing in the wings. The revels of autumn have now ended.

Expiation asks, "How much will it all add up to?" and this becomes as well the question asked by the poet, who has been waiting in vain for fifty years. He has been reading an anthology of pre-Socratic philosophy, and here and there in his local journal he pastes brief passages from the early Greeks—Pythagoras (as reported by Aristotle), Parmenides and Melissus (as reported by St. Simplicius), Democritus, and Heraclitus. The poet does not comment on the two quotations from Heraclitus ("If you don't expect the unexpected, you'll never find it" and "You can't escape the attention of what you can't see"), but he would affirm the wisdom of both epigrams. He is less certain that Democritus has got it right. Democritus believed that atoms, the unchangeable substance of the universe, could be rearranged into different forms. The atoms of the void interact with the atoms in our bodies so as to produce the appearance of certain qualities. Atoms are round, pointed, solid, oily, and the like. When different atoms interact with the atoms of the tongue, they give the illusion of taste. "Still, you could have fooled me," the poet says in response to Democritus's statement about the conventions of taste, meaning that the juniper and rhododendron, the garbage cans and river rock, and the cross of the power pole are objects of real existence. What are the conventions of perception involved in the experience of these things?

It is a time for pruning the rhododendron, which in *May Journal* had metaphored wildly. The mood, especially after the setting changes to the James River, is one of diminishment, inactivity, and absence. There are no birds, no signs, and no news. No one comes forth. Autumn disappears. Everything darkens to "fine ash and a white coal" here at year's end.

p. 228, l. 8–9. "The Pythagoreans, too, said that void exists, and that it enters the universe from the infinite breath as if it were being inhaled. It is the void which keeps things distinct, being a kind of separation and division of things that are next to each other. This is true first and foremost of numbers, for the void keeps them distinct" (Aristotle, *Physics*, 213b22). Wright is silent on the matter of separation, and he changes "universe" to "heaven," the alterations intended apparently to make room for the line about punishment: whatever the means of atonement and reparation, the sheep will be separated from the goats (Matthew 25:31–46).

p. 228, l. 12. *Objects do not exist*. "Melissus thus clearly explains why they [i.e. Parmenides *and* Melissus] say that perceptible objects do not exist but seem to exist" (Simplicius, "Commentary on *On the Heavens*," 559.13, qtd. in Jonathan Barnes, *Early Greek Philosophy* [Harmondsworth: Penguin, 1987], 98).

p. 228, l. 12. "By convention sweet, by convention bitter, by convention hot, by convention cold, by convention colored, but in truth atoms and void" (Democritus, *Sextus Empiricus*, Fragment 9, qtd. in Jonathan Barnes, *Early Greek Philosophy* [Harmondsworth: Penguin, 1987], 209).

p. 229, l. 1. Cf. "Again waking, I stretch a hand out / to stop the warning clock. // Time is another country" (Denise Levertov, *Broken Ghazals*, ll. 22–4).

p. 229, l. 2. *If you don't ... find it.* Heraclitus, Fragment 7

p. 229, l. 14. *You can't ... see*. Heraclitus, Fragment 27.

Last Journal

Xionia, 38; WTTT, 230
Pattern: 1-1-2-1

The last of the twenty-five journals is a final judgment. We will be sentenced according to the words we've used to recreate the things of this world, which have been a matter of both trust and lust. In the context of "mouths" and "word" perhaps "sentenced" contains a trace of "spoken": by their words shall you know them. But as death will soon cause us to forget the world and it us, what then? In the face of such a bleak awareness, the poet concludes this leg of his pilgrimage with an affirmation, which is that there is a continuity between this world and the next. This continuity is represented by a single word of the wind. We're not told what this word is, but the suggestion is that it's *spirit*. Breathing is what keeps us alive in this world, and in several of our languages, as noted before, the words for *breath/wind* are the same as those for *spirit*: *ruach* (Hebrew), *pneuma* (Greek), *spiritus* (Latin), *akasha* (Sanscrit), *gandr* (Old Norse), *chi* (Chinese), among others. If it is the spirit that unites our lives as they pass "from this one to that one," then Wright's *Last Journal* acknowledges something quite close to Paul's *soma pneumatikon*, the spiritual body (1 Corinthians 15:44).

Appendix 1: Reviews of Wright's Books, 1968–1990

Note: Giannelli = *High Lonesome: On the Poetry of Charles Wright*, ed. Adam Giannelli. Oberlin, Ohio: Oberlin College, 2006. Andrews = *The Point Where All Things Meet: Essays on Charles Wright*, ed. Tom Andrews. Oberlin, Ohio: Oberlin College Press, 1995. Reviews of Wright's books from 1995 to 2007 are listed in Robert D. Denham, *Charles Wright: A Companion to the Late Poetry, 1988-2007*. Jefferson, NC, and London: McFarland & Co., 2008. 239–43.

The Dream Animal. Toronto: House of Anansi, 1968.
Poetry (February 1971): 322.

The Grave of the Right Hand. Middletown, CT: Wesleyan University Press, 1970.
Agena, Kathleen. "The Mad Sense of Language." *Partisan Review* 43, no. 4 (1976): 625–30.
Anon. *Kirkus Reviews* (1 February 1970): 168.
Library Journal (15 March 1970): 1036.

The Venice Notebook. Boston: Barn Dream Press, 1971.
Library Journal (15 November 1972): 3717.

Hard Freight. Middletown, CT: Wesleyan University Press, 1973.
Agena, Kathleen. "The Mad Sense of Language." *Partisan Review* 43, no. 4 (1976): 625–30.
Anon. *Times Literary Supplement* (29 March 1974): 339.
Carpenter, John R. "The Big Machine." *Poetry* 125, no. 3 (1974): 166–73.
Choice 11 (April 1974): 264.
Gall, Sally M. "Seven from Wesleyan." *Shenandoah* 21, no. 1 (1974): 54–70.
Kennedy, X.J. "Lovers of Greece, Women, and Tennessee." *New York Times Book Review* (17 February 1974): 6.
Kessler, Edward. "The Shortest Distance between Two Poets." *Washington Post Book World* (5 May 1974): 3
Meinke, Peter. *New Republic* 169 (24 November 1973): 26–7.
Morris, John N. "Making More Sense than Omaha." *Hudson Review* 27, no. 1 (1974): 106–18.
National Observer (9 February 1974): 25.
Pinsky, Robert. "Description and the Virtuous Use of Words." *Parnassus* 3, no. 2 (1975): 134–46. Revised version rpt. in *The Situation of Poetry: Contemporary Poetry and Its Traditions*. Princeton: Princeton University Press, 1976. 111–18.
Ramsey, Paul. "American Poetry in 1973." *Sewanee Review* 82 (Spring 1974): 399.
Smith, Dave. *Library Journal* 99 (1 February 1974): 368.

Bloodlines. Middletown, CT: Wesleyan University Press, 1975.

Agena, Kathleen. "The Mad Sense of Language." *Partisan Review* 43, no. 4 (1976): 625–30. Partially rpt. in "Charles Wright," *Contemporary Literary Criticism*, Volume 13. Detroit: Gale Research Company, 1984. 613.
Anon. *Kirkus Reviews* (1 January 1975): 67.
Choice (September 1975): 848.
D'Aguiar, Fred. *Library Journal* (July 2001): 95.
Garrison, Joseph. *Library Journal* 100, no. 4 (15 February 1975): 398.
McClatchy, J.D. "Recent Poetry: New Designs on Life." *Yale Review* 65, no. 1 (Autumn 1975): 103–5.
Morris, John N. "The Songs Protect Us, in a Way." *Hudson Review* 28, no. 3 (1975): 446–58.
New York Times Book Review (7 September 1975): 6.
North American Review 261 (Fall 1976): 91.
Sewanee Review 84 (July 1976): 533.
Stitt, Peter. "The Inward Journey." *Ohio Review* 17 (1976): 91–2. Rpt. as part of "Five Reviews" in Andrews, 53–4.
Vendler, Helen. *New Yorker* 55 (29 October 1979): 160–9.

China Trace. Middletown, CT: Wesleyan University Press, 1977.

America 138 (8 April 1978): 283.
Booklist (1 January 1978): 891.
Book World (11 December 1977): E6.
Bromwich, David. "I Showed Her My Darkness, She Gave Me a Stone." *Poetry* 133, no. 3 (1978): 169–76.
Choice (March 1978): 75.
Garrison, Joseph. *Library Journal* 102, no. 14 (1 August 1977): 1654.
Jackson, Richard. "Worlds Created, Worlds Perceived." *Michigan Quarterly Review* 17, no. 4 (Fall 1978): 555–6.
Kirkus Reviews (15 August 1977): 924.
Kliatt (Winter 1978): 19.
New Republic 177 (26 November 1977): 26.
New York Times Book Review (1 January 1978): 10.
North American Review 264 (Fall 1979): 71.
Sadoff, Ira. *American Book Review* 1, no. 4 (October 1978): 8.
Sewanee Review 86 (July 1978): 454.
Stitt, Peter. *Georgia Review* 32, no. 2 (1978): 474–80. Rpt. as part of "Five Reviews" in Andrews, 54–7.
Vendler, Helen. *New Yorker* 55 (29 October 1979): 160–9.

Wright: A Profile. New Poems by Charles Wright with an Interview and a Critical Essay by David St. John. Iowa City: Grilled Flowers Press, 1979.

Booklist (15 January 1980): 703.

Dead Color. San Francisco: Meadow Press, 1980.

Anon. *American Book Collector* (May 1983): 27.
_____. *Fine Print* (January 1981): 20.

Country Music. Middletown, CT.: Wesleyan University Press, 1982. 2nd ed. Hanover, NH: Wesleyan/New England Press, 1991.

Atlas, James. "New Voices in American Poetry." *New York Times* 129 (3 February 1980): sec. 6, p. 16.
New York Times 132 (12 June 1983): 38.
New York Times Book Review 88 (12 December 1982): 14.
Parini, Jay. "From Scene to Fiery Scene." *Times Literary Supplement* (1 March 1985): 239.
St. John, David. "Charles Wright's *Country Music*." In *Country Music*, 2nd ed. Hanover, NH: Wesleyan / New England Press, 1991. xiii–xxi. Rpt. in Andrews, 86–93; in St. John's *Where the Angels Come Toward Us: Selected Essays, Reviews & Interviews*. Fredonia, NY: White Pine Press, 1995; and in Giannelli, 3–9.
Stitt, Peter. "Words, Book Words, What Are You?" *Georgia Review* 37, no. 2 (Summer 1983): 428–38.
Tillinghast, Richard. "From Michigan and Tennessee." *New York Times Book Review* 12 December 1982: 14.

The Southern Cross. New York: Random House, 1981.

Anon. *Western American Literature* 17 (Fall 1982): 268.
Axelrod, Steven Gould. *World Literature Today* 57 (Winter 1983): 111.
Bedient, Calvin. "Tracing Charles Wright." *Parnassus* 10 (Spring–Summer 1982): 55–74. Rpt. in Andrews, 21–38, and in Giannelli, 126–41.
Brown, Gary. *Library Journal* 106, no. 20 (15 November 1981): 2240–1.
Buckley, Christopher. "From Here To There: A Review of Charles Wright's *The Southern Cross.*" *Telescope* 4, no. 1 (1985): 81–94. Rpt. in Buckley's *Appreciations: Selected Reviews, Views & Interviews, 1975-2000*. Santa Barbara, CA: Millie Grazie Press, 2001. 39–51.
Conarroe, Joel. *Washington Post Book World* (27 June 1982): 10.
Kennedy, X.J. "A Tenth and Four-Fifths." *Poetry* 141, no. 6 (March 1983): 349–58.
Kirkus Reviews (15 September 1981): 1230.
Lodge, Sally. *Publishers Weekly* 220 (October 1981): 110.
Prado, Holly. "Respecting Poetry's Possibilities." *Los Angeles Times Book Review* 7 February 1982: 3.
St. John. "Raised Voices in the Choir: A Review of 1981 Poetry Selections." *Antioch Review* 40, no. 2 (Spring 1982): 225–34. Rpt. in *Where the Angels Come toward Us: Selected Essays, Reviews, and Interviews*. Fredonia, NY: White Pine Press, 1995.
Stewart, Pamela. "In All Places at Once." *Ironwood*, 19 (1982): 162–6.
Stitt, Peter. "Problems of Youth ... and Age." *Georgia Review* 36, no. 1 (1982): 183–93. Rpt. as part of "Five Reviews" in Andrews, 57–60.
Walker, David. "*One for the Rose* and *The Southern Cross.*" *Field* 26 (Spring 1982): 87–97. Rpt. in Andrews, 67–71, and in Giannelli, 10–14.

The Other Side of the River. New York: Vintage, 1984.

Anon. *Publishers Weekly* 225 (10 February 1984): 192.
Bell, Madison. *New York Times Book Review* 89 (20 May 1984): 26.
Buckley, Christopher. "A Light in Our Eyes—*The Other Side of the River* by Charles Wright." *Bluefish* 2, nos. 3–4 (Spring 1984–85): 147–57. Rpt. in Buckley's *Appreciations: Selected Reviews, Views & Interviews, 1975-2000*. Santa Barbara, CA: Millie Grazie Press, 2001. 53–60
Burris, Sidney. *Kenyon Review* 6 (Summer 1984): 127–34.
Eschelman, Clayton. "Life as a Poetic Puzzlement." *Los Angeles Times* 103 (19 August 1984): B7.
Frank, Elizabeth. "The Middle of the Journey." *The Nation* 238, no. 13 (7 April 1984): 421–3.
Hemstath, James B. *Library Journal* 109 (1 March 1984): 51.
Jarman, Mark. "The Trace of a Story Line." *Ohio Review* 37 (Fall 1986), 129–47. Rpt. in Andrews, 96–104, and in Giannelli, 17–24. Also rpt. in Jarman's *Body and Soul: Essays on Poetry*. Ann Arbor: University of Michigan Press, 2000. 71–90.
Kalstone, David. "Lives in a Rearview Mirror." *New York Times Book Review* 89 (1 July 1984): 14. Material on Wright rpt. in Andrews, 94–5, and in Giannelli, 15–16.
Koontz, Thomas. *Library Journal* 109, no. 4 (1 March 1984): 495.
Pettingell, Phoebe. *New Leader* 67 (20 August 1984): 17–18.
Stitt, Peter. "The Circle of the Meditative Moment." *Georgia Review* 38, no. 2 (Summer 1984): 402–12. Rpt. as part of "Five Reviews" in Andrews, 60–3.
St. John, David. *Washington Post Book World* 107 (20 May 1984): 6.

Five Journals. New York: Red Ozier Press, 1986.

Bringhurst, Robert. *Fine Print* 13, no. 2 (April 1987): 93–8.

Zone Journals. New York: Farrar Straus Giroux, 1988.

American Book Review 11 (March 1989): 6.
Clark, Kevin. "Stature." *Café Solo* 5, nos. 3–4 (1989): 63–8. Rpt. in Andrews, 163–6.
Corbett, William. *Harvard Book Review* 9–10 (Fall–Winter 1988): 11.
Enconomou, George. *World Literature Today* 62 (Autumn 1988): 660.
Galvin, B. *Choice* 25 (May 1988): 1407.
Gregerson, Linda. "Short Reviews." *Poetry* 155, no. 3 (December 1989): 229–31. Rpt. as "God's Concern for America" in *Negative Capability: Contemporary American Poetry*. Ann Arbor: University of Michigan Press, 2001. 120–2. Rpt. in *Contemporary Literary Criticism* 146 (2001).
Harris, Roger. "Place to Place." *Star Ledger* [Newark, NJ] 10 January 1988.

Jarman, Mark. "The Pragmatic Imagination and the Secret of Poetry." *Gettysburg Review* 1, no. 4 (Autumn 1988): 647–60. Material on Wright rpt. in Andrews, 105–9, and in Giannelli, 25–8.
J.S. *Booklist* (15 December 1987).
Logan, William. "Season to Season, Day to Day." *New York Times Book Review* (4 September 1988): 9–10.
Pankey, Eric. "The Form of Concentration." *Iowa Review* 19, no. 2 (Spring–Summer 1989): 175–87.
Santos, Sherod. "*Zone Journals.*" *New Virginia Review* 8 (Spring 1991): 369–72. Rpt. in Andrews, 155–9, and in Giannelli, 36–9.
Shreve, Jack. *Library Journal* 112, no. 19 (15 November 1987): 84.
Smock, Frederick. "Tennessee: Burnished Edges." *American Book Review* 11, no. 1 (March–April 1989): 6.
Stitt, Peter. "To Enlighten, To Embody." *Georgia Review* 41, no. 4 (Winter 1987), 800–13. Rpt. as part of "Five Reviews" in Andrews, 64–6.
Stuttaford, Genevieve. *Publishers Weekly* 232 (27 November 1987): 76.
Thorpe, Peter. "Life's Answers Lie in Rhetorical Question." *Rocky Mountain News Sunday Magazine* (5 June 1988).
Van Winckel, Nance. "Charles Wright and the Landscape of the Lyric." *New England Review and Bread Loaf Quarterly* 12, no. 3 (Spring 1990): 308–12. Rpt. in Andrews, 167–71.
Vendler, Helen. "Travels in Time." *New Republic* 198, no. 3 (18 January 1988): 34–6. Revised version appears as "Charles Wright" in *The Music of What Happens: Poems, Poets, Critics*. Cambridge: Harvard University Press, 1988. Rpt. in Andrews, 13–20; and in Giannelli, 29–35.
Virginia Quarterly Review 64 (Spring 1988): 62.

A Journal of the Year of the Ox. New York: Farrar Straus Giroux, 1988.

Fine Print 15 (January 1989): 41.

Xionia. Iowa City: Windhover Press, 1990.

Buckley, Christopher. "Charles Wright's Hymn." *Poet Lore* 86, no. 3 (Fall 1991): 59–65. Rpt. in Andrews, *The Point Where All Things Meet*, 204–11; in Giannelli, 61–7; and in Buckley's *Appreciations: Selected Reviews, Views & Interviews, 1975–2000*. Santa Barbara, CA: Millie Grazie Press, 2001. 121–7.

The World of the Ten Thousand Things: Poems 1980–1990. New York: Farrar Straus Giroux, 1990.

Andrews, Tom. "The Point Where All Things Meet: Improvisations on Charles Wright's *The World of the Ten Thousand Things*." *Iron Mountain Review* 8 (Spring 1992): 9–13. Rpt. as "Improvisations on Charles Wright's *The World of the Ten Thousand Things*" in Andrews, 212–21, and in Giannelli, 52–60.
Bedient, Calvin. "Slide-Wheeling around the Curves." *Southern Review* 27 (1991): 221–34. Rpt. in Andrews, 39–52.
Blasing, Mutlu Konuk. "The American Sublime, c. 1992: What Clothes Does One Wear?" *Michigan Quarterly Review* 31 (Summer 1992): 425–41. Material on Wright (pp. 436–41) rpt. in Andrews, 198–203.
Collins, Floyd. "Metamorphosis within the Poetry of Charles Wright." *Gettysburg Review* 4, no. 3 (Summer 1991): 464–79.
Costello, Bonnie. "Voices from the Other Side." *Newsday* 23 December 1990: 19 ("Currents" section).
Garrison, David. *Choice* 28 (February 1991): 936.
Koeppel, Fredric. "Poems Register the Cosmic Touch." *Commercial Appeal* [Memphis] 23 December 1990: G3.
McClatchy, J.D. "Amid the Groves, Under the Shadowy Hill, the Generations Are Prepared." *Poetry* 158, no. 5 (August 1991): 280–95.
Sampson, Dennis. "Poetry Chronicle." *Hudson Review* 44, no. 2 (Summer 1991), 333–42.
Stocking, Marion. *Beloit Poetry Journal* 41, no. 2 (Winter 1990–91): 38.
Tillinghast, Richard. "An Elegist's New England, a Buddhist's Dante." *New York Times Book Review* 96 (24 February 1991): 18–19. Rpt. in Andrews, 195–7, and in Giannelli, 40–1.
Unsino, Stephen. *America* 166, no. 14 (25 April 1992): 361–2.
Virginia Quarterly Review 67, no. 2 (Spring 1991): 63.
Young, David. "The Blood Bees of Paradise." *Field*, No. 44 (Spring 1991): 77–90. Rpt. in Andrews, 184–94, and in Giannelli, 42–51.

Appendix 2: Secondary Sources on Wright's Poetry

Books

Andrews, Tom, ed. *The Point Where All Things Meet: Essays on Charles Wright*. Oberlin, Ohio: Oberlin College Press, 1995.
Denham, Robert D. *Charles Wright: A Companion to the Late Poetry, 1988-2007*. Jefferson, NC, and London: McFarland & Co., 2008.
Giannelli, Adam, ed. *High Lonesome: On the Poetry of Charles Wright,*. Oberlin, Ohio: Oberlin College, 2006.
Moffett, Joe. *Understanding Charles Wright*. Columbia: University of South Carolina Press, forthcoming, 2009.

Theses and Dissertations

Devine, Kelly Anne. *Language Journal: A Study of Charles Wright and Deconstruction*. B.A. thesis, California State Polytechnic University, San Luis Obispo, 1997.
Dewett, Shawn. *We're Out Here*. M.A. thesis, University of North Carolina, Chapel Hill, 2007. On Wright's *Homage to Paul Cézanne*.
Francini, Antonella. *In the Longfellow Line: Some Contemporary American Poets as Translators of Eugenio Montale: A Study in Theory and Practice*. Ph.D. dissertation, Drew University, 1985.
Franzek, Phyllis Jean. *Political Poetics: Revisionist Form in Adrienne Rich, John Ashbery, Charles Wright, and Jorie Graham*. Ph.D. dissertation, University of Southern California, 1996.
Gilchrist, David William. *Greening the Lyre: Environmental Poetics and Ethics (Poetry, Robert Frost, Wallace Stevens, Adrienne Rich, A.R. Ammons, Charles Wright)*. Ph.D. dissertation, University of Oregon, 1996.
Hart, George Leslie. *The Poetics of Postmodernist and Neoromantic Nature Poetry*. Ph.D. dissertation, Stanford University, 1997.
Holland, Diane. *Focusing the Dream: Image, Sequence and Pattern in Poems by Charles Wright*. M.F.A. thesis, Warren Wilson College, 2002.
Johnson, Andrew. *Back to Splendour: Charles Wright's Poetry*. Ph. D. thesis, Monash University, 2005.
Johnston, Geranl Gordon. *The Poetry of Charles Wright*. Honors thesis, University of Redlands, 1981.
McCorkle, James. *Gaze, Memory, and Discourse: Self-reflexivity in Recent American Poetry (Bishop, Ashbery, Merwin, Wright)*. Ph. D. dissertation, University of Iowa, 1984.
McCurry, Sara Kathleen. *The Places of Contemporary American Poetry*. Ph.D. dissertation, University of Oregon, 2005. Chapter Two, "Transcending Place: Charles Wright and 'The Things That Must Fall Away.'"
Merriman, Emily Taylor. *"Whatever": God as Absent Presence in the Poetry of Geoffrey Hill, Derek Walcott, and Charles Wright*. Ph.D. dissertation, Boston University, 2007.
Monacell, Peter. *Poetry of the American Suburbs (Louis Simpson, James Dickey, Donald Justice, Charles Wright)*. M.A. thesis, University of Missouri, 2004.
Pugh, Christina Anne. *Revising the Pictorial: Ekphrasis and the Nature of Modern Lyric*. Ph.D. dissertation, Harvard University, 1998.
Rivara, Sara. *Forever Joined: Images of Landscape in the Poems of Charles Wright and Kay Stripling Byer*. M.F.A. thesis, Warren Wilson College, 2002.
Roman, Camile. *Postmodern Homemaking (Poetry)*. Ph.D. dissertation, Brown University, 1990.

Essays, Articles, and Papers

Allbery, Debra. "Lives of the Artists: Line, Landscape and the Poet's Calling in the Work of Charles Wright." Warren Wilson College Audiotape, January 2000.

Albright, Daniel. "Noble Savages in Armani Suits: Recent American Art: Proceedings of the XV Biennial Conference, Siracusa, November 4–7, 1999." *America Today: Highways and Labyrinths*, ed. Gigliola Nocera. Siracusa, Italy: Grafià, 2003. 51–65.
Altieri, Charles. "The Dominant Poetic Mode of the Late Seventies." In *Self and Sensibility in Contemporary American Poetry*. Cambridge: Cambridge University Press, 1984. 32–51.
Anon. "Charles Wright." *Contemporary Authors. New Revision Series*. Vol. 62. Detroit: Gale Research, 1998. 447–50.
———. *Contemporary Authors: Autobiography Series*. Vol. 7. Detroit: Gale Research, 1988. 287–303.
———. "Charles Wright." *Poetry Foundation*. http://www.poetryfoundation.org/archive/poet.html?id=7560.
———. "Wright, Charles. *Encyclopedia Britannica*. 2003.
Bedient, Calvin. "Coloring Nature Big and Wet, Dry and Varied, and Pushed Aside." *Antioch Review* 52 (Winter 1994): 15–33.
———. "The Predicament of Modern Poetry (The Lyric at the Pinch-Gate)." *Chicago Review* 51/52 (Spring 2006): 135–54.
Bond, Bruce. "Metaphysics of the Image in Charles Wright and Paul Cézanne." *The Southern Review* 30 (Winter 1994): 116–25. Rpt. in Andrews, 264–73, and in Giannelli, 221–9. Also available at http://www.english.uiuc.edu/maps/poets/s_z/c_wright/bond.htm.
Boyle, Peter. "Tradition and Wisdom in Charles Wright's *Black Zodiac* and *Chickamauga*. *Verse* 15–16, no. 3/1 (1998): 102–8.
Bratcher, Drew. "Charles Wright's Poetry of Place." *Washingtonian.com* http://www.washingtonian.com/blogarticles/mediapolitics/capitalcomment/3436.html.
Buck, Paula Closson. "A Deeper Disregard: Thoughts on Reading Charles Wright." Paper presented at the annual meeting of the Associated Writing Programs on a panel "Charles Wright at 70: A Celebration and Retrospective," Vancouver, BC, 31 March 2005. Typescript. 8 pp.
Butterick, George F. "Charles Wright." *Dictionary of Literary Biography Yearbook 1982*. Ed. Richard Ziegfeld. Detroit: Gale Research, 1983. 389–400. On CD-ROM, Version 3.1, 1997.
Cain, Stephen. "Two in T.O.: The Canadian Publications of Allen Ginsberg and Charles Wright." Paper presented at the conference of the National Poetry Foundation, University of Maine, Orono, ME, 28 June–2 July, 2002.
Carls, Alice-Catherine. "Charles Wright, poète da la transparence." *Poesie premiere* no. 12 (Winter 1998–1999): 3–24.
———. "Charles Wright." *Le Journal des Poètes* 68, no. 8 (December 1998): 9–11. Translation of seven poems, with a brief biographical introduction.
Chitwood, Michael. "Gospel Music: Charles Wright and the High Lonesome." *Iron Mountain Review* 8 (Spring 1992): 23–5. Rpt. in Andrews, 241–7, and in Giannelli, 186–91.
Chollet, Laurence. "Poetry Set in Motion." *The Record* (Bergen County, NJ), 13 June 1993.
Conte, Joseph Mark. *American Poets since World War II, Fourth Series*. [*Dictionary of Literary Biography*, vol. 165]. Detroit: Gale Research, 1996.
Cooperman, Matthew. "Echolocation and the Imperative of Landscape: Charles Wright's Late Appalachian Trilogy." Paper presented at the Twentieth Century Literature Conference, Louisville, KY, February 2001.
Costello, Bonnie. "Charles Wright, Giorgio Morandi, and the Metaphysics of the Line." *Mosaic* 35, no. 1 (March 2002): 149–71. Rpt. in Giannelli, 304–24.
———. "Charles Wright's *Via Negativa*: Language, Landscape, and the Idea of God." *Contemporary Literature* 36, no. 2 (2000): 325–46.
———. "Introduction: Flame and Flux." *Shifting Ground: Reinventing Landscape in Modern American Poetry*. Cambridge: Harvard University Press, 2003. 3–5.
———. "The Passions of Charles Wright." Paper presented at the 1999 Association of Literary Scholars and Critics, 31 October 1999.
———. "The Soil and Man's Intelligence: Three Contemporary Landscape Poets." *Contemporary Literature* 30, no. 3 (1989): 412–33. Material on Wright rpt. in Andrews, 145–54.
Crenshaw, Brad. "Charles Wright." *Critical Survey of Poetry*. Vol. 7. Ed. Frank N. Magill. Englewood Cliffs, NJ: Salem Press, 1982. 3147–54.
Cushman, Stephen. "The Capabilities of Charles Wright." *Iron Mountain Review* 8 (Spring 1992): 14–22. Rpt. in Andrews, 222–40; and in Giannelli, 203–20.
Daniels, Kate. "Porch-Sitting and Southern Poetry." In *The Future of Southern Letters*. Ed. Jefferson Humphries and John Lowe. New York: Oxford University Press, 1996. 61–71.
Davis, William V. "Bruised by God: Charles Wright's Apocalyptic Pilgrimages." Paper presented at the Swansea Conference (2000) in a session on "Walt Whitman and His Legacy." See *American Studies in Britain* 82 (Spring–Summer) 2000.
———. "Making the World with Words: A Reading of Charles Wright's Appalachian Book of the Dead." *Latitude 63° North: Proceedings of the 8th International Region and Nation Literature Conference, Östersund, Sweden 2–6 August 2000*. Ed. David Bell. Östersund, Sweden: Mid-Sweden University College, 2002. 255–70.
Dodd, Elizabeth. "'Looking Around': A Fidelity of Attention in Charles Wright's Transcendental Journals." Paper presented at the annual meeting of the Associated Writing Programs on a panel "Charles Wright at 70: A Celebration and Retrospective," Vancouver, BC, 31 March 2005. Typescript. 14 pp.
Finch, Annie. *The Ghost of Meter*. Ann Arbor: University of Michigan Press, 1993. 132–5.

Francini, Antonella. "Chronicle of a Long Fidelity: The Case of the American Poets." *Rivista di Poesia Comparata* Nos. 16–17 (1997): 11–16.
____. "Crepuscolo americano: la poesia di Charles Wright." *Poesia* 149 (April 2001): 18–22.
____. "'The pale hems of the masters' gown': Mediterranean Voices and Shadows in the Poetry of Charles Wright." *America and the Mediterranean: AISNA, Associazione Italiana di Studi Nord-Americani, Proceedings of the Sixteenth Biennial International Conference, Genova, November 8–11, 2001*. Ed. Massimo Bacigalupo and Pierangelo Gastegneto. Torino: Otto Editore, 2003. 85–92.
____. "A Poet's Workshop: Charles Wright Translating Eugenio Montale." *L'Anello che non tiene: Journal of Modern Italian Literature* 4, nos. 1–2 (Spring–Fall 1992): 44–71.
____. "Trilogia triplice: riflessioni sulla poesia di Charles Wright." In Wright's *Crepuscolo americano e altre poesie (1980-2000)*, trans. Antonella Francini. Milan: Jaca Book, 2001. 261–81.
Franzek, Phyllis Jean. "Charles Wright's Half-Life: Elegiacally Inventive." *Pacific Coast Philology* 40 (2005): 138–57.
____. "Ibn 'Arabi to Charles Wright: Luminous Longings and Related Matters." Paper presented at the annual conference of the Pacific Ancient and Modern Language Association, 10–11 November 2006.
Gardner, Thomas. "Restructured and Restrung: Charles Wright's *Zone Journals* and Emily Dickinson." *Kenyon Review* 26, no. 2 (Spring 2004): 149–74. Revised for inclusion in Gardner's *A Door Ajar: Contemporary Writers and Emily Dickinson* (New York: Oxford University Press, 2006).
Garrison, David. "'An Old Song Handles My Heart': Charles Wright and the Sweet Failure of Music." *Kentucky Philological Review* 6 (1991): 9–14.
____. "From Feeling to Form: Image as Translation in the Poetry of Charles Wright." *Midwest Quarterly* 4, no. 1 (Autumn 1999): 33–47.
Gewirtz, Ken. "The Age of Ozzy Osbourne." *Harvard Gazette*, 6 June 2002.
Gibson, Lydiaile. "'Not Dark, Not Dark, But Almost' Lurking in Shadows: Charles Wright's Poetry Wonders about History, Memory, and the Rest of Time." *Chicago Journal Poetry Center*. http://poetrycenter.org/involved/news/wrightjournal.html.
Gitzen, Julian. "Charles Wright and Presences in Absence." *Mid-American Review* 14, no. 2 (1994): 110–21. Rpt. in Andrews, 172–83, and in Giannelli, 192–202.
Guilford, Chuck. "Beyond the Great Wall of Language: Charles Wright's *The World of the Ten Thousand Things*. http://chuckguilford.com/uncollected/GRT_WALL_LNG.pdf.
Hahn, Robert. "The Mockingbird's Chops: Charles Wright in Italian." *Parnassus: Poetry in Review* 29, nos.1–2 (2006): 349–69.
____. "Versions of the Mediterranean in American Poetry." *America and the Mediterranean: AISNA, Associazione Italiana di Studi Nord-Americani, Proceedings of the Sixteenth Biennial International Conference, Genova, November 8–11, 2001*. Ed. Massimo Bacigalupo and Pierangelo Gastegneto. Torino: Otto Editore, 2003. 57–64. Revised version in *Poetry International* 6 (2002).
Hammer, Langdon. "The Latches of Paradise: Charles Wright's Meditations and Memories at Year's End." *American Scholar* 74, no. 4 (Autumn 2005): 73–4.
Harper, Margaret Mills. "Charles Wright (1935–)." *Contemporary Poets, Dramatists, Essayists, and Novelists of the South: A Bio-Bibliographical Sourcebook*, ed. Robert Bain and Joseph M. Flora. Westport, CT: Greenwood Press, 1994. pp. 553–61.
Hart, Henry. "Charles Wright." *American Writers: A Collection of Literary Biographies, Supplement V: Russell Banks to Charles Wright*. Ed. Jay Parini. New York: Scribner's, 2000. 331–46.
____. "Charles Wright." *Oxford Encyclopedia of American Literature*. New York: Oxford University Press, 2004. 465–72.
____. "Charles Wright's *Via Mystica*." *Georgia Review* 58, no. 2 (Summer 2004): 409–32. Rpt. in Giannelli, 325–44.
Hart, Kevin. "'La poesia è scala a dio': On Reading Charles Wright," *Heat* [Artarmon, New South Wales] 1, no. 6 (1997): 92–109. Rpt. in *Religion and the Arts* 8, no. 2 (June 2004): 174–99.
____. "Poetry and Transcendence." 25 November 1997. http://home.vicnet.net.au/~ozlit/news9711.html.
Hawkins, Peter, and Rachel Jacoff. "Still Here: Dante after Modernism." *Yale Review* 89 (July 2001): 11–24.
Henry, Brian. "Exquisite Disjunctions, Exquisite Arrangements." *Antioch Review* 56 (Summer 1998): 281–93.
____. "New Scaffolding for New Arrangements: Charles Wright's Low Riders." *Virginia Quarterly Review* 80, no. 2 (Spring 2004): 98–112.
____. "Southern Cross: The Inheritance of Charles Wright." *Quarterly West* 46 (1998): 196–202.
Hirsch, Edward. "The Visionary Poetics of Philip Levine and Charles Wright." *The Columbia History of American Poetry*, ed. Jay Parini. New York: Columbia University Press, 1994. 777–805. Rpt. in Andrews, 248–63.
Hix, H.L. "Charles Wright and a Case of Foreshortened Influence." *Notes on Contemporary Literature* 18, no. 1 (January 1988): 4–6.
Hoagland, Sadie. "Poet Charles Wright Reinterprets Reality." *The Middlebury Campus*, 15 January 2004. http://www.middleburycampus.com/news/2003/10/10/Arts/Poet-Charles.Wright.Reinterprets.Reality-524165.shtml.
Holland, Gill. "Charles Wright and the Presence of Chinese Poetry in Contemporary U.S. Poetry." *Crossing Borders: Interdisciplinary Intercultural Interaction*. Ed. Bernhard Ketterman and Georg Marko. Tübingen: Gunter Narr Verlag, 1999. 313–23.

Ingalls, Zoe. "Charles Wright, Poet of Landscape, Melds Tradition and Innovation." *Chronicle of Higher Education* 45, no. 4 (18 September 1998), B10–11.
Irons-Georges, Tracy, and Philip K. Jason, eds. On *Homage to Paul Cézanne*, *Laguna Blues*, and *Reading Lao Tzu Again in the New Year*. *Masterplots II Poetry*. Pasadena, CA: Salem Press, 2002. vol. 4, pp. 1731, 2135; vol. 6, p. 3143.
Jarman, Mark. "The Pragmatic Imagination and the Secret of Poetry." *Gettysburg Review* 1, no. 4 (Autumn 1988): 647–77. Rpt. in Andrews, 105–9; and in Jarman's *The Secret of Poetry: Essays*. Ashland, OR: Story Line Press, 2001.
_____. "The Trace of a Story Line." *Ohio Review* 37 (1986):129–47. Rpt. in Andrews, 96–104.
_____. "'I Have Seen What I Have Seen': Charles Wright's 'Tattoos' and the Problem of Autobiography." *Colloquy: Text Theory Critique* 7 (May 2003). http://www.arts.monash.edu.au/others/colloquy/current/Issue%20Seven/Johnson.htm.
Kenzie, Mary. "Haunting." *American Poetry Review* 11, no. 5 (September–October 1982): 40–1.
King, Arthur H., Jr. *American Scholar* 75 (Winter 2006): 142. Letter to the editor.
Kirby, David. "Upward, Toward." *What Is a Book?* Athens: University of Georgia Press, 2002. 60–70.
Kondracki, Elena. "Poets Sherod Santos and Charles Wright at the 'Y.'" *nycBigCityLit.com*, February 2001. http://www.nycbigcitylit.com/feb2001/contents/SeriesReviews.htmlSeries.
LaBlanc, Michael, ed. "Black Zodiac." *Poetry for Students. Volume 10: Presenting Analysis, Context and Criticism on Commonly Studied Poetry*. Detroit: Gale Research, 2001. 46–61.
Lake, Paul. "Return to Metaphor: From Deep Imagist to New Formalist." *Southwest Review* 74, no. 4 (Autumn 1989): 515–29. Rpt. in *New Expansive Poetry: Theory, Criticism, History*, ed. R.S. Gwynn. Ashland, OR: Story Line, 1999.
Levine, Philip. "Citation: 1996 Lenore Marshall Poetry Prize." *American Poet*, Winter 1996–97: 25 Also at http://www.poets.org/poems/prose.cfm?45442B7C000C0702007A.
Longenbach, James. "Disjunction in Poetry." *Raritan* 20, no. 4 (2001): 20–36. Incorporates "The Landscapes of Charles Wright," a paper presented at the meeting of the Association of Literary Scholars and Critics, 31 October 1999.
McClatchy, J.D. "Reading." *White Paper on Contemporary American Poetry*. New York: Columbia University Press, 1989. 26–44. Rpt. as "Under the Sign of the Cross" in Andrews, 72–85, and in Giannelli, 142–53.
McCorkle, James. "Charles Wright." *Dictionary of Literary Biography: American Poets Since World War II, Fourth Series*. Vol. 165, ed. Joseph Conte. Detroit: Gale, 1966. 267–82.
_____. "Local Habitations." *American Poetry Review* 32, no. 5 (September–October 2003): 13.
_____. "'Things That Lock Our Wrists to the Past': Self-Portraiture and Autobiography in Charles Wright's Poetry." *The Still Performance: Writing, Self, and Interconnections in Five Postmodernist American Poets*. Charlottesville: University Press of Virginia, 1989. 171–211. Rpt. in Andrews, 110–44, and in Giannelli, 154–85.
McDonald, Jeanne. "Charles Wright and the Talking Eternity Blues." *Appalachian Life* 62 (December–January 2003): 26–8.
McFee, Michael. "Charles Wright's Pilgrimage." *Seneca Review* 14, no. 2 (1984): 85–97.
McGuiness, Daniel. "The Long Line in Contemporary American Poetry." *Antioch Review* 47, no. 3 (Summer 1989): 269–86. Rpt. as "The Long Line in Jorie Graham and Charles Wright," in *Holding Patterns: Temporary Poetics in Contemporary Poetry* (Albany: State University of New York Press, 2001), 139–54.
Morris, John. "Making More Sense than Omaha." *Hudson Review* 27 (Spring 1974): 106–7.
_____. "The Songs Protect Us in a Way." *Hudson Review* 27 (Autumn 1974): 453–5.
Mulvania, Andrew. "Confessions of St. Charles: Confession as Spiritual Autobiography in the Work of Charles Wright." *Valparaiso Poetry Review: Contemporary Poetry and Poetics* 4, no. 1 (Fall-Winter 2002-2003). http://www.valpo.edu/english/vpr/mulvaniaessaywright.html.
Muske, Carol. "Ourselves as History." *Parnassus: Poetry in Review* 4, no. 2 (Spring–Summer 1976): 116–21.
Ormsby, Eric. "Of Lapdogs and Loners: American Poetry Today." *New Criterion* 22, no. 8 (April 2004): 5–18.
Parini, Jay. "Charles Wright: The Remembered Earth." *Some Necessary Angels: Essays on Writing and Politics*. New York: Columbia University Press, 1997. 181–200.
Parisi, Joseph. "Charles Wright." *Poets in Person: A Listener's Guide*. 2nd ed. N.p.: Poetry Press, 1997. 168–83.
Perloff, Marjorie. "Charles Wright." *Contemporary Poets*, 4th ed. Ed. James Vinson and D.L. Patrick. New York: St. Martin's Press, 1985. 947–8.
Perkins, David. *A History of Modern Poetry: Modernism and After*. Cambridge: Harvard University Press, 1987. 561–2.
Pittard, Shawn. "Charles Wright and 'The Minor Art of Self-Defense." *The Great American Pinup*, 5 May 2005. http://greatamericanpinup.blogspot.com/2005/05/charles-wright-and-minor-art-of-self.html.
Prampolini, Gaetano. "Charles Wright: Tre poesie e nota bio-bibliografica." *I poeti dell'antico fattore*, (1999): 40–5, 52–4.
_____. "Nota" to a translation of *The Secret of Poetry*; *Is*; and *Nostalgia*. "Charles Wright: Il segreto della poesia." *La Luna*, Pensiero 12 [1999]. Poems with a graphic by Rossano Guerra laid in stiff paper wrapper.
_____. "Nota del curatore." *Testo a fronte* 16 (March 1997): 136–7. Accompanies the translation of Wright's poem *The Southern Cross*.
_____. "Poeti americani in Italia: Richard Hugo e Charles Wright." *Il Veltro: Rivista della Civilta Italiana* 38 (September–December 1994): 397–416.

———. "Postfazione." *L'altra riva del fiume*, trans. Gaetano Prampolini. Milano: ExCogita Editore, 2001. 135–45.
Prunty, Wyatt. "At Home and Abroad: Southern Poets with Passports and Memory." *Southern Review*, 30 (Fall 1994), 745–50.
Przybyszewski, Chris. "The Wright Words." *Memphis Flyer*, 29 March 2001. http://www.memphisflyer.com/MFSearch/full_results.asp?xt_from=1&aID=923.
Rosenthal, M.L. "Sensibilities, Ltd." *Parnassus: Poetry in Review* 7, no. 2 (Spring–Summer 1979): 119.
Rowan, Tori. "A Wright-er's Landscape of the Impersonal." *The Declaration* November 1990.
Runciman, Lex. "Belief, Nonbelief, Invention: The Recent Poetry of Charles Wright." *Poet Lore* 78, no.1 (Spring 1983): 41.
Santos, Sherod. "A Solving Emptiness: C.K. Williams and Charles Wright." *A Poetry of Two Minds*. Athens: University of Georgia Press, 2000. 125–38.
St. John, David. "The Poetry of Charles Wright." *Wright: A Profile*. Iowa City: Grilled Flowers Press, 1979. 51–65. Part 1 of the essay first appeared in the *Seneca Review*.
Smith, R.T. "The Appellations Yet Rising: A Birdseye View of Poetry from the Appalachians." *Poetry Daily* [Charlottesville, VA]. http://www.poems.com/essartsm.htm.
Spiegelman, Willard. "Landscape and Identity: Charles Wright's Backyard Metaphysics." *Southern Review* 40, no. 1 (Winter 2004): 172–96. A slightly different version of the essay rpt. in *"The Way Things Looks Each Day": How Poets See the World*. New York: Oxford University Press, 2005. 82–111. Rpt. in Giannelli, 345–73.
———. "The Nineties Revisited." *Contemporary Literature* 42, no. 2 (Summer 2001): 206–37.
———. "The Vision of Charles Wright." Paper presented at the 1999 Association of Literary Scholars and Critics, 31 October 1999.
Stitt, Peter. "Resurrecting the Baroque." *Uncertainty and Plenitude*. Iowa City: University of Iowa Press, 1997. Rpt. in Giannelli, 230–54.
Swerdlow, David. "The Unknown Master of the Pure Poem Walks Nightly Among His Roses: Traveling Toward the Idea of God with Charles Wright." Paper presented at the annual meeting of the Associated Writing Programs on a panel "Charles Wright at 70: A Celebration and Retrospective," Vancouver, BC, 31 March 2005.
Swift, Todd. "Commedia del Arte." *Eyewear* [London], 7 June 2007. http://toddswift.blogspot.com/2007/06/commedia-del-arte.html.
Theune, Michael. "The Dark Wood of Reading: The Diminished Pilgrimage of Charles Wright's Chickamauga." Paper presented at the 15th Annual Conference of the American Literature Association, 29 May 2004.
T[onge], J[ennifer]. "Wright, Charles." *Who's Who in Twentieth-Century World Poetry*, ed. Mark Willhardt and Alan Michael Parker. London: Routledge, 2000. 345.
Upton, Lee. "Charles Wright's Self-Portraiture: The Lyric Poet as Self-Traitor." *Poesis* 7, no. 5 (1987): 1–12.
———. "The Doubting Penitent: Charles Wright's Epiphanies of Abandonment." *The Muse of Abandonment: Origin, Identity, Mastery in Five American Poets*. 23–53. Lewisburg, PA: Bucknell University Press, 1998. Rpt. in Giannelli, 255–84.
Vendler, Helen. "The Transcendent 'I.'" *New Yorker*, 29 October 1979, 160–74. Rpt. in *Part of Nature, Part of Us: Modern American Poets*. Cambridge: Harvard University Press, 1988. 277–88; in Andrews, 1–12, and in Giannelli, 115–25.
Walton, Anthony. "The Journey Within." *Oxford American* 37 (2001): 67–73.
West, Robert. "Everywhere but His Own Country: Three Essays on Charles Wright and the American South." *Asheville Poetry Review* 9, no. 1 (Spring–Summer 2002): 93–103.
———. "'Take Me as a Southern Writer, Please': Contextualizing Charles Wright in Southern Literature." Southern Writers Symposium, Fayetteville, NC, September 2000.
Wright, Stuart. "Charles Wright: A Bibliographic Chronicle, 1963–1985." *Bulletin of Bibliography* 43, no. 1 (1986): 3–12.
Young, David. "Language: The Poet as Master and Servant." *Field* 14 (1976): 68–90. Rpt. in *A Field Guide to Contemporary Poetry and Poetics*, ed. Stuart Friebert and David Young. Oberlin, OH: Oberlin College, 1997. 179–97.
———. "Looking for Landscapes." *Field* 58 (Spring 1998): 74–90. Rpt. in Giannelli, 87–93.
Zawacki, Andrew. "Reading Wright in the Wrong Country." *Thumbscrew* 8 (Summer 1997).

Index

Numbers in **bold italics** indicate the primary entries for individual poems.

A Lume Spento (Pound) 140
Abraham (Ooskiah) (Cherokee chief) 158
Acts, Book of 40, 43, 100, 128
Adams, Andy (1859–1935) 48–9
American Twilight 122
Among School Children (Yeats) 117
Analects (Confucius) 76
Andalusian Dog 74
Andreis, Yola 107
Angel Playing a Tambourine (Fra Angelico) 135
The Annals of Tennessee (J.G.M. Ramsey) 158
Anniversary **70–1**
Annunciation (Cosimo Tura) 126
Antonioni, Michelangelo (1921–2007) 129
"A.P. and E.D." 118
Apologia Pro Vita Sua 62, 87, 161, 168
Appalachia Dog 63
Appalachian Book of the Dead III 122
April **77–8**
Arbus, Diane (1923–71) 46
Arkansas 132–3
Arkansas Traveller **132–3**
Arnold, Matthew (1822–88) 14, 24
Ars Poetica **107**
Ars Poetica III 22
At Zero 67
Aubade **17–18**
Auden, W.H. (1907–73) 22, 43
Auguries of Innocence (Blake) 168, 174
Augustine, St. (354–430) 14, 92, 146, 168
Aurélia (Nerval) 68
Autumn **83**
Autumn of the Lonely (Trakl) 80
axis mundi, as a structural archetype 14, 53, 60, 75–6, 85, 90, 99, 103, 109, 162

Back Yard Boogie Woogie 87
Backtrack 38
Bacon, Francis (1909–92) 97
Bar Giamaica, 1959–60 **107–8**
Basic Dialogue 62
Bays Mountain Covenant **56**
Beddoes, Thomas (1760–1808) 61
Bend in the Road (Cézanne) 87

Berenson, Bernard (1865–1959) 43, 149
Bicoastal Journal **166–7**
Binder, August (1876–1962) 92, 119
Bingham, Edgar (1921–99) 152
Biographia Literaria (Coleridge) 14
The Black Château (Cézanne) 95, 96, 135
Black Zodiac (book) 111, 154, 160
Blackwater Mountain **33–4**
Blake, William (1757–1827) 51, 76, 93, 97, 116, 118, 168, 174
Blandula, Tenulla, Vagula (Pound) 18–19, 21, 28, 173
Bloodlines (book) 10, 13, 33, 39–57
Body and Soul 122
Boehme, Jakob (1575–1624) 51, 129
Book of Common Prayer 60
The Book of Thel (Blake) 118
Born Again **73**
Borsuk, Chuck 107
Brunelleschi, Filippo (1377–1446) 164
Bruno, Giordano (1548–1600) 113
Buffalo Yoga (book) 12, 22
Buffalo Yoga (poem) 22, 122
The Business of Living (Pavese) 130
"By the Banks of the Holston" (Marion) 153
Bygones 59, **69**

Cá Paruta, Villa 155, 156–7
Cacciaguida degli Elisei (ca. 1091–ca. 1148) 111
Caffè Dante (Verona) 126
Cage, John (1912–92) 97
California Dreaming **136–7**, 167
California Spring 102
California Twilight 70
Called Back 63, 91, **96**
Calvino, Italo (1923–85) 59
Campana, Dino (1885–1932) 22, 29–31, 71–2, 110, 145, 146
Campo dei Fiori 113, 146
Can Grande della Scala (1291–1329) 28, 110
Cancer Rising 10, **40**
Canis Major 63, 103, 132
Cantos (Pound) 42, 92, 112, 114, 141, 174
Captain Dog 63, **73–4**

Carpaccio, Vittore (ca. 1460–1526) 92, 129, 156
Carter Family 118
Carver, Raymond (1938–88) 144
Caserma Passalacqua 124, 125, 149
Catherine of Alexandria (d. 305) 156
Cato, Publius Valerius (fl. 1st cent. B.C.E.) 19
Catullus (84–54 B.C.E.) 19, 28, 110, 151
Cézanne, Paul (1839–1906) 22, 87, 88–90, 95, 105–6, 135, 139, 140, 141, 164
Charlottesville, Virginia 160, 172
Château Noir (Cézanne) see *Black Château*
Ch'en Jung 58
Cherokee 38
Cherokee Indians 138, 148, 151–2, 158, 161–2
Chi K'ang-tzu (223–63) 76
Chickamauga (book) 43, 154
Chickamauga, Battle of 132
Childhood **60**, 62
Childhood's Body 99
The Chimney-Sweeper (Blake) 93
China Journal **175**
China Trace (book) 10, 12, 13, 58–85
Chinese Journal 62, **163**
Chinoiserie **26**
Chitwood, Michael 34
Christ School 34, 44, 110, 132
Christianity 36, 53, 60, 77, 81–2, 83, 99, 115, 146, 168
Cimabue (1240–1302) 164
Clare, John (1793–1864) 164
Clarke County, Virginia 94–5, 158
Clear Night **82–3**
Clinchfield Station **37**
Cloud of Unknowing (anon., 14th cent.) 129, 159
Cloud River **79–80**
Coleridge, Samuel Taylor (1772–1834) 143
College Days 45
Composition in Grey and Pink **97–8**, 99
Confessions (Augustine) 14, 146
Confucius (551–479 B.C.E.) 76
Congenital **36–7**

187

Index

Constable, John (1776–1837) 142
Corfu 17
Corinth, Mississippi 45
Corinthians, Epistle to the 115, 176
Corvo, Baron (Frederick Rolfe) (1860–1913) 22–3
Cosimo Tura (ca. 1430–95) 125, 155, 156
Country Music (book) 10, 13, 17–85
Crane, Hart (1889–1932) 22, 103–4, 169
crystal image in Pound 56, 69, 81, 92, 140
Custis, Nelly (1779–1852) 95
Cyropexy **130**

danse macabre 56, 61
Dante Alighieri (1265–1321) 28, 31, 36, 51, 88, 90, 102–3, 111, 124, 139, 148, 154, 155, 160
Davidson College 108
De Amore (Marsilio Ficino) 154
Dead Color **105–6**
Death **66–7**
Death and the Earth (Pavese) 130
Death Will Come and Will Wear Your Eyes (Pavese) 129–30
December Journal 11, **167–8**, 174
Decline of Summer (Trakl) 80
Deep Water 58
Definitions 38
Delos, Greece 46–7
Delta Traveller **48–9**
Democritus (ca. 460–ca. 370 B.C.E.) 176
Depression Before the Solstice 59, **74–5**
The Desire and Pursuit of the Whole (Corvo) 22
de Staël, Nicolas (1914–55) 103
d'Este, Borso (1413–71) 155
d'Este, Isabella (1475–1539) 126
deus absconditis 73, 129
Deuteronomy, Book of 128
Diaries 1914–1923 (Kafka) 23
DiCenzo, Ed 124
Dickinson, Emily (1830–86) 22, 80, 91, 96, 146, 148, 153, 170
Dillard, Annie (1945–) 11
Dino Campana **71–2**
The Divine Comedy (Dante) 28, 33, 102–3, 111
Dog **62–3**
Dog Creek Mainline 10, 17, 19, 20, **31–3**, 63
Dog Day Vespers 63, **103**
Dog Yoga 63, 74, **101**
Dogana di Mare 20
Dogen Zenji (1200–53) 174
Donaldson, Agnes 117
Donati, Piccarda 102
Donelson, John (ca. 1718–75) 152
Donne, John (1572–1631) 61, 82, 91, 96–7
Dowling, Constance 129–30
Dragging Canoe (ca. 1732–92) 148, 158
A Dream (Blake) 93
The Dream Animal (book) 10
Driving through Tennessee **99–100**

Driving to Passalacqua **124**
dropped-down line 12, 71
Druckerwerkstatt (von Werdt) 25
The Drunken Boat (Rimbaud) 21
du Bellay, Joachin (1522–60) 128
Du Fu *see* Tu Fu
Dürer, Albrecht (1471–1528) 145

Early One Summer (Merwin) 68
East of the Blue Ridge, Our Tombs Are in the Dove's Throat 77
Easter, 1974 **40**
Ecclesiastes, Book of 128, 142
Ed è subito sera (Quasimodo) 163
Edvard Munch **69**
The Egyptian Book of the Dead 77
Eliot, T.S. (1888–1965) 20
Emblems 38
The Enchiridion (Augustine) 158
Entertaining Literary Men in My Official Residence on a Rainy Day (Wêi Ying-wu) 132
Entries 38
Epithalamion 38
Equation **69–70**
Ercole de' Roberti (1450–96) 155, 156
Erigena, John Scotus (ca. 810–ca. 877) 27
Essay on Criticism (Pope) 149
Essays in Idleness (Kenkō) 119
Eucharist 50, 73, 99, 134
Exile's Letter (Pound) 19

Fall, myth of 60
Faulkner, William (1897–1962) 41
The Fever Toy **29**
Ficino, Marsilio (1433–99) 154
Firstborn 10, **27**
Five Journals (book) 11
Flatt (Lester) and Scruggs (Earl) 123
Folgóre da San Gimignano (1270–1332) 153
For an "Homage to Rimbaud" (Montale) 22
Forio d'Ischia 112
the four elements 44, 53, 79, 84, 90, 164, 165
Fra Angelico (1395–1455) 30, 135
Francesco del Cossa (1430–77) 155–6
From a Swiss Lake (Montale) 34
From Ch'in Country to the Buddhist Priest Yuan (Mêng Hao-jan) 131
Frost, Robert (1874–1963) 20
Fucile, Tom 127
Fulbright 42, 112, 118, 128, 129
Fulke Greville, Lord Brooke (1554–1628) 140
Funeral of St. Jerome (Carpaccio) 129

The Garden of the Golden Valley (Tu Mu) 132
Gate City Breakdown **108**
Gates, Jim 107, 108, 127
General Kê-shu (Mêng Hao-jan) 131
Genesis, Book of 23, 72, 106, 163, 172
George Trakl Journal **169–70**

Gianni, Lapo (ca. 1250–1328) 80
Giorgio Morandi and the Talking Eternity Blues 62
Glass, Carl 107
Godfrey, David (1938–) 127
Going Home **79**
Goldstein, Arnie 107, 108, 126
Gould, Glenn (1932–82) 136
Govino Bay 17
Grace **28**
The Grand Grimoire 52
The Grave of the Right Hand (book) 10, 17–19
Graves, Robert (1895–1985) 68
The Green Hills of Africa (Hemingway) 15
Greene, Graham (1904–91) 22
Guilt 58

Hadrian VII (Corvo) 22, 23
Han Shan (Cold Mountain) 71, 171
Han Yu (768–824) 131
Hard Freight (book) 10, 13, 19–38
Hardin County **47–8**
Hawaii Dantesca 106
Hebrews, Epistle to the 93
Heidegger, Martin (1889–1976) 129, 147, 174
Hemingway, Ernest (1899–1961) 15, 20, 119
Heraclitus (535–475 B.C.E.) 176
High Lonesome (Giannelli) 9
Him **84–5**
Hiwassee Village 32, 43, 109
Hix, H.L. 66
Hobart, Peter 107, 108, 149
Holston River 35, 55
Holy Thursday **93**
Holy Thursday (Blake) 93
Homage to Arthur Rimbaud **21–2**
Homage to Baron Corvo **22–3**
Homage to Cesare Pavese **129–30**
Homage to Claude Lorrain **123**
Homage to Ezra Pound **20–1**
Homage to Giorgio Morandi 62
Homage to Paul Cézanne **88–91**, 114
Homage to X **23–4**
Homecoming 40
Homer 90
Hopkins, Gerard Manley (1844–89) 61, 141
Huang Kêng (Sung Dynasty) 26
Hugunin, James R. (1947–) 94
"The Hunger Artist" (Kafka) 23

Illuminations (Rimbaud) 21
In a Station of the Metro (Pound) 66
Indaco, Major 149
Indian Summer **64**
Inferno (Dante) 102, 124
The Infinite (Leopardi) 134
interpenetration 45, 59, 112, 168, 174
Invisible Cities (Calvino) 59
Invisible Landscape **72**
Iowa City 67
Iron Mountain Review 152
Isaiah, Book of 82
Issa (1763–1827) 147
Italian Days 11, 122, **125–7**

January **67–8**
Jarman, Mark (1952–) 109
Jerusalem (Blake) 79
Jesus 100
Job, Book of 54–5, 106, 114, 149, 161
John, Gospel of 83, 84, 101, 114, 170
John Scotus Erigena *see* Erigena
John the Baptist 115, 122
Joshua, Book of 122
Journal of a Voyage (Donelson) 152
A Journal of English Days 87, 122, **140–3**
A Journal of One Significant Landscape 122, 139, **163–5**
A Journal of Southern Rivers **173–5**
A Journal of the Year of the Ox 11, 12, 87, **148–63**
A Journal of Three Questions **169**
A Journal of True Confessions 62, 87, **143–7**
Justice, Donald (1925–2004) 97

Kafka, Franz (1883–1924) 23–4, 45
Keats, John (1795–1821) 14, 95, 129, 140, 141, 160
Kenkō, Yoshida (ca. 1283?–ca. 1350) 119, 120
Kingsport, Tennessee 55, 56, 57, 60, 77, 108, 115, 117, 119, 121
Knoxville, Tennessee 109
The Koran 135

Laguna Beach, California 28, 55, 59, 79, 98, 103, 108, 112, 121, 125, 133, 137
Laguna Blues **98**
Laguna Dantesca **102–3**, 106
Lake Garda 18, 44, 50, 95, 110, 116, 173
Lake Hiwassee 32
Lake Llewellyn 35, 120, 123
Lamentations, Book of 100
"Landscape of the Holston" (Bingham) 152
Landscape with Seated Figure and Olive Trees **100–1**
Langland, Joe (1917–2007) 153
Language Journal **170–2**
Language poets 170–1
Lao Tzu (ca. 600–300 B.C.E.) 129, 139
Last Journal **176**
Lawrence, D.H. (1885–1930) 22
Leonardo da Vinci (1452–1519) 146
Leopardi, Giacomo (1798–1837) 133–4
Letters on Cézanne (Rilke) 164
Li Po (701–62) 19, 71, 104–5, 146
Liberman, Peter 33
light, image of 20, 21, 27, 32, 33–4, 35–7, 39, 41, 43, 45, 50, 51, 54, 60, 64, 65, 66, 67, 73, 74, 76, 79, 81, 84, 85, 89, 92, 96, 99, 103, 104, 110, 112, 114, 118, 121, 126, 127, 130, 136, 138, 145, 150, 153, 159, 161, 162, 163, 167, 171, 174
Light Journal **163**

Lines on Seeing a Photograph for the First Time in Thirty Years 108
Link Chain **55–6**
Lips 58
Littlefoot (book) 12, 108, 122
Lives of the Artists (Vasari) 146, 164
Local Journal **175–6**
The Log of a Cowboy (Adams) 48–9
Lonesome Pine Special **118–20**, 122
Long Island of the Holston 56, 138, 148, 152–3, 158, 162
Looking Around 62
Looking at Pictures **135–6**
Looking East at Night (Merwin) 67
Lorrain, Claude (ca. 1600–82) 123
Lost Bodies **115–16**
Lost Souls **117–18**
Lucciola, Joe 124
Luke, Gospel of 42, 115

MacLeish, Archibald (1892–1982) 20
Madonna del Ortolo (Stephano da Verona) 42, 95
Madonna del Parto (Piero della Francesca) 43, 127
Madonna dell'Orto (church) 124
Mallarmé, Stéphane (1842–98) 53
Mancini, George 144
Mantegna (ca. 1421–1506) 72
Mantova **123–4**
March Journal **143**, 144
Marion, Jeff Daniel (1940–) 153
Mark, Gospel of 42
Martel, Charles (688–741) 111
Marvell, Andrew (1621–78) 115
Mastino della Scala (d. 1277) 28
Matisse, Henri (1869–1954) 139
Matthew, Gospel of 50, 77, 117, 149
May Journal **172–3**, 176
McClatchy, J.D. (1945–) 20, 33, 88, 174
McIntire, John (1907–91) 91, 113
Memories (Leopardi) 135
Mêng Hao-jan (Meng Haoran) (689–740) 71, 131
Merwin, W.S. (1927–) 66–7, 68
Messerli, Douglas (1947–) 171
Il Mestiere di vivere (Pavese) 129–30
Metamorphoses (Ovid) 145
Mingliaotse 59
"Miseducation of the Poet," 118
Modugno, Domenico (1928–94) 126
The Monastery at Vršac **105**
Mondrian, Piet (1872–1944) 139
Montale, Eugenio (1896–1981) 22, 31, 33–4, 47, 71
Montana 59, 60, 70, 80, 91, 113, 114, 119, 120, 125
Monte Grappa 127
Mooring at Twilight in Yü-yi District (Wêi Ying-wu) 132
Morandi **61–2**
Morandi II 62
Morandi, Giorgio (1890–1964) 50, 61–2, 65, 139, 165
Mount Caribou at Night **91–2**, 119
Mt. Leconte, Tennessee 121
Moving On **81–2**

Mulas, Ugo (1928–73) 107–8
Munch, Edvard (1863–1944) 69, 93
My Own Little Civil War 132

Nashe, Thomas (1567–1601) 149
Nashville, Tennessee 117
natura naturans and *natura naturata* 61, 75
Naxian Lions 46–7
Near the Li-Chou Ferry (Wên T'ing-yun) 132
Negative Blue (book) 10, 12, 13, 111
Negatives **29**
Neo-surrealism 63
Nerval, Gérard de (1808–55) 68
Nerval's Mirror **68–9**
The New Ancestors (Godfrey) 141
The New Poem **24**
New Year's Eve, 1979 **108–9**
Next **67**
Nietzsche, Friedrich (1844–1900) 61
Night (Blake) 93
A Night Abroad (Tu Fu) 131
Night Journal 11, **147**
Night Journal II 144, **165–6**
Night Song of a Wandering Asian Shepherd (Leopardi) 134
A Night-Vigil in the Left Court of the Palace (Tu Fu) 131
Nightdream **36**
Nightletter 38
Nine Dragon Scroll (Ch'en Jung) 58
1975 **68**
1960, Landscape (Morandi) 15
Nocturne [1] **18–19**, 21
Nocturne [2] **29–31**
Nolan, Jeanette (1911–98) 91, 113
Noon **78**
North American Bear (book) 111
Northhanger Ridge **35**, 62
Notes for Oscar Wilde at San Miniato **29–31**
Notturno teppista (Campana) 31
Nouns 38
Nurse's Song (Blake) 93

October **98–9**
Odyssey (Homer) 90
O'Grady, Desmond (1935–) 93–4, 146
On an Ancient Sepulchral Bas-Relief (Leopardi) 135
On the Festival of the Moon to Sub-Official Zhang (Han Yu) 131
On the Portrait of a Fair Lady (Leopardi) 135
On True Religion (Augustine) 168
One Two Three **26**
Opus Posthumous 122
Orphic Songs (Campana) 145
Oscar Wilde at San Miniato **29–31**
The Other Side 38, 122
The Other Side of the River (book) 13, 115–37
The Other Side of the River (poem) **121–3**
Ovid (43 B.C.E.–17 C.E.) 51, 145

Padua, University of 111
Painters of the Italian Renaissance (Berenson) 43
Palazzo del Tè 124
Il Palazzo di Schifanoia (Varese) 138
Palazzo Schifanoia (Ferrara) 138
Palmer, Michael (1943–) 171
Paradiso (Dante) 36, 51, 106, 111, 114, 124, 154
Passing Through Hua-Yin (Ts'uêi Hao) 131
Patanjali (2nd cent. B.C.E) 101
Paul of Thebes 171
Pavese, Cesare (1908–50) 20, 129–30
Pecchiar, Grace 107, 108, 126
Penzel, Charles F. (1840–1906) 132
Perrault, Solo Joe (d. 1925) 120
Perry, Anne 34
Perry, Jim 34
Petrarch, Francesco (1304–74) 148, 156–7
Philippians, Epistle to the 116, 129
La Pia de Tolomei 111
Piccarda Donati 102
Pickwick Dam, Tennessee 37, 114
Piero della Francesca (1420–92) 42–3, 50, 161
pilgrimage, Wright's poetic 10, 13–14, 49, 54, 58, 73, 84–5, 99, 148, 160, 162
Pisan Cantos (Pound) 21
Pisanello, Antonio (1394–1455) 28, 88
Platonic Theology (Marsilio Ficino) 154
Poe, Edgar Allan (1808–49) 148, 154
The Poet Grows Older **18**
poète maudit 21, 128
The Point Where All Things Meet (Andrews) 9
Pope, Alexander (1688–1744) 149
Portrait of the Artist as a Young Dog 74
Portrait of the Artist with Hart Crane **103–4**
Portrait of the Artist with Li Po **104–5**
Portrait of the Poet in Abraham von Werdt's Dream **24–5**, 91
Positano 19, 44
Postscript 38
Pound, Ezra (1885–1972) 18, 19, 20–1, 31, 43, 44, 56, 66, 81, 92, 101, 111, 114, 119, 128, 140, 141, 151, 173–4, 175
Pre-Socratics 175–6
Primitive Journal **170**
Primitive Journal II **172**
Primogeniture **36**
Psalms, Book of 67, 128, 162
Purgatorio (Dante) 88, 90, 102, 103, 106, 111, 124, 160

Quasimodo, Salvatore (1901–68) 163
The Quest for Corvo (Symons) 23

A Quinzaine for This Yule (Pound) 140
Quotidiana **64–5**, 67

Ramsey, J.G.M. (1797–1884) 158
Reading Rorty and Paul Celan One Morning in Early June 150
Red Ochre Black on Red (Rothko) 135
religion, natural vs. revealed 50, 73, 82, 83, 115
Remembering San Zeno **72–3**
Reply to Chi K'ang **76**
Reply to Lapo Gianni **80**
The Resurrection (Piero della Francesca) 43–4
The Return (Pound) 151
Reunion **76–7**, 83
Revelation, Book of 114, 143, 145
Richard of St. Victor (ca. 1123–1173) 167
Rilke, Rainer Maria (1875–1926) 157, 163
Rimbaud, Arthur (1854–91) 21–2, 23, 53, 128, 169
River Run 122
Rocchio, Elena 107
Roethke, Theodore (1908–63) 174
Rolfe, Frederick *see* Corvo
Roma I **128–9**
Roma II **129**
Romano, Giulio (ca. 1499–1546) 124
Rome (Pound) 128
Rome, Italy 46, 113
Rosso Venexiana 23
Rothko, Mark (1903–70) 135
Rudge, Olga (1895–1986) 20–1, 101
Runyan, Sam (1892–1947) 92, 119
Rural Route **56–7**
Ruysbroeck, John of (1273–1381) 164

St. Catherine of Alexandria 156
St. Francis of Assisi 171
St. George Liberating the Princess of Trebizond (Pisanello) 28, 88
St. Jerome 92, 171
Saint Jerome Leading the Lions into the Monastery (Carpaccio) 92
St. John, David (1949–) 15
St. John of the Cross (1542–91) 129
St. Paul 60
St. Paul's Episcopal Church (Kingsport) 41, 42, 55
Saint Spiridion 17–18
Salamun, Tomas 43
Salon des Months (Francesco del Cossa) 155–6
salvation, motif of 34, 35, 83, 84
San Miniato (Wilde) 30
Santa Maria Antica (church) 28
Santa Maria in Organo (church) 124
Sant'Anastasia (church) 110
San Zeno Maggiore (basilica) 28, 72–3, 95, 127, 163
Saturday Morning Journal **167**
Saturday 6 a.m. **84**
Scalp Mountain 58

Scar Tissue (book) 12
Scar Tissue II 108, 123
Schimmel, Harold (1935–) 44, 107, 108
Schneeman, George 107, 108, 149
Science and the Modern World (Whitehead) 112
Scuderi, Roberto (d. 1961) 126, 127
A Season in Hell (Rimbaud) 21
Les Secrets Merveilleaux de la Lagic Nayurelle du Petit Albert Lyons 53
Seeing Li Po in a Dream II (Tu Fu) 131
Selected Poems (Pound) 19, 21
Self-Portrait [1] **91**
Self-Portrait [2] 22, **92**
Self-Portrait [3] **93**
Self-Portrait [4] **95–6**, 87
Self-Portrait [5] **96–7**
Self-Portrait in 2035 **61**, 91
Sentences 59, **65–6**, 67
Serenata Indiana (Montale) 47
The Setting of the Moon (Leopardi) 135
Sex **35**
She Was a Phantom of Delight (Wordsworth) 141
Shipley, Harold 116
A Short History of the Shadow (book) 12
A Short Life of Trouble (Flatt and Scruggs) 123
Sidney, Sir Philip (1554–86) 14, 140
Sienkiewicz, Henryk (1846–1916) 129
Signature 59, **78**
The Silent Generation 55
Silent Journal **166**
Sirmione 18–19, 21, 28, 116, 151
Sitting at Night on the Front Porch **83–4**
Skins 14, **49–55**
Sky Diving 154
Sky Valley, North Carolina 10, 33, 35, 60, 77, 122–3
Sky Valley Rider 10, **34**
Slides of Verona 21, **27–8**
Smoot, Joseph Walter (1882–1946) 91–2
Smythe [Smyth], Ellison 132, 133
Snapshot **63**
Snow **60**
The Snow Man (Stevens) 166
The Solitary Life (Leopardi) 134
The Solitary Thrush (Leopardi) 134
A Solitary Wildgoose (Ts'uêi Hao) 131
soma pneumatikon (spiritual man) 115, 116, 176
soma psychikon (natural man) 115
Something Is Crook in Middlebrook (Hugunin) 94
Song of Myself (Whitman) 145
Song of Songs 114
A Song of White Snow in Farewell to Field-Clerk Wu Going Home (Ts'ên Ts'an) 131
Songs of Experience (Blake) 79
Songs of Innocence (Blake) 93

Index

sottonarrativa (submerged narrative) 12
The Southern Cross (book) 13, 88–114
The Southern Cross (poem) **109–14**, 122
Spider Crystal Ascension 61, **80–1**
Spiegelman, Willard 121
Spiritual Espousals (Ruysbroeck) 164
Spring Abstract 100
Spring Storm 122
Ssŭ-k'ung Shu (740–ca. 790) 132
stanzaic form 12–13
Stephano da Verona (ca.1375–1438) 95
Stephen Martyr 100
Stevens, Wallace (1879–1955) 25, 66, 115, 119, 129, 172
Still Life with Stick and Word 62
Stone Canyon Nocturne **75–6**
Storm **19**
The Storm and Other Poems (Montale) 22
Strand, Mark 50, 138, 144, 155
Sunday Morning (Stevens) 115, 119, 172
Symons, A.J.A. (1900–41) 23
Synopsis 38

Talk in the Mountains (Li Po) 104
T'ang Notebook **131–2**
T'ang poets 58, 71, 125, 165
T'ang Yin (Ming Dynasty) 26
Tao Te Ching (Lao-Tzu) 11, 129, 164
Taoism 11, 77, 99
Tate, James (1943–) 43, 111, 153
Tattoos 32, **41–7**, 62, 73, 108, 111
Teaching a Stone to Talk (Dillard) 147
The Tempest (Shakespeare) 121
Terra e la morte, La (Pavese) 129–30
Terry, James Y., Jr. 33
There Is a Balm in Gilead 77, 112
Thinking of George Trakl **80**
Thinking of Marsilio Ficino at the First Hint of Autumn 154
Thomas, Dylan (1914–53) 89
Thompson, Captain James 158
Thorp, Winfrid 107, 108
Thoughts of Old Time I (Tu Fu) 131
Three Poems for the New Year 22, 125, **127–8**
Three Poems of Departure **125**, 127
Tian Wen: A Chinese Book of Origins 169
Tintoretto (Jacobo Comin) (1518–94) 42
To a Friend Bound North after the Rebellion (Ssŭ-k'ung Shu) 132
To Giacomo Leopardi in the Sky 122, **133–5**

To Himself (Leopardi) 134
To His Lady (Leopardi) 134, 135
To Juan at the Winter Solstice (Graves) 68
Tongues 38
Torri del Benaco 115, 116
Trakl, Georg (1887–1914) 59, 169
Tre poeti per Morandi (Pasquali et al.) 62
The Tribe That Time Forgot 52
trilogies, Wright's series of 10, 33
Tsali (Cherokee hero) 158
Ts'ên Ts'an (8th cent. C.E.) 131
Ts'uêi Hao (Cui Hao) (704–54) 131
Tu Fu (Du Fu) (712–70) 58, 131
T'u Lung (1542–1605) 59
Tu Mu (803–52) 132
Tuktens, Ingrid 107, 108
Turner, J.M.W. (1775–1851) 42
12 Lines at Midnight **71**
Twickenham Garden (Donne) 97
Two Stories **120–1**
Twombly, Cy (1928) 138

Uccello, Paolo (1397–1475) 164

Valmarana, Count Giustino (d. 1757) 157
Varese, Ranieri (1941–) 156
Vasari, Giorgio (1511–74) 146, 164
Vaughan, George 117
Venetian Dog 23, 63
Venexia I 111
Venexia II 22, 111
Venezia, Dick 107, 126
Venice, Italy 20, 42, 111
The Venice Notebook (book) 10
Verona, Italy 19, 27–8, 95, 110, 123, 125
Verrà la morte e avrà i tuoi occhi (Pavese) 129–30
Vesper Journal **173**
via negativa 139
Vico, Giambattista (1668–1744) 50
Victor Emmanuel II (1820–78) 157
Victory Garden 38
Vietnam War 24
Virgil (70–19 B.C.E.) 37, 88, 106, 139
The Virgin of Tenderness (icon) 94
Virginia Reel **94–5**
Virgo Descending **39–40**
Vision of St. Augustine (Carpaccio) 92
Vitti, Monica (1931–) 129
Vollard, Ambrose (1966–1939) 105
von Werdt, Abraham (1594–1671) 25, 50
The Voyage (book) 10, 17
The Voyage (poem) **18**
Vršac, Serbia 105

Wang Chi-wu (Ch'ing Dynasty) 26
Wang Wei (701–61) 71
Wêi Ying-wu (737–92) 132
Wên T'ing-yun (ca. 813–70) 132
"Where Moth and Rust Doth Corrupt" **77**, 75
Whistler, James Abbott McNeill (1834–1903) 142
White **26–7**
Whitehead, Alfred North (1861–1947) 112
Whitman, Walt (1819–92) 95, 146
Wickliffe Church (Clarke Co., Virginia) 94
Wier, Dara (1949–) 43
Wilde, Oscar (1854–1900) 29–31
Williams, Susan 107
Williams, William Carlos (1883–1963) 66
wind, archetype of 54, 79, 84, 114, 115, 176
Wishes **64**
With Eddie and Nancy in Arezzo at the Caffe Grande 43
Wordsworth, William (1770–1850) 141, 174
The World of the Ten Thousand Things 10, 11, 12, 13
Wright, Charles Penzel (father) (1904–72) 36, 37, 39–40, 41, 47–8, 111
Wright, Holly (wife) (1941–) 15, 125
Wright, Luke (son) (1970–) 27, 58, 143, 162
Wright, Mary Winter (mother) 36, 39, 46, 48–9, 58, 111, 118
Wright, Moorhead (grandfather) (1872–1945) 132, 133
Wright, Winter (brother) 39, 122
wu wei 77

Xavier, St. Francis (1506–52) 146
Xionia (book) 11, 166–76

Yard Journal **138–9**
Yeats, William Butler (1865–1939) 54, 56, 115, 117
Yellow **31**
The Yellow Crane Terrace (Ts'uêi Hao) 131
Yoga Sutras (Patanjali) 101
Young, David (1936–) 103

Zajac, Jack (1929–) 113
Zechariah, Book of 55
Zeppa, Mary 31
Zone Journals (book) 11, 12, 13, 138–66

www.ingramcontent.com/pod-product-compliance
Lightning Source LLC
Chambersburg PA
CBHW081559300426
44116CB00015B/2936